DEAD RECKONING

The Art of Forensic Detection

DEAD RECKONING

The Art of Forensic Detection

by
Jon J. Nordby, Ph.D.

CRC Press
Boca Raton London New York Washington, D.C.

Library of Congress Cataloging-in-Publication Data

Nordby, Jon J.
Dead reckoning : the art of forensic detection / Jon J. Nordby.
p. cm.
Includes bibliographical references and index.
ISBN 0-8493-8122-3
1. Forensic pathology Case studies. 2. Death—Causes Case studies. 3. Homicide investigation Case studies. I. Title.
RA1063.4.N67 1999
614'.1—dc21

99-40308
CIP

Direct all inquiries to CRC Press LLC, 2000 N.W. Corporate Blvd., Boca Raton, Florida 33431.

International Standard Book Number 0-8493-8122-3
Library of Congress Card Number 99-40308
Printed in the United States of America 2 3 4 5 6 7 8 9 0
Printed on acid-free paper

1. Aristotle, 2. William Whewell, 3. Joseph Bell, M.D., 4. J.S. Mill, 5. Charles Sanders Peirce, 6. Sir Arthur Conan Doyle, 7. Sherlock Holmes

Introduction

The Art of Detection

Rhymes of Ancient Mariners

> I propose to devote my declining years to the composition of a textbook which shall focus the whole art of detection into one volume.
>
> Sherlock Holmes, *The Adventure of the Copper Beaches*

Most suspicious deaths arouse little public interest. Many never involve trials. Others pass for natural deaths, perfect crimes because they remain forever unnoticed. The murderer escapes detection, lurking behind a fog of subterfuge, deceit, and ordinary circumstance. Death investigators must penetrate this fog to discover hidden clues to explain the death and follow the path to the killer. Like mariners navigating without landmarks under a starless sky, investigators lacking reliable witnesses and coherent confessions plot their course through the clues by applying their own style of dead reckoning.

"Dead reckoning," first described in *Bourne's Regiment for the Sea* published in 1577, became a useful method to determine a ship's position when adverse conditions prevented navigating by the stars with a sextant. Under a dark sky, a sailor could estimate position by considering the distance recorded in the log, the course steered according to the compass, the specific effects of the currents, and different signs of land, such as gulls, or smells carried by prevailing winds. The seasoned mariner also had to know when the ship had drifted too much to allow an accurate estimate of its position or course. The method's accuracy depended upon the knowledge, skill, and experience of the sailor. As Lowell said, "The mind, when it sails by dead reckoning . . . will sometimes bring up in strange latitudes."[1]

Following the course of ancient mariners, investigators and forensic scientists also reckon their way through cases in the daily work of death investigation. As with sailors, sometimes the method fails them, too, but more often, Lowell's "strange latitudes" turn out to signal a successful end to the voyage, a correct explanation of the death. In an age blinded by misconceptions of science and illusions about technology, this art of detection often remains as invisible as the clues it uncovers.

Many practitioners of this art go quietly about their business without much public acknowledgment. Many of the people who die the sudden, unexpected, or violent deaths investigated also remain invisible. They seldom lead glamorous lives, or enjoy the notoriety and fortune of interest to an increasingly fickle and fame-focused public. What makes a case interesting for those doing this work has little to do with what makes a case interesting for tabloid-television producers.

Applications of logic and science forming the heart of an investigator's method lack the sound bites and segue important to the death-as-entertainment industry. But they do supply investigators with the kind of stimulation that Sir Arthur Conan Doyle used to animate his fictional 19th-century scientific detective, Sherlock Holmes. The effect of solving a difficult case through reconstructing the crime by disciplined observation, careful reason, and practiced sagacity supplies the rush of a powerful drug. Holmes became so addicted to this intellectual pleasure that Doyle has his character resort to a 7% solution of cocaine between cases just to fill the void that its absence created. Holmes no doubt would have become just another overdose statistic, another passive passenger on a cold morgue gurney, if he had not been saved from drug abuse by the rush derived from the applied logic I call dead reckoning.

The intellectual pleasure supplied by applied logic often must remain its own reward. The pleasure grows as a byproduct of hard work over a long time through diligent exercise. The work demands internally motivated persistence and effort. Albert Einstein said, "It is a grave mistake to think that the joy of seeing and searching can be prompted by [an external] means of coercion or a sense of duty [motivated by outward pressures]." While those familiar with such intellectual rewards fill the 10 different cases detailed in the following pages, they can merely invite others to witness this logic in action for themselves, and to develop its exercise on their own.

These cases represent years of work by many dedicated men and women: judges, coroners, prosecutors, defense attorneys, investigators, forensic pathologists, and other forensic scientists with whom I have had the privilege to work during my career. To simplify the presentation, some characters combine two or more individuals; at least one character usually incorporates my own point of view. Names have been changed—the focus is to show method, not to develop characters. When a case remains legally "open," some details, including names and places, have been altered. However, the essential features of each case regarding the thinking behind forensic science, forensic medicine, and detection remain intact.

Sherlock Holmes comes closest to illustrating this thinking in Doyle's popular detective stories.[2] Doyle, a physician, patterned his hero after Joseph Bell, M.D., Doyle's professor of medicine at Edinburgh. The logic Holmes employed as the most famous solitary scientific sleuth of fiction survives in the daily casework of detectives, forensic scientists, and medical examiners. It helps us recognize clues, sort evidence from coincidence, distinguish truth from falsehood, and evaluate guilt or innocence. This logic of explanation soon became the focus of my professional interest as both a philosopher and as a member of various death investigation teams over the years.

As an enthusiastic young fan of Doyle's Holmes, I planned a career as a physician, hoping to develop the ability to observe a patient's symptoms, and magically, to diagnose the underlying disease. My father, an orthopedic surgeon, stimulated my interest in medicine and amazed me by reading X-rays, deciphering mysterious ghosts of injury and explaining the likely outcomes of treatment. My mother, an artist, nurtured my empathetic powers and sharpened my eye for detail.

But I soon found that premedical study offered little to help me investigate the intrigues of medical diagnosis. I turned to philosophy, the only discipline I found that expressed an interest in thinking about thinking itself, and to art, the field I chose to help me train as a careful observer.

Throughout my training, this interest in medical diagnosis and an eventual disinterest in medical treatment led me from clinical medicine to death investigation. I never have lost my fascination with logical methods applied to decipher chaotic death scenes, and to derive orderly explanations from their jumbled clues, and that interest accompanies me while I work death cases as an investigator. I have followed this interest for 20 years, studying and applying logic and the forensic sciences as an investigator involved with each of the 10 cases described in the following chapters.

These cases come from my experience as one member of a larger death investigation team working together to explain a death. I dissect each investigation from my own philosophical viewpoint. Unlike the rigid rules used to define modern formal logic, the methods of dead reckoning do not reduce to a set of procedures to be followed blindly.

Some philosophers of science have attempted to supply an account of scientific reasoning as a middle ground between overly rigid rules and the methodological equivalent of a birthday celebration at a McDonald's Playland.[3] We seek a philosophically robust distinction between science and pseudoscience; between methodically defensible explanations, and utter nonsense. Useful dead reckoning must be distinguished from useless random guessing which ignores relevant signs, even when such random guesses coincidentally reach the right answer.

The specific challenges in these 10 cases reveal both the strengths and weaknesses of applied logical methods. The powerful abstractions of science often hang helplessly from a web spun of ordinary circumstance. At some point, under some of these circumstances, even the fictional master of the method, Sherlock Holmes, may have to admit defeat.

Holmes, like his contemporary nonfiction counterparts, operates with what 19th- and early 20th-century American philosopher Charles Sanders Peirce [pronounced purse] calls the logic of abduction. Abduction provides a method of reasoning from presented signs to their probable explanations. A cloak of interpretive uncertainty shadows both the method and its result. As in navigating by dead reckoning, correctly reading the signs forms the heart of the process. This abductive process, displayed by Doyle through Holmes' uncanny ability to read the signs correctly, has its limits.

Each chapter's case approach exhibits the logical methods of the forensic sciences, forensic medicine, and detection in specific contexts facing specific challenges. Some challenges provide insurmountable limits. If Peirce is right, such practical contexts are required for any accurate glimpse of the logic of a scientific method having dead reckoning at its center. Without the framework of real cases, the search for scientific method degenerates into the logically impossible quest for a non-existent abstraction, akin to attempts to view form without shape.

The powers of observation exercised in reading the signs, identifying them as clues, and reasoning from them to the best explanation, develop slowly through experience and training. The ability to determine the number of blows striking a bludgeoning victim from blood spatter, or to estimate time of death from decomposition and ambient conditions cannot be learned from treatises on fluid mechanics, biochemistry, or microbiology. Such abilities come from paying attention to the details, from seeing and doing while thinking, from learning when and how to trust one's own eyes through the fog of subterfuge, deceit, and coincidence. Sometimes familiar fictional characters other than Sherlock Holmes help model the process.

As Batman and Robin hang from their "Bat Ropes," walking up the side of a warehouse in search of the Joker, Riddler, Penguin, and Catwoman, Robin breaks the determined silence. "Think, Batman, with four super crooks in weird outfits hanging around, it's amazing someone hasn't reported them to the police." Batman explains by saying, "It's a low-brow neighborhood, Robin, full of saloons. Citizens attribute any curious sights to alcoholic delusions." Robin replies, "Golly, drink is a dirty thing—I'd rather die than be unable to trust my own eyes!"[4]

The 10 cases in the following chapters each display elements of learning how to trust one's own eyes, learning how to navigate the turbulent and ancient sea of clashing opinion and hazardous belief, noticeably rougher in modern science's powerful wake.[5]

NOTES

1. Lowell, Witchcraft Prose, WKS, 1890, ii, p. 372.
2. All references to Doyle's Sherlock Holmes stories cited here may be found in Sir Arthur Conan Doyle, *The Complete Sherlock Holmes [In Two Volumes]*, Doubleday & Company, Inc., Garden City, NY, N.D.
3. (A bibliography of relevant philosophical works appears in the Appendix). For details on this book's philosophical motivations, see note 4 below.
4. Paraphrased by the author from Lorenzo Semple, Jr., *Batman: The Movie*, Twentieth Century Fox, 1966.

5. The need to identify suitable scientific methodology arises whenever so-called scientific experts testify in court. In Fry v. United States, 1923, the Supreme Court set the standard for admitting scientific evidence. Any scientific finding, procedure, or test requires "general acceptance" by members of the relevant scientific community. The so-called Fry Test thereby excluded polygraph, or "lie detection" evidence as unscientific. But in 1993, in Daubert v. Merrell Dow Pharmaceuticals, Inc., 113 S. Ct. 2786 (1993), the Supreme Court embraced Rule 702 of the Federal Rules of Evidence to exclude unscientific conjectures. [Rule 702: "If scientific, technical, or otherwise specialized knowledge will assist the trier of fact to understand the evidence or to determine a fact at issue, a witness qualified as an expert by knowledge, skill, experience, training, or education may testify thereto in the form of an opinion or otherwise." *Federal Rules of Evidence For United States Courts and Magistrates, as Amended to March 1, 1993.* West Pub. Co., St. Paul, MN, 1993]. Trial judges now separate the scientific wheat from the unscientific chaff.

   To help judges, the Supreme Court supplied four criteria for legitimate scientific evidence: testability, peer review, error rates associated with standard techniques, and general acceptance. The focus for admissibility becomes "correct methodology." Forensic scientist John Thornton of the University of California, Berkeley [in "Courts of Law v. Courts of Science: A Forensic Scientist's Reaction to Daulbert," *Shepard's Expert and Scientific Evidence Quarterly,* Vol. 1, No. 3, 1994, pp. 475–485] argues that while it's up to the law to decide how science is used in court, it's up to science to decide what counts as good science.

   Leaving the quest for correct scientific method to either attorneys or to scientists raises problems dating back to the roots of Western science in ancient Athens. Puzzles *about* method don't fit with either lawyers or scientists. Lawyers deal with principled resolutions to human conflicts. Thorton argues that many competent forensic scientists may have a poor theoretical grasp of what constitutes appropriate scientific method. I believe that the quest to grasp method must turn toward philosophy of science.

   The search for method goes beyond examples of good science, or illusive rules defining scientific practice. [Parallels can be discovered in Plato's *Euthyphro* regarding instances of a practice vs. principles of a practice, or the Meno, regarding rules of a practice vs. understanding the practice]. Both ancient dialogues cover issues again raised by 'knowledge engineers' and rule-based expert system computer programs. However, this takes us nowhere toward an adequate understanding of scientific method.

   Mere examples of 'good science' reduce to anecdote, and abstract rules either become too specific to apply to novel instances, or too general to help. Scientific experts experience the frustration of both Socrates and Euthyphro: no such rules appear to exist. Expert knowledge seems to reduce to a collection of special cases, exceptions, and novelties with no unifying thread. This book presents a scientifically practical, yet philosophically respectable alternative to such quests to clarify a more robust picture of scientific method.

About the Author

Jon J. Nordby, Ph.D., works as a forensic science investigative consultant for Final Analysis, an independent consulting practice in forensic science and forensic medicine. He specializes in scene reconstruction, evidence recognition, collection, and analysis, as well as bloodstain pattern analysis. He serves the National Disaster Medical System as a death investigator and forensic specialist with the Region X DMORT team. He is also an associate professor and former department chair with Pacific Lutheran University, a consultant with the B.C. Coroner's Service Forensic Unit, the King County Medical Examiner's Office, the Pierce County Medical Examiner's Office, and the Puyallup Police Department's Homicide Investigation Section. He formerly worked as a medical investigator with the Pierce County Medical Examiner's Office.

Dr. Nordby received his bachelor's degree from St. Olaf College, Northfield, MN, and his master's and Ph.D. from the University of Massachusetts-Amherst. He spent a postdoctoral year as a visiting scholar, studying at Stanford University. He was awarded membership in Phi Beta Kappa, and received both Woodrow Wilson and Rockefeller Brothers postgraduate fellowships. In 1994, he received a Senior Research Fellowship from the Department of Forensic Medicine, Guy's Hospital, London, England. His extensive in-service training includes courses in forensic medicine, criminalistics, and homicide investigation from medical schools, scientific organizations, and investigative agencies throughout the U.S., Canada, and the U.K. For example, he studied elements of crime scene analysis and death investigation with the FBI at Quantico, VA, the Royal Canadian Mounted Police in Canada, and the Metropolitan Police Training Academy, Hendon, England.

Active in professional organizations, Dr. Nordby is a Fellow of the American Academy of Forensic Sciences, serving as General Section chair and as a member of the Ethics Committee. He is also a member of the Association for Crime Scene Reconstruction, the Canadian Society of Forensic Science, the International Association of Bloodstain Pattern Analysts, the Pacific Northwest Forensic Science Study Group, and the Philosophy of Science Association. He formerly served as chair of the

International Criminal Justice Law Enforcement Expert Systems Association (FBI, Home Office, Interpol, Metropolitan Police, Berlin Police, and U.S. Police jurisdictions). In recognition for his service, he received the American Academy of Forensic Sciences General Section Meritorious Service Award, as well as other acknowledgements from various professional groups. He also enjoys teaching undergraduates as well as law-enforcement and other medical-legal professionals.

Acknowledgements

> My grandfather once told me that there were two kinds of people: those who do the work and those who take the credit. He told me to try to be in the first group; there was much less competition.
>
> Indira Gandhi

My appreciation extends to many for help with, and support for, this project. Even a partial list risks serious omission.

Despite the peril, I acknowledge Det. Edward Hanson, formerly of the Washington State Patrol; Maria Strange, Jackie Shelton, Teresa Terpin, Nancy Kendall, Peg Shaffer, John Walker, Clifford Jo, and the Rev. George Walker; Lt. Gary Hendrickson, Detectives Richard Josephson, and Merle Ziegler of the Dane County Sheriff's Dept.; Phillip Little, Dane County. Coroner's Office: The Rev. Lowell Mays, Sgt. Steven Harb, and the Hamilton Wentworth Regional Police; Rowland Rebusan, and David Icove, FBI Behavioral Sciences Unit; Agent Gregg McCrary of the FBI, formerly from NCAVC, and Robert Siebert, FBI Laboratory; Joan Jacoby, Heike Gramakau, and the now dispersed members of the International Criminal Justice Law Enforcement Expert Systems Association (FBI, Home Office, Interpol, Metropolitan Police, Berlin Police, and U.S. Police jurisdictions); Dick Shepherd, M.D., formerly of Guy's Hospital Department of Forensic Medicine, and Dereck Tremain; Detective Inspector Kenneth Gallagher, Graham Kempson, and John Childerly, of London's Metropolitan Police; Andrew Clapworthy, Metropolitan Police Lab; HRM Coroners Dr. David Paul, Dr. J. H. P. Roberts, and Dr. R. Levine; former Pierce County Medical Examiner E. Q. Lacsina, M.D., Jane Webber, Ed Duke, John Reish, Mari DeTracy, Paul Jay, and current Pierce County Medical Examiner John Howard, M.D.; Sgt. Mark Mann, Tacoma Police Department; Gerry Horne, Pierce County Prosecutor's Office; Chief Investigator Robert Keppel, Washington State Attorney General's Office; King County Medical Examiner Donald T. Reay, M.D., William Haglund, Ph.D., Vaughn Vanzant, and Joseph Frasino; T. E. Chico Newell, and Bart Bastien of the B.C. Coroner's Service Forensic Unit; David Sweet, D.D.S., Peter Hampel, D.D.S., James Young, M.D., Norman "Skip" Sperber, D.D.S., Professor James E. Starrs, Tom Bevel, Ross Gardner, Bart Epstein, and my many colleagues in the American Academy of Forensic Sciences, the International Association of Bloodstain Pattern Analysis, and the Association for Crime Scene Reconstruction; Philosophers Susan Allard, Nancy Cartwright, Lynn Stephens, Scott Arnold, and Keith Cooper; readers Peg and Dan Shaffer, Barbara Evans, Karen Brandt, Janet Prichard, and Steven Brunette, E. J. Nordby, M.D., and Olive M. Nordby; authors Jack Cady, and Ann Rule; Pacific Lutheran University and the ELCA for some financial support; a special indebtedness to B. G. Brogdon, M.D., for his exceptionally valuable mentoring, CRC Press editors George Novotney, Harvey Kane, and especially Becky McEldowney; and an astounding debt to my wife Kim for her extensive critical comments, editorial advice, and her patience with me and my focus on this project.

Despite this invaluable critical support, the slant of the material with any errors of omission or commission, rest solely with the author.

Dedication

To my mom & dad

This work is dedicated to my parents, who have always stood by me. For all the good you bring to my life, the gifts of love, support, friendship, and respect, I am eternally grateful.

JJN
July 1, 1999

Author's Note

With several exceptions in Chapters Four, Five, Six, and Eight, the names, locations, irrelevant circumstances, and characters have been changed to protect personal and professional privacy. The characters presented here often embody characteristics of more than one individual, but in all cases, the methodological approaches are faithfully preserved, and presented. To further focus the reader on *Dead Reckoning: The Art of Forensic Detection,* the graphic detail of photographs, so customary in forensic science texts, have been omitted in favor of black and white line drawings, provided by my mom, the best artist I know.

Table of Contents

> All that you can find in print of my work on logic are simply scattered outcroppings here and there of a rich vein which remains unpublished. Most of it I suppose has been written down; but no human being could ever put together the fragments. I could not myself do so.
>
> Charles Sanders Peirce, 1903

Logic always lurks among the chaos of violent death.

chapter one

Method—The Andrews Case

Reasoning Backward Analytically

> Like all other arts, the Science of Deduction and Analysis is one which can only be acquired by long and patient study, nor is life long enough to allow any mortal to attain the highest possible perfection in it.
>
> Sherlock Holmes

"Dead body found" means a long night for everyone including my wife. Whether in dry summer twilight or wet winter night, she'll attend to our dog's bladder by herself in a long walk around our neighborhood. I won't get home to eat or sleep. My attentions focus on a stranger in a strange place, someone whose death demands investigation.

I never know what to expect when a call comes. Not all deaths are homicides and not all deaths occur in comfortable places. Few people die worshipping on church pews; more die sitting on bus station toilets. I like not knowing what to expect, and I carry tools to handle whatever happens. The powerful abstractions of logic help me understand the colors, odors, and sounds pointing toward an explanation for a stranger's death. My job is to scour the scene for clues, initiate scientific analyses, conduct interviews, and with the results, produce a logical reconstruction of a particular death based on fact.

When a late call comes, I roll out of bed and gather my gear. As a naturally modest investigator, I ask my wife to help me find my keys. Then I'm on my own as I make my way in the van to a trailer park, Space 15.

Intermittent flashes from Ident cameras supply the only brightness in the damp doublewide mobile home decorated in orange '70s shag, lighted by rattan swag lamps, and littered with the debris of careless living. Distant secondhand conversations echo from several sources through speakers too small for clarity and too large to fit comfortably onto any belt. The regenerating cameras whine between flashes, and static crackles punctuate the monotone radio exchanges. The wet air smells of stale cigarette butts and warm beer. A sweet smell, familiar as the taste of a nosebleed and just as sickening, permeates the postpartylike odors; a good sign that the victim bled considerably. Still he had not been dead long enough for smells of decay to overpower the pungent odors wafting through the dwelling.

I never get used to death, although some people say they do. I can never ignore the stillness of the corpse as it lies surrounded by the businesslike motions of the Crime Scene Processing Unit, the ritualistic protocols of the deputies securing the scene, and the cryptic exchanges among hovering detectives. The dead silence, more telling than blood, never makes it to court.

I usually wear a white shirt with a dark tie and it's a matter of pride to keep both clean. I always carry a microcassette recorder as a notebook for my observations because it fits into my pocket where it doesn't get lost. I withdraw the recorder as I approach the body that lies face down in a dark pool as on a bier of once-bright linoleum. The body is male, dressed only in white cotton briefs.

I wonder to myself how he looked the day he was born, whether his mother held him during a baptism, how he liked the second grade, and who gave him his first job. Who was his first love? What did his buddies call him? Where did he work? Did anyone miss him when he left town? Who would miss him now? For the recorder, I supply a case number, date, time, place, and a list of personnel present.

I kneel by the body. The red light on the recorder disappears as Ident finishes photographing the kitchen floor. Rubber gloves stretch over my hands, creaking like balloons at a birthday party. Serum and hemoglobin decorating the linoleum continue to separate, leaving a pink and watery edge to the dark pool surrounding the left side of the corpse.

I withdraw a latex-covered finger after poking an area of pinkish discoloration on the right thigh touching the floor. Post-mortem lividity, the settling of blood in the body by gravity once the heartbeat ceases, appears minimal, but does not blanch to my finger's moderate pressure. Rigor mortis, the chemical process resulting in muscular stiffness, is noticeable: The arm and leg joints move slightly but the neck does not as my gloved hand tests for motion.

It's hard to establish time-of-death. It lies between the time the decedent was last seen alive and first found dead. Factors offer clues but no specifics. Lividity varies with temperature, massive bleeding, or medications such as Coumadin, a cardiac drug that thins the blood to prevent clotting. With lots of blood on the floor, not much settles in the body for finger pressure to detect. Muscular exertion before death increases the rate of rigor's stiffening. Varying temperatures also vary this effect. Estimating "time of death" isn't a precise calculation.

The recorder reappears, and the red light glows. "It is now 2330 hours. Decedent, discovered by a neighbor about 2230 hours, appears to have been dead about eight hours, plus or minus. Time of death about 1530, plus or minus." I turn my attention to the area around the body and through an open door into a room behind the kitchen.

I notice a glass in the dish drainer beneath two open cupboard doors. In the back bedroom, above the tangle of unwashed pants, shirts, and sheets, I see an oily rag smelling faintly of nitrocellulose and a dishtowel smelling of alcohol. My eyes pass over the arsenal in the closet: one 30–30 rifle, a 22 semiautomatic rifle, three shotguns and two revolvers, a 32 and a 22. They rest on a 9mm semiautomatic pistol placed on the closet shelf behind a box of Winchester shotgun shells. It was the only clean weapon there, and the arsenal included no 9mm cartridges.

A small triangular impression, flattened in the orange shag floor, pointed from the closet door toward its back wall. The ghost of a pleasant scent lingered with stronger odors in the musty closet. Logic always lurks among the chaos of violent death linking its signs to help show me the way. Once observed, clues must be followed.

Sherlock Holmes was the fictional master of clues. If relaxed in his Baker Street quarters and seated in his wing-back chair puffing his pipe, he might insist that scientific reasoning represents the investigator's only hope of explaining mysterious deaths. It supplies our ability to recognize, understand, organize, and evaluate information, he would say. To read words, we must recognize the signs on paper, interpret their meanings, and notice the organization and relations among the ideas presented. To read clues, investigators must recognize the signs at the scene, interpret their significance and cleverly test them.

To read the scene of this murder, Holmes would recognize the glass, the towel, the 9mm weapon, the footprint, and a faint odor as natural signs among the chaos of haphazard life and violent death. He must decode the stories they tell, relate the stories, and evaluate the resulting account. He must use this reasoning to organize the scene, relate the physical evidence with the dead man's history and the testimony of witnesses, and design tests to allay or develop his emerging suspicions. Similarly, we must read from the book of nature and separate the relevant evidence from a trailer full of coincidences competing for our attention.

On the trailer's makeshift front porch, county detectives David Germaine and Roger Shipley watch through the open front door. I've found that official distance from bodies increases with unpleasant odors. Shipley leans against a door jamb and smokes. Germaine, who is sometimes too efficient for his own good, stops in front of me.

"Before this screws up," he says, "let's get our look-through coordinated." He's tall enough that he bumps his head going from room to room if he's not careful. At present, he is being careful, and his tan face keeps trying to come awake. Still, I know him well. When the work starts his eyes will be open.

We moved through the trailer room by room. First things first. A name had to connect with the body lying on the kitchen floor. With it, family, friends, associates, and even enemies would appear. Who saw him when, his state of mind, and his movements before his death would become visible. Corroboration or contradiction would be supplied by physical evidence. The task of explaining the body on the linoleum had many parts. Relevant evidence had to be gleaned from a trailer full of coincidences. We echo the form of the ancient hunter, knee in the mud, spear in hand, and eyes to the ground in pursuit of his quarry. We began our hunt in the bedroom.

A brown highboy dresser facing the door on the opposite wall beside an unmade bed lacked knobs on two of the six drawers. A piece of wire that looped through one of the holes and out the other supplied a makeshift handle for the top drawer. The second drawer, already open, overflowed with pajama tops, plaid shirts, underwear, and colored handkerchiefs. Germaine pulled the wire, searching for the dead man's identity in the top drawer. He would work his way down.

"Hey, look here," he says, closing the bottom dresser drawer, holding a creased photo of a man, woman, and two children, one male and one female. "And I got a canceled check and phone bill," he adds, smiling like a kid with a buck in a candy store.

I examine a wallet from a pair of pants on the rumpled bed finding a driver's license and social security card. But we both know that licenses can be forged or stolen, and traumatized or decomposed bodies rarely resemble photographs taken in happier times. If the victim had a criminal record, his fingerprints may be on file. We compare postmortem prints with antemortem records to make the identification. If that fails, X-rays of his teeth could be compared with known dental records. Again, that presupposes finding the right antemortem record. But this identification won't be that difficult. Suitably sanitized, the dead man could probably be identified by family or friends.

Outside, the others continue to work illuminated by the mercury lamp lighting the yard and road. One uniformed deputy logs access to the trailer. Another controls the perimeter of the scene, defined by yellow tape with black letters reading "Crime Scene Keep Out." She keeps back curious residents attracted by the two patrol cars, two unmarked county cars with telltale antennas, and two white vans.

Shipley, a cigarette pinched between his lips, stands on the porch squinting at the responding deputy's handwritten report. He has the weathered face of the Marlboro man, and I'd bet the lungs to match. He's shorter than Germaine and heavier than both of us put together. He looks up at us through wisps of smoke.

"Whadaya got?" Germaine asks.

"One Bernice Heldon, age 52, found the body," he answers behind his flopping cigarette. "Our boy is one Norbert Andrews, an unemployed shipyard worker. She says she had a date with him at seven. He didn't show. At 10:20 she says she looked in and saw his feet."

I walk off the porch and peer through the window beside the front door to see what she claimed to see.

I figure she might be expecting to see him asleep on the couch in front of the 25-inch RCA. The set cast no moving shadows on the empty couch. The cramped living room, piled with old newspapers and magazines, led to the dining area on the right and the kitchen behind. A mercury yard light provided the only illumination. I could see the bare white feet on the linoleum, legs disappearing into the shadow cast by the windowsill. An irregular pool to the ankle's left reflected the colorless light. Stepping past Shipley through the front door I could see where the responding deputy broke a window in the front door to unlock the knob. The windowless back door remained locked and bolted.

While Shipley chews on the deputy's report, I bag the dead man's hands in paper to secure any trace evidence such as blood, hair, or skin from the attacker, if there had been one. The bare feet may also supply trace evidence. Bags, tied with string, protect the hands and feet from contact with other surfaces when transporting the body to the medical examiner's office. Paper prevents any contamination from the moisture released by the body. My gloved hands reach for the bare left arm and, assisted by rigor, the corpse tips to the right away from the bloody puddle, with head, trunk, and legs following in the graceless choreography of death.

As the body completes its tip, more blood dribbles from the middle of the chest. After a careful inspection of the body's anterior surface, and the patch of linoleum once underneath, the recorder reappears: "Small scratches on right arm above elbow. Large bloody injury present about the midline in the center of the chest. No other obvious signs of injury are observed at this time. Tentative ID is Norbert Andrews, visual ID by drivers license found in bedroom and other photos in residence, to be confirmed by relatives, fingerprints, or dental. Personal effects indicate two children and one wife or ex-wife as possible next-of-kin. No notifications known or made at this time."

Germaine helps unfold a new white cotton sheet along the right side of the body. Our gloved hands grasp the decedent's ankles and wrists above the bags, placing him in the middle of his fresh shroud. They fold the uncontaminated sheet over the body, wrapping the contents like a giant burrito to contain any possible trace evidence that may tag along for the ride. Red stains wick through the top of the sheet as I unzip a white body bag, and we lift the body onto the opened container then zip the contents securely in place. Little more can be done with the 6-foot, 228-pound, 57-year-old dead man at the scene. He rides with me to the county morgue, where I confirm identification, locate the family, and write my report for the chief medical examiner.

In the medical examiner's office, 0600 hours the day after Norbert Andrew's death, forensic pathologist Howard E. Manning, M.D., unzips the body bag after reading my report over a cup of black coffee. The white cloth sheet and paper bags from hands and feet, with any adhering trace evidence, will accompany the items he sends to the crime lab for further analysis. Wheeled from the morgue refrigerator and now unwrapped, Norbert rides to his various appointments on a stainless steel gurney.

He arrives at his first stop beneath a surgical lamp. Manning examines the dead man under the bright light in exacting detail, recording his observations with both pen and camera. The notes and photos eventually join my report in a gradually growing case file.

Norbert lay on his back atop the white sheet, his salt and pepper medium-length hair matted with blood. The gray stubble on both pale cheeks held blood wiped from the linoleum pool. The pathologist removes the blood soaked undershorts from Norbert's uncooperative body, now much stiffer after a few hours at 38 degrees Fahrenheit, allowing them to air dry before their trip to the laboratory. He records identifying marks, scars, moles, and tattoos; any injuries, old or new, bruises, scratches, or injection sites, distinguishing those occurring before death from those inflicted after. The scratches on the right arm above the elbow show healing. A tattoo on the left arm artfully depicts a large-breasted mermaid, presumably not Mr. Andrews' mother. On the right arm, a red and blue heart circled by a greenish snake announces "Ruthie forever."

Lowering the lamp and adjusting its angle, Manning collects trace evidence including hairs and fibers adhering to the body. He scrapes under each fingernail and cuts them, putting the material in evidence envelopes. He moves the light again to examine the bullet's entry wound.

"I don't see any powder burns or stippling on the skin," he says, partly to himself and partly to me. "No clothing besides the underwear, right?" he asks both to double-check his memory and to cite a firsthand source.

"No clothing besides the briefs," I say.

"This looks like an intermediate-range entry wound," he says while leaning over his patient like a dentist examining a cavity. "No clothing to absorb the unburned powder and no stippling on the skin," he adds with the same tone in the same breath.

He swabs the hands to collect any possible gunshot residue. I fingerprint the body and wheel the gurney to X-ray.

Ghostly black and white skeletal shadows display an opaque projectile lodged in the fifth thoracic vertebra. Manning will dig it out for possible ballistic comparison with any suspect gun. Comparisons may be difficult given this bullet's apparent deformity. The freshly developed films accompany the gurney to one of the office's four stainless steel autopsy stations. Detective Germaine stands at Station Three, apron in hand, awaiting Norbert Andrews.

With the sheet, bags, and underwear removed, the body on the gurney lies beside a scale, instrument tray, and Stryker saw, perpendicular to a stainless steel sink. The medical examiner's autopsy assistant places a block under Norbert's neck, and raises the gurney one notch at the head end so blood and debris will wash down to the sink's drain at the other. With Detective Germaine well back, the technician makes a Y-shaped incision, starting below both shoulders meeting at about the second rib by the sternum, and continues down the midline, carefully avoiding the gunshot wound, ending the Y just above the pubic region. With the scalpel, he deflects the skin, muscle, and a layer of yellow fat, which looks like buttered popcorn. With a garden lopper, he cuts the collar bones and ribs on each side, scissoring toward the hips, and removes the bone and cartilage held together by what looks like filaments of strapping tape. The internal organs now appear beneath the opened flaps of skin, muscle, and fat.

Looking up at the X-rays glowing from fluorescent display boxes to the table's left, the medical examiner traces the bullet's path from the sternum through the aorta to bone, and notes a slight upward trajectory. He removes, weighs, examines, sections, and describes all of the internal organs, including the brain, saving samples for microscopic analysis and for any further tests the investigation warrants. With the internal organs out of the way, he removes the bullet from the vertebra, places it in a marked evidence container, and hands it to Detective Germaine.

"Should be able to match the bullet to a gun," Germaine says hopefully, "if we can find the gun it goes with."

While Manning continues to chat with Germaine, I experience a wave of what I call the Humpty-Dumpty effect. I've attended hundreds of autopsies. I still feel it every time. This amazing and complex human body opened for viewing, organs removed for weighing, can never be put back together again. Maybe it's the chatter over the silence of death that brings it on. The feeling helps focus my attention on the case before me.

I see that the coronary arteries remained open, but brittle reinforcements replaced once flexible supply lines, hardened by calcification. The cirrhotic liver, hard and yellowed with fatty nodules, did not resemble the smooth, deep burgundy organ supplied as original equipment. The lungs, discolored by carbon, heavy and wet like an unwrung dishrag, showed the signs of emphysema. This complex wonder had covered some hard miles.

Dr. Manning, looking up, his hands occupied with knife, needle, or scale, would occasionally present his results dramatically. But he never received the immediate confirmation that a fictional scientific sleuth like Holmes enjoyed. His patients simply no longer participated in his examinations. They could not applaud his remarkable conclusions. As usual, his conclusions appeared for our benefit.

"Well, my man, you've served in the Navy, or Merchant Marines." Silence. "A heavy smoker, and a heavy drinker, too." More silence. "Shot from a distance by a person that you knew, probably quite well." Continued silence. Detective Germaine, standing front row center, became Manning's attentive Watson stand-in. I stood back to enjoy the logical show.

"You see, Dave, the tattoos have a design popular with merchant seamen 30 years ago. The first and second fingers on both hands show yellowing characteristic of heavy cigarette smokers and his lungs show alveolar collapse and fluid infiltration. His arteries and liver show the effects of chronic alcohol abuse. The entry wound has no evidence of fouling, placing the muzzle some distance from his chest. He wore only his underwear, indicating a familiar relationship with the shooter."

Germaine nodded, took it all in, and smiled appreciatively. Conjectures about the shooter remained to be tested.

"Cause of death: a single penetrating gunshot wound to the chest," Manning continued. "The shot lacerated the pericardial sac, entered the aorta and lodged in the fifth thoracic vertebra. His position and the hole account for the blood on the floor."

"Could he have moved after the shot?" Germaine asked.

"He dropped like a sack of sand. A big old hole in the pipes drops blood pressure quick. That interrupts heart function, and unconsciousness follows in seconds." Germaine nodded again.

In my work, death's cause is usually easier to find than its manner. Through a large enough hole in a proper position, blood abandons the body like profligate fathers ditching dependent children. But did the gun fire accidentally? Did he shoot himself, or did someone else pull the trigger? Maybe we can't answer the question, or maybe we can. Our answer may not meet the standard of proof established by risk-averse prosecutors. But clues from the autopsy, when added to the signs at the scene usually point toward the answers.

Dr. Manning finished dictating his report by noon. Toxicology, histology, ballistics, and trace evidence analysis would take at least another several weeks. The death certificate, the final report card, brings the bad news home for the last time a week or so after that. The body, with its organs collected in a plastic bag stuffed into the thoracic cavity, topped by the pruned ribs and secured by four sutures under the gaping Y-shaped incision, can be released to a funeral home. In the meantime, wrapped in white plastic with a yellow toe tag, Norbert Andrews rejoined the prefuneral holding pattern in the morgue refrigerator. I sat down at my desk, replayed my taped observations, and called Ident for their report.

The report described their search for minute traces of blood on the furniture, carpets, walls, ceilings, and floors of the trailer's other rooms. They found none. One patch of linoleum about two-feet in diameter, located three feet behind where Norbert lay, lacked the dust, dirt, and grease found everywhere else on the kitchen floor. Signs central to the logic of explanation began to point more clearly.

Meanwhile, Shipley interviewed neighbors, hoping to identify potential suspects. Bernice Heldon, still dazed from her brief introduction to Norbert's white feet, added little to her first interview. She said he drank too much, smoked too much, and had a temper, but added nothing further. She saw Norbert through heavy mascara and powder blue eye shadow as a potential paramour. By dying, Andrews probably avoided an even worse fate.

Mrs. Hilda Orson lived in her mobile home parked on the living room side of the dead man's trailer. Her brown eyes, deeply set in a pudgy face and magnified by thick glasses, expressed permanent surprise. Curly gray hair wrapped around pink sponge rollers lacked only an occasion for such increasingly haphazard ministrations.

Hilda talked nonstop, as only the lonely can, relishing her newfound importance. Shipley reduced her statement to coherent English and gave Germaine and me the bottom line before we met to notify Andrews' next-of-kin. She had walked past her window during a commercial break between *As The World Turns* and *Guiding Light,* making it about 2:00 P.M., and had seen a faded red sedan pull up in front of her neighbor's trailer. A woman, carrying a purse, had gotten out and headed toward his front door.

Carrying these pieces of the puzzle, the three of us, now into our second day with little sleep, met at Mrs. Andrews' home about 12:30 P.M. the afternoon after Bernice Heldon's surprising discovery. With no divorce on record, the legal chain remained intact. Mrs. Norbert Andrews and her children count as family regardless of fractures in the emotional bond.

"Hey look," Germaine said under his breath, nodding toward a faded burgundy 1965 Chevrolet sedan parked in front of the small one-story rambler. Inside, the Andrews family assembled on the couch. Mrs. Andrews with puffy red eyes sat flanked by her son with his wife on the left, and her daughter on the right. A small child, about three scattering Lego blocks on the floor appeared oblivious to the somber scene.

"This is hard to say and hard to hear. Your husband is dead." I saw no sign of surprise when I officially delivered the news. The composition of the family portrait changed little. Lego distribution continued uninterrupted. No one asked how he died. No one said, "it can't be true."

My eyes remained on Mrs. Andrews. Tired and drawn, she sat motionless, her eyes refusing contact with mine. Uneven face powder revealed purple and yellow discoloration around her left eye and cheek. Her daughter, Helen, wearing stone washed Levis too tight for her ample figure, a western style shirt, and cowboy boots, stared intently at her own folded hands. A blue tattoo on her left wrist peeked from underneath the western cuff. I smelled perfume. The son, smoking a cigarette, resembled his father, feet and all. More of the puzzle's missing pieces.

Amateur sleuths hone their skills by reading page turning whodunnits. They become accomplished investigators of literary plots. But the signs in the trailer, at the lab, on the body, or seated on Mrs. Andrews' couch do not organize by literary rules. Fiction is orderly. Reality isn't. The genres differ. Shipley, the interrogator, asked the questions.

"How long have you lived apart?" he asked.

"Must be most of five years," she said. "He don't believe in divorce. Still, seems like he always wants money er . . . " her voice trailed off and finally added " . . . er sumpthin'," her eyes even further away from Shipley, and he was hard to miss.

"When did you last drive your car?" Unresponsive, she began sobbing. Tears soon eroded the thick cosmetics under her eye. Tears appeared in the younger Mrs. Andrews' eyes as she stared at her son playing on the floor. Her husband looked out the window, blowing smoke through his nose. Helen stepped in and took over answering questions for her mother.

"I come over from Kalispell 'bout a week ago," she said, looking directly into Shipley's eyes. "Yesterday, I guess it was, I went an' seen him," she added, shifting her eyes to the ground. Shipley remained quiet. Uncomfortable silences were an interrogator's strongest ally.

"I wanted him to quit beatin' up on Ma." More silence.

Finally Shipley asked "When did you go to see him?"

"Got there 'bout 2 o'clock. I go in and he's on the couch, drinkin'. As usual," she added after a slight pause. "I tell the pig to keep away from Ma, or I'll get the cops to toss his sorry ass in jail."

"What'd he do then?" Shipley asked without leaving the cushion that silence provides.

"The bastard said he'd blow his fuckin' brains out if we done that." She shifted her eyes from the floor to the Lego structure rising off the carpet. More silence. No one moved.

"He pulls a gun from under the couch and started throwin' one o' his fits. He gets up, goes ta the kitchen, stops, turns 'n' points it at me. I'm scared shitless. So he yells, then I hear this bang. I think, shit, I'm dead. Then he drops to the floor. He don't say nothin', he just lays there."

"What did you do then?"

"I just look. I finally figure he shot himself. It was like slow motion. Seemed like hours. I just kep' starin'."

"You just looked?"

"Well, no. I pick up the gun, wipe it with a rag, and put it in the closet."

"Why?"

"'Cause I wanted Ma ta git his union insurance. I figure they don't pay if he done it to himself."

She explained how she left the trailer, locking the front door on the way out and drove around for a few hours. She finished her story saying that she called her brother, and told the family that Norbert Andrews, husband and father, had committed suicide. I could tell from his frown that Shipley remained unimpressed.

Not just words, but inflections, ineffectively concealed bruises, tears, and body language all tell a story. This family portrait when fit together with clues from the scene and autopsy pose two timeless puzzles: how to distill the correct solution from them, and how to prove its truth.

Creative discovery seems to have a mystical quality. Shipley says that he just has "a gut feeling." He thinks that science just tests these inspired discoveries. Held hostage to the muses, science becomes window dressing for courtroom theatrics.

But I'm not persuaded. Forensic scientists don't work as slaves to Shipley's brilliant hunches. I find a deeper relationship between these signs and the solution, the problem and the proof. What counts as a clue suggesting and supporting the best explanation requires confirmation.

As a student, I read the father of American Pragmatism, Charles Sanders Peirce,[1] who lived from 1846 to 1914. He devoted his life to studying the logic of science, a method he called "critical logic." He established logical relationships between the signs that suggest an explanation and the methods that prove or disprove it.

Peirce insisted that scientists reason from specific details, not from abstract generalities. He also insisted that scientific testing first requires discovering something to test, as cooking a fish dinner begins with catching a fish. I revisit his insights at every death scene I attend. My wife uses critical logic to find mislaid keys.

If I asked Shipley the right questions, his "gut feeling" might appear as a series of identifiable steps that distinguish relevant evidence from coincidental items, and help suggest tests to provide proof. Germaine must assemble the case for the prosecutor, and he must identify relevant items from the interrogations, witness statements, the lab, and the medical examiner. In this case, Shipley's gut, though ample, doesn't count as relevant evidence.

Tangible evidence also comes from bench scientists far removed from smelly trailers and tortured families. I never think that this distance from chaos makes their work any easier than mine. I'd miss the artifacts of daily life interrupted by violent death that help me humanize the contents of a test tube filled with blood, now identified only by a case number.

Crime lab toxicologist Susan Stanley examined the blood collected by Dr. Manning at the autopsy. I listened as she reported her results about a week after our interview with Mrs. Andrews and her children.

"I'll fax you my report after we get off the phone," she said as politely as she could, considering that she has hundreds of drug screens to perform, document, and report. My call took valuable lab time. She remained, as always, gracious. "Norbert Andrews' blood alcohol read .15% w/v," she said. That means 0.15 grams of alcohol per 100 milliliters of blood.

So he was legally drunk in most jurisdictions, but that's not a high level for a practiced drinker with a liver like his. All other drug screens read negative. Hairs and fibers depend on comparisons. With nothing to compare recovered hairs or fibers with, and no reason for suggesting comparisons, lab personnel performed no analyses on either the underwear, or the fingernail material. That evidence must wait for the appropriate question before revealing any answer.

The paper bags and white sheet also headed toward perpetual storage in the county evidence locker. The decedent's prints appeared on the glass taken from the table; a single smudged print, lifted from the glass in the dish rack, lacked identifiable features. The decedent's prints covered all weapons except the 9mm semi-automatic: No prints, identifiable or otherwise, remain on the gun. That gun, the absence of a shell casing at the scene, the cartridges remaining in the clip, and the deformed bullet removed at autopsy, became the focus of further testing. Germaine's case required these supporting scientific details before he could charge his prime suspect with murder.

Reviewing the details can be as simple as a making a list of facts, and imagining what they might mean. Any little kid can do that better than the average grownup. List: the 9mm weapon had no prints. Hmm. Any smooth, hard surface like a gun's barrel, trigger, trigger guard, or clip takes prints easily. Rough handles rarely reveal prints. Loading, shooting, and putting the gun in the closet should leave prints, even if they remain unidentifiable smears. Hmm. So someone wiped the gun clean and put it away without leaving prints. Why? I love being a kid.

Helen Andrews' account that she wiped the gun to conceal Norbert's suicide depended on the fatal shot being self-inflicted. Unlikely she'd take the gun apart and wipe the clip in her supposed state of shock. But no prints. Not even smudges.

Sometimes the listing and the imagining put someone to work. Germaine wanted to know if Norbert Andrews fired a gun. That's a question for Shelly Herbert.

When a gun fires, residue shoots from the weapon's barrel, and both gunpowder and primer blow back toward the shooter. How much depends on the gun's design and wear. Gunshot residue tests look for barium and antimony from the primer that ignites the gunpowder. It usually deposits on the thumb web and the back of the firing hand, or on areas closest to the gun's side and back.

But positive results even from known shooters are rare. Primer residues usually endure for only a few hours. They dissipate by wiping and washing. Residue samples, taken from living suspects more than six hours after a shooting, answer few questions. The hands of the dead, however, do tell tales.

Shelly Herbert returned Germaine's call. Barium and antimony were absent from Norbert Andrews' hands. Some answers stimulate the imagination and add facts to the list. Thank you forensic science. Detective Germaine had his sign. Helen's story had a problem.

But sometimes, even great questions have lousy answers. Real science has limits. Germaine hoped to link the bullet from the body to the gun from the closet. A 9mm weapon in a closet with no 9mm ammunition raised a question. Suppose the killer brought the gun and left it at the trailer. Link the bullet with the gun, and the gun with the suspect, and the case becomes stronger. Or link identical 9mm ammo to the suspect, and the signs also point toward the killer.

But as luck would have it, the bullet removed from Norbert Andrews, too mutilated by striking bone, could not be linked positively to the 9mm semiautomatic found in the closet. The bullet could still be compared by spectrographic analysis to any source of ammunition later recovered, but that only happens with divine intervention or luck, depending on your theological preference. It doesn't matter either way. Neither seems to appear with any predictable regularity.

The list of facts included no sign of fouling on the entrance wound. Another occasion for imagination. Hmm. This fact suggested a shooting scenario and more questions, leaving Helen's story with a hole in it about the size of the one found in Norbert's chest. More work for someone. Dr. Shelly Herbert from the lab conducted more tests.

The discharge distances of unburned gunpowder, flame, and other residues determine the distance from a gun to its target. When the gun fires up to an inch away from a target, a halo of vaporous lead, unburned powder, and scorch marks decorate the bullet entry site. If the gun contacts skin over bone, the gasses blown under the skin shred hunks of tissue from surrounding bone. Any gunpowder stippling suggests a discharge distance of about 20 inches or less, depending on the weapon. Herbert test fired the 9mm semiautomatic found in the closet.

"The weapon," she told us, "produces stippling patterns beginning 18 inches from the target." Germaine had another sign pointing toward the shooter.

Doyle's Sherlock Holmes demonstrated the value of discovering and then reasoning from such signs. He reasoned from small and apparently inconsequential observations, constructing a chain of evidence strong enough to secure the solution. Holmes had the luxury of sufficient time and abundant resources to follow the evidence, and he always solved the mystery. Real-life investigators of violent death, whose radios intrude with new calls and new mysteries every few hours, are rarely as fortunate. But every investigator, medical examiner, and forensic scientist applies the same peculiar brand of reasoning that Sir Arthur Conan Doyle's Sherlock Holmes first made famous. As Holmes himself says, "Most people, if you describe a turn of events to them, will tell you the result . . . there are few people . . . who if you told them a result, would be able to evolve . . . the steps which led up to (it). This power is what I mean when I talk of reasoning backward, or analytically." The corpse on the kitchen linoleum, a silent result demanding explanation, invites this reasoning characteristic of the investigators and forensic scientists who must "evolve the steps" which lead to the true story of the death in this trailer.

This story, built from list of facts, questions, imaginings, and their eventual answers, form the case. Germaine now could add another fact to his list. Based on answers to questions about the gun and the wound, Dr. Manning ruled the manner of Norbert Andrews' death to be homicide.

"Homicide" doesn't mean exclusively "murder," except on TV. "Homicide," on a death certificate, means another person caused the death. "Murder" adds that the killing is both wrong and unjustified. That decision rests with the prosecutor. Germaine's list pointed to murder. He brought it to the county's chief deputy criminal prosecutor, Jerry Barron.

"Norbert beat both Ruth and Helen." Germaine said, looking at Jerry across a pile of papers, files, and open books stacked on the prosecutor's desk. He continued without looking at the folder he had added to Barren's piles.

"Michael, the youngest, left home after eighth grade. Norbert's battering allied mother with daughter. Daughter Helen moved to Montana six months before the shooting. The move put pressure on mom, but everyone, even mom, denies that Norbert caused trouble."

"Same old thing," he added after a pause. A person's capacity to improve on reality never ceases to amaze, even after years of measuring self-deception with a yardstick of injury and death. Such experience teaches, but the student must learn the correct lesson. Statistics don't explain anything, especially particular deaths.

A week after the shooting, detectives Germaine and Shipley arrested Helen Andrews and prosecutor Jerry Barron charged her with first-degree murder. From there, Justice moved slowly. Three months after Helen traded her jeans for a county jail jumpsuit her jury trial began. In two days, it was over.

Like many in forensic science, I rarely hear what happens after my work is done. I'm busy working new cases. But the signs in Norbert's trailer and the nature of his wound remained points at issue, so I followed developments even after my part ended.

At trial, the prosecution argued that Helen Andrews drove her mother's car to her father's trailer about 2:00 P.M. the day he died. She brought the 9mm semi-automatic with her to kill him. Norbert, drinking and sitting on his couch while arguing with Helen, got up and walked toward the kitchen to get her a drink. He left his glass on the table. He got a glass from the cupboard and filled it. Helen stood on the shag carpet between the linoleum and the front door, and when he walked toward the living room carrying her drink, she shot him in the chest from about four feet away.

After she shot him, she picked up the unbroken glass, wiped up its contents, washed the glass, and put it in the dish drainer. She picked up the shell case ejected from the weapon onto the orange shag carpet, wiped the gun with a rag from the bedroom arsenal, and put it on the closet shelf. She locked the front door knob at about 2:45 P.M. and closed the door, leaving her dead father on the kitchen floor. For motive, the prosecutor painted a picture of abuse, alcoholism, and the need to break free on a canvas of long-smoldering anger, fear, and financial gain. "Abuse that does not pose an immediate threat," he concluded, " does not justify a cold-blooded execution."

The prosecution witnesses included a Montana gun shop owner. He positively identified Helen from photographs as the woman who purchased a 9mm semi-automatic with the identical serial number as the gun found in the trailer, and a single box of 9mm ammunition, later found with her things at her mother's home. Two scientific experts, Dr. Manning and Dr. Herbert, presented the physical evidence.

The defense lawyer countered the prosecution scenario by arguing that Norbert Andrews' tragic life ended in a tragic suicidal death. The defense is paid to create doubt. In our adversarial system, the prosecution's case must withstand the attack. The jury must decide if the doubt created is reasonable or not.

According to the defense, Helen did not murder her father. No one did because he shot himself. Yes, Helen drove to her father's trailer about 2:00 P.M.

the day he died. She brought no gun with her. Norbert, drinking and sitting on his couch, screamed at her. He walked toward the kitchen to fill his drink, waving the gun. He forgot his glass on the table. He kept yelling from the kitchen. Helen stood in fear on the carpet, ready to go out the front door. He walked toward the living room and shot himself in the chest.

In shock, she picked up the shell case from the kitchen floor, wiped the gun with the rag from the bedroom, and put it in the closet. She locked the front door and closed it, leaving at 2:45 P.M. She threw the shell case down the storm drain. Helen's only crimes, hindering a death investigation by failing to report a death, and altering the scene of a suicide, fit her history of covering up for her father and protecting her mother.

Dr. Manning testified that he saw no powder burns, stippling, or flash marks of any kind on the chest wound. "This," he said, "is consistent with a shot fired at an intermediate range, but inconsistent with a shot fired at close range." He concluded that the decedent's wounds could not have been self-inflicted. No evidence supported the supposition. He based this conclusion on the autopsy and his observations of the wound. The decedent's right arm measured 27 inches from the tip of his middle finger to his armpit. His left spanned 26 inches between the same points. Even held out as far as possible with both hands, using the right thumb to pull the trigger, the tip of the barrel would be at most 10 inches from the chest and probably closer. There would be powder marks on any self-inflicted wound fired from those distances. There were none.

Shelly Herbert, Ph.D., presented the prosecution's next lesson in physical science. She explained gunshots for the jury. Experts must educate, not pontificate. Her tests showed that the 9mm handgun leaves stippling patterns 18 inches from a target. In her opinion, based on test firing the weapon, the shot that struck Norbert Andrews in the chest was fired from a distance more than three feet away.

The defense battle for juror sympathy included a direct attack on the scientific findings. Some legal scholars call the process "Socratic." In many cases, it appears to ordinary folks as fancy manipulation. Two defense experts countered Dr. Manning's and Dr. Herbert's conclusions. It's up to the jury to resolve contradictory testimony, including scientific conflicts. Ultimately, whatever the jury says, is so. Emotion plays well against dry scientific litany.

The defense designs the cross of scientific witnesses to strengthen its own case and weaken their adversary's. Experts must explain their objective findings simply and coherently, or risk their deliberate distortion by advocates for one side or the other. Casting doubt was fair game; that's the defense attorney's job. Any scientific testimony, whether focused on alcohol or guns, becomes a delicate balance between too much and too little. Either extreme can lose the jury. And in ether case, advocacy for anything but sound logic and scientific truth evaporates expert credibility.

The defense argued that the facts supported an alternative explanation at least as likely as the prosecution's. No one could prove that Helen carried the gun to her father's trailer the day of his death. When the bet is 50-50 either way the law calls that "reasonable doubt." The prosecution case compared favorably with the flip of a coin. Innocent until proven guilty. Therefore, by defense argument, innocent. The fog first formed around hypothetical 9mm cartridges "shorted" gunpowder.

The defense ballistics expert testified that a bullet propelled by too little gunpowder in the cartridge produced no stippling at short range. He test fired the weapon with "short loads" at targets 10 inches from the muzzle. He found no stippling pattern. He recited statistics showing that less than half a percent end up shorted powder, but added that such manufacturing defects couldn't be ruled out in any case. He concluded, given a "short load," a slightly defective primer cap, and the backward position of the gun in both hands, that no gunshot residues would be recovered from the shooter's hands. To test for stippling, he removed powder until no stippling appeared at 10 inches from the target. To test for gun shot residues, he fired a series of special cartridges, decreasing the primer charge in each until no residues deposited.

Charges of careless testing affect the weight of the evidence, but not its admissibility. The defense expert did not state the facts in this case. He stated that the absence of both stippling on the wound and primer residue on Norbert's hands *could be* explained by his experiments. And he testified that his experiments amply demonstrated the possibility of such a shot. The actual facts in Norbert Andrews' death were separate issues before the jury. No wonder jurors get confused. Neither Manning nor Herbert could swear that a short load played no role in Norbert Andrews' death. Nor could the defense expert swear that it did. The jury's opinion was what counted.

Unlike high profile cases filling the tabloids, the public didn't care enough in this case to have opinions. Except for the usual fleeting murder trial curiosity, this case, like most such violent deaths, did not excite public interest. I can imagine a tabloid headline: "Fat repulsive unemployed alcoholic resident of trailer park dressed only in dirty underwear, found shot." Story line: "Homely daughter, truck stop waitress from Montana, charged. Did she do it?!!!" No true crime writers attended this two-day trial. No high-priced experts volunteered their services. Even Jerry Springer would have no interest.

The defense team offered one more player, a therapist who specialized in treating dysfunctional alcoholic families. She explained the slick of lies coating family relationships floundering in a sea of alcohol. She described concealing suicides, transferring blame, denying problems, and shielding the alcoholic himself. Norbert acted as the alcoholic in final despair when he took his life. Helen acted codependently when she covered it up. Her testimony came off like an episode of *Oprah.* I suspect that the therapist told the same story repeatedly. Different cases; same explanations.

Even though psychological testimony remains speculative, psychologists supply it, and lawyers accept it. Psychologists take the stand and defend opposite sides of an issue, often turning judges into talk show hosts and juries into emotionally divided audiences. For the defense, the payoff is reasonable doubt.

After the summations, repeats of the opening statements, the judge told jurors about burden of proof, reasonable doubt, and the preponderance of evidence. They retired to deliberate. I went home to mow the lawn.

We have a small yard and a hand mower. The quiet whir as I walk lets me think. I thought about the details I saw at the scene that never entered the court record. The triangular impression on the trailer's orange shag carpet suggested the pointed toe of a cowboy boot. Helen Andrews habitually wore cowboy boots. The lingering scent of perfume in the closet matched the fragrance I smelled both at our first meeting and again in court.

These signs of Helen's visit pointed at both the towel and the gun. The more I mowed, the more I thought that the towel's informative power had escaped both sides.

If I'm right, the towel shows traces of barium and antimony from the primer mixed with residues from a drink and a dirty kitchen floor. Given positive gunshot residue results, only the shooter could have handled that towel, and only after the shot was fired. The clean linoleum patch suggested that the shooter wiped up a spilled drink. Norbert Andrews lay dying on the floor. If the towel carried those signs, with only two people present, elimination identified the shooter.

The logic is risky and uncertain. Many shoes leave triangular impressions like cowboy boots. Perhaps Helen left the impression, but made it with other pointed-toe shoes. Or the impression relates to the 9mm but not the towel. The lingering scent may have another source, or come from Helen's admitted visit to that room. Even if the towel were tested, and no traces of primer residue appeared, my musings could still be fact. But if such traces appeared, their presence could be explained some other way. But not all doubts are reasonable, and not everything possible becomes probable.

The towel remains in perpetual storage in the county evidence locker, forever untested. The country's budget doesn't always support my inspirations. The actual deliberations of these jurors remain a mystery to me. All I know is that our lawn eventually gets mowed.

Two days after receiving the case, this jury of Helen Andrews' peers returned a verdict of not guilty. I found the story in the local section, page B-11, of our morning paper. The prosecutor appeared as disappointed as the defense appeared elated. The jury foreman was quoted: "Both the defense's psychological and ballistics evidence raised reasonable doubt about her guilt."

Helen returned to Montana to resume her career as a truck stop waitress. After an independent insurance company investigation, her mother Ruth collected a $35,000 death benefit. The Longshoremen's union-issued policy had no relevant suicide clause. Anyway, Norbert Andrews' death certificate still lists "homicide" as the manner of death. Ruth spent most of the money on Helen's defense.

Four and one-half years after the trial, I ran across Helen again. While returning to Montana after visiting her mother, Helen Andrews' beat-up Ford Maverick left the road and hit a tree. I found no skid marks on the pavement. In the nontechnical language of ordinary death, she died instantly. Her autopsy revealed basal skull fractures, a transected spinal cord at C1–C2 and massive internal injuries. She had the early stages of her father's liver. Her blood alcohol read .20.

In death, we achieve some equality. The stockbroker lies between the minister and the mugger, waiting on gurneys, shoulder to shoulder with the Helen Andrewses of the world, wrapped in white plastic from the same roll. Only yellow toe tags distinguish one bundle from another. Some of their stories read clearly, while others remain opaque. Helen's one-car fatality is one of the latter. Officially recorded as an accidental death, she may have intentionally ended her life. We may suspect one way or the other, but we'll never know.

Physical evidence, witnesses, and confessions supply our only clues. In her father's death, Helen did not confess under Shipley's expertly applied pressure. Norbert, shot in the chest, was unavailable for comment. Helen denied she did it, and only the physical evidence remained to make sense of it all. There, if I'm correct, the clues made sense, and pointed toward the correct explanation. But the signs of Helen's own death pointed in too many directions, making sense of too many possibilities, opening the door for too many solutions with few facts to support one alternative over another. That's reasonable doubt.

Through my cases, I continually learn what science can tell us, and what it can not; what experts know and what they don't; where reason works and where it fails; where it applies and where it is misapplied. Either Helen shot Norbert, or she didn't. Either Helen intended to die, or she didn't. In our scientific work, we try to discover reasons to select correctly between such options. Rarely, if ever, can we know "for sure." Instead, we face the question "Which alternative is *justified* in the face of this uncertainty?" Our abilities to answer depend upon understanding the scope and limits of a complex scientific method. The following chapters serve to demonstrate its central logical features.

NOTES

1. Harvard University first assembled Peirce's collected works. The numbers which appear after brief quotations here refer to specific places within these collected manuscripts. See *Collected Papers of Charles Sanders Peirce,* edited by Paul Weiss and Charles Hartshorne, Harvard University Press, Cambridge, 1934.

Betting is not guessing.
Deduction, like hind sight, is twenty-twenty.

chapter two

Signs—The Duffy Case

Reading Signs

> "Those who have dissected many bodies have at least learned to doubt, while those who are ignorant of anatomy and do not take the trouble to attend to it, are in no doubt at all."
>
> Giovanni Battista Morgagni
> (Seventeenth-century morbid anatomist)

Dead bodies do not habitually collect in kitchens of doublewide trailers. While trailer parks and mobile home courts attract more than their fair share of disaster, they have not become exclusive magnets for unexpected death. Bodies routinely appear elsewhere singly or grouped, mangled by machinery, shot, stabbed, strangled, hanged, bludgeoned, dismembered, or otherwise dispatched. They may be found confined in buildings or vehicles, dumped in alleys or woods, or set adrift on oceans, lakes, or rivers. The deaths may be immediately witnessed, discovered in mere moments, or it may take days, weeks, or years for the body's discovery. These circumstances, shuffled by fate, form the deck with which investigators play. They read the cards dealt and place their bets on how the death occurred and who bears the responsibility.

Most investigators don't hesitate to take a piece of the action with a fresh body found in a house. A decomposed body discovered in an alley, however, shakes a wagerer's confidence. And with the discovery of a skeletonized body dumped in the woods or a body found in the water, all bets are off. Without an identified scene, the signs become progressively harder to read. The questions become increasingly difficult to identify and to ask. The odds lower since getting the right answers depends on asking the right questions.

A building preserves the scene's details, protects them from the elements, and supplies immediate questions. Who owns the building? Who lives there? Who visits? Why is the victim present? It also supplies immediate witnesses to answer those obvious questions: residents, family, neighbors, workers; delivery, repair, or maintenance personnel. If the building is a home like Norbert Andrews' trailer, either the killer entered by invitation or by guile. Absent signs of forced entry or no opportunities for secret access suggest a relationship between the victim and the killer. What relationship? While entering, moving around, and killing, what did the killer touch? What signs did the killer leave for investigators to read?

Nineteenth-century French criminalist Edmond Locard said, "Every contact leaves a trace." Fingerprints, hairs, fibers, bullets, blood spatter, and the body itself all supply questions. Which prints belong to an intruder? Which hairs? What did the intruder wear? What weapons were used? What blood types made the stains? What does the blood's distribution pattern reveal? And what can the body tell us about who died, and the time, cause, and manner of its death?

Good investigators know that lists of questions from officially issued procedure manuals have limited use. Reading the signs and asking the questions at a scene or in an interrogation room does not involve completing a bureaucratic form, chanting some Miranda-like litany, or responding to circumstances by following pre-established rules. Each scene, indoors or out, perfectly preserved or irrevocably compromised, has unique elements that modify the questions and define the playing rules for that particular scene or interrogation game. Asking the right questions depends on identifying the rules of each new contest.

Reasoning backward analytically at a death scene involves discovering the rules while playing the game. No one who sits in on an unidentified card game for a few minutes confuses playing Draw poker with playing Go Fish. At least not after losing a few hands. The same signs read differently. When the game is "Dead Body Found," good players develop an instinct for calling a killer's bluff, and identifying the rules of homicide by doubting false moves accurately. Signs common at a suicide, accident or natural death, or signs obliterated by efforts to alter a homicide scene read suspiciously when used by a killer to bluff or confuse investigators.

When the game is poker, good players develop an instinct for reading the signs of a bluff. Whether the "Dead Body Found" game to be identified turns out to be homicide, suicide, accident, natural, or undetermined, good investigators, like good poker players, learn to doubt by knowing how to be surprised and how best to explain surprising signs. In this sense, Detective Joseph E. Richards, Jr., ace poker player, is a master of surprises.

Detective Richards, dubbed "Junior" behind his back by the uniforms, reclines in his chair with both hands behind his head. Like a king on his throne, Richards is master of his domain: a standard issue metal desk, matching gray metal file cabinet, stacks of case files, and his third cup of office coffee now leaving the royal seal on the uppermost folder.

He abandoned his regular poker night, Friday, over 20 years ago when he joined the county homicide unit. He could never clear Fridays, paydays for most workers and welfare recipients. When loaded with the alcohol made possible by their paycheck, someone always managed to turn someone else into a case file on his desk.

The file cabinet housed the remains he managed to clear off the desk. Any case off the desk and into the cabinet counted as a cleared or solved case. His clear rate was the best in the unit because he took more calls than anyone else. With no county medical examiner, Richards handled all the suspicious, sudden or unexpected death investigations in the area for the county coroner. Many of his cleared cases turned out to be accidents, suicides, or natural deaths. He enjoyed death investigations that turned out to be naturals just as much as he enjoyed browbeating a confession from a tight-lipped homicide suspect.

Richards had no equal in the interrogation room. He could hold his own with the likes of Shipley any day. He used physical evidence effectively. The facts in the universe do not conspire to hide a lie. Sooner or later, a lie collides with hard uncooperative facts. Unless, of course, he could get away with it himself for the greater good, using what the courts have called "reasonable deception." Facing a suspect and lacking physical evidence, Richards puts on his best poker face to browbeat and manipulate. After listening to a pack of lies, he slowly reaches into his county-issue brown polyester sport coat, withdraws a folded piece of white paper, ceremoniously opens it, and frowns toward its printed surface. "Not what it says here," he adds sadly while shaking his head. More often than not, the suspect breaks down and supplies a version closer to the truth, or at least a different lie. He leaves the interrogation room with a smile, and the uniforms who see him know that Junior has once again pressed his wife's grocery list into official service.

Scenes as well as suspects often conceal the truth. When a call comes from the communications center requesting his royal presence with the arson squad at an outlying rural farmhouse, his hands leave the back of his head, and long legs carry his tall frame toward one of the unit's Plymouth Horizons parked in the county garage. A small roof antenna wiggles in time with the cranking starter, and after three tries the best car he finds smokes to life. Behind the wheel, Richards contemplates the endless variety of possible circumstances in store for him. He can't even be sure that a death has been properly identified. He may have a 50-minute drive for a dead St. Bernard.

From a mile away he sees black smoke mixed with white from the county firefighters' efforts to douse a blaze in a four bedroom two-story wood frame farmhouse. He parks the Horizon in a long driveway next to Lt. Dick Littlefield's new burgundy Chevy Suburban, finagled from tight-fisted bureaucrats on behalf of the county's one-man arson squad. He steps out of his small, oxidized econo-box initially glimpsing the scene via its reflection in the massive Suburban's shiny paint.

The farmhouse sits about 200 yards from a two-lane county road, officially named County Trunk D. Corn, about waist high, fills a field across the road and a weathered red barn stands to the house's left. A large oak tree in the front yard dangles a tire from a long rope that disappears into its leaves. Two bikes, one small, one larger, lie on their sides beside the swing. The gravel driveway leads from the road between the house and barn, becoming a large graveled area beside two open barn doors. A green John Deere tractor, a tin can covering its upright exhaust, shares the space with two red fire trucks pointed toward the house. Below, a gold county radio car blocks the driveway by the tree. The Suburban and Horizon now close the driveway entrance below the radio car. Josephs notices a tan Dodge van, a white Chevrolet, a farm wagon pulled by a tractor, and a light green pickup truck parked on the side of County D by the corn field. A small crowd clusters by the vehicles, each face looking across the road and up the driveway toward the now smoldering house.

The fire appears confined to the rear of the 50-year-old building. Josephs walks slowly up the drive toward the house, stopping at the radio car. Dick Littlefield leans on the car, holding an aluminum clipboard. Referring to the clipboard, Lt. Littlefield updates Richards on the specific circumstances now known. The call came in, he says, at 11:45 A.M. A neighbor driving by saw a fire on the back porch and flames inside the kitchen window toward the rear of the house. She used her CB radio to call for county firefighters. She did not see Joan Duffy's black Buick station wagon parked in its usual place between the tractor and the back porch. Nor did she see Joan's sons Bill and Chuck playing in the yard. So she assumed that Joan and family went to do errands, probably at the little IGA market four miles down County D. He raises one eyebrow to suggest a hidden flaw in her assumption, and to indicate that her story will continue in due time.

He says that the firetrucks, one pumper, and an extra water truck, arrived at noon and started pumping about 12:05 P.M. controlling the blaze by 12:30 P.M. Two firefighters assessing the damage to the kitchen and looking for the fire's possible cause smelled gasoline and called for the county arson investigator. Then they found what looked like a body in the kitchen, and called the county coroner. Richards adds that homicide got the call at 12:50 P.M. and he notes his time of arrival as 1:45 P.M. he would have arrived even sooner, he says, nodding toward the end of the driveway, if he had a fancy new vehicle.

Junior's normal caseload takes him to death investigations that would be handled by a medical examiner's office in other jurisdictions. But like the county where Richards works, many counties across the U.S. have coroners, not medical examiners. Bodies discovered in these different jurisdictions may get radically different treatment. Treatments range from a thorough medical-legal death investigation, supplying a lasting record to address future questions, to a worthless piece of paper attesting to death by "stopped breathing," or "cardiac arrest," neither of which is a cause or a manner of death.

The coroner system originated in England with "crowners" appointed by the king to collect taxes pinched by crooked sheriffs' profiteering in the shires. Soon the crowners cut in on the sheriffs' action. Their function remained legal and pecuniary, not medical. An interest in the manner of a death focused on its tax implications. An ox cart accident killing a peasant netted the king an ox cart. A murder netted the king all the murderer's property. A suicide, defined by kingly statute as "self-murder," netted the king all the victim's property. The crowners soon discovered their own entrepreneurial niche. For a fee, a homicide would officially become a natural death, or a suicide would become an accident.

The system evolved for the better over about nine centuries through stubborn British insistence on institutional reform rather than wholesale replacement. Similar refinements and improvements carried over to coroner's jurisdictions in British Columbia, Canada. But in the U.S., jurisdictional competition, budgetary constraint, and the resulting piecemeal approach to death investigation make uniformity difficult. Without a king, and with no uniform refinements, many, both in and outside of government, question the value of official "crowners."

In some U.S. jurisdictions, to be a qualified coroner one must be 18 years old, alive, and elected. No medical, legal, or investigative training requirements exist. Coroners sign death certificates, attesting to the manner of death, much as their medieval predecessors did. Many elected coroners come from the ranks of retired police officers. In other jurisdictions, the county prosecutor or sheriff doubles as coroner. How well or badly this system works often depends upon the personalities involved.

Many U.S. coroners do have medical or legal backgrounds and add to them extensive death investigation training. Unless their own medical background happens to be forensic pathology, they use consulting forensic pathologists to perform autopsies and to testify as medical experts in court. They also rely on qualified investigators to process death scenes. Many county councils willing to pay for Chevy Suburbans aren't willing to pay for a medical examiner's office, and many other rural counties across the U.S. can afford neither given limited tax bases. They rely on elected coroners and investigators from homicide like Detective Joseph Richards.

While Richards lacks formal medical training, he makes up for this defect by attending every autopsy performed by the coroner's consulting forensic pathologist, Dr. Harry Hunter, M.D. He learned the signs of death early by working many natural deaths and observing hospital deaths. He knew his own limitations and resisted overstepping his medical bounds. The county could do a lot worse than Detective Joseph E. Richards, Jr. at a death scene.

Richards looks in the two large open barn doors and sees a black Buick wagon, the driver's door slightly ajar, parked in the middle between animal stalls on the left and several bales of hay on the right. He walks toward the Buick while Littlefield remains just outside the doors. A film of dust along the driver's side appears wiped from the rear door in the rear wheel well. Touching nothing, Richards peers through the open driver's window and notices that the front bench seat adjustment is all the way back. Littlefield's previous eyebrow signal, inviting questions about reported circumstances, starts to sink in.

Richards leaves the barn and Littlefield continues his report as they walk around the outside of the farmhouse. He says that he contacted the woman who reported the fire on her CB. She described the flames from the kitchen and on the porch as white, not red, pink, or yellow. Consistent, he says, with gasoline used as an accelerant.

A wood frame home any older than 15 years generates temperatures of up to 1,650 degrees Fahrenheit about 20 minutes into the fire. Temperatures may be as low as 1,450 degrees. Flames at 1,450 degrees or below appear red. Up to 1,650 degrees, the flames look salmon pink, purple or turn orange at about 1,700 degrees. But to get white flames, temperatures have to reach at least 2,000 degrees. Gasoline burns at about 2,400 degrees. Combined with the firefighters' report of a gasoline smell in the kitchen, white flames suggest an arson fire.

Junior deadpans a defense attorney: "Maybe they stored the gas for their snowmobiles in the kitchen over the summer beside a defective propane heater." Littlefield winces at the sarcasm. Both investigators appreciate the importance of a careful investigation. They approach the house and enter what used to be the back porch.

The porch leads directly into the kitchen through a solid core wooden door with a half-window, broken in tiny fragments and scattered inside the kitchen over the blackened but intact entry carpet. The investigators see an aluminum frame kitchen window, an update from the original wood window, to the left of the entry door. The glass is crazed and fragmented, its pieces scattered inside the kitchen. The aluminum frame sags like candle wax. The floor appears heavily burned, while the ceiling appears less consumed by the flames. Water drips into the kitchen from the second story. Steam rises from the scorched remains of the floor. The charred room smells like a poorly run self-serve truck stop selling greasy burgers and cut rate gasoline from leaky pumps. In a single row, side by side like cordwood at the center of the conflagration, Richards recognizes what used to be at least three human beings. His 50-minute drive was not for the family pet.

The three unrecognizable bodies mimic the same position: thin black arms raised toward the face, and legs drawn toward the trunk in what pathologists call the pugilistic attitude, a condition caused by prolonged exposure to heat. They look like Giacametti sculptures of boxers frozen in a fighting stance, yet down for the count. He walks around the bodies, staying carefully away from a quick visit to the basement through the compromised floor. He notices that each of the three appear to have skull fractures.

He knows enough forensic medicine to know that heat fractures of the skull frequently appear on fire victims. Usually such victims have irregular linear fractures, a separated suture line, or less often, stellate fractures. Most heat fractures of the skull involve the parietal bone at the rear of the skull, and most involve herniation of the cooking brain. There also may be an extradural heat haematoma or bruise which mimics an antemortem injury. But there will be no other signs of blunt force trauma. He knows that these fractures require Dr. Hunter's autopsy to sort out. But the fractures he sees on all three skulls cover the occipital, temporal and frontal areas. They appear as circular depressions and the outer layers appear torn. That surprises him.

Despite the damage to at least three victims and the floor, the rest of the kitchen remains remarkably intact. Though black, the cupboards, counters, sink, dishwasher, and stove remain undamaged. On the counter beside the sink rests a burned grocery bag, identifiable only by a loaf of charred bread, several unidentified bulging black cans, and a couple of broken jars collected in a pile of ash. Next to the bag sits the remains of a pocketbook with two open metal clasps and a collection of credit cards exposed by the flames. A kitchen knife block sitting under cupboard next to the stove has a round handled sharpener, cleaver, and butcher knife present, with three empty slots.

The door from the kitchen to the dining room shows charring on the kitchen side. Richards and Littlefield carefully walk around the bodies, still cautious not to break through to the basement, visible between two joists exposed by a patch of burned-out flooring. The hinges on the dining room door show the early stages of transformation from solid to liquid, arrested by the firefighters' efforts. The hinges still swing the door open to the dining room.

Smoky, sooty, and wet, the dining room remains otherwise undamaged. Six chairs surround a large table in the middle of the room. Richards notices that the chair closest to the kitchen doorway lies on its side, the back broken free from the seat. He sees what looks like a carpenter's framing hammer sliding the blackened, wet tablecloth away from the broken chair, exposing half of the table's wooden top. The wet wood surface also wears a layer of muddy soot. He leans over the cloth, looking at the head of the hammer. Thin fibers attached by red clumps adhere to the hammer's waffled head. Similar colored stains appear mixed with soot and diluted by water on the tablecloth. The investigators continue from the dining room into the living room, the connected front porch, and up the stairs to the right of the front door.

Their slow walk through the rest of the first floor and the upstairs bath and bedrooms reveals no serious fire damage. The front door remains closed and unlocked, but on this clear summer day, all the downstairs and upstairs windows are shut. Richards parts the curtain and glances out the front bedroom window across County D toward the cornfield. The tractor pulling the farm wagon has disappeared. The Dodge van and the Chevrolet have been joined by another car, a white Ford. The aging green International pickup also remains parked on the shoulder furthest from the driveway. One man, dressed in blue coveralls, plaid shirt, and a mesh DeKalb Corn cap leans against the pickup with his arms crossed looking up at the house. The other spectators, joined by the Ford's occupants, cluster in front of the van, closer to the driveway.

The two investigators retrace their steps to the kitchen. Both Richards and Littlefield have been dealt a good hand, and they prepare to play it carefully. Littlefield begins planning his sample collection, making a mental list of the equipment he needs from the Suburban. Richards stands staring at the bodies from the kitchen door, steam rising from below, and water dripping from above.

After the quiet meditation, he moves toward the spectators gathered before the Dodge van. He introduces himself as a county investigator, and asks if anyone knows the people who live here. He asks those who do to explain how they know them. The group comprises some of the Duffys' friends and neighbors. While artfully ducking their questions, Richards learns that Joan's husband Jerry died late last winter after a four-year battle with cancer, and that Joan's brother, Earl Thompson, is standing by his green pickup truck just down from the white Ford.

Richards motions to the deputy in the radio car securing the scene and instructs him to call for the state crime lab techs to process the physical evidence, and Dr. Hunter to observe the bodies at the scene. He asks another deputy to escort Earl Thompson, family member and helpful witness, to the office for questioning. He will meet him there later. The uniform grasps the implication clearly.

Richards slowly walks toward Earl Thompson, who continues to lean against his truck. On Earl's coveralls he sees a streak of dust across the left thigh and hip. Nothing in the truck appears fair game for a plain view search. Whatever rests in the pickup's bed is covered by a dark tarp. He asks Earl for his cooperation with the investigation of the fire. Earl assents. Unlike the friends and neighbors, he asks Richards no question of his own.

Slow and deliberate of speech, Earl Thompson, Joan's youngest brother, answers Richards' preliminary questions. He currently does odd jobs, repair work, and remodeling. He recently quit his job as a fieldhand. He can't remember when he last saw his sister or his nephews. He just happened to drive by and he saw fire engines. The smell of alcohol accompanies the sounds from his mouth. Richards, working the consent-search routine for all he can get, asks Earl if he would mind emptying his pockets on the hood of his truck.

Earl slips a billfold with a built-in coin purse from his back pocket. He empties the contents on the hood: the usual driver's license, Social Security card, a Texaco credit card and a 10-dollar bill, two fives, and three ones, smoothly placed in descending order. The coin purse contains three quarters, two dimes, a nickel, and four pennies. His left front pocket has a red paisley handkerchief. His right front pocket holds four wadded up one-dollar bills, a dime, a nickel, two pennies, and a pocketknife. Richards stares at the contents of the right front pocket. Earl does not know it yet, but he will spend the next 12 hours in an interrogation room either waiting alone or talking with the detective.

Richards assembles relevant evidence when preparing to interrogate both witnesses and suspects. Only on unfortunate occasions does he resort to his wife's grocery list. Often his witnesses become suspects in the interrogation room, sometimes the reverse happens. Sometimes he treats suspects like witnesses to aid his manipulations again, sometimes the reverse. Sometimes he uses physical evidence in his interrogations long before it can be collected, processed, or interpreted by state crime laboratory forensic scientists or the coroner's forensic pathologist. That may come later, the step that Shipley calls window dressing for the trial. Richards processes it in his mind and applies the imagined results immediately in questioning his witnesses and suspects. His imagination now prepares for Earl Thompson.

Some would say that he guesses at these imagined results. Richards insists that he does not guess. He bets. Betting is not guessing. Guessing is blind and riddled with doubt. Betting is sighted and filled with belief. Both are uncertain. We guess wrong. Bets are lost. But informed betting is methodical. Guessing is merely desperate.

No one needs to guess or bet in the face of ordinary facts. Usual facts raise no doubts. When Richards sees the tin can over the tractor exhaust he has no need for what C. S. Peirce called "critical logic" to interfere with his belief that the can keeps rain from entering the muffler. Nothing unusual presents itself. For someone without his rural experience, the can on the exhaust may be unusual. The context of the fact and the experience of the observer often determine whether or not the given fact is usual or unusual. For Peirce, "critical logic" begins with doubt raised by an unusual fact, and the source of that doubt is surprise (5.512, 5.43). Whatever raises doubts and occasions surprise requires explanation. Whatever suggests an explanation relates to what proves it.

Junior does not face an unusual fact when he sees three severely burned bodies at the farmhouse fire scene. His surprise roots in finding them in the kitchen, lined up in a row with severely fractured skulls. This unusual finding raises doubt. He must resolve the doubt to explain the observation. He could merely guess: Maybe the three family members, lined up to admire their cache of gasoline stored in the kitchen, set their snowmobile fuel on fire with a defective propane heater. The headlines read: Three Stooges incinerated in hapless accident.

But the universe conspires to cheat groundless guesses. Lawyers call it reasonable doubt. Signs woven into a pattern form an explanation. Surprise, then doubt, generates questions. Find the snowmobile. Find the fuel cans. Find the heater. Explain the skull fractures. What about the hammer? When Richards sees something unusual raising doubt, he asks himself what explanation makes that fact usual, believable.

Detective Richards does not always have unlimited time for his reflections. Deliberate, decisive actions often speed a case folder from Richards' desk to the gray metal file. Bets placed during the first 24 hours of a homicide investigation often determine the outcome. Some things at a scene—the bodies, the hammer, and the gasoline residue—can wait for the crime lab and Dr. Hunter. Other things, Earl Thompson, his pockets, and his pickup are less enduring. Richards now bets on the $4.17 found in Earl Thompson's right front pocket. It's a long shot. But as with all bets, the greater the risk and the higher the stakes, the better the payoff.

He studies the pocket contents on the hood as another deputy pulls up in a gold patrol car to escort Joan Duffy's still-cooperative brother to the office. With the scene secure, the arson investigation started, the crime lab techs, and Dr. Hunter on the way, and Thompson en route to the interrogation room, Richards heads across County D and back up the driveway to chat with Littlefield, who stands behind the open rear doors of the Suburban assembling his camera equipment.

They briefly discuss their observations. Littlefield points out that fires burn up and out from a source. Excessive low-level damage is surprising and needs explanation. The damage to the kitchen floor and to the bodies becomes usual when explained by some accelerant, probably gasoline. That also accounts for the obvious smell.

Ordinary house fires exert positive pressure on closed windows and break the glass outward. Long cracks with sharp edges are usual. The broken glass lands outside the building. With accelerant fires, however, the fire sucks oxygen rapidly, and windows break inward as the room implodes to satiate the fires' growing oxygen appetite. Initially, thermal shock crazes the glass when hot vapors from the fire hit the relatively cold surface. Then it fragments, breaking inward as the air rushes in to feed the starving flames. Littlefield also notes that with the windows closed, the oxygen supply diminishes rapidly, increasing the chance that the fire will extinguish, starving itself by running out of oxygen.

Also note, he says, that the kitchen floor burned through to the joists, and that the joists have also burned. A wood fire usually burns about one inch in 45 minutes. The white ash on the joists indicates that the fire craved oxygen, sucking it from the wood fibers. That also points to accelerants.

Testing in this case should be relatively straightforward. If present, gasoline residues will be found on the inside of the broken glass, and in the wood. Testing should be even easier because of good luck. The initial witness happened to have a CB radio, and the rural fire station happened to be within a couple of miles from the scene. The windows happened to be closed, and the fire happened to be quickly controlled. Richards says that despite Littlefield's single-digit IQ, and his good luck, he knows arson. "Chance," he says quoting Louis Pasteur, "favors the prepared mind." He had met the quote by chance in a gaming book.

Even after their first hour on the scene, both Richards and Littlefield believe that the people in the kitchen died homicidally, that the killer attempted to conceal his crime by starting an arson fire, and that the killer lacks a basic understanding of the physics and chemistry of fire. Richards also wagers that the killer watched the house from a vantage point across County D. While he may lose the bet, it provides added incentive to secure the most fragile part of this scene. The signs that suggest these conclusions and present the odds for the wager relate directly to what ultimately proves or disproves them.

Even before Dr. Hunter's autopsy, Richards is ready to bet that the bodies in the kitchen are what remain of Joan, Bill, and Chuck Duffy. He also bets that the hammer explains the apparent skull fractures and is, in fact, the murder weapon. If he is lucky, confirming identity with dental records may take a few days. A consulting forensic odontologist compares postmortem X-rays with the antemortem dental record, assuming that one exists. Analyzing samples from the hammer for blood, typing it, and identifying hairs will take time. Impact injury confirmations also wait for the autopsy.

Richards also bets that Earl Thompson used the hammer on the Duffys. The smear in the Buick's dust and the dust on Earl's left hip and thigh connect, but testing could only establish similarity of the dust, unless he got lucky with some other more exotic transfer of trace evidence. From a lawyer's viewpoint, dust is dust. Earl had access to dust. Big deal. But that one sign links Earl to the Buick. So does the seat position, unless Joan had very long legs. Find his fingerprints on the car. Cement the link. That may take the state crime lab a couple of weeks, but confirmation remains an outside chance. What business did Earl have driving Joan's Buick? Thompson does odd jobs—construction. The framing hammer on the dining room table might be Earl's. Does his tool belt or chest lack a hammer? Check the hammer for latent prints. Compare latents with Earl's prints. Where did the gasoline come from? Did Earl buy gasoline? What did he use to carry it to the kitchen? Richards bets that some answers lie under the dark tarp in Earl's pickup.

Richards uses Littlefield's cellular telephone to order a tow truck to impound the green International. For now, it's an official traffic hazard. If testing his bets becomes necessary, it will merit a search warrant. Either way, it will be secured in the county garage, ready for his search and for processing by crime lab personnel. He returns the phone to its dashboard cradle, and thanks Littlefield. On his way to meet Earl, he plays his long shot. He plans to go grocery shopping.

His Horizon rolls toward the IGA market at about 1600 hours, 4:00 P.M. for normal timekeepers. The side trip will give Earl another hour or so to get nervous while seated in the small interrogation room. Richards bets that the extra time will make his task easier. He hopes that the same clerk working now worked about 9 o'clock this morning. The store has two gas pumps out front, no service island, a large white ice machine beside the door, and a red and white IGA sign on top of its brown T-111 plywood siding. A bell dangling from the push bar on the door jingles as he enters. A sturdy woman stands behind a counter, her back to the door, restocking cigarettes in single-pack dispensers.

As she turns, he identifies himself as a county investigator, and asks her when she came to work. Her eyes open slightly wider, her mouth gapes, and no words come out. His ability to disarm and disable hit the wrong target. Smiling, he explains that he is investigating a fire and needs her help. She visibly relaxes, returns his smile, and says that she came to work early, about 6:00 A.M., and will leave about 6 o'clock tonight. She covers for her sister who, in her ninth month, has trouble staying on her feet behind the counter. She runs the IGA with her sister and her sister's husband who earlier left for town to pick up some parts for the freezer. He keeps the store open until about 9:00 P.M.

He asks more questions. She knows Joan Duffy well. They belong to the same church. Richards asks if she came to the store today. Why, yes she did. She and her two sons came in about 9:00 A.M. or so. They picked up some groceries. He asks if she can remember what they bought. She screws up her face and shakes her head. She opens the side of the cash register, unreeling the day's tape. The tape is short. Business, from the look of the store, is slow. Her eyes brighten as her face resumes its normal contours. She reports that Joan bought bread, three cans of soup, a jar of peanut butter, a jar of jelly, and a soap opera magazine. Richards struggles to mask his delight. Did she write a check, he asks. No, she paid cash, the clerk-owner replies. Her total, she says in reply to his next question, came to $5.83. She paid with what she said was her last money, a 10-dollar bill. Her change: $4.17.

She remembers, she says, because Joan remarked that she would have to drive to town and go the bank before church this Sunday. Richards asks for a copy of the tape. She offers to make one, and explains that they record their totals at the end of the day, and that the tape must be intact for the process. The customer, she says, gets the only copy the machine generates. She says that she always hands the tape to her customers. She does not just drop it in the bag. The rural personal touch. Richards asks her to save the tape. He bends down to retrieve a short cash register tape some careless customer discarded on the way out. Before she can ask questions of her own, Richards walks out the door and drives toward the interrogation room to pursue Earl Thompson.

C. S. Peirce calls the logic of this pursuit "abduction." Luckily for Richards, stuck with a clunker from the aging Horizon fleet, this pursuit does not depend on a maneuverable high-speed vehicle. Peirce writes:

> "Nothing has so much contributed to the present chaotic or erroneous ideas in the logic of science as failure to distinguish the essentially different characters of different elements of scientific reasoning; and one of the worst of these confusions, as well as one of the commonest, consists in regarding abduction and induction taken together . . . as a simple argument (7.218)."

Scientists and philosophers may be confused, but Richards the death investigator hones the skill as the main tool of his trade.

Abduction, Pierce says, is the process of proposing some explanation that is likely in itself (7.202) but that must be tested before anyone can be fully justified in accepting it. Abduction is Richards' informed betting. Induction, on the other hand, involves observing some sign and noting the frequency of its association with another. Every observed raven is black, so probably all ravens are black. The numbers count. The more ravens the better. Induction is statistical. But Pierce notes a gaping hole: What explains the association? Why are ravens black? Inductions, without abductions, explain nothing.

Despite their uncertainty, abductions are fundamental to any increase in knowledge. They have a definite rational structure to be treated by critical logic. Richards, Littlefield, and any investigator worth his salt makes a career operating within that rational structure. The structure rests in links between signs and sign makers, and the promise for knowledge lies in supplying new links to test. Observing those links provides the basis of the bet, and opportunities to test supply the odds. Guessing has no such structure. Richards, now holding the cash register tape with his other cards, antes up and opens the interrogation room door, ready to play his hand.

Earl Thompson sits in the homicide interrogation room, a half-full white foam coffee cup on a table in front of him. Beside the cup, an ashtray holds freshly incinerated tobacco remains. Another cigarette rests between the first two fingers of Earl's right hand. The room, uniformly painted yellow, has acoustical tile walls. A mirror faces the table opposite the door. Thompson stares at the ashtray, a thin ribbon of smoke tying his yellow fingers to the yellow ceiling. Richards says he would like to continue their conversation about the bodies in the kitchen. Earl continues to stare at the ashtray.

If he were smart, which he is not, Earl Thompson would merely continue to stare at the ashtray. Call the investigator's bluff. Raise the stakes by demanding the presence of an attorney. Any good defense attorney knows that no good comes from a suspect saying anything to a detective in an interrogation room. But so far, Earl enjoys witness status, part of Richards' manipulation to get him talking. At Thompson's first utterance of anything incriminating, Richards will read him his rights.

While the 1966 Miranda decision underscores a suspect's rights in an interrogation room and removes the threat of physical coercion, it does not remove compelled and manipulated admissions and confessions. If it did, even more guilty people would escape arrest and conviction. Detective Richards has to convince the room's occupant that it is in that person's interest to confide things that will in turn be used to lock him away for life. Richards has a hard sell. He has been carefully trained in what others call the art of deception.

The detective eyes Earl, and reads a hint of fear and perhaps remorse. Remorse is a bonus card of great value to practitioners of the deceitful art. The vast majority of murderers have none. Or worse, their remorse centers on any inconvenience they now face. Ralph Waldo Emerson observed that the act of murder "is no such ruinous thought as poets and romancers will have it; it does not unsettle him, or frighten him from his ordinary notice of trifles." Murderers of family members sometimes behave more like Hamlet in the remorse department, though less eloquently. Richards counts on the trifles of his abductions to probe and test Earl's story, seeking the confirmation that will help put the Duffy case file in his metal file cabinet. Three cleared in one blow.

Earl continues to stare at the ash tray. Despite the cloak of cigarette smoke, an unmistakable gasoline odor hangs in the atmosphere. Richards pulls up a chair across the table and sits down. He plays his imaginary royal flush, the unbeatable detective's hand that takes a murder case down. Richards asks Thompson about Joan, playing the remorse angle. Get him thinking about Joan while he stares at the ashtray. Thompson says he has not seen her for weeks. He snuffs out the remains of this cigarette with the others. Richards senses Thompson's anger. Remorse probably won't work. He tries using the boys, shifting gears, giving Thompson some cards to play. "Did those boys of hers, what are their names . . . ?"

Thompson's eyes move up. "Bill and Chuck."

"Yeah," Richards continues, "Bill and Chuck. Did you ever know them to play with matches or fire?" Richards wants to give Thompson the illusion of an escape, an out, to get him going, and then to keep him thinking. Blame the boys. He senses that Thompson can play the blame-game well. Thinking is foreign territory to him. Keep him off balance.

"Chuck had a lighter," Thompson volunteered. "They was always play'en' with matches." Thompson's face shows the strain his thinking creates while he concentrates on producing speech.

"The reason I ask, Earl," Richards says, "is that the fire you saw burn up the kitchen burned up Joan, Chuck, and Bill, too. And I have a problem, Earl." He sees Thompson realize that Richards' problem has now become his problem. "You said you hadn't seen Joan for a couple weeks, but your fingerprints are all over her Buick. She last drove it this morning. Your prints overlap hers. How's that Earl?" Richards prepares to play his Miranda speech.

Thompson wavers, his anger getting the better of him. "OK, I borrowed her wagon."

"Why?" Almost time for the speech.

"I had to haul lumber for a job." As the words leave Thompson's mouth, he wishes they would return.

"You have a pickup, Thompson. Why use the wagon?"

Thompson remains silent, returning his eyes to the ashtray. They dart among the confines of the glass and ash.

"I know about the money." Richards stares intently at Thompson, who now visibly slumps in the chair. Junior fingers the receipt he picked up at the IGA. "You got pissed off. Really pissed off. I can understand that." Richards again dangles the illusion of justification, an out, the goal of the blame-game.

"OK," Thompson continues in his slump, relieved of the obvious strain of thinking. "I was there."

Richards interrupts Thompson and explains his rights. He brings out the Miranda sheet, asking Thompson to initial each section if he understands. Thompson has seen cop shows on TV. He can recite the words himself. He initials each section as Richards patiently explains it like a father helping his child with a homework assignment.

Far from harming interrogations, Miranda warnings can bridge the natural gap between the hunter and his prey. Thompson needs help. He needs help to understand this mess, and help to feel better about it. Richards does the helping. Junior can be very helpful. The spider helps the fly into its web.

Thompson takes out a soft pack of Marlboros from his pocket, puts one between his lips, and slips out his matches, stored just inside the pack's cellophane wrapper. As Richards watches intently, Thompson opens the matches, and Richards sees a bloody thumb print on the inside cover. Richards grabs Thompson's arm, forcing the matches onto the table.

In one brain-dead move, Thompson has all but laid the murder weapon on the table. Richards does not enjoy playing a royal flush against such a witless opponent. But Thompson is not the real opponent. Richards' real battle will be against whomever Thompson gets as an attorney, the judge, and 12 of whomever cannot avoid the indignity of being called one of Earl Thompson's peers.

Richards lets him have it. "Your hammer didn't burn, Earl. You hit Joan with the hammer. Her blood and your prints are on that hammer." He places his abductive bets. He leaves out Chuck and Bill for the moment, working on the anger. "You killed Joan in the kitchen, hit the boys in the dining room, dragged them into the kitchen, shut the windows, covered all three, poured gas on them, and lit the match, didn't you, Earl? Your prints are all over the windows. Their blood stains your matchbook. You washed your hands at the sink, and took the money from her purse by the groceries, didn't you, Earl? Your prints are all over the sink. We traced that $4.17 in your front pocket to Joan."

Thompson spends the next few hours dictating his confession, which was witnessed by two other detectives, typed up, and then signed. His court-appointed attorney scowls at the detectives upon arrival. The legal chain, beginning with crime and ending with punishment, faces a test of each link. A confession in the chain stands up best when physical evidence tempers it. No legal document, no matter how carefully crafted, seems immune from some sort of procedural attack. With a confession, Richards bets that Thompson's attorney and the prosecutor will work some kind of plea bargain. On the strength of the evidence, Thompson won't have the cards to stay in that game more than one hand.

Back at his desk the next afternoon, Richards meets a crime lab tech who takes Thompson's clothing as evidence, and accompanies Junior to the impound garage. They execute a search warrant issued for the truck. With Thompson locked up, and the prosecutor's office now involved, the first set of Richards' abductions gets its test.

Walking through the tiled hallway to the stairwell on the way to the garage, Junior says that in the truck they will find a tool belt, missing a hammer. Gasoline cans, now empty, will appear in the pickup's bed. Somewhere in the cab, probably in the jockey box, a receipt for $5.83 will turn up. The tech looks skeptically amused. The embodied spirit of Watson walks with Richards down the cement stairwell to the impound parking area carrying his black evidence-collection camera bag.

The green International faces a cement wall on the lower level of the police parking garage. Rows of quartz lights high atop 10-foot metal stands on both sides illuminate the truck as if it were a high school football field. Deposited by the tow truck, it sits just as Thompson parked it on County D beside the cornfield. Gold-colored radio cars park one layer up in the garage at street level. The Horizon armada moors one floor above the radio cars. No police vehicle contamination reaches the lower level. Contract tow trucks bring vehicles to the impound area. All impounded vehicles parked inside enjoy evidential status. The hulks and derelicts rest in private tow truck yards outside in the weather. Joan's Buick will be processed in her barn.

After taking initial overall photographs, the investigators remove the tarp. The bed contains a tool chest, several buckets of drywall compound, a chain saw, two quart cans of wood stain, and two five-gallon military-style, red-metal gas cans. They lay on their sides. Both have no fuel. Flexible metal spouts screw into the tops of both cans. The bed smells of gasoline.

After photographing and collecting the gas cans for possible fingerprint processing and contents analysis at the state crime lab, they open the tool chest that bolts to the front of the bed and the rear of the cab. Three tool belts hang from pegs on the back of the custom-made wooden box. The first contains a nail pouch filled with 16-penny galvanized framing nails and has an empty hammer loop. The second has a nail pouch filled with finishing nails, and a finishing hammer hangs from a loop on its side. A small-, medium- and large-size nailset fills each of three small side holsters. The third belt has a pouch filled with sheetrock screws and an assortment of screwdriver bits in side loops. Several cordless drills, a circular saw, a sawsall, handsaws, paintbrushes, and extension cords fill the rest of the chest. The hammerless belt enters a plastic evidence bag.

A portable spotlight shines into the open driver's door illuminating the cab's contents. A Thermos rests on the front seat filled with vodka-spiked coffee strong enough to raise anyone's blood alcohol to lethal levels. In the glove box, a pile of gas and oil receipts lies next to a notebook recording gas purchases. On top of the notebook Richards finds an IGA receipt for $5.83, listing purchases reported by the clerk to be Joan's, dated the day of the fire at 9:03 A.M. The clutch, brake, and accelerator pedals show traces of what appear to be blood. To preserve the sample, the tech performs no hemodent test to determine the positive presence of blood. The tech instead merely removes them for laboratory analysis.

With the truck photographed, analyzed, and sampled, each of Richards' bets pays off. Within two hours of his predictions, the lab tech expresses the amazement characteristic of the incredulous Dr. Watson. It's simple, says Richards, especially when dealing with the likes of Earl Thompson. With the evidence collected and sent off to the lab, Richards returns to his desk, the king back in his kingdom, to finish the paperwork that he regards as a royal pain.

The county prosecutor benefits most from his written work. But a solid feel for the case against Earl Thompson requires a personal visit. She favors a second-degree murder charge in Joan's death, and two aggravated first degree murder charges in the boys' cases. Before she gets additional reports, she needs to assess the admissibility of the evidence.

Richards gladly regales the prosecutor. He recounts the steps he would never put in his terse report. He explains that gasoline soaked the bodies and the kitchen floor. The murderer used fire in an attempt to hide his crime, but failed to understand that fire needs oxygen to burn. Thompson used gasoline to magnify the fire, thinking that closing the windows would increase the inferno's intensity. Instead, closing the windows made the gasoline-fueled blaze easier to control.

The gasoline had to be poured onto the bodies and kitchen floor from some container. No cans or containers appear at the scene. Thompson smelled of gasoline. So odds favored that these containers could be found in Thompson's truck. Headspace gas chromatography and mass spectrometry should identify the gasoline from the scene, Thompson's clothing, and the residue from these cans as having the identical composition. By Richards' reckoning, that would link Thompson both to the bodies and to the fire through the gasoline.

The framing hammer supplies another link between Thompson and the bodies. No remodeling or visible projects at Joan's farm explain a framing hammer's presence on the dining room table. Thompson works as a handyman and would be expected to use a framing hammer. Its absence from his tools would be expected if he used his hammer to murder the Duffys, then laid it on the table and planned for it to disappear in the fire. Blood, hair and tissue samples as well as possible pattern injuries to the skulls may link the hammer to the victims. Richards rhetorically asks himself what links the hammer to Thompson for the prosecutor's benefit. The link, he says, turned out to be Thompson himself.

Thompson's wallet reveals a surprising order, Richards continues, a slow, deliberate neatness which Richards says that he expects to find in all things Thompson values. He organizes his money. He values money. He values tools. He organizes his tools. That organization makes it easy to expect some empty slot, some void in the pattern, for the missing hammer. Methodical but not quick, Thompson's order roots in habit, not thought. Richards points to a photo of Thompson's tool belt. These nails are galvanized 16-penny framing nails but there is no hammer. His other tool belt has a finish hammer and finishing nails with three nailsets. So, Richards says, the hammer in the kitchen must be his. Fingerprints or some other trace evidence found on the belt and the hammer may establish the connection. Retrieving his coffee cup, Richards says that given his bet on Thompson's organization, any breaks in his plodding routines require an explanation.

For example, he continues, Thompson's carefully organized wallet has all the bills in order of value and his change in a coin compartment. Why have four crumpled one-dollar bills, a dime, a nickel, and two pennies stuffed into the front pocket? Why have money in his right front pocket when he also had a carefully organized billfold with a coin purse in his back pocket? What explains it? The $4.17 in Thompson's right front pocket would not be surprising if Thompson pocketed the money hurriedly, without taking time to open his billfold. But now why did Thompson pocket the money hurriedly?

So far, Richards' discoveries are both clever and legal. Her job may be either to overwhelm the defense attorney with the strength of the case against Thompson, or to present the case in court. She interrupts Richards. As a lawyer, she knows that his question has several parts. To ask this question is to ask why Thompson and not someone else, why in his pocket and not in his wallet and coin purse, and why in a hurry, and not leisurely, or methodically? How did you answer those questions, she asks, expressing mild interest, posing a friendly cross-examination.

Richards tells her that he pursues the explanations with the greatest payoff. First, he says, Thompson had more money neatly organized in his billfold than disorganized in his pockets. That would be usual if whenever he got change, he put the bills in his wallet and the coins in the snap compartment. Thompson behaves out of habit. When hurried, or when forced to think, he derails. Betting that he did habitually organize his money, why didn't Thompson have time to organize these bills and change? Hurriedly pocketing the money would be usual if he took it from one of the Duffys during or after the murders, or during or before the fire. So the problem now involves improving the odds that Thompson took the money from one of the Duffys.

Having \$4.17, an odd amount in itself, could be usual if that amount came in change after shopping. The roasted groceries on the counter by the burned pocketbook signaled a recent shopping trip. So the problem became finding some merchant who gave \$4.17 to one of the Duffys after a shopping trip. A long shot. The single grocery bag indicated a short trip to some nearby market for a few items rather than an extended supply run into town. Joan's open pocketbook beside the bag suggested a source for the change. No money, burned or unburned, lay near the bag on the counter. Few people carry bills higher than \$20; most carry \$10s, \$5s, and \$1s. The grocery bag looked to hold purchases of under \$10. A trip to the little country IGA confirmed that Joan Duffy received \$4.17 change that morning. The receipt found in Thompson's truck and the clerk's statement all scream "read 'em and weep."

The prosecutor smiles, mildly entertained by what she calls Richards' brilliant deductions. But if C. S. Peirce could hear her comments, he would step away from his 19th-century coast and geological survey pendulum experiments to correct her. Powerful abductions make Richards' reasoning brilliant, not deduction. By abduction, Richards initially proposes an explanation, or bet, likely in itself (7.202). Peirce identifies the form for "critical logic" as follows:

"The surprising fact, C, is observed; but if A were true, C would be a matter of course. Hence there is reason to suspect A is true." (5.189, also cf. 2.624).

Richards appears to deduce his result because his bets become proven winners, resolving initial doubts about their wisdom. Deduction, like hindsight, is 20/20. Abduction, like foresight, is cloudier and carries more risk. Abductions presume a great deal. But testing their presumptions provides great insight into the problem at hand. Abductions amplify, adding something new that is not present in the original sign. Deductions do not amplify. They draw out something that is already before us in the original sign. Low risk, high odds, low payoff. Not the exclusive domain of detective Richards, the gambler.

Even Littlefield would scarcely merit his Suburban if he merely deduced his results. The sign "gasoline fire" already contains the sign "white flames." By deduction, if all gasoline fires have white flames and this is a gasoline fire, then this fire has white flames. But the reported sign "white flames" does not contain the sign "gasoline fire." White flames can have other sources. Induction might associate gasoline fires and white flames, but white flames may associate with other combustibles as well. The two investigators read the signs and then place their bets. What best explains these white flames? Peirce would say "that all this universe is perfused with signs if it is not composed exclusively of signs." Reading those signs goes beyond brilliant deduction. Reading those signs goes beyond merely associating them statistically. Reading signs requires abduction.

Good abductions lessen doubt by best explaining the surprising sign in context, but they can never completely resolve doubt on their own. If the bet that gasoline explains the white flames is correct, then gasoline residues will be present on the windows and in the wood. Littlefield finds such residues. He can now deduce that the bet on gasoline wins. Not all inferences work to lessen doubt the same way. The deduction would not be possible unless preceded by the abduction.

The process of inference from signs appears deceptively straightforward. Abduction yields some conjecture, a bet. Investigators explore various results deduced from it, and then test for the expected consequences by applying inductively derived associations. In Richards' reasoning this integrates abduction, deduction and induction into a unified process. The steps begin with abduction.

Richards' bet about the origin and significance of the $4.17 originates with reasoned abductions, not with desperate guesses. Peirce says that "according to the doctrine of chances it would be practically impossible for any being, by pure chance to guess the cause of any phenomenon . . . man's mind, having been developed under the influence of the laws of nature, for that reason naturally thinks somewhat after nature's pattern (1929:269)."

The sign, Peirce says, in some sense resembles what it signifies. The logic of pursuit, the logical compass of the process called scientific method, is directed by what one hopes to learn.

What Detective Joseph E. Richards, Jr., hopes to learn depends on the context before him. He makes his bets cautiously like a good oddsmaker. He could truthfully display a bumper sticker quoting Sherlock Holmes in *The Sign of Four,* "I never guess." Richards' mind, if not always his attitude, has evolved after nature's pattern, prepared to take advantage of any lucky chance that comes his way. In the Duffy case, the lucky chance that supplied a good hand stayed with the manila folder all the way to his file cabinet.

Richards retrieves the Duffy case file to append a supplemental report, summarizing his meeting with the prosecutor. He cranks a C.Y.A. report form into his ancient Underwood, and uses a single finger to type date, time, name, and place. His report reads "Discussed case with above named prosecutor." No details. His signature follows. He adds the report to the file.

Before returning the folder, Richards looks over Thompson's confession. He hit a nerve when he first mentioned the money in the interrogation room. The sign may resemble what it signifies, but it isn't necessarily identical. Thompson had thought that Richards was referring to the money he borrowed to buy his fishing boat.

Joan, the responsible older sister, cosigned a loan for irresponsible Thompson so he could buy the boat. When Thompson quit his job, he failed to pay the monthly installments. Joan did not hide her anger and frustration when Thompson repeatedly asked for more money, and demanded that she make payments on the boat. She refused. The boat became bank property. Thompson began drinking heavily. He constantly attacked Joan for failing to help him and wasting money on her boys. She bought them each a new bike the week before they died. Money. One of the oldest, simplest and strongest motives for murder.

Motive often plays as window dressing at a trial. Prosecutors and juries love to hear the motive. But Thompson's pathetic and insignificant motive plays no role in closing the case. The apparent motive merely fits in the pattern of Thompson's life. Richards does not attribute self-awareness or introspection, the ability to examine one's own reasons, to the likes of Earl Thompson. Richards bets that even Thompson remains unaware why he murdered the woman and two boys that he called family. He doubts that it had to do with money.

The details of the rambling confession and the mechanics of the murder fit Richards' and Littlefield's reconstruction. Thompson said that he went to the Duffy farm about 9:00 A.M. to talk with Joan about the boat. He waited on the back porch. Joan and the boys drove up in the Buick, parked in the usual spot, and passed Thompson on the porch. Joan accused him of being drunk and asked him to leave. He followed the family into the kitchen. Joan put her pocketbook and grocery bag on the counter by the sink. They began a heated argument, Joan finally struggling to push Thompson out the kitchen door, off the porch and out into the yard.

The struggle got as far as the porch. Thompson said that he'd had the framing hammer in a loop on his coveralls on the right side. He remembered hitting Joan, knocking her down on the porch. He dragged her into the kitchen, blood covering the floor. The two boys peered through the partly open dining room door. He went after them, fighting first with Bill, breaking the chair in the struggle. He hit him with the hammer. He could not remember how many times. He went after Chuck, who tried to fight him off and help his brother. Thompson hit him, too. He tossed the hammer onto the table, and dragged both boys into the kitchen with their mother.

The blood continued to flow on the kitchen floor, and Thompson said he got the idea to burn up the evidence. He moved the Buick into the barn to make it look like no one was home. He got the gas cans from his truck, put some newspapers from the porch on the bodies and soaked them with gas from both of the five-gallon cans. He poured gas on the porch to cover Joan's blood, and put the cans back in his truck. He shut the windows in the house, rinsed his bloody hands in the sink, pulled out his cigarette matches, opened the book, lit one and tossed it toward the gasoline-soaked newspapers. As the paper exploded into flames, Thompson grabbed at Joan's open pocketbook, planning to take all her money as an afterthought, he said. He did. He got $4.17, plus the receipt.

Richards still found problems with Thompson's story. Even confessions of guilt smell of self-serving lies. Why, he thinks, did Thompson have a framing hammer in the hammer loop of his coveralls? He didn't have a job. Why did he have damn near 10 gallons of gasoline in his truck, unmixed with oil? His chain saw has a two-cycle engine. It uses gas mixed with oil. His truck's gas tank was nearly full. The gas cans were not permanent accessories attached to the truck. He needed more time to get the truth from Thompson. But he had to be satisfied with his bet that Thompson would never get out of prison, regardless. Doomed to a life of 57 channels and nothing to watch.

Given Thompson's mental prowess, Richards doubted that the prosecutor would go for the death penalty. He pictured some psychologist testifying that because Thompson had the intellectual stamina of a withered geranium and a problem with alcohol he should be spared. He failed to see how diminished intellectual capacity translated into a moral excuse for murder. Brutally killing two children and their mother can have the same moral status whether a genius or a dolt delivers the blows. Besides, Richards remains convinced that Thompson planned the whole thing. Everything except the $4.17. The signs all pointed in that direction.

The prosecutor negotiated a plea bargain with Thompson and his attorney. Thompson did not appear to get much of a bargain. The physical evidence alone overwhelmed his public defender. Thompson's prints covered the Buick, the windows, the kitchen sink, the counter, and the hammer. The gasoline from the kitchen, the five-gallon cans, and Thompson's coveralls had the identical composition. His clothing had traces of blood from all three victims. The blood and hair on the hammer came from the two boys. The lab reports did not mention the dust on his coveralls, or the $4.17.

The coroner's pathologist, Dr. Hunter, reported that the bodies all had multiple skull fractures caused by the hammer, which left a wafflelike pattern injury on Joan's and Chuck's skull identical to the pattern on the hammer's head. All three victims died from the blows, not from the fire. Dr. Hunter found no soot in the airways, a sign that the victims stopped breathing before the fire burned.

With the confession added to the physical evidence, the prosecutor offered a plea bargain of second-degree murder for Joan's death, and aggravated first-degree murder for killing Bill and Chuck. Thompson struck out in anger at Joan, killing her in the heat of the moment, she said, then coldly murdered the boys, planning to burn the home and destroy the evidence. She would not seek the death penalty, provided he pleaded guilty. Thompson would spend the rest of his next three consecutive lives in prison with no possibility of parole. He took the deal. He got a bargain after all.

Detective Richards got no overtime pay working on the Duffy murder case. He attended Thompson's sentencing on his own time, and watched as the judge put him away forever. No extra investigation, and no time-consuming trial. But for every case that moves quickly from desk to file, three never make it at all. In the two weeks following his call to the farmhouse fire, he had six more cases. Three homicides remain on his desk.

A partially skeletonized unidentified female found in the bushes near a freeway interchange still lacks a name. Despite distinctive jewelry and dental work, no clues surfaced to identify her. She had a ligature around her neck and her hands tied behind her back. She occupied her spot in the bushes by the busy intersection for at least three weeks, according to the coroner's consulting forensic entomologist. Flies and maggots tell tales, too. But no one meeting her description resides in the N.C.I.C. computer's list of the missing and mutilated. No cards left to play in that game.

Another bad hand lay face down in a back alley dumpster. The victim, identified as a known drug dealer, had a single .38-caliber bullet in his brain. Predictably, none of his associates admits to knowing anything. Richards uncovered at least 30 people who had very good reason to put the dealer out with the other trash. No lanes and grooves could be identified on the mushroomed bullet. About half of the 30 "persons of interest" owned .38-caliber weapons. None could be linked to the crime. No meaningful physical evidence. Too many signs pointing in too many different directions.

Later the same day another losing set of circumstances collected in a new case. Kids hunting for frogs in a small spring-fed rural lake found a body weighted down with rocks near the shore. Saponification, a chemical process that turns body fat into soaplike adipocere, indicated to Dr. Hunter that the body had been under the cold water for some time. The body had been stabbed in the chest. Richards finally identified the corpse. The out-of-state victim was last seen alive eating alone in a roadside diner, five years before his discovery 200 miles from his rocky landing in the lake.

All three ongoing contests demand Richards' time and thought even as he answers new calls. Richards knows he can't win them all. Not even guessing has helped move these three folders from his desk to the peaceful confines of his gray file cabinet. In these unfinished games he faces the hardest move critical logic teaches. Go Fish.

NOTES

1. In a famous illustration, Peirce gives examples of three types of inference (2.623, 1878). Consider a bag of beans in a room. A nonampliative inference from the signs might look like this:

   Deduction

   Rule All the beans from this bag are white.
   Case These beans are from this bag.
   Result These beans are white.

The result, that these beans are white, is certain given that the rule and the case are true. But this relation does not hold for ampliative inferences from the signs. Reshuffle the Rule, Case, and Result cards, and consider induction:

Induction

Case These beans are from this bag.
Result These beans are white.
Rule All the beans from this bag are white.

Induction rests on relative frequencies. Being from this bag is associated with being white. The reliability of the association depends on how many beans have been examined and the conditions of examination. Induction is statistical inference. Finally, reshuffle again to consider abduction as ampliative inference:

Abduction

Rule All the beans from this bag are white.
Result These beans are white.
Case These beans are from this bag.

Abduction rests on explanation. Explaining the result depends on finding mechanisms, manners, and causes. Abductions enable uncertain predictions. They provide, according to Peirce, "the only possible hope of regulating our future conduct rationally. (2.270)" They uncover conjectures to be proved or disproved by future testing. They constitute the heart of reasoning backward analytically.

2. The word ampliate comes from the Latin *ampliatus,* meaning adding, not contained in, or adding in the predicate something not contained in the meaning of the subject term. Synthetic, not analytic.

"Likelihood"...does more harm than yellow fever ever did.

chapter three

Chance—The Davenport Case

Probability and Serendipity

"I'd rather have you think me a damn fool than to be one."

Hopalong Cassidy

Any poker player loves to play a royal flush, especially in spades during a high stakes game. Its rarity accounts for its power. The chance of getting one appears remote when considering all the possible combinations a 52-card deck provides. The Duffy case dealt Richards good cards and he played them well. But it doesn't take a royal flush just to win. Winning cards in a death case are not as rare as Richards' royal flush. But unlike poker, what counts as "winning" in death cases varies considerably.

In natural deaths, the signs often clearly point to the correct medical explanation—a long history of heart problems; a sudden collapse while gardening; 90% stenosis of the left descending coronary artery. In accidents, the circumstances frequently defy misinterpretation—playing golf, standing under a tree wearing golf shoes during a thunderstorm when struck by lightning. In suicides, the signs may point in one direction—a history of serious depression; previous attempts, an explanatory note, an overdose of antidepressant medication. Often in homicides, unambiguous signs point toward the killer—found kneeling over the victim, murder weapon in hand, cursing the evil bastard who needed killing while swearing gladly to murder the devil again.

However, the three cases added to the others on Richards' desk, like all vague or ambiguous death cases, fare less well. Their signs present gambles with higher, even unacceptable, risks. The cards just aren't there. The decomposed body by the freeway, the executed drug dealer in the dumpster, or the saponified corpse in the lake each present many isolated signs with many possible links among them. They don't point toward any clear path to follow.

Solving such cases requires recognizing coincidental signs for discard while distinguishing from them coincidental clues for play. Apparently ignoring this step, Dashiell Hammett said that:

> "This business of a detective endlessly poring over clues to solve a crime is overdone. The difference between the knotty problem confronting the detective of fiction and that facing the real detective is that in the former there is usually a paucity of clues and in the latter altogether too many."[1]

In a sense, Hammett is right. There may be plenty of signs. But they may not turn into clues to help explain the death. They may turn into the saliva test that Germaine waited weeks for from the cigarette butt left by his own deputy; a sign but a sign unrelated to the problem at hand—not a clue; not even relevant. Richards' tested bets can eliminate the coincidental signs from the freeway, dumpster, or lake death scenes, and leave him holding the clues. But after all the work there may be little left in his hand to call a clue. Unlike the Duffy case, these cases require investigators wait for more cards to play.

Fishing for clue cards involves reading signs pulled in from informants, unidentified citizens supplying tips, or from unwilling anonymous witnesses. The bait could be rewards offered in Crime Stopper ads, appeals to social responsibility, or offers of a reduced sentence for those more self-interested than civic minded. Investigators hope for a strike that will close the case. But they throw back most results from these fishing expeditions.

The demand for new clues adds pressure to the forensic scientists analyzing the signs already in hand. This pressure demands "endlessly poring over the clues (read 'signs')" until the investigation gains a productive direction. Besides adding pressure to the trace evidence analyst, serologist, and toxicologist, the forensic pathologist must squeeze more information from an already unyielding body. Pathologists may come to regret any Holmes-like displays of reasoning performed for approving audiences of Watson-like detectives. The investigative demand for exotic signs from the autopsy indicating medical and social history increases when supplies of signs from the body approache zero. The pathologist remains unable to supply either an identifying feature or time and cause of death.

To satisfy the demand for signs, the forensic entomologist may count the number of maggot generations feeding off the host to help provide time of death estimates. The forensic anthropologist may search for and analyze skeletal remains to help identify the body, distinguish antemortem injuries from postmortem animal scavenging, and supply age, sex, and stature information. The forensic odontologist may examine any teeth or dental work and help locate antemortem dental records. Forensic botanists may examine surrounding plant life and compare divergent or immature vegetation found under the corpse to link the victim with other locations, or to determine the season of the body's deposit. Forensic psychologist "profilers," called criminal investigative analysts by the FBI, may analyze a homicide scene to profile the perpetrator, suggesting personality, social, and occupational characteristics based on signs left at the scene.

Catching additional signs with these specialties depends on discovering the body or locating a sequence of crime scenes. In some cases, even with a recovered body, these hooks come up empty. If EMT's could magically resuscitate the dead to ask, "Who killed you?", the answer may be, "No idea." Investigators lack an obvious connection between the victim and the killer, and the crime scene remains undiscovered. The site of initial contact, the assault site, the murder site, and the dumpsite may each be separate scenes miles apart. The odds for discovery diminish considerably over time. When that happens, or in presumptive death cases without a body, investigators must change the bait. The only remaining signs for pursuit come from applying previous investigative experience and hoping for parallels.

Detectives may connect elements of cases from their own files to develop clues, such as "Women killed in bedrooms are murdered by lovers," "Women killed in living rooms are murdered by less intimate acquaintances," or "Homicide victims are killed by family members or friends." When lacking individual experience, investigators may appeal to collective relative frequencies supplied by crime statistics: "Bodies found dumped in the woods are deposited by sexual predators." "Multiple stab wounds on a male implicate a gay lover."

Such statistical associations qualify neither as laws of nature, nor as explanatory narratives. As signs, they must be read with caution. Peirce would say that mere induction lacks imagination. The problem remains to discover which of the available experiences proves relevant to the case under investigation. That involves proposing alternative abductions from the statistical signs, then following and testing the different signs each supply. As Sherlock Holmes says, "I have devised seven separate explanations, each of which would cover the facts as far as we know them. But which of these is correct can only be determined by the fresh information which we shall no doubt find waiting for us." Similar nonfictional pursuits take heroic commitments of time and money and a healthy dose of good luck. For real investigators, it may be a long wait for fresh information.

Germaine, Shipley, Moretti, Dr. Manning, Richards, and Dr. Hunter have neither unlimited time nor unlimited funds to pursue such cases. New cases arrive daily and soon these files become inactive. Chance fails to favor minds otherwise occupied. In jurisdictions lacking experience with difficult death cases, inactive files often pass from local to county to state investigative agencies. As these dead-end cases move and age, the case file is often all that remains. After several years, the file itself may be the only sign left to pursue. By then the trail is colder than the corpse it chronicles. It takes a hero or a fool to pick up one of these cases. Only a damn fool would do it on his own time. But Detective Edward W. Levine, nobody's fool, did just that.

Sept. 1, 1981, 5:15 P.M.

Detective Levine ambles in his cowboy boots toward his own garage-tack room from an unmarked State Police Mustang with a box under his arm. The box holds the official remains of a 10-year-old boy named William Davenport, called Willie by family and friends. Levine carries a jumble of papers, envelopes, and folders jammed rather precariously into an aging Coors beer box. William Davenport, if he had lived past that October night in 1971, would now be 20 years old.

The case file of the little boy they said never made it home from Mr. Hargrove's pee-wee football practice smelled like a mixture of firecrackers, ashtrays after a wild party, and damp basements—the kind with dirt floors. Supplemental reports, handwritten on dog-eared legal paper, crowd notes on napkins, tip sheets, letters, suspect files, photographs, and D.M.V. reports. Indistinguishable tan Xeroxes of God-knows-what stick out among the reports, all in no apparent order and for no identifiable purpose. Four cassette tapes squeeze together in front.

Levine looks through these remains, now as old as the victim they represent, in his detached garage-tack room turned into a home office. Cases like this, as the fictional detective Hercule Poirot might say, challenge "the little gray cells." Like many of his generation, Detective Levine does not attempt to think for extended periods without an adequate supply of both coffee and smokes. The bundle in the beer box had been given a lot of thought by other members of his generation. That's how a case earns its own peculiar odor.

Detective Levine assigned to the State Police Crime Analysis Section and a local resident since 1968 lives on a small ranch East of town. Middle age has been kinder to him than to many: He stands about 6 feet with graying temples and gray streaks in neatly trimmed mustache. Three of his daughters played with Willie as children. So it seemed natural for the local police and the county sheriff to ask him to review the case, and, if possible, help bridge a 10-year gap in an investigation briefly rekindled only last year, but now as stone-cold as ever.

Levine and his three daughters assemble around the box in his office, looking like a spoof of a Rembrandt medical painting. They gaze down at a picture of William, taken in 1970, as if paying last respects to the contents of a casket. The picture shows a kid who could pass for cute, but would always look as though he needed cleaning. His smile masked tired but expectant eyes and his full-sized teeth looked like uncomfortable strangers in his half-sized mouth. Any power and independence of spirit showed itself in his hair—not through the willfulness of adolescent rebellion, but through the genetic forces that caused a tuft on the back of his head to defy the lesser forces of gravity.

The eyes might have faded with time and disappointment—one more beating from a bully, one more snub from a classmate, or a face full of pimples turned to scars. His dreams might eventually have been gelded by absent talents and waning ambitions. If he had lived, he might have grown up to be very ordinary, like most people. His death would not be the kind to immortalize in film or song, certainly not a topic with Shakespearean interest. It would have gone unnoticed by Tennessee Williams. But it would have been his life and he might have made something of it, however humble or grand. Regardless, no one should have taken it from him, turning his life into this death in a beer box.

His case, packaged in cardboard, moved through predictable stages of decomposition. First, it became inactive after a year or so, but not unforgotten. New successes quickly replace old failures. That's one feature of human resilience. Humans have the capacity to forget, to go on. Win a few, lose a few. After a year or two, it was tabled, like an old lover—memories of it dulled by new conquests and new demands. Corpus delicti No. 711011 embodied another frustrating unsolved missing person case, a check in the debt column of the justice ledger. The case, ruled a presumptive death in 1978 by the county coroner, did not officially count as a homicide. The manner had been formally ruled "undetermined."

The last known likeness of this 10-year-old smiles awkwardly up from the wrinkled photo. This postmortem of a cardboard box filled with records has no stainless steel gurney, no autopsy assistant, and no forensic pathologist. No evidence has been collected or sent to the crime lab for analysis. No body has been recovered, and no scene has been identified. The records in the box are all that remain. The *corpus delicti,* literally the body of the case, consists of these reports, records and tapes. This autopsy requires different tools, different skills but similar methods. Like a good pathologist facing a body, Ed Levine's diagnostic experience applies to this kind of corpse.

Levine relies on his imagination in problem cases to develop a novel approach, to suggest what might have happened, and to test his conjectures. In his first difficult murder case, he realized that "yes" and "no" did not exhaust the possible replies to questions about the truth of its details. Some questions could not be answered accurately by either reply. Given the uncertainties of the case, he added "maybe" to complete the options. He thereby discovered "probability," the word used variously to measure human uncertainty.

Through a fitting fog of irony, few things appear as uncertain as the nature of probability. Ambiguous uses of the word "probability" pepper legal practice like shots at the victim of a drive by shooting. The "beyond a reasonable doubt" requirement presents one source of befuddlement. When asked what measure of probability must be met for a defendant to be found guilty "beyond a reasonable doubt," a survey of 347 judges uncovered some who thought that this meant a 70% chance of a defendant's guilt, one who thought this meant only a 50% chance, and nearly a third who thought it required a 100% chance. A group of 69 jurors gave equally diverse responses on the measure of chance sufficient either to convict or to acquit. When asked what "probable" meant, all responses included the phrase "most likely."

To say that "the most probable event" is "the most likely event" defines the remotely unclear with the utterly mysterious—unhelpful even for lawyers accustomed to tortured language and vacuous definition. According to C. S. Peirce,

> "The term 'likelihood' is the most deceptive thing in the world, being nothing but the degree of conformity of a proposition with our preconceived ideas. When this is dignified by the name of probability, as if it were something on which vast Insurance Companies could risk their hundreds of millions, it does more harm than the yellow fever ever did." (7.220).

Probability theory seeks to demystify the concept by defining what it means to say that one event is more likely than another.

Modern accounts of probability began with a correspondence between Blaise Pascal (1623–1662) and Pierre de Fermat (1608–1665) over the division of stakes in an interrupted gambling session. The classical theory of probability, formulated by Laplace, DeMorgan, Keynes, and others, holds that probability measures degree of belief. In this view, probability always results from partial knowledge and partial ignorance. (We only know certain things about coin tosses, not everything.) The so-called *priori* view holds that to compute the probability of an event, divide the number of different paths leading to its occurrence by the total number of possible paths. (So the probability of the first card in a normal deck being a spade is 13/52.) In the relative frequency view, probability measures the number of times something associates with something else. (For instance in one population, 971 of 1,000 women live at least one year beyond their 25th birthday.)

Probability predictions of the chance for future events can be made from past experience. Every baseball fan knows when asked what a hitter batting .500 will likely do his next trip to the plate, that the hitter has a 50% probability of getting a hit. These probabilities describe relative frequencies, empirical generalizations that result from past correlation of "at bat" and "getting a hit." However, saying that a batter hitting .500 has a 1 in 2 chance of getting a hit the next trip to the plate says more than that his future performance resembles his past attempts. It includes tacit appeals to special circumstances affecting performance that lurk in the background. Illness, personal problems, a troublesome contract dispute, or a special nemesis on the mound affect the probability in a specific "at bat."

C. S. Peirce provides an analysis of what more needs to be said about context in the logic of chance. Context, he thinks, shows probability's abductive component, treating the observed relative frequency as one sign to be read among others. The batting average remains only one consideration to be weighed in any specific "at bat" when predicting future performance.

Levine's practical need to know the best bet despite conditions of uncertainty mixes abduction with induction as Peirce describes. As Peirce warned that treating abduction and induction as one simple inference mirrors a common confusion. Relative frequencies and their associations depend upon abductions for their relevance. Without explanation, statistics become coincidental oddity.

Levine began developing devices and techniques to organize, refine and measure his uncertainty about criminal cases. In William's case he expected many "maybes" requiring a bet that one event more likely occurred than another. Like Holmes, he began to organize this missing person case according to alternative explanations for William's disappearance. Reviewing statistics, he proposed abductive bets to explain the unusual fact that William never made it home that October night. Unlike Holmes, he proposed only six. The alternatives gave direction to his file review and supplied significance to new signs.

He proposed to consider runaway, relative kidnap, relative homicide, accident, stranger kidnap, and stranger kidnap-homicide scenarios. Like horses in a race, one explanation may get an early lead. But the first from the gate does not always cross the finish line first. Like handicapping horses, the problem becomes ranking the scenarios from most to least likely to hedge the bet. Peirce's caution about "likelihood" serves to marshal existing data into these alternative explanations. Mere prejudice does not play well in the logic of probability.

The best bet may not always have the lowest risk or the highest payoff. To compare bets, statisticians use what they call "the expected value theorem." A bet's expected value becomes a number derived formally so that the risk and payoff of one bet can be compared with another. A dollar bet on "heads" in a coin toss purchases an expected value. If heads appears, the bettor gets \$2 (the \$1 originally bet, plus \$1 in winnings). If tails appears, there is no return. The probability of heads is 1/2, and the same for tails. Thus, the expected value of a one dollar bet that heads will appear equals $(1/2 \times \$2) + (1/2 \times \$0) = \$1$. With the odds even, the expected value equals the purchase price. That defines a good bet. In many games of chance, the expected value may be less than the purchase price, one condition for a foolish bet. While this sounds powerful, its application to Case No. 711011 reaches a predictable limitation.

Many foolish bets beat the odds and many mutually exclusive bets have the same expected values. But Detective Levine's calculations lack the numerical formality of probability theory, a formality largely appropriate for cards and coins but inappropriate for missing children. The bets differ. Levine's uncertainty does not concern betting on a future unknown outcome. He does not bet on predictions about similar little boys not coming home in the future. Whatever happened to William Davenport occurred long ago. No uncertainty surrounds the outcome itself. Levine's uncertainty focuses on choosing the best explanation of this specific past event from abductively proposed alternatives. His task is not to predict an uncertain future but to explain the foggy past. Detective Levine's problem begins with too many explanations that appear to cover the same data. He must reason backward analytically to find the best explanation in Case No. 711011. Levine must fish upstream, against the current.

He finished unpacking the file in his garage office, and switched on his PC to help with his autopsy. In difficult cases lacking clues, meticulous persistence works better than flashes of cunning. In a bet between the tortoise and the hare, Levine bets on the reptile every time. Perhaps because he prefers to amble, or perhaps because he figured out a way to handicap the race. He may lose some bets, anger impatient superiors, and vex overburdened co-workers, but he's still a sucker for the underdog. Difficult cases, he says, take time.

He takes his own time, evenings, weekends, and slack days in the office, to work the case. He works through midnight the first day, organizing categories for information, sorting the reports, and piling the papers in some order. At 2:30 A.M. he ambles across his driveway, takes off his boots, and crawls into bed beside his sleeping wife. She has managed to put up with him and with this for 24 years. She will put up with his work on this case for another 10.

Detective Levine sleeps fitfully, often dreaming about Monday, October 11, 1971, the birthday of Case No. 711011. In his dream, the face in the picture stares up at nothing with unseeing eyes. He hears a soft whimper punctuated by shallow breathing, then longer spaces between shallower breaths. No soft whimper. Then only space. The dream recurs for the next 10 years.

Living in the community, knowing police work, and interviewing long-retired investigators helps him move beyond the terse reports in the file. He struggles to reconstruct the events of October 11, 1971. An image of that Columbus Day slowly focuses.

Monday, October 11, 1971, 8:10 P.M.

The phone rang for the 42nd time this swing shift. Morgan had the desk, replacing Jepson, who had a family potluck planned for the Columbus Day holiday. About time for the first big fight of the evening, he thought to himself. He parked his latest cigarette in a black ashtray heaped with proof that he was almost through for the night.

People who worked in this community worked hard and drank hard. Those out of work drank hard longer. And most of the hard drinkers in this town, dominated by sun and range, also packed a hard punch. The holiday just mixed the hard-working and non-working drinkers earlier, and the mixture usually turned to trouble.

"Police Department, Morgan," the tired voice spoke into the black receiver.

"It's my boy William. He missed dinner. I'm s'pposed to take'm to the basketball game at school and he's not here . . ." The woman's voice trembled, obviously worried. Morgan knew you could go by the voice in these cases more than anything else.

"Name?" Morgan asked, hoping to regiment a potentially long and misdirected conversation. He whisked a stray cigarette ash from the yellow legal pad while he spoke.

"Davenport," she said. "Betty Davenport."

"Address and phone?" He scribbled notes on the yellow pad, linking the spaces between two circular brown coffee stains.

"1614 North Dawson Creek, 555-7241," she said.

"What's your son's full name, Mrs. Davenport?"

"William James Davenport, but everyone just calls him Willie."

Morgan, speaking from years of experience finding misplaced cats, dogs, children, and an occasional horse or chicken, said "When and where was he last seen?" Cigarette smoke escaping his lungs made it look like he was talking in a deep freeze.

"He came home after school at 3:30 to change his shoes for practice; he left about 3:35 or so to go to the playfield."

"How old is he?"

"Ten. He's excited about the exhibition basketball game at school tonight, the teachers are playing some women's team to raise money . . . he'd never miss it . . . unless . . ." The voice now wavered between worried and scared. This call demanded calming, reasonable, compassionate common sense.

"Give me a little more information, like his height and weight."

"He's about four-feet, six-inches and weighs about 58 pounds. Do you think you'll be able to find him? Have there been any accidents?"

"We have a couple of cars out tonight and they'll keep an eye out for him. Now, how about the color of his hair and eyes?" Morgan scrubbed out the latest evidence of his long shift in the black ashtray.

"He's got black straight hair with a cowlick in back and gray eyes. You don't think anything has happened to him, do you?" she asked.

"What was he wearing today?"

"When he left for practice, he had the shirt his gramma made for him, his gray corduroy bell bottoms, and sneakers. Has something happened to William?"

"Has he ever done anything like this before?" Morgan asked quickly, to evade inevitable questions from a mother fearing the worst.

"No, never! He always comes home for supper about 5 o'clock . . ." The voice at the other end of the black handset now mixed anger and frustration with fear.

The next question always added resentment to the already volatile mixture: "Has your son ever run away before?"

A gasp preceded the explosion: "No!" Morgan's instinct sensed credibility.

"Maybe he got to playing and forgot to come home." Said aloud, it didn't sound nearly as reasonable or calming as Morgan had hoped.

A long silence at the other end assured Morgan that his common sense was being carefully considered. He thought his next words should give her something productive to do. "Just go where he usually does, call his buddies . . . maybe they've seen him. He probably just forgot the time. Kids are like that . . . got four o' ma own with their own sense of time," he said compassionately.

"Siskel's out lookin for him now. That's my husband. Don't worry he said. I know he's worried . . ." Betty's voice trailed off; less anger, more frustration, but now further from panic.

"You help him look. I'll call it to the cars, and if we find out anything, I'll call you. If you find him, call back right away." The other phone line was now on its third ring, the white light of line two flashing in Morgan's face. He covered it with his finger, poised to quiet the rings.

"Thanks," the slightly reassured but unconvinced voice said in his ear. The rings were silenced and line two was receiving official attention. The light on line one was now dark. It was 8:15 P.M. Monday, October 11, 1971, Columbus Day.

Monday, October 11, 1971, Police Dept. Graveyard Shift

When Siskel Davenport called Sgt. Cairns, Morgan's swing shift partner, at 10:10 P.M., William had been missing for over five hours. The official complaint from the box in Ed Levine's garage reads: "Son failed to return from football practice." Hardly an alarm bell signaling a homicide, especially in 1971. Betty and Siskel exhausted every alternative they knew. Wherever he was, he was not with any friends or at any of the places they looked. It could only become an official police matter, Case No. 711011 after 72 hours. It's not a crime to be missing. But to their credit, the police treated the case seriously from the start. They wasted no time worrying about formalities. This case did not go bad because the local police either failed to do something, or did something incompetently.

Officers Byrd, Covington, and Read worked the graveyard shift. They searched the playfield bleachers and bushes. When small town kids are missing, unusual patterns and the activities of strangers become two of the first categories entering a cop's mind. Two motels host visitors to town, a good first source of strangers. And one unusual activity: the exhibition basketball game. Officer Byrd first rousted the City Center Motel's groggy manager at 3:15 A.M.; checked all vacant rooms, the two storerooms, and recorded the license numbers of every vehicle at the motel.

At 4:00 A.M. Officers Covington and Read visited the Sands Motel, brought their combined list of license numbers to 28, woke up the basketball team's coach, and contacted each of the nine players. Coach Cogins and the athletes remembered William watching them practice at the school gym with 10 other boys. The boys walked them from the gym to their motel around 5:30 P.M. William, described by the players as a tiny charmer, talked briefly with the women at the door, and was invited to sit on their bench at the game, an honor not to be missed in the life of any 10-year-old sports fan. Neither the players nor the coach saw William at the game, despite looking for him. His spot on the bench remained vacant.

This information placed William at the Sands Motel around 5:30 P.M. The Motel sits on the corner of La Cassa Avenue and Dawson Creek Road, just four blocks away from his home at 1514 Dawson Creek Road. Ordinarily, William could not have waited to tell his family the exciting news about being invited to sit on the bench during the game. So something extraordinary happened. Toward the end of his shift, Officer Covington checked from Dawson Creek to the edge of town. He found nothing.

Tuesday, October 12, 1971, Police Dept.

The flurry of activity that would put dark circles under many eyes over the next weeks began with a radio broadcast describing William, where he was last seen given the graveyard shift's work, and asking for any information. At 7:18 A.M. a call came in from Mrs. G. T. Evans, an employee of Shane Hardware Supply. She heard the radio request on her way to work and called to say that she saw a boy fitting William's description talking to a man in a light-colored VW Bug on Dawson Creek Road yesterday about 5:30 P.M. when she drove by and looked in her rear view mirror, she saw the boy get into the car.

At 8:15 A.M. after talking with the 10 boys who were with William at the Sands Motel, and checking with his school to see if William showed up for class at 9:00 A.M. officers Johnson and Covington visited the Shane Hardware to interview Mrs. Evans. She identified a photograph of William as a picture of the boy she saw get into the VW. "I saw the boy talking to the driver from the passenger side, and then he walked around to the driver's side. The driver's side door was open, and he appeared to get in the car." She didn't see the car leave. The driver was a white male, with dark messy hair, wearing a dark shirt.

While officers Johnson and Covington worked on this angle, the police department intensified its investigative efforts by calling the county sheriff department into the case. Police Sgt. Ogalla and Officers Johnson, Read, Byrd, and McLain joined forces with county deputy McPhearson, and county detectives Ramirez and LaStella. They combined their efforts to check railroad schedules, boxcars, truck stops, and interview neighbors, friends, and relatives.

Tuesday, October 12, through Friday October 15, 1971

At the same time, the county Civil Defense Unit and Explorer Scouts from two adjacent counties line-searched areas along Dawson Creek, the city dump, 100 yards either side of every major county road near town, and several square miles of desert cut through by many intersecting area cattle roads.

In addition to the foot searches, four-wheel-drive vehicles from a club of self-professed naturalists who experience desert beauty while crushing it with knobby tires, searched more remote outlying areas. An aerial survey firm flew fixed-wing aircraft over the entire region. Tracking dogs joined in the search, assisted by a Search and Rescue Unit that provided radio communications among the various searchers. Church groups pitched in to supply food and refreshments for the hundreds of volunteers stomping, wheeling, soaring over, and sniffing the area. But by Friday, October 15, it ended. Betty and Siskel Davenport knew no more about what happened to their son William than they had Monday night.

James Grange, county civil defense coordinator, said, "The ground search could be resumed on short notice if law enforcement officials come up with any ideas as to where searching might be worthwhile." So far, no areas had been isolated. It was like looking for an overdue canoe in the middle of the Pacific Ocean.

Meanwhile, much police work remained to be done. Standard procedure included eliminating nonstranger suspects by discreetly investigating family relationships, and thoroughly searching Siskel and Betty's house and yard. Statistics favored some sort of domestic involvement. If not the immediate family, then the extended family, including grandparents, aunts, uncles, and their circle of associates. In the guise of learning more about William, detectives learned more about the Davenports.

The Davenport family's collective life centered on their church and its strict Bible-centered fundamentalist faith. Men commanded and women served. Siskel worked hard at a local shipping firm, off-loading box cars. Betty worked harder at home, sewing, cooking, cleaning, and raising both their vegetables and their children. The kids, Karen, Jack, and Jody did chores, homework, and church work. Each toiled according to God's master plan to save them from current sin and reward them with future glory. Careful work eliminated them, their extended family, and their associates as suspects. Whatever sins they carried, none involved William's disappearance.

After the extensive family investigation, which stopped just short of digging in Betty's garden, other leads and tips required equally thorough follow-up treatment. Twenty-eight vehicles had to be run through various D.M.U.'s, and a light-colored VW Bug had to be located. The plan included listing sex offenders on probation, paroled, or released who might have been in the area at the time and who might have access to a light-colored VW Bug, or who might be connected to one of the 28 cars at the two motels.

The sheer tedium of these tasks provokes frequent reassessment of such plans. Just physically collecting motor vehicle, court, prison, and mental health records from multiple jurisdictions can melt a dedicated detective's mind, forming a mental slush incapable of originating civil speech. Once the data rests on someone's desk, correlation must be attempted among the multiple six-inch piles of fan-fold paper. Pencils guided by nicotine-stained fingers record the painful progress. Even if computers could be used, no agency's system ever communicates with any other. Mere silicon slush.

On a television program, one sex offender record buried in one six-inch pile would match with one motel registration record and one suspect would emerge with access to a VW bug. An investigator stuffing a shoulder-holstered arm through a sport coat sleeve while running from desk to car would speed to make the arrest. But off camera, the piles of paperwork present too many signs, but too few clues. No less than 12 sex offenders of one species or another visited town that night, some stayed in one of the two motels, and at least five had access to VW bugs. In the Disneyland version of this investigative ride, annoying little voices chant, "It's a small world after all." Each of the dirty dozen had to be worked as a potential suspect.

After all this labor, four good suspects emerged, any one of whom had the personality and the credentials to kill William. One owned a light blue VW Bug and all were in the area on Monday, October 11. The problem became sorting the clues from the coincidences.

County detectives Ramirez and LaStella each took two. They followed phone bills, credit card slips, and traffic citations. They interviewed waitresses, bartenders, and mechanics. They questioned co-workers, cellmates, friends, family, and the suspects themselves. More off-camera police work netted the same unreal result.

It may be disheartening to discover in the course of a criminal investigation how many people, through personality, criminal history, and circumstance, could easily be guilty. But it is positively depressing to discover that none of the prime suspects who otherwise match the crime perfectly bear the guilt. The local police and county sheriff investigators concluded, after careful work, that none of these four prime suspects could be involved in William's disappearance.

One received an excuse from a drunken bar fight. Another entertained himself by raping a juvenile male in his rooming house. The other two lacked dramatic excuses leading to jail time, but circumstances placed them too far away between 5 and 6 P.M. to take their possible role seriously. The correlations sifted from the perp-paper piles explained nothing. Investigators hit zero for 12. After this much effort, this zero result often leads detectives to desperate measures.

Hypnotism does not ordinarily qualify as a desperate measure. Its use aids the recall of a witness who has seen something but does not remember certain details. It's as if memories cover with frost in the mind's freezer. Hypnotism works like a kind of mental defrosting. Through hypnosis, the memories thaw and the frost clears so that they can be identified. Like defrosting frozen food, one can't take anything out of memory that didn't at one time go in. Dr. Salvatori of the state crime lab hypnotized Mrs. Evans from the hardware supply store. She recalled under hypnosis that the VW had a rusty front bumper, a broken taillight, and faded light paint. This information could be valuable, should the vehicle ever be recovered. But it did not help distinguish one rusty, bashed, faded VW from any other of the thousands on the road.

Unlike using hypnotists, using psychics can safely be considered a desperate measure, even when resorting to those as successful as Dorothy Allison. No one contacted Dorothy. Betty's sister Evelyn worked with a professional psychic named Maria Garcia, who called her house the "Parapsychology Research Clinic." She and Evelyn gave demonstrations of "psychic powers, progression, regression, clairvoyance, mind control, habit control, and subconscious sight." Admission was $2.50. But when the session with Betty began in the conference room of the police department, admission was by invitation only.

After being around the station almost all week, Betty was tired and worried. Garcia calmed her down, worked her wonders, and claimed to have her deep in a trance. Through the psychic energy of a mother's love for her son, she explained, he would have Betty spiritually fly over William and observe what happened to him after he left home at 3:30 P.M. to go to practice. She could then lead investigators to her son. From the vantage-point of his garage, Detective Levine could see a willingness to try anything, no matter how loony it sounded. The tape recorder's microphone in the middle of the conference room table pointed directly at Betty. All eyes focused on her with skeptical anticipation.

As she flew over William, she described his movements and his mood. On the four cassette tapes from the box in Levine's garage, she described William getting into a car, and riding, with the driver putting his hand on William's leg. "Would you say he is making advances toward William?" Garcia asked in as delicate a manner as circumstances warranted. "Yeah." Betty replied. "What is William's reaction?" she asked. "He's scared," she answered.

Investigators followed her spiritual trip on county road maps. She described roads and notable landmarks that led investigators to an area just off the Tumbleweed Road to a point 50 feet off the end of Meghan Trail Road, one of the many crisscrossing cattle trails cutting up this area. "I'm going to ask you in a couple seconds to open your eyes," Garcia said, "and when you do, you're going to remember everything that you stated to me. Do you understand? And I want you . . . to take us to the spot that you last saw William." "All right," Betty said. And she did. But William was not there.

September 17, 1980, 3:18 P.M. County Sheriff Department

Time has a way of healing some wounds. But the cruelty of William's disappearance eventually destroyed Betty and Siskel's marriage. Despite their brand of religion-made-simple, or perhaps because of it, they divorced and Siskel moved out of the state. Its rigid and mechanical cause-effect theological structure supplied no room for chance, and no room for tragedy with its attendant undeserved suffering. The guilt becomes too much for any human to bear when the only choice is between blaming God or blaming humans. With no other human in focus, blame shuttled between Betty and Siskel until the game became too painful to continue.

Even creators of scientific explanations covering complex events often confuse reasons or statistical associations with causes. Associations have many scientific functions, but they don't serve to *explain* concrete events. Nor are reasons functionally equivalent to causes. The metaphysical fact remains that some processes forming a "single event" occur *coincidentally.* That's an important element of explaining and locating missing children like William. An unequivocally mechanical example such as an airplane crash illustrates.

Suppose that a small corporate jet crashes, killing all aboard. The family and the media keep pressing investigators for *the cause.* While we certainly understand the request, good investigators don't let it color the method for producing and defending the best explanation of the crash. The fact remains that media and family alike confuse *causes* with *explanations.* Scientists don't confuse ordinary language accounts such as "the sun rises every morning" with concrete explanations of celestial motions such as "the sun, relative to the earth, remains motionless." The sun cannot rise since it does not move. Nor do complex events like air crashes or kidnapping have *a cause.*

Investigators discovered that over several years, fueling the jet introduced small cracks in the fuel tank's neck. The aircraft's assembly process failed to secure a sheath over a wire bundle in the left wing. Vibrations over the several years moved the sheath exposing wires in the bundle. During routine maintenance, a service technician nicked the insulation on an exposed wire. During a long-past repair, a mechanic lost a steel washer in the right wing. Designers provided a passageway between wings for wires and hydraulic lines. To comply with tower instructions, the pilot switched on the landing lights and banked steeply left to land. Spilled jet fuel and the washer slid to the left wing. The nicked wire powered the landing lights. The fuel, the washer, and the nick produced a sustained spark that ignited the fuel. The resulting fire melted wires and hydraulic lines. The pilot lost control and the plane crashed.

While tempting to postulate *a cause* for the crash, there isn't one. Each of these events, the cracks, the misassembly, the nick, the washer, the design, the switching, and the banking, remain causally unconnected. They're independent events occurring coincidentally (literally at the same instant). Their simultaneous occurrence *explains* the crash, but no single event *caused* it. Switching on the landing lights did not *cause* the crash any more than dropping the washer did.

Coincidence relates events not themselves causally related. To ignore coincidence and to embrace a world of simplistic causation commits one to holding absurd positions such as "a dropped washer causes hydraulic failure" or "birth causes death." Such reasoning appears when parents blame themselves or each other for causing their child's death, when all they did was let him go to school. It remains metaphysically inaccurate and scientifically flawed. So do relative frequency measures of coincidence.

When told that her mother died of a heroin overdose, a child says, "Mama shot heroin her whole life and never died," offering a version of the she-can't-be-dead-she-never-died-before argument for human immortality. "Injecting heroin" and "being alive" are neither reasons nor causes of continued life, regardless of the frequency with which they associate. Inductive associations alone explain nothing. In fact, they demand explanations of their significance.

Peirce observes that " . . . any two things resemble one another just as strongly as any two others, if recondite resemblances are admitted (2.634)." The relevant regularities to be tested must be specified by abduction. Mere associations such as the fuel tank cracks and the short themselves require *explanation.* Several similar explanations of air crashes in the same make of plane associate only after each has been already explained. In this sense abduction must precede induction. According to Peirce,

> "A chemist notices a surprising phenomenon. Now if he has a high admiration of (John Stuart) Mill's Logic, as many chemists have, he will remember that Mill tells him that he must work on the principle that, under precisely the same circumstances, like phenomena are produced. Why does he then not note that this phenomenon was produced on such a day of the week, the planets presenting a certain configuration, his daughter having on a blue dress, the milkman being late that morning and so on? The answer will be that in early days chemists did use to attend to some such circumstances, but that they have (since) learned better." (6.413)

The mere association of events with the passage of time does not always permit us to learn better. Peirce's "critical logic" does not share the rigid mechanical structures favored by nature's simplifiers.

Nor does the mere passage of time permit us to forget past events. For the Davenports, life eventually returned, after nine years, to the new version of normal that results after sustaining a great loss. But their spiritual and emotional wounds did not heal. Betty, Siskel, Karen, Jack, Jody, and the rest of the family still didn't know what happened to William. Phone calls still came, but from nameless, faceless tormenters, asking, "Is William there?" Pornographic magazine subscription forms arrived addressed to "William Davenport." It would be easier if they knew he was dead. They could have no funeral to lay William or their grief to rest. Betty sometimes imagined him a prisoner, like a GI in a Southeast Asian bamboo cage, suffering unspeakable torture while she sat by, unable to help. Time, in this case, simply served to deepen the wounds.

Investigators had not given up hope, but Case No. 711011 became inactive. Nothing new could be done. Local police and county sheriff phones keep ringing, bringing new tragedies that demand attention. But not giving up links present calls with past cases. Some attribute these links to luck. But as Pasteur pointed out, "Chance favors the prepared mind." And Deputy

Bennett was prepared when the phone rang in the county sheriff department at 8:56 A.M., September 17, 1980.

The call came from a bulldozer operator named Pritchard who reported finding a human skull in the sand. Bennett dispatched Deputy Dale Matheson, and asked the caller for the location. "My dozer is right across from the spot," Pritchard said. "What's your location?" asked Bennett. "Oh, it's just off Tumbleweed Road, at the end of Meghan Trail Road. The skull is no more than 50 feet off the end of Meghan Trail Road." Deputy Bennett recalled the ground searches nine years earlier. He linked the call to William's case. Now, he thought, an area had been isolated. The ground search could be resumed.

The area had been searched first in 1971 when Betty Davenport led investigators to this same spot after her spiritual flight. Nothing had turned up. On October 2, 1980 the county's Mounted Search and Rescue Unit removed tumbleweeds from the area where the skull was found, and looked for a buried body. They found no body. Another fullscale Search and Rescue mission, including units from the same two adjacent counties, mobilized on October 12, 1980. After a long grid search of the surrounding area, they again found nothing. Investigators expressed extreme disappointment. But they had a skull, the first real bit of physical evidence after a long dry spell.

The skull itself proved disappointing as evidence goes. Only a partial cranial vault rested on the county coroner's desk. No mandible and no teeth accompanied the bone. Ruts from animal gnawing roughened the margins and covered the flat surfaces of this bit of parietal bone. No frontal bone, no temporal bones, and no occipital bone articulated with the find. The bones had separated at the sutures (the natural junctions that grow together over time), and had gone their separate ways. The bone looked bleached and dry, indicating its long stay in the desert.

The best forensic anthropologists, including a forensic anthropologist from a nearby medical examiner's office, could only say that the skull probably came from a juvenile, did not originate with an ancient Native American burial, and had been exposed to the elements for some time. Even sex could not be established with any confidence. The gnawing activity indicated that animals might have dropped the bone found some distance away. The body probably did not decompose where Pritchard found the bone.

An X-ray of the bone, they said, could supply positive identification. The meningeal artery leaves a distinct pattern on the parietal bone, like a fingerprint, with no two marks alike. The X-ray could be compared with antemortem X-rays of William's skull. Identical patterns on both antemortem and postmortem X-rays could positively identify the bone. But no antemortem X-rays existed for comparison. The meningeal artery reached another dead end, like one fingerprint with neither prints nor fingers for comparison. The best bets tendered about the bone itself appeared to lead nowhere. Dissatisfied investigators stood alone, needing to explain the bone's origin.

Explaining animal remains had occupied physical anthropologist C. K. Brain for most of his lifetime. He noted that caves containing human bones mixed with nonhuman remains required careful explanation. Some less cautious anthropologists reasoned that since the caves housed the humans, the presence of the other bones could be explained by the human occupants' taste for meat. Presumably the humans then died in their own kitchens on their own compost piles.

According to Brain, the same associations of human with nonhuman bones in caves have a better explanation. Suppose that saber-toothed tigers, not humans, lived in those caves. The tigers brought both humans and nonhumans to their caves as food. Sorting out the hunters from the hunted became his exercise in reasoning backward analytically. Predictions from the signs could help. Tooth marks on the skulls, signs of fires, or the presence or absence of cave art might help establish a pattern of signs and ownership of the caves.

In some cases, the same data support conflicting explanations and reasons need to be developed for preferring one to another. Brain knew that those reasons might not always be conclusive. Without additional signs in the caves or on the bones, the commingling of human with non-human remains became an unusual finding. It would be usual, however, if both humans and nonhumans were the quarry, hunted as food by tigers living in the caves. The nature of the commingled remains became evidence supporting the explanation that they suggested. Signs suggesting explanations often closely relate to its proof.

Similarly, the investigators knew that either the bone on the coroner's desk came from William or it did not. Establishing which became their exercise in reasoning backward analytically from the bone. No physical features displayed by the bone counted against it being from William's skull. But mere consistency does not provide sufficient proof. The bone's features conform equally to thousands of other missing humans. Only a confirmed negative instance supplies definitive evidence. Yet the lack of definitive evidence itself provided some support for the bone's belonging to William. Finding a juvenile parietal bone in the desert is unusual. Ask Mr. Pritchard. That discovery just off the Tumbleweed Road near Meghan Trail Road would be less unusual if the bone came from the little boy who disappeared from the nearby town. As Peirce would say, that hypothesis appears initially plausible in itself.

Peirce discusses such initially plausible hypotheses and their pitfalls. Discovering the fossil remains of a fish far inland suggests that the sea once covered the area. Paleontological tradition encourages the abduction. "But why not privilege some other explanations . . . [like ancient fisherman transported the fish inland]. *Ceteris paribus,* with nothing else to go on such as the fossilized remains of plant life once prominent in the sea, sandstone, salt, and other signs of sea life the paleontological explanation seems the most economic" . . . but there were many false scientific explanations which seemed very economic . . ." ((2.265), Brent, p. 204). Without signs pointing to the activities of the fishermen, without their fishhooks or nets, without the remains of their culture, the best explanation, while risky, rests on relevant paleontological traditions. Absence of proof is not proof of absence, but the absence of signs can itself be a sign.

Despite the disappointment carried with the skull bone, not one investigator seriously doubted that it belonged to William. But it brought them no closer to identifying William, proving his death, or finding his killer than they'd been before the bone's discovery. Even if the skull belonged to William, without further physical evidence neither time, cause, nor manner of death could be established. The investigation again reached an apparently unbridgeable gulf. Detective Levine worked to bridge that gulf the hard way.

Without further physical evidence to establish that the recovered bone belonged to William, Levine chose to show that it could not belong to anyone else. To show that William's disappearance is best explained as a homicide, he chose to show that it could not be a natural, suicidal, or accidental death. To paraphrase Sherlock Holmes' tribute to the power of negative instances, eliminate what ain't so, and what's left, no matter how strange, is probably true. The investigation floated above the gulf, like Betty Davenport's psychic flight, on the gossamer wings of risky inference, guided from a suburban garage control tower. For weary investigators, and for Levine, the stranger kidnap-homicide scenario remained the sentimental favorite.

Saturday, May 23, 1987, Levine's garage

Detective Levine's work supported Byrd, Covington, and Read's initial instincts on October 11, 1971—his search now focused on a stranger. The scenario had sexual assault as a motive, since no ransom had been demanded and no other motive seemed to fit the facts. Levine reexamined the searches done for sex offenders and mental patients with a history of sexual abuse and Covington checked the results with the list of VW bugs.

No shortage of sex offenders existed in the local area. Less than five miles from town, a state correctional facility housed 344 inmates, and 179 served their time for sex-related violence. In addition, the state mental health system operated a state mental hospital 38 miles south. Of the 587 patients, over half received treatment for disorders whose symptoms included sexual violence. Levine reconsidered the offenders and patients both paroled and released by October 11, 1971. Again, like the investigators before him, he came up empty. He checked escapes with the same result. But late one May night, while poring over *The State Mental Hospital Annual Report for 1971,* his eye caught the first reward for his efforts—a sign. He discovered that the investigation had missed a major category for leads. Statistics could mislead as well as guide future research.

The potential for misdirection increases when more records in a given area hide under unexpected categories. The U.K. enjoys one of the lowest suicide rates in the world. However this low rate results directly from their method of recording data. Deaths without a suicide note and without a clearly established intent to kill oneself become "death by misadventure," another category entirely. A person known to be depressed steps out a tenth-floor window. By Floor Eight, the victim may come to change his mind and regret his action. No note. No intent clearly established (See Floor Eight). Misadventure. Welcome to the healthy, happy U.K., and to the world of bureaucratic statistics.

The state hospital annual report that lay open before Levine also belonged to the genre of bureaucratic record keeping. The political goal of the report became clear: to demonstrate the success of treatment programs for violent offenders. Such success appeared by measuring the number of mentally ill offenders admitted against the number released. The more released, given responsibility, and reentered in society, the better the program. One model for such a program, The Voluntary Sex Offender Treatment Program, looked good on paper. It took offenders from the involuntary program and collected them in another category, improving the data profiles for each treatment option. It looked especially good to Detective Levine. No one had noticed it before.

In the voluntary version in 1971, participants could simply sign out of the hospital on what administrators called "TV"—travel and visitation. Detective Levine requested both general information on this program, and specific records of people signing out on October 11, 1971. He spoke with Charles Cistern, M.D., Clinical Director of the Legal Offender Unit, who assured Levine of his cooperation. Levine explained the case, and gave Dr. Cistern the brief version of the investigation's history. The records would take some time to recover from archives, Cistern said. Levine, the patient hunter, said he could wait.

August 11, 1987 State Mental Hospital

Ancient humans survived by tracking their prey while ducking their predators. Although some became tiger food, others tracked the unseen quarry, identifying the prey and its movement through sand, rock, and brush by reading impressions, scuffs, blood, hair, feathers, excrement, sounds, and smells. They read apparently insignificant trifles and formed a mental picture of the as yet unseen beast. Those who read too slowly ended up in unfriendly caves among the mixed remains studied by Brain.

An ancient Middle Eastern tale presents the skills of such hunters through the three sons of Serendippo's king, who were traveling in the desert. They meet a man who has lost a camel. The three immediately describe the camel: white, blind in one eye, under the saddle it carries two skins, one full of oil, the other full of wine. But they claim not to have seen it. The man accuses them of theft, and brings them before a judge.

They prove their innocence by showing how they reconstructed the appearance of an animal that they had never seen from the traces it left in the desert sand. The camel's tracks, they explained, circled left toward an oasis palm tree. The tree's bark held traces of white camel hair where it struck the tree.

The tracks pulled away from the tree, then curved toward the water. By the pool where the camel knelt to drink, on one side of the saddle strap impression left on the ground, oil residue remained. On the other side wine residue appeared.

When the makers of tracks in the sand can't be observed, they must be inferred from their effects. The sons of Serendippo's king did so to prove their innocence and save their lives. They met both the tracks and the man searching for his camel by chance. They used their own sagacity to identify the camel and to prove their innocence. This led Horace Walpole, in 1745, to use the word "serendipity" to mean making happy and unexpected discoveries "by accident and sagacity." "Finding valuable or agreeable things by chance" now bears the name "serendipitous discovery."

Chance has a part in serendipity, but Nobel laureate chemist Paul Flory said that significant discoveries do not occur as mere accidents. "Unless the mind is thoroughly charged beforehand, the proverbial spark of genius, if it should manifest itself, probably will find nothing to ignite." (*Serendipity: Accidental Discoveries in Science,* Royston M. Roberts, John Wiley, 1989.)

A letter postmarked August 8, 1987, reached Dr. Charles Cistern's desk three days later, on August 11. It led to a serendipitous discovery. Levine had a spark, and his mind carried a full load of powder.

The letter came from a 54-year-old former participant in the voluntary sexual offenders program. In it, he recounted his sexual molestation and requested readmittance to the program. He was, he said, currently "scouting children." He participated in the program in 1971. In a letter, dated August 19, Dr. Cistern wrote back that the program no longer admits sex offenders on a voluntary basis. The man would have to contact a local mental health center for help. The doctor contacted Detective Levine. Now Levine had at least one name to follow through the piles of records.

August 12, 1987, Police Department

Levine wasted no time checking hospital files, focusing on October 11, 1971. The "person of interest, Skids a.k.a. Charles Sidney Smith then lived on P Ward. He received a travel and visitation pass at 10:30 A.M. and nursing records showed that he returned at 9:30 P.M. smelling of alcohol. The records also noted a fight that morning between Smith and another patient, Robert Terry Bowman, over some car keys. Smith wanted to use Bowman's car for the day. Bowman owned a cream-colored VW bug. Detective Levine immediately contacted the police department with the news. Smith looked like a good suspect. The gossamer wings of inference again took flight.

Police Detective Bill Kane already spent many hours of his own time in Levine's dark garage sorting through the remains of No. 711011. No one in the department spoke of Levine's obsession with the case. No one saw it that way. Levine, like Kane, merely refused to let go. Persistence and obsession do not equate. When the slow-talking cowboy called with his discovery, Kane could begin working on city time. He ran criminal history checks on Smith, and hit pay dirt. Incoming criminal history reports added to the piles of wide computer paper that were already overflowing from suspect's folders. Smith merited a file of his own.

His record began with car theft in Osland, NM, at age 14. He served a year in Sand County Jail in 1951 for petty larceny. In 1954, he went to the Nevada State Hospital for observation when charged with breaking into a tavern. While at the institution, Smith secured a weekend pass, picked up a little girl from a playground, drove her to a remote area, and sodomized her for several hours.

He served six years for this offence in the Nevada State Penitentiary and was released January 12, 1960. By March 12, the same year, he was arrested in California for assault and indecent liberties. Sentenced May 11, he served another five years, this time in Vacaville State Penitentiary. He was released February 8, 1965. On June 21, the same year, he was arrested just outside town by the county sheriff department for picking up two minor girls, ages 9 and 11, driving them to a cattle road towards Tumbleweed, and committing oral sodomy on the 11-year-old. He threatened to kill them with a razor.

Detective Kane noted that after this offense on August 23, 1965, a judge committed Smith to the state mental hospital for observation as a suspected sexual psychopath. Diagnosed as a pedophile, he underwent what hospital records called "successful treatment" for 22 months, success confirmed when he obtained his release from the hospital June 1, 1967. By October 13, the same year, he was arrested for kidnapping a young boy. On October 14, he was recommitted to the State Mental Hospital for additional "successful" treatments.

After four years in the violent sexual offender program, on February 10, 1971, Smith went AWOL from the state mental hospital for three days. On March 5, the same year, Smith appeared in superior court to ask for revocation of his probation because of his dissatisfaction with the state mental hospital. The record showed that he was again committed on June 14 and released on June 15, the same year. July 19, 1971, after a parole violation, Smith entered the voluntary sexual offender program at the state mental hospital.

As Kane checked the records, he noted that Smith had worked as a range hand off and on since 1952, first as a cattle cutter for Western Beef Co. and later mending fences for the Barclay Ranch. His brother also worked as a range hand. Kane's eyes caught the locations of the cattle roads where Smith had taken some of the previous victims of his sexual aberrations. The June 21, 1965 assault occurred in an area near the skull bone's 1980 recovery site. Time to question Charles Sidney Smith.

August 13, 1987 Sundown Group Home

At a county group home southwest of town, Detectives Levine and Kane stared at Sid a.k.a. "Skids" Smith. Smith carried 152 pounds of pathetic disorder on his 5-foot 11-inch frame. His wizened face showed mostly nose and mouth. His fawnlike brown eyes floated too far apart for a human but about right for a fish. Long, tight lips forming a vacant smile made his cheeks stack up in front of long protruding ears like soiled drapes against open French doors. He had short brown hair and bushy eyebrows. Long, thin arms and sloping shoulders mimicked a horseshoe. The hands, hanging too low from bony wrists, looked like canoe paddles. Thin legs clad in faded jeans ended in oversized feet covered by worn black boots. He wore a filthy fiberfill coat that might have been blue. Nothing, including Skids, had been washed in 10 years. He smelled like spoiled vegetable soup.

Smith did not look anything like a Ted Bundy-style boy-next-door serial killer. Rookie detectives may have assumed that Smith's powers matched his appearance: a helpless incompetent living at public expense. But detectives Kane and Levine had learned through years of experience to read the signs before them. He looked like everything that thousands of parents taught their children to fear. Smith had at least one area of demonstrated competence: molesting children. His record proved it. And that record only catalogued the times he got caught.

At 10:30 A.M. Detective Kane read Smith his rights. He explained them as he would to a five-year-old. At 10:49 A.M. Kane depressed the record button and the questioning began. As Kane started the tape recorder, Levine started a cigarette. On tape, Smith granted permission for the interview, acknowledged an understanding of his rights, and agreed to talk without an attorney present. When Levine asked if Smith knew why he and Kane had come to question him, his reply nearly toppled the two slightly overweight detectives out the windows they'd been leaning against.

Smith said, "You're here to question me for killing the Davenport boy."

He admitted killing a boy he called "Willie" whose last name, he said, was Davenport. He did it, he said, in 1968, or 1970, he wasn't sure of the date. He said that he was now taking medications that affect his memory and that slow him down quite a bit. The confession taped that day in the Sundown Group home coffee room proved to be as goofy as Smith himself, and as much work to sort out as his own tangled psyche. The confession demanded that Detective Levine crystallize an exact image of the events on October 11, 1971, he had worked so long to reconstruct.

Monday, October 11, 1971

William flew home down Dawson Creek Road with all the speed that he could muster from his leather school shoes. As he ran, his Thermos beat once against the inside of his Partridge Family lunch box for every two of his breaths. His fifth grade notebook, parted by the wind, looked dangerously close to scattering it's contents along the sidewalk. The precarious position of the violin in his right hand would have given his music teacher a stroke. But the rumble from his corduroy pants played bass to the song in his heart. Today, following his afterschool football practice, he could watch the visiting women's basketball team prepare for tonight's big game against the teachers. And then he got to go to the game! William's loves were typical for a 10-year-old boy: his mother and father, his brothers and sisters, their dog Rex, his friends and teachers, and sports.

He caught up with his sister Karen just across the bridge on Dawson Creek Road and Rex came out of the gate, barking to greet them. He passed Karen, bounded up the steps, opened the front door, yelled, "Hi Mom, I'm home!" and at the same time dropped lunch box, notebook, instrument, and jacket on a chair near the foot of the stairs. Up the stairs two at a time, in his room, he pulled off his school shoes and put on his white Keds with the red circle on the ankles. Now he could really fly! They were just like the shoes that real basketball players wore, he thought to himself. Down the stairs two at a time, he grabbed his jacket, yelled, "Bye, Mom!" a cry, as always, punctuated by the slam of the front door, and William was gone forever.

September 13, 1987 Levine's garage

The snap of the rewind and play buttons on the Panasonic replayed the confession against Levine's vision of William's movements on October 11 from school dismissal on. The first problem became sorting out just what Smith had confessed. Levine again pressed "Play" and the recorder went to work.

Asked why he decided to confess now, Smith said, "Well I just like to get my life straightened out . . . I would like to go back to P Ward and write an autobiography of myself, you know, and get straightened out. I don't want to be running, hiding, peaking around doors, straightening myself up all the time, and back down again."

Levine says, " . . . this kinda to relieve your conscience?"

"Not kinda," Smith replies, "but it does."

"Did you have the use of a car?" Kane asks of Smith's stay at the state hospital.

"Well, I stole one . . . the keys was in the ignition, so I stole it."

"OK, that was the one you were talking about that you stole in Victorville?" Kane asked.

"Um, ha."

Later, while giving a litany of his many crimes, he said that he stole this car in Victorville in 1948 or 1949.

In the course of the interview, Smith confused times and tended to blend events from his criminal history. "And that's something that I don't remember too well is things, I am taking medication."

"OK. Does this medication affect your memory?" asks Kane.

"It slows me down," says Smith.

"OK, how did you get to Victorville?" asks Kane.

"I drove."

"In what car?"

"In a Volkswagen."

"What kind of Volkswagen?"

"It was a cream-colored Volkswagen."

"A Volkswagen bus?" asked Kane.

"No, just a ordinary small car, looks like a bug," replies Smith.

"Where did you get it?"

"I stole it," he says. "It was on state mental hospital grounds."

Hudson then says he drove the VW bug down to Victorville and to Ontario. He picked up the Davenport boy, he said, in Victorville.

"Do you remember his first name?" asks Kane.

"Willie. Willie Davenport," says Smith.

He remembered nothing about Davenport's appearance except that he wore a jacket, had brown hair and was about five feet tall. He told Kane and Levine that he picked up William as a hitchhiker from town, killed him in Ontario, and then drove his body back to town.

"Why did you take it back there rather than just leaving it in Ontario?" asks Kane.

"I don't know . . . I just done it that way," answers Smith.

He did not know the month he killed William. He placed it in December, but then said it could have been February. He said he just wasn't sure and couldn't remember. He had a weekend pass from the hospital.

Kane asks Smith if he read about the Davenport case in the newspapers. Smith says that he read one article in the paper about the Davenport boy having run away. He spotted the picture but never bothered to finish reading the article. He said he wasn't interested.

No need to, thought Kane. Smith knew what happened to him. Smith took the picture, and kept it for a while by the magazines and catalogs he used for sexual stimulation. "I'd look at the picture, remember his prick and strangling him, then jack off."

"What kind of catalogs?" asked Levine.

"Well, just magazines, books, Sears and Roebuck catalogs, Montgomery Ward catalogs . . . I remember when I was, oh gosh, 11, 12 years old, and I would take a shit out in the country, you know, . . . I would jack off to the little girls in the catalog . . . of course at that time, you got to consider my age too. I was only 11, 12 years old then, but I remember doing it, but somehow, or some reason, I never came up out of it here until the last 10 or 12 years. Since then, you know, I've been doing pretty good." Ten years ago Smith would have been 44 years old.

"Did you see any other news accounts of it?" asked Kane.

"No, that was the only one," said Smith.

He said he picked up William as they both walked by a restaurant in Victorville, and killed him in Victorville. Smith said he picked up William as William hitchhiked by the roadside and Smith drove by in Ontario, and killed him in Ontario. Smith said that William was hitchhiking to Los Angeles. Hudson said he strangled William in the car, as he was parked beside a big statue of a rearing horse in Ontario. Smith said that they smoked cigarettes, drank beer, and ate hamburgers in the car. Smith said that they smoked, drank beer, and ate at a tavern. Hudson said William told him he was running away because he didn't like his Dad. Hudson said William didn't tell him why he was running away, and if he did, he forgot the reason.

"What kind of medication are you taking?" asked Levine.

"Well, let's see . . . I'm taking four, five kinds of medications, five kinds. Oh yeah, I play the guitar," said Smith.

In response to Kane's questions, Smith admitted strangling William for the sexual thrill when he was a patient at the state mental hospital. Having no car, he stole one from the hospital grounds, a cream-colored VW bug. He said he killed him in the car. In response to Levine's questions, he said that he dumped the body outside of town about 50 feet off an old cattle road. He thought that he could find the spot, if it hadn't been paved.

"How did you feel after you killed him?" asked Kane.

"Well, guilty and ah, I just thought it was the wrong thing to do."

"Were you scared?"

"Oh, yes, I was."

"Scared of being caught?"

"Yes."

Monday, October 11, 1971

William ran, he imagined, as gracefully and as fast as Wilt Chamberlain would have, if Wilt were weaving his way down Dawson Creek Road crossing La Cassa and cutting the corner on La Cassa. He saw Bill, Siskelmy, Frank, Timmy, Dave and four other friends waiting on the corner of El Toro Play Field for him and for Mr. Hargrove with his silver whistle. For an hour the boys ran, jumped, walked, passed, kicked, caught, yelled, and listened in a magical dance to the tune of that whistle.

When the final whistle blew, the day's magic continued. The guys were going to watch the All-American Red Heads girls' basketball team practice. "They beat the Globe Trotters, you know," said Timmy. William knew the date they played, the city, and the final score.

The All-American Red Heads were southern goodwill ambassadors for the virtues of hard work, service to others, honesty, honor, integrity, and positive thinking. Their message, through athletics, stressed self-esteem, confidence, and character for service to others. Orwell Moore, owner and executive director of the team, also owned Camp Courage, a sports camp devoted to the development of young women's sports. These virtues, and the camp, both were promoted by inspirational halftime messages delivered during their games.

William struck Jolene as a fine example of these values: He appeared confident, yet honest; gregarious, yet helpful. She never tired of meeting these wonderful children who would be tomorrow's leaders. The little boys followed the women out of the gym as they walked in their sweatsuits across La Cassa to their Motel on the corner of La Cassa and Dawson Creek Road.

William jabbered the whole way about sports, his love of basketball, and answered questions about his family. Goodwill ambassadors Jolene and Mary often asked about families. They wondered why some kids turned out nice, like William, while others didn't. Families seemed to them important for the answer.

About 5:15 P.M. Dave, Timmy, and Siskelmy left the front door of Room 14, Sands Motel, to join the others on the corner to wait for their mothers to pick them up. William was still talking animatedly with the players. Impressed by him, Jolene, the team captain, invited him to sit on the player's bench during the game. William rushed down the motel's side stairs and rejoined his friends on the corner of La Cassa and Dawson Creek to tell them his exciting news.

"I get to sit with the team! They asked me to!" His friends knew it was true. William never lied, at least not about something important like that. Besides, he'd look like a jerk tonight if they saw him in the bleachers. Siskelmy's mother pulled up in the Chevy wagon, and after all the "see ya's" William stood alone on the corner of Dawson Creek and La Cassa, four long blocks from home, one short block from eternity.

September 13, 1987 Levine's garage

Corroborating Smith's confession required both explaining its confusions, and testing its essential veracity. The work required voluminous research, and the cooperation of both the criminal justice and the mental health systems of at least three states.

Smith's medical records read like a *Physician's Desk Reference:* Stelazine, Chloral Hydrate, Tera Cambex, and Haldol, since 1954, to control his undifferentiated type of schizophrenia. The long-term effect of these medications on a 55-year-old ninth-grade dropout like Smith served to confuse perception of time and place, to distort memory, and to cause memory loss for unimportant events in his life. He also had drunk fortified wine all day long for seven years. Understanding his medications and history of alcohol abuse helped to sort out the contradictory confession.

The apparent inconsistencies in the confession and the criminal history Kane studied began to correspond. Observed through his drug haze, the confession shows a recollection of events that he participated in, but a confusion over person, time, and place. He confessed to killing "Willie Davenport" in Ontario, California, and parking near the statue of a big horse. On September 12, 1956, Smith received five years in the Nevada State Penitentiary, for molesting a child. He was caught beside a monument to Nevada's equestrian heritage near the state capitol.

Hudson confessed to picking up "Willie Davenport," age 14 or 15, in Victorville, NV—that time he did not say Victorville, CA. On April 15, 1947, Charles Sidney Smith, age 14, was arrested while riding in a stolen vehicle. He was himself sexually molested by his father until age 17. In his confession,

Smith said that William was hitchhiking and that he took him for hamburgers, beer, and cigarettes. March 12, 1960, Smith offered two boys a ride, purchased beer, and attempted to molest them. He said that William was hitchhiking, headed for Los Angeles, CA. In the March 12 incident, he tried to talk the two boys into riding with him to California to assist him in picking up tires. He offered them $10.

While events scramble and conflate, they also correspond with reality. Snatching William fits consistently with his previous captures. He said that he drove around schools, playgrounds, neighborhoods, and shopping centers looking for the smallest unsupervised children, separated from a group. William, at four feet seven inches and 60 pounds stood alone on the corner of Dawson Creek and La Cassa, walking toward home. In his previous cases, Smith enticed children into his car and drove them to a secluded spot.

In September 1954 while on a weekend pass from Nevada State Hospital, Smith had sexually molested a seven-year-old girl. He took two boys to a secluded cattle road and threatened to kill them unless they had sex with him. He enticed a girl, seven, and a boy, three, into his car, sexually molested the girl, cut her with a razor, and threatened to kill them both. Smith picked up two girls, ages nine and 11, took them to a secluded cattle road toward Tumbleweed, and sexually molested the 11-year-old. A trend was developing. On June 16, 1960, Dr. Walter Richards says in his psychological evaluation report that "his attacks on young children appear to be accompanied by increasing hostility, and increasing aggressive actions on his part."

Monday, October 11, 1971

William wanted to play on a team just like the Red Heads. But on a boy's team, of course. The magic Keds, the silver whistle, the messages of service and reward mixed with his joy and propelled him across La Cassa, down Dawson Creek toward home. At the corner of Dawson Creek and Trail Head Lane, a man's voice broke into his reverie. He saw one of those funny German cars pull toward him along the curb from its parking spot on Dawson Creek. The man was talking to him from the driver's side. He couldn't hear what he said. His joy kept him moving, but his sense of helpfulness slowed his pace. The man motioned him to come to the driver's side window. With a mix of frustration and a 10-year-old's subjugation to adult authority, William reluctantly walked into the street toward the driver of the VW Bug.

"What's your name, boy?" the driver asked. William noted a smell that his uncle sometimes brought with him to dinner on Fridays after work.

"William. William Davenport," William said properly, as he noticed the driver's need for a shave.

"William, how about a beer with me?" the driver asked, shoving an open can in his direction. William recoiled from the very thought because of his love of athletics, and his love for God and God's church. He stepped back.

"No." Nancy Reagan would have been proud. A car passed on Dawson Creek, and turned the corner left onto La Cassa.

"OK. Hey, how about getting in. Show me where your school is. My kid is going to go there. If you do, I'll give you a ride home. You look like you're in a hurry," said the driver.

"I'm going home for dinner. I'm going to sit with the team tonight," William said.

"You just get in, tell me all about it, show me the school, and I'll get you home before you finish your story."

"Well, I guess so," William said, reluctantly but helpfully, ready to take on one last responsibility before his reward. He got in the car and it drove up to La Cassa, turned left, and headed out of town.

Tumbleweed Road had little traffic this time of night. Sitting in the car on the side of Meghan Trail Road with his fallen prey, he finished the last beer and lit another cigarette. The kid felt dead, but he wasn't sure. He'd sucked and fucked lots of 'em, but never offed one before. This kid's neck was so small, and his big hands felt so good around it—like around a giant prick. The memory thickened his penis and he masturbated again.

The VW slowly squeaked to a stop. The driver got out, dragging his burden like a sack of dog chow. He walked about 50 feet and leaned his load against a boulder. The head hit the rock like a watermelon thumped by a careful shopper. Relieved of extra resistance, the driver staggered gamely back to the car, shut the VW's door, and clattered down the road toward the highway. Cool darkness fell over the arroyo like a shroud.

May 15, 1991 County Courthouse

"Sorting out inconsistencies in a confession and showing capacities for violence against children doesn't prove that Smith is guilty of murder," says the county prosecutor. He looks up over his half glasses and stares intently into Detective Levine's eyes as he speaks. The papers in his hands summarized the ten years of Levine's work on the Davenport case, No. 711025. "We have no shortage of people who would kill children given the opportunity. But proving that Smith fits in that category along with thousands of others does not prove that Smith killed William. Past crimes don't prove a current charge."

"Any first year law student could make him sound like a typical indigent who wants back on the gravy train." His eyes glance again at the summary. Three more pages turn. After a pause, his eyes refocus on Levine. "And look," he says, "there's no body. The area was searched over the years, what, half a dozen times? We can't even prove that we have a homicide. The skull bone can't be identified as male, let alone as William's. And when Smith takes you to this magic spot, you find the area has become a housing development. What evidence could anyone hope to find there? We've got no time, manner, nor cause of death. Except for the coroner's presumptive death ruling, we have no evidence of death. We've got nothing. End of case."

The prosecutor's eyes again return to the printed pages now spread out on his desk. He speaks slowly toward the wood surface without raising his eyes. "If Smith did commit murder, he couldn't have been luckier. If this case really is a homicide," he says, tapping his pencil eraser on the paper closest to him, "it's another perfect murder, with another moron-murderer blown to freedom by the winds of chance."

The prosecutor does his job impeccably. Levine and Kane requested the meeting to sort out their case, and get an opinion about possible action against Smith. So far, they're selling arrest and prosecution, but the lawyer's not buying. There is nothing for sale. He won't buy what he can't resell to a judge and jury. The gray-blue eyes now gazing above the glasses at the two detectives invite a reply. Kane and Levine look at each other the way naughty boys' exchange glances in the vice principal's office.

No one knows better than Levine what evidence they have and what they lack in this case. He also knows what can happen to a detective's investigation even after an arrest: The prosecutor files no charges, the best suspect goes free, and the casework moves into boxes stored behind little-used janitorial supplies. Prosecutors assign cases to this paper-towel wasteland based on their best guess about what some jury will likely believe about the uncertainties involved. They have to produce more to secure a conviction than the sons of Serendippo's king had to produce to prove their innocence. Jurors' expectations add another dimension to the burden of proof shouldered by the prosecution in court.

Jurors raised on heavy doses of television expect definitive resolutions. For that reason, prosecutors like to produce eyewitnesses to murders. Levine could produce no eyewitnesses to William's death. Prosecutors also like hard indisputable physical evidence. Levine had none. Prosecutors like indisputable confessions. Levine had a tortured tale that read like a Heideggerian acid trip. Prosecutors hate potential claims of mental incompetence or insanity. Levine had Smith. A defense attorney could display him in court dressed in his filthy fiberfill jacket, dismiss his confession as the ramblings of a pathetic incompetent, and rest his case. Prosecutors hate convoluted reasoning that makes jurors into witless narcoleptics. Yet despite these obstacles, Levine and Kane believed that they had William's case closed, his death explained as a murder, and his killer identified as Skids, a.k.a. Charles Sidney Smith.

"I think we all know what we don't have, now let's go over what we do have," said Levine, his soft brown eyes scanning the papers on the desk and in the prosecutor's hands. "What we do have we gained by a process of elimination." The prosecutor looks up from the desk, but says nothing. "Let's start with the evidence that William is dead." Kane realigns the papers on the desktop exposing the relevant documents.

Levine's 10-year chronicle read like a textbook for a missing person investigation. The hard road to proving someone's death involves eliminating all other possible explanations of his disappearance. Ten-year-old kids don't have Social Security accounts, make insurance claims, use checking accounts, or have credit cards to track, so the standard search for activity in these areas didn't pay off. But Levine organized his investigation into other manageable chunks.

To prove William's death, he first needed to show that William did not run away, or go to live with some other relative or stranger. William enjoyed a happy yet strict home, looked forward to the basketball game that night and behaved like a normal well-adjusted 10-year-old kid. Investigators evaluated reports of his being seen as far away as Montana and evaluated every description of kidnapped, runaway, or other missing juveniles presumed alive. Nothing turned up. No one in the Davenport clan had William under wraps. No custody issues plagued the family. Like all families, the Davenports had their share of conflict, but the evidence showed that both love and support graced the kid who visited the Sands Motel that October night. No relative remained unexamined.

"So some stranger snatched him and still has him in Alaska, raising him as his own," says the prosecutor. "How do you get him dead?" His eyes focus on the graying cowboy. Kane's hands shuffle more papers on the desk.

Levine recounted his work with the skull bone. He collected data on all children reported missing in October and November of 1971 in a six-state region. After eliminating those who had been found, alive or otherwise, four names remained to investigate as possible sources for the skull. Armed with the X-ray of the parietal bone recovered by Prichard, he located antemortem X-rays for two from California, and one from Nevada. The meningeal artery pattern ruled out all three. One child, missing from Arizona, and William, remained without antemortem exemplars. Both children, officially missing and presumed dead by their respective coroners, remained undiscovered. Levine needed to establish some meaningful measurement of the chance that the bone belonged to William.

Population bases offer statistical support for such inferences. In a larger population base, with greater numbers of relevantly similar individuals, the chances of an artifact like a bone belonging to one individual and no other decline. The smaller and more diverse the population, the better the chance that ownership can be narrowed. Levine understood that specific chance events checker the most mathematically pure populations. While the numbers from a small-town population base favor the inference that the skull belongs to William by apparently increasing its probability, this result depends upon a prior abduction.

Like reading a batting average as a prediction of a given future performance at bat, abduction reads the numbers as one sign among many in the specific context. The other signs must be weighted along with the numbers to explain any uncertain event. When statistics alleged to measure the chance of an event serve as its *explanation*, trouble results. Mere associations muddle legitimate reasons in any proof of the case. Levine would not be able to impress the prosecutor with a numerical probability that the bone belonged to William derived from population statistics. Courts, already skeptical about inappropriately derived probability figures, do not play justice by the numbers.

This skepticism became legal precedent in California's People v. Collins. An elderly San Pedro resident saw a young blond woman running away after being assaulted and robbed in an alley. Other witnesses saw a Caucasian woman with blond hair and a ponytail run from the alley, enter a yellow car driven by a black male with a full beard, and drive away. These descriptions lead to the Collins' arrest a few days later. At trial, the prosecutor called a statistician. He testified that the probability of any randomly chosen Los Angeles area couple being interracial, in a partly yellow car, one a Caucasian female with a blond ponytail, the other a black male with a full beard, equaled one in 12 million. On the strength of this testimony alone the accused pair went to jail for assault and robbery.

The court of appeals overturned this statistical conviction. The fallacious probability calculation, it found, merely assumed the mutual independence of the six characteristics, ignoring, for example, the number of men with variously trimmed yet full beards. The prosecutor's statistician also falsely equated the probability that a randomly selected couple would have the six characteristics with the probability of their guilt or innocence in the San Pedro assault. Given a population of 24 million, at least two couples might share the six characteristics described by witnesses. If so, the numbers prove that the chance of either couple being innocent is one in two, the results of a fair coin toss, a statistical fact about anyone in the population selected at random.

Anyone, including the judge, is either guilty or not guilty of the San Pedro assault. The witness descriptions, while evidence, provided no statistical bite. The numbers meant nothing. The prosecutor's case amounted to no more than the irrelevant smoke once produced by a suspect in a murder case described by G. K. Chesterton. When told that a witness had seen him commit murder, the suspect replied that he could produce a hundred witnesses who had not seen him commit it.

The issue before the court remains the interpretation of other factors given provisional significance as evidence in the case by the witnesses' descriptions. Could the Collins' account for their activities during the assault? Did any physical evidence link them with the alley, the victim, or her property? Either they assaulted the victim, or not. Either the suspect Chesterton describes committed murder or not. Either the skull bone belongs to William or it does not. The numbers favor Levine's assessment of the chance. But more than mere population statistics in Levine's case increase the probability that the bone belongs to William.

The bone's belonging to William best explains the total evidence. While several hypotheses might explain the bone, all but one alternative falls short, contradicting what he knows or has good reason to believe. The surviving hypothesis attributing the parietal bone to William then has the best chance of being true. Gilbert Harmon named this form of abduction "inference to the best explanation." The best explanation survives the tests that each considered alternative supplies. Being the best in that sense, it holds neither the investigator nor the Juror hostage to formalized probability theory, fallaciously applied in California vs. Collins.

When tests remain inconclusive, one explanation still may emerge from the data as the single best alternative. Such initially plausible hypotheses must withstand any future challenges, including confrontations in court.

Jurors charged to determine the facts of a case on this battleground must decide which explanation is the best. Mathematical sophistication is not a prerequisite. As Oliver Wendell Holmes put it, "Even a dog can distinguish between being tripped over and being kicked."

Levine kept restating the obvious. The prosecutor kept looking for evidence. Levine continued developing his case.

"The bone's recovery occurred in an area connected with William's disappearance, within several miles of where he was last seen," the detective said. "He never made it home. Later, the partial cranial vault turns up excavation. It belongs to a juvenile skull. It's not an ancient Indian artifact. No other juveniles missing in a three-state area account for it. Is it dumped from some unreported kidnap-murder in California, Nevada or Arizona? Maybe, but unlikely. We have an unaccounted for kid missing in this neighborhood. It is more probably his."

"Remember," Kane said, "we have a witness who saw William talking to a stranger in a light-colored VW bug less than four blocks from his home."

"And our boy Smith had a cream-colored VW that day, left the state Mental Hospital on TV, and fits the description given by Mrs. Evans," said Levine. He continued "So, why does a stranger snatch a 10-year-old kid? Let's rule out to raise him, send him to college, and better his life. Statistically, it's sexual assault, or ransom. No ransom demand, no note, no phone call, nothing indicates ransom. That leaves sexual assault."

"And," Kane added, "we do have the confession."

"Take a look at that," invited Levine. "We read him his rights, and he gave his statements voluntarily. Despite the medicated haze, he took us to the location 50 feet from an old arroyo never described in any news story. He knew cattle and cattle trails in the vicinity. He took previous victims to the same general area. We collected every newspaper article ever published on the case. Smith knew things not published anywhere. He knew where Pritchard found the skull. Unless he searched the area with the Explorer Scouts, that supplies more evidence that the skull bone belongs to William and that Smith deposited him in the woods."

"Consider that he lied, and confessed just to get what he wants: to be back on the hospital gravy train," Levine continued. "Why confess to an ancient case, and a homicide at that? Plenty of crimes out there could get him what he wants with less risk and more speed. This could get him hung."

Levine's increasingly forceful voice began to sound like his film hero the Duke, John Wayne. He almost said "Pilgrim." "We've got who, what, where, why, when, and how. That, to me, sounds like we have a good case."

"So," the prosecutor interjected, "the kid is kidnapped, and sexually assaulted. After the assault, he gets lost walking home, falls, hitting his head and dies. Animals take care of the rest, and Prichard finds what's left."

"Then," replied Levine, "you and I both know that whoever assaulted him and turned him loose in the woods committed murder."

"Yes, that's what the law says all right." The prosecutor allowed a faint smile to warm his cool blue eyes. "Let me keep your file for a few days, and

I'll spend some time with it. I'll keep looking for proof, evidence, something solid. No promises," he said, addressing both Levine and Kane while rising from his desk chair, signaling an end to the meeting.

Both detectives, walking silently from the county office building, know that the end of the meeting signals the end of their case. As a suspect, Smith lurks among the amorphous brambles between the state's criminal justice system and its mental health program. When its wayward denizens break the law, overburdened courts usually banish such transgressors to the land of halfway houses, therapy, medication, or maybe involuntary commitment. With his citizenship in the briar patch firmly established, Smith's mental state became the major sticking point in what little there was of the case against him.

Prisons and mental hospitals supposedly protect the public. But the problem of getting any prosecutor's office to take such an ambiguous case to court is legendary in police circles. The standards of proof differ between "knowing in your heart," and "proving in court." Cases always lack some necessary ingredient. For the prosecutor, the solution to the Davenport case rests on uncertain inference and incoherent confession. No crime scene, no identifiable body, and neither time, nor cause, of death. The presumptive death certificate lists the manner of William's death as "undetermined." Even if Smith committed the murder, were charged, tried, and found guilty, he would be recommitted to the mental hospital with probable release to a halfway house, like the Sundown Group Home. A waste of court time and county money. Either way, throw him back to the briar patch.

After his review, the prosecutor declined the case. "You're a damn fool to work a case this hard this long. It's a lost cause," the prosecutor said over the phone. Levine, smiling to himself, quoted Claude Raines in *Mr. Smith Goes to Washington:* "The only causes worth fighting for," he said, "are lost causes."

Fresh from the prosecutor's call reporting his decision, Levine contacted the former Betty Davenport, now Betty Strickler, and Siskel Davenport. He told them of his 10-year saga, of two broken humans, both destroyed very young: one suddenly by a slayer's hands, and the other, the slayer, over a longer period by abuse, genetics, drugs, disease, indifference, and capitulation to evil. The satisfaction he felt both reopening and resolving a case that remained legally untouched failed to balance the pain at the other end of the line.

After briefing the divided family Friday, Detective Ed Levine went on a pack trip. That night, Betty Strickler had another dream about William being tortured. Across the country in Arkansas, Siskel Davenport woke up in a cold sweat. Unaffected by anything other than his medications, Skids Smith stared out the window of the Sundown Group Home and smiled as a school bus passed by on the street below.

NOTES

1. Johnson, Diane, *Dashiell Hammett: A Life*, pp. 44–50; quotes from *Hammett's Memoirs of a Private Detective*, Fawcett Columbine-Ballantine Books, NY, NY. July 1987.

A really good scientist is one who knows how to draw correct conclusions from incorrect assumptions.

Chapter four

Elimination—The Homberg Case

Inductivism, Best Explanations, and Testing Alternatives

"It is an old maxim of mine that when you have excluded the impossible, whatever remains, however improbable, must be the truth."

Sherlock Holmes

From his first meeting with Deputy Anderson three weeks after Ruth Ann Homberg's disappearance, the story sounded wrong. Now he had to work out its problems. Discovering the crime and proving its solution became two stages of the same task. Everyone heaped sympathy on poor Gary Homberg, the grieving husband anxious for news of his missing wife Ruth. Everyone except Merle Ziegler. "Columbo," as they called Ziegler, had just one or two little questions that bothered him. He always did. They would not go away, and neither would he.

Ziegler's rumpled trench coat, black hair, short cigar, and unassuming manner made him an easy stand-in for Peter Falk's TV detective. Like Columbo, references to his unseen wife infuse his conversation and underscore her strong presence. Driving an unreliable Horizon, faded and dented by county service, did little to circumvent comparison with the aging Peugeot driven by Columbo. He and his wife had three cats but no basset hound. That and the sheer drudgery of real police work seemed to separate his life from a made-for-TV movie putting Columbo back on the streets.

Piles of papers, files, and books appear randomly mixed in layers on his desk, but Ziegler can find anything there faster than any computer could bring it to a screen or printer. "It only looks messy," he always tells new visitors. "Appearances can be deceiving," he routinely adds with a smile, holding his cigar just so.

Worn copies of Aristotle's *Prior Analytics,* Bacon's *Novum Organum,* Mill's *System of Logic* and Peirce's *Collected Papers, Vol. II Elements of Logic,* lean against a copy of Dr. Lester Adleson's *Pathology of Homicide.* What at first appears to be a model of Rodin's *The Thinker,* at second glance turns out to be a monkey contemplating a human skull. A bust of Socrates sits on the right rear edge of the desk.

The so-called Socratic method of question and answer long ago worked its way into law schools. Ziegler found that his intellectual hero also supplied a useful approach to homicide investigation. Throughout Plato's dialogues, Socrates appears through his questions to be alone in his ignorance. Others appear to have all the answers. But one small detail, one nagging question raised by Socrates unravels the fabric of deception posing as knowledge. If wisdom consisted in knowing that one does not know already, then Detective Merle Ziegler was the wisest of men.

He deepened his ignorance by reading philosophy. He focused on the intertwining natures of discovery and proof, and on issues of human moral character. His business was to find things out and to support his discoveries with evidence suitable for courts of law. For Ziegler, this took him beyond his network of informants and past the many tricks of his trade that the Greeks would call *techne,* knowing how. He wanted to understand, to know why. He never hid the fact when he didn't.

His humility remains genuine, his quest sincere. A faded piece of paper above his desk quotes C. S. Peirce:

> "The development of my ideas has been the industry of thirty years . . . For years in the course of this ripening process, I used for myself to collect my ideas under the designation fallibilism; and indeed the first step toward finding out is to acknowledge you do not satisfactorily know already; so that no blight can so surely arrest all intellectual growth as the blight of cocksureness; and ninety-nine out of every hundred good heads are reduced to impotence by that malady—of whose inroads they are most strangely unaware!
>
> Indeed, out of a contrite fallibilism, combined with a high faith in the reality of knowledge, and an intense desire to find things out, all my philosophy has always seemed to me to grow . . ."

Detectives, deputies, medical examiners and forensic scientists live daily with that intense desire to find things out. That's one reason Ziegler finds himself heading an investigation that so far raises more questions than it answers. Ziegler's Socrates approaches Deputy Anderson's slave boy who, with select questions from the master, will gradually produce the Homberg theorem.

Ziegler's questions cover Anderson's initial steps into a maze soon to involve the county district attorney's chief investigator, and the state department of revenue, along with the local police department having original jurisdiction. Like all major investigations, this case did not become Ziegler's exclusive domain. He worked with others searching for answers. From Deputy Anderson's initial response to the home at 8:10 P.M. Saturday,

November 5, 1983, the Homberg case presented nagging questions that would take a team of nine investigators six years to answer. To Ziegler's lasting dismay, after those six years one answer still eludes them.

Unobtrusive questions soon help Deputy Anderson establish his rhythm. He responded to the Homberg's country estate, he says, after Mr. Homberg called local police at 5 P.M. Saturday, November 5, 1983, to report his wife, Ruth Ann Homberg, missing. Patrolling in the area, Anderson got the call. When he pulled into the long driveway, the English Tudor-style home looked like a photo from an ad for a luxury vacation.

Anderson says that Gary William Homberg invited him into the carpeted family room appointed with the latest in home entertainment technology. The couches smelled like real leather. Homberg, dressed in a crisp white shirt open at the neck and navy slacks, had a military air. Neatly cut dark hair and a slim but powerful 6-foot 2-inch 180-pound build hid his 44 years well. He went to the room's wet bar, filled a glass with ice and mixed himself a drink. He spoke in response to Anderson's questions with a thick German accent.

He said that he and his wife had been out to dinner with another couple Friday evening and returned home about 1 o'clock Saturday morning. He said he left for Millfab Inc., a wood products company, about 6:30 A.M. and when he returned to meet Ruth for lunch about noon, he found both his wife and her car gone. Their custom, he said, was to work Saturdays. She occasionally ran errands before work but he expected to see her that morning at Millfab where she worked as the office manager and company bookkeeper. As 49% stockholder, Mr. Homberg said that he served as the company's president. He said that he last saw Ruth in bed when he left for the plant after breakfast.

Listening to Gary Homberg, Anderson heard a balanced concern for the lunch, the car, and the wife. The signs of worry appeared subtly out of focus, at least not what Anderson expected from a husband concerned for his missing spouse. Maybe the heavy scent of cologne wafting from the Gestapo-like figure before him merely clouded his judgment. Putting instinct aside and pencil to paper, he recorded a description of both Mrs. Homberg and her missing vehicle.

Homberg described his wife clinically without hesitation. Forty-three-year-old Ruth Ann Homberg stood 5 feet 4 inches and weighed 120 pounds, with blond hair and blue eyes. She drove a 1974 Buick Century two-door, maroon with a beige top. Homberg said that he'd called his in-laws, Art and Sally Nelson, since Ruth had a close relationship with her parents, but that they had not seen or spoken with their daughter Saturday. When she had not returned by 5:00 P.M. he called the local police department dispatcher. Beyond that, he said, he knew nothing. It reminded Anderson of a Sgt. Shultz-style protestation of ignorance rather than of a confession laced with genuine puzzlement.

Homberg described his wife's mood as "upbeat" when he left for work, and said he found it unusual that she neither came to work nor told him that she would be late. Anderson looked up from his note pad to see Homberg standing above him asking if he wanted to look around the house. Anderson asked him if he noticed anything abnormal or wrong. Like a teenager who managed to get party stains off the family couch, Homberg said, almost proudly, that nothing appeared out of place.

Five hours into Deputy Anderson's next shift, at 8:45 P.M. November 6, 1983, Gary Homberg's disciplined voice reported from the other end of a telephone that Ruth's Buick had been found in the long-term parking area of the Dane County Regional Airport. Anderson's terse reports record the facts. In the meeting with Ziegler he also communicated his undocumented insights. Deputy Anderson says he thought that Gary Homberg's behavior appeared abnormal. His instincts told him that something odd and unspoken lurked beneath the surface of Homberg's story.

That feeling, Anderson said, together with the Hombergs' civic prominence in the town of Stoughton, kept both the county deputies and the Stoughton Police searching diligently since being informed of Mrs. Homberg's disappearance. Anderson's difficulties with Homberg's demeanor, and other puzzling aspects of the now three-week-old investigation brought Ziegler as point man into the case.

He studied all the reports detailing the investigation's progress over this three-week period. They documented how police officers, deputies, and detectives followed up Mr. Homberg's original complaint. Police dispatcher David "Buck" Christianson of the Stoughton P.D. contacted several local restaurants looking for Ruth Ann Homberg after Gary Homberg's 5 P.M. call. He found nothing. No family members had seen Ruth, but interviews with both family and friends opened new doors.

Reports relayed that when Ruth's mother, Sally Nelson, called the Homberg home about 10:00 A.M. Saturday, November 5, 1983, no one answered the phone. When Ruth's former sister-in-law Roseanne Johnson telephoned for Ruth about 6:15 P.M. Gary answered. When she asked for her friend, Gary said, "She's not here." He did not ask Roseanne if she had seen Ruth, or knew where she might be. He did not call Ruth's daughter Roxanne Nordness, nor did he call her son, Rick, and his wife, Sharon Jacobson Nordness. When Ruth's other son, Rob, returned to the Homberg's home from a hunting trip about 1 P.M. that Saturday, Gary told him that his mother went on a shopping trip. He did not call Lee Brusegar, Ruth's cousin, or his wife, Nancy, with whom she often socialized. He did not call any of their friends, including Carlton and Kenlynn Pokrandt with whom they had dinner Friday evening. Yet at about 5 P.M. he called police dispatcher Buck Christianson. Ziegler knew that clues do not always involve something present at a scene. Like a man missing his wallet or a woman her purse, important clues often center on something absent.

According to small-town gossip in Stoughton, something essential for marriage vacated the Homberg's relationship. Rumors circulated about Gary cheating on Ruth. Local police, including Chief Grady, learned as much from questioning Carlton and Kenlynn Pokrandt about their Friday evening with Ruth and Gary Homberg.

According to the Pokrandts, they began the evening with drinks and appetizers at their home. They drove with the Hombergs to Madison in one car, had a quiet dinner at a fancy German restaurant called the Essen House and danced after their meal. They all returned to the Pokrandt home about 11:30, mixed after-dinner drinks, and visited in their living room. Kenlynn said that Carlton invited Gary, the wood expert, to admire a dresser that she had refinished for their bedroom. When the men left the living room, Ruth slid along the couch toward where Kenlynn sat in her rocking chair and asked in a quiet voice if she would tell her what was going on. "If you are any friend of mine, you'll tell me," Kenlynn quoted Ruth as saying.

After polite protests, Kenlynn did tell Ruth what she knew. In August she heard that Gary continued an affair with a younger woman, who also worked as a secretary at Millfab. The woman, she said, was Ruth's daughter-in-law Sharon Jacobson Nordness. Ruth said nothing, but her pale face showed the pain carried with the crushing news. When Carlton and Gary returned to the living room, conversation dwindled and the Hombergs left for home a little after midnight. No one beside Gary Homberg ever saw Ruth after that evening.

Kenlynn said that recent months had been difficult for the Hombergs, both professionally, given the recession in the building industry that had slowed business at Millfab, and personally, given growing strains in their relationship. She reported that Ruth had bared her soul to her in the spring of 1983, complaining that Gary spent evenings at Millfab, missed meals, and even told her that he didn't need her anymore. She said that Ruth called her from home that evening and told Kenlynn that she and Gary planned a divorce. But she called the next day, saying that plans had changed. There would be no divorce. But the Hombergs obviously had problems, according to the Pokrandts. Investigators had some problems of their own.

Ziegler and Anderson revisited Homberg's answers to the deputy's questions November 5, 1983. Ziegler wanted to know what his eyes looked like, whether he moved his hands or held them still, folded them in his lap or dropped them at his sides. They covered the hair, clothing, and cologne. He asked more about the house, and about Homberg's offer to show off the place that Saturday evening three weeks ago, and about the car at the airport. Something bothered both men. Together they explored the alternatives.

One explanation of Homberg's odd behavior could be that he had nothing to hide. Another alternative could be that he felt in absolute control and had already hidden any incriminating signs of foul play. It could all be a macho or cultural artifact from his German roots. Mrs. Ziegler always says that men don't know how to grieve properly the way women do. Maybe he just kept to himself, not wanting to admit that his wife finally had left him.

So far, by questioning Anderson and reading the reports, Ziegler suspected that a midlife crisis and another woman produced a marital tiff that explained the signs at the fancy English Tudor estate and in the airport's long-term parking lot. Ruth Ann Homberg probably needed some breathing room. One hypothesis may take the lead, but good investigators develop evidence not only to support it, but to refute it as well. The alternatives running on the rail could move up in the pack given any new information that failed to fit the current leader. He needed to allow Ruth time to cool off, and to return from any trip. The fast three weeks' work uncovered information justifying a wait. But how much time?

Members of both the local police and the Sheriff's Department followed all possible leads to locate Ruth Homberg. On November 10, 1983, Detective Kenneth Pledger went to the airport to learn if Ruth Homberg had tickets on any outbound flights on November 5. He arrived too late. Passenger information goes to main airline offices three days after flight time for a date with the shredder. Computerized operations demand purging such records for maximum efficiency. No evidence existed to prove that Ruth either did or did not board some departing flight. And even if records could be located, she may have used an assumed name. Tracking down every female passenger on each departing flight would be an exercise in futility. The car at the airport and a possible trip originally dictated the three-week wait. Now the wait ended. Investigators explored both Ruth and Gary Homberg's backgrounds, following standard routes through family, friends, and others associated with their lives. Their perspective began to broaden.

Gary William Homberg entered the U.S. as a penniless emigrant from his native Germany in 1961. His father died in the family's shoe store during an Allied bombing raid on Berlin. Born Gerhard Wilhelm Homberg in 1939, he became a naturalized U.S. citizen in 1966. After a stint in the Air Force, he worked for the Conney Safety Products Co. in Madison, where he met his first wife, Sara. Married in 1967, they had a son Nathon and a daughter Elizabeth. The marriage endured six years. Sara divorced Gary in 1974. The split lacked the acrimony characteristic of many divorces. He and Sara remained friends. Now he had more time for his career, which began to develop in earnest by the early 1970s.

By 1971, Stoughton businessman Don Wahlin, owner of both Millfab Manufacturing, producers of wood moldings, and Stoughton Trailers, builders of truck cargo containers, hired Homberg as a salesman. By 1972, his good looks, confident manner, and organized competence persuaded Wahlin to appoint him president of Millfab, boss of 70 employees, and trustee of a business that turned a tidy profit each year. Gary put in long hours, working his way to company president.

Ruth Ann Nordness took a job as secretary at Millfab in 1975, and divorced her husband Richard in 1976. They had three children, two boys Rick and Rob, and a daughter, Roxanne. She and Gary Homberg soon became lovers and married on June 4, 1976. After the wedding, her Millfab responsibilities increased from secretary to Gary's executive assistant, then office manager and bookkeeper. Rick, Rob, Roxanne, and Rick's wife Sharon all eventually came to work for Millfab.

Above all else, Ruth lived for her family. She remained devoted both to her children and to her parents, Art and Sally Nelson. The Nelsons deeded Ruth and Gary four acres of land near their own country estate for a wedding gift, and in 1976 the newlyweds began building their English Tudor home on the property. The couple appeared to be happy and devoted to each other.

Gary remained the classic workaholic, gradually becoming an even greater consumaholic. In 1979, he traveled to Germany on business, invested in two separate tracts of land in the county near Stoughton, and by 1980 had a large garage built on the estate which would eventually house a new $40,000 Mercedes and an antique Mercedes of even greater value. He dressed in expensive suits, bought Ruth expensive jewelry, furnished their home in high fashion and appeared to enjoy each material addition to the life he shared with his family. But in 1983, Ruth's son, Rick, discovered that Gary shared more with his family than increasing wealth.

When interviewed after his mother's disappearance, Rick Nordness told Ziegler that early one Sunday morning in August 1983 he picked up his wife Sharon's purse looking for a calendar and found a letter written to Sharon by his mother's husband, Gary. In clinical terms, the explicit letter praised his wife's sexual abilities, and expressed impatience for their continued enjoyment. When he confronted Sharon, she admitted to an affair with Gary but swore that it had ended. That Monday after work Gary called Rick saying, "We've got to talk." Rick said that he simply replied, "I got nothing to say to you," and hung up. He said nothing to his mother about Gary's behavior. He thought Gary had something to do with his mother's disappearance.

Roxanne Nordness also gave Ziegler an earful. She said that in 1980, Homberg lost his temper and hit her with a closed fist three or four times during an argument about her living at their home. By January 1983, he tried to throw her out of the house. She moved out, but remained close to her mother. Late one night in December 1983, she called Gary Homberg and asked bitterly, "How did you kill her, and where did you put the body?" She said that Gary began to sob, then asked, "What makes you think I did it?" Ziegler saw that at least Gary had asked the right question. His job became providing and assessing an answer that rose above overheated family emotions. The job took him to Millfab and casual conversations with employees.

Millfab workers Richard Scheel and Bonnie Sampson both painted the same picture for Ziegler. Sharon Jacobson Nordness worked as a secretary in the office shared by Gary and Ruth. According to Scheel, she flirted with Gary and the flirtation grew more obvious by 1982. Both Scheel and Sampson saw Gary and Sharon kissing, embracing, or touching both before and after Ruth disappeared. Many in the Millfab office saw Gary touch and fondle her. Gary apparently continued his relentless pursuit of the finer things.

Bonnie Sampson also said that one day Ruth came into her office, closed the door and said, "I don't want to burden you . . ." then began crying. Ruth apparently did not share Gary's vision of what counted as the finer things. She called her former sister-in-law Roseanne Johnson, obviously troubled according to Mrs. Johnson, and complained about men wanting only one thing, about men being ruled by their desires, and about greed and insensitivity. She never mentioned Gary. Her conversation with Kenlynn Pokrandt and their last evening together came into clearer focus for Ziegler. But as much as he had learned, he still had little to explain what happened to Ruth. Almost everything appeared to support her running away from Gary: everything except Ziegler's suspicions.

Neither Rick's, Roxanne's, Deputy Anderson's, nor his own feelings counted as evidence. From Ziegler's latest conversation with Millfab employees, and another hour with his growing case file, he began to develop his own misgivings about their midlife crisis scenario. Still his reasons paralleled a mountain climber's response justifying the activity: "because the mountains are there." Nonclimbers go around the mountain for the same reason. The reason supports either alternative, failing to eliminate one view in favor of the other. With several contending hypotheses available to explain Ruth Homberg's absence, the search for further evidence to rank them one over another had a long way to go. Clues needed sorting from the growing maze of potentially unconnected circumstances.

Sorting clues from coincidence seldom centers on merely unraveling a complex motive, especially given the possibility of a murder. Motives for murder remain boringly simple. Sex, money, power, anger, greed, love, jealousy, hate, or any of their various combinations usually supply an adequate motive for such crimes. Many murders have motives that first appear quite illogical. Whatever lacks logic cannot be explained logically. Mass murders at a fast food restaurant or the local grade school playground supply obvious examples. But as their investigations proceed, detectives discover that even these random killings possess their own logic.

Finding and following this thread of logic leads investigators to clues supporting the best explanation of the case. Usually the thread becomes visible once surrounding events have been reconstructed. Discovering evidence by unraveling the crime becomes the real difficulty. And overcoming that difficulty presupposes solving a puzzle about method addressed by the philosophers Ziegler enjoyed.

Nothing less than the methods of science could serve Ziegler's dual tasks of discovery and proof. Both the nature of, and requirements for, these rational activities, driven by inference and advanced by evidence, have remained central topics of philosophy since Aristotle's day. The sciences have developed many techniques but appear to share only one method, one complex logical skeleton supporting newly emerging and increasingly diverse techniques from physics, biology, chemistry, and specialized subfields such as genetics. Any unity to these sciences must rest in their common method to understand and explain in the face of uncertainty. The aims and goals of various sciences may differ, but the method underlying their various techniques supplies the common logical thread. Like an osteologist who studies bones, philosophers attempt to understand and explain the structures of natural science, the method itself.

Philosophers and scientists hold that mere description and classification no longer exhaust the scientific enterprise. Describing Ziegler's inventory of witness statements would do little to explain Ruth's disappearance. The exact nature of acceptable scientific explanations that go beyond merely describing unsupported guesses and untested hunches remains a noteworthy puzzle about the logic of the sciences, the framework of the method. Rick and Roxanne, impatient for action, felt they knew the explanation of their mother's disappearance. But feelings and beliefs don't count as *justified* until the path of discovery and its proof can be charted clearly for others to follow. To investigate a maze like the Homberg case, Ziegler had to fashion nothing less than a practical solution to an ancient theoretical puzzle about acceptable explanations. Formulating that solution through explaining Ruth Ann Homberg's disappearance involved learning from what worked in this powerful method, and what did not.

Belief in powerful methods to solve every type of problem both infuses human history and documents human gullibility. From seeing the future in the stars to curing disease and building wealth, the sophistic pretenders to wisdom prey on their uncritical victims. The method of the sciences calcified in the bones of its logic offers a less universal claim to solve all problems and explain every mystery. But over the centuries, its chroniclers have offered immodest accounts of its power, exaggerated claims of its objectivity, and inaccurate assessments of its nature. Dead, dry textbook abstractions characterizing rational method fracture under the weight of a living inquiry like Ziegler's search for Ruth Homberg. The first cracks appear in characterizations of science as an inductive method. That analysis, modified by Francis Bacon and J. S. Mill, began with the inductive method of science first described by Aristotle.

In the *Prior Analytics*,[1] Aristotle supplied a comprehensive analysis of nonampliative inference, a form of deduction that he called the syllogism. The appeal of deduction lies in its certainty. When accepting the premises, the conclusion cannot be denied without contradiction. His familiar example holds that:

All men are mortal.
Socrates is a man.
Therefore, Socrates is mortal.

While its application raises questions, the power of deduction remains indisputable. But Aristotle also described forms of ampliative reasoning to carry thinkers beyond the claims of given premises. This feature characterizes the method of uncertain discovery and proof in science. According to Otto Frisch, "A really good scientist is one who knows how to draw correct conclusions from incorrect assumptions."[2]

In the *Topics,* Aristotle characterizes this ampliative inference soon synonymous with the logic of scientific method:

> We must distinguish how many species there are of dialectical arguments. There is, on the one hand, induction (epagoge), on the other deduction (syllogismos) . . . Induction is a passage from individuals to universals. For example, the argument that supposing the skilled pilot is the most effective, and likewise the skilled charioteer, then in general the skilled man is the best at his particular task." (105.a. 10–19)

Tradition holds that this version of inductive logic reasons from particular cases to general conclusions or from the part to the whole. The name "enumerative induction" sticks to this reasoning as the basis for statistical inference. A commonly used illustration involves birds: All crows that have been observed are black, therefore all crows are black.

The enormous frequency of "black" associating with "crow" supplies a reason to think that all crows are black, but the uncertainty rests in the wait for one nonblack crow to vitiate the generalization. If enumerative induction characterized the method of science, scientific conclusions would be generalizations forever held hostage to a single contrary instance. But not all science involves generalizations of that kind. The aims differ. Induction required recasting to survive as a meaningful inference characteristic of practical scientific pursuits.

Francis Bacon set out to establish this new approach to science in his *Novum Organum* (1620). Bacon rejected simple enumeration and introduced a replacement called "eliminative induction," a new form that he said would "separate nature by proper rejections and exclusions," eliminating all false hypotheses, leaving the one remaining true claim. Such reasoning would be of obvious help to Ziegler facing his alternative scenarios. But just how competing hypotheses were "properly rejected" became Bacon's difficulty. Merely eliminating any number of hypotheses does not guarantee that the next to be considered will be acceptable. The method only works given a complete set of available alternatives: It supplies no guidance for producing the original set or rooting out the imposters. If Gilligan is murdered on the island bearing his name, if the island has only six other inhabitants, and if Ginger, the Professor, Mary Ann, and the Howells all have alibis, then the Skipper should be charged with murder. But rarely do real scientific or criminal investigations come supplied with such restricted alternatives, nor do they apply such limited reasoning methods. Ruth Homberg did not disappear from Gilligan's Island. Bacon's advance did not help define a rigorous method to produce or defend "scientific" explanations elevated above other conjectures by their methodical derivation.

In his *System of Logic* (1843) John Stuart Mill attempted to rectify the problem by recasting induction using the notion of "cause." When someone dies, or a disease spreads, causes of the phenomena exist and Mill saw the scientist's task as identifying and distinguishing causes from the tangle of antecedent factors mixed with them. Perhaps something as yet unidentified "caused" Ruth Homberg's disappearance. Mill sought rules for identifying causes parallel with rules for solving mathematical equations. He thought that the weakness of both Aristotle's and Bacon's approach lay in restricting induction to a single rule. Scientists might use enumeration in one setting and elimination in another. He set out what he called "four experimental methods" to detect "causes."

The first he called the "Method of Agreement." When only one antecedent condition remains common to all occurrences of the puzzling effect, then that condition probably causes the effect. If a peculiar cancer occurs only when exposure to asbestos also occurs, then asbestos likely causes the cancer. The second, the "Method of Difference," involves tests eliminating one antecedent condition to learn if the effect disappears. If Lyme disease does not occur when deer tick bites are prevented, then deer tick bites are necessary for the spread of Lyme disease. The third, the "Method of Concomitant Variation," relates variations in cause with parallel changes in effect. If eating more fat increases the risk of heart disease, and eating less fat decreases the risk, a causal link between fat intake and heart disease appears through the variation. The fourth, the "Method of Residues," compares sets of causes and effects to identify the cause of one particular phenomenon. An obese alcoholic smoker develops heart disease, cirrhosis of the liver, and lung cancer. A nonobese alcoholic smoker develops cirrhosis and lung cancer, while a nonobese nondrinking smoker develops only lung cancer. Heart disease, as the "residue," appears to be caused by obesity.

Each of Mill's four methods defines a relation between cause and effect to distinguish a given effect's cause from many antecedent events. The methods rest on two principles, one holding that a cause sufficient for a given effect cannot be present when that effect is absent, and the other holding that a cause necessary for a given effect cannot be absent when the effect is present.

Given the right examples, Mill's four methods appear to identify appropriate "causes." But Mill's nemesis, William Whewell, objected in 1849 that the methods "take for granted the very thing which is most difficult to discover, the reduction of the phenomena to formulae such as are here presented to us." (*Of induction*, p. 44) He sees Mill's methods as presenting causal discoveries already made and not as a procedure for discovering unknown causes. They aid in testing results but do little to derive the results to be tested in the first place.

Whewell pointed out that the method presupposes selecting the correct antecedent conditions to test as possible causes. But this assumes a solution to the problem of causal discovery the method was designed to solve. Without the correct inventory of causal candidates to begin testing, the method fails. Often our lack of understanding, the reason for applying the method in the first place, limits this list of alternatives. Accordingly, Hoblyn's *Medical Dictionary of 1878* defines "malaria" as a disease caused by "certain effluvia or emanations from marshy ground." Mill's four methods support this result. By "agreement" malaria occurs where marshlands exist. By "difference" malaria does not occur where no marshlands exist; sailors at sea, mountain residents, or desert dwellers do not develop the disease. By "concomitant variation," the frequency of malaria in a population varies with the size of the surrounding marshland. By "residues," only marshland dwellers or visitors developed malaria. Until mosquitoes joined the list of conditions to be tested, no further application of Mill's methods, or any other inductive rules, could improve the result identifying marshland as the "cause" of malaria (See Gjertsen, pp. 95–96).[3]

Forensic science and investigative work refute inductive method as a mechanical means of discovery. Routine applications of Mill's methods would support the conclusions that "cardiac arrest" caused Norbert Andrews' death, that oxygen caused the fire in the Duffy's kitchen, and that being under 18 years old caused Smith's victims' injuries. Good detectives and reputable forensic scientists know better. Peirce would say that they know better because they can read the signs, formulate abductions, and then test the relevant hypotheses. Some hypotheses involve causes, but most do not. When most people use the verb "caused" they really mean "explained." They do not confuse complex explanations and reasons with simplistic causes and effects. They know better because they do not confuse induction and abduction taken together as one simple inference. They refuse to play science by the numbers.

Contemporary inductive logicians use artificial manipulations to patch persistent holes in inductive methods. Their abstract attempts confuse even mathematical geniuses. They play the traveling Sophist to Peirce's questioning Socrates. Their work consistently ignores the practice of science and the application of its method in the trenches. Those like Ziegler, fighting in the muddy mix of science with nonscience, focus on reading the signs, physical or statistical, and formulating hypotheses that define appropriate tests.

Some combination of Mill's methods may organize tests and present results once the discoveries occur. Some discoveries may occur by chance aided by investigative preparation. Others take persistence mixed with chance. Ziegler approaches Ruth Homberg's missing person investigation with several alternative explanations in mind. His instincts agreed with Anderson's initial feeling that the signs show something as yet uncovered lurking beneath the surface. He began to view Gary Homberg as a potential suspect, somehow linked to Ruth Ann's disappearance. Given this hypothesis, both confirming and refuting evidence could be organized, developed, and tested. The logical thread of crime, if it existed, could be revealed and followed. But not by "induction" alone.

To discover what happened to Ruth Ann Homberg and to prove this discovery correct demanded implementing a practical answer to the ancient puzzle of acceptable scientific arguments. Gary Homberg's behavior, the bedroom, and the circumstances all held unusual signs. Those signs would be usual given certain explanations. Alternative explanations must be proposed and critically investigated. Ziegler's strong faith in the reality of knowledge, his intense desire to find things out, and his immunity to the blight of cocksureness infuse his method of discovery and proof. A reliable method must not create a thread of crime where none existed, but must discover and confirm the best explanation of mysterious events. The method involved investigators' personal integrity, a moral dimension defined by some notion of "good character." It did not parallel rules for solving mathematical equations. The blind application of rules misses the mosquitoes for the marshland. This uncertain Columbo began to buzz the all-knowing Millfab president with annoying questions.

Homberg sat stiffly behind his desk dressed in a three-piece suit when Ziegler entered his Millfab office, escorted by Sharon Jacobson Nordness. He introduced himself, and said how sorry he was that Ruth was missing, but managed not to extend sympathy to Homberg. He first asked about the Buick found at the airport. Mr. Homberg said that his wife's son, Rob, discovered the car Sunday morning when he went to the airport to search for it. Homberg said that he sent him there because he felt that Ruth had left him, and might have taken a plane to Florida or Mexico. Lee and Nancy Brusegar, Ruth's cousins, also spotted the car in the long-term parking area of the airport Sunday a little after noon. A few days later, Homberg said that he took his in-laws Art and Sally Nelson to see the car. Later, they moved it back home.

Ziegler followed the trail that Gary Homberg blazed. He asked if Ruth had taken any money for her trip. Homberg answered yes, she had taken between $7,000 and $10,000 from their home. From where in your home did she take it? Homberg answered that they kept their money in separate spots, his in the study and hers in the master bedroom. He said that about $4,000 of his money was missing from its spot in the den and all of her money from the bedroom was gone. Ziegler asked if she had taken anything else of value. He said that he noticed nothing but the sizable sum of money missing. His knowledge, Homberg said, went no further. Ziegler couldn't help but feel otherwise. At the door, Ziegler turned and asked again about the car, then he decided to give his suspect a rest. He would return to ask more about the money another day. He needed to learn more about living arrangements at the Hombergs' country estate. He thought that the best source for that information might be the maid.

Beverly DeGroot had cleaned the Homberg home once a week since before the first coat of paint dried in 1976. The hard-working woman had a sharp eye for detail and a clear memory for family members and their possessions. Her powers had been reinforced during more than eight years of duty in the Homberg household. She said that she cleaned for the Hombergs every Monday, but on Monday, November 7, 1983, something odd happened just as she prepared to leave for their home. The telephone rang and Sharon Nordness told her to stay home.

"Don't bother to clean today," Sharon had said, adding, "Ruth's out of town and we don't know when she's coming back."

DeGroot said to Detective Ziegler that she found that odd. Wouldn't Mr. Homberg want the house clean even if Ruth were away? Besides, she knew

Mr. Homberg to be even more fanatic about a clean and tidy home than Mrs. Homberg. Still she waited until the following Monday to return to duty.

DeGroot told Ziegler that she arrived Monday, November 14, 1983, more than one week after Ruth disappeared. She said that she did not think that Ruth would go anywhere without telling her parents or her children. She was too close to them for that. She would never leave without at least telling her mother how to contact her, yet Ruth had not done so. DeGroot sensed something wrong for that reason. She told Ziegler that she searched the house for signs of Ruth's packing and moving to escape an increasingly unhappy marriage. She walked through the house and into the cavernous bedroom seeing fanatical neatness everywhere.

She described the scene to Ziegler from memory. DeGroot described a king-size bed with dark Mediterranean-style accents, two octagonal bedside tables with gold shaded lamps, and two matching dressers that hardly began to fill the space. The walk-in closet that she described to the left of the entrance first sounded like another bedroom. A marble-floored bathroom to the right had the dimensions of a normal kitchen. She said that her eyes first focused on the dressing table to the right just inside the bathroom door.

Ruth's makeup accessories covered the table. He pictured liners for eyes and lips coexisting with line-removers for face and neck. Three pairs of false eyelashes filled two cards neatly hung from hooks in the middle of a wig stand. A dark blond wig rested on top. From the maid's description, he visualized a collection of brushes for hair, powders, and pastes adequate to help restore the ceiling of the Sistine Chapel. Also present on the expansive table were Ruth's blow dryer and curling iron. She said that she'd also looked in the medicine chest over Ruth's sink and saw the prescription medications Ruth regularly took to treat the symptoms of early menopause. She saw Ruth's toothbrush, dental floss, and tartar-control toothpaste all poised and ready for use.

DeGroot detailed the rows of clothes across the room dividing the closet into "his" and "hers" sides. Both halves appeared to her to be fully loaded. She saw Ruth's pink Samsonite travel bags resting on shelves above the clothing. A small matching makeup case sat on top. Rows of shoes on racks extended from entry door to far wall above a white carpeted closet floor. The carpet covered the bedroom, extending into the entry hall and ending by the bathroom entrance.

Answering Ziegler's unobtrusive questions about the room's details, DeGroot expressed surprise that the thick pile carpet showed wheel tracks from a recent vacuuming. DeGroot also noted a faint odor that she thought may have been carpet cleaner. Ziegler opened his eyes and asked if she noticed any of Ruth's outfits missing. The maid said that she saw nothing missing except Ruth's jewelry box. She said Ruth usually kept it on the vanity. As far as she knew, Ruth stored her diamond bracelet, a watch and other assorted jewelry in the box. She always wore her big diamond wedding ring. To her knowledge, that box alone was gone. That, together with the woman who always wore the big diamond ring.

If TV's Columbo were hunting for Ruth Homberg, he would hover and intrude, soliciting his suspects' cooperation to help him answer one little question, to understand one thing that still bothers him, then another, and another. Eventually the suspect, stung repeatedly in diverse areas, falls victim to his own grandiose manipulations, or he cuts and runs from the pressure. Ziegler's little questions required knowing some answers before testing Gary Homberg's replies. Some of those answers would have to come from other investigative specialists. If a guilty Gary Homberg fell, he would fall by his own weight, crushing the rickety bones of falsehood and deceit assembled to support his crime. By December 3, 1983, the investigation focused on Gary Homberg, traded on his potential arrogant confidence, and pursued his activities relentlessly. Fortunately, tests built into the strategy would help eliminate the incorrect explanations of Ruth's disappearance. Unfortunately, the eliminative tests depended on the passage of time.

On December 3, 1983, a short article in *The Capital Times*, published by Madison Newspapers, Inc., appeared on the bottom of page 1.

> Family Seeks News of Missing Woman
>
> Stoughton—The family of 43-year old Ruth Ann Homberg is offering a reward for information about her whereabouts. She was reported missing on Nov. 5.
>
> Her husband, Gary Homberg of Stoughton, said he went to work on Nov. 5 and, when he returned home for lunch, discovered her missing. He telephoned local police at 5 P.M. that evening.
>
> The Hombergs' car was found at the Dane County Regional Airport on Nov. 6. Sheriff's Detective Merle Ziegler said he does not suspect foul play, but added that he had no further information about the circumstances of Mrs. Homberg's disappearance.
>
> Persons with any information about her whereabouts can contact the Dane County Sheriff's Department.

The game, as Holmes would say, is afoot. The quiet hunters kept their distance and waited for their prey to make a move.

Ziegler and Lieutenant Gary Hendrickson had reasons to support their hunch that Homberg would move forward with his plan, whatever it might turn out to be. Homberg appeared too organized not to have one. Hendrickson shrewdly judged that Homberg felt superior to the various investigators he viewed as low-life, groveling peasants. That hubris played well against Ziegler's gadfly Socratic approach. They counted on Homberg's superiority complex to move him along despite his sense that he may have become a suspect in his wife's disappearance. For people like Homberg, right becomes "whatever I want" and wrong is "whatever gets in my way." *Good* means "good for me" and *bad* means "bad for me." The resulting Homberg jokes soon wore thin. Nothing about evil stays funny for long.

On December 19, 1983, Detective Ziegler parked his Horizon in front of Rick and Sharon Nordness' apartment. He spoke with Sharon. She wore tight-fitting jeans and a man's white shirt unbuttoned just enough to invite weaker men than Ziegler to stare at the middle of her chest. Heavy eye shadow and lipstick hid what might have been soft eyes and sensitive lips.

Spray-stiffened bleached hair curled from her head toward her shoulders. She wore the scent of insecurity. Beauty, he thought to himself, rests in the soul. The false art of cosmetics duels with the true art of health. Sharon may one day become beautiful, he thought, but not today.

He apologized for bothering her, and said that he had to follow up on every possible lead in her mother-in-law's disappearance for his report. Without revealing his cards, he asked Sharon if she had a romantic relationship with Gary Homberg. He watched her carefully. She looked at the carpet, her hands on her lap, then she looked at the living room wall. She had been seeing him romantically, she said. They had a brief affair, but it ended in August of 1983. They were through, and she had returned her affections to Rick. She licked her lower lip slightly as she waited for a reply. After a pause, Ziegler thanked her for her help with his case. He said that he was sure Rick's mother would turn up, and that if she learned anything to please contact him. He gave her a card and left her in the apartment. In the Horizon he could still smell the perfume on his normally cigar-tainted overcoat.

At the office, leaning back in his chair, he thought about Sharon's interview and the work that had been done to follow her moves. He looked at the time line worksheet for Case No. 157694. About two and one-half months before Ruth vanished, August 22, 1983, Sharon leased a condominium at 1015 Sunnyvale Lane, Unit G, Foxwood Hills, for $495 per month, according to the property supervisor, Karen Danner. On that same day, she opened an IRA account for $2,000 and a checking account with $805 at Valley Bank. The next day she paid the first month's rent on the condo with a check from her new account.

The timeline got more interesting by September. The Dane County District Attorney's Chief Investigator, William Drenkhahn, now as involved in the investigation as Ziegler, found that a telephone installed in the condo and listed in Sharon Nordness' name had been billed to Gary Homberg. The property manager told Ziegler that Sharon moved into the condo on September 1, 1983. Homberg visited frequently. On October 12, Sharon deposited a $1,000 check from Gary Homberg into her Valley Bank checking account, and on October 28 she made another $1,000 deposit with another check from Homberg. According to police chief Grady, on November 4, Sharon charged her gasoline at an East Side service station to Millfab's account. Any of the alternative hypotheses explaining these facts and Sharon's December statements to Ziegler raised the same questions. He sat up and punched Line 4 to call Drenkhahn.

Ziegler and Drenkhahn decided to have another talk with Rick Nordness. Rick wore his flannel shirt rolled up at the sleeves, and would make an honorable sidekick on any TV hunting, fishing, or woodshop show. He said that on September 9, he and Sharon had another fight about her frequent absences from home. He saw her coming from Millfab on that Saturday morning after she told him that she was staying with her friend Joan Murphy. Rick looked both hurt and unprepared for the punishing self-doubt that lies can create in trusting people. The investigators thanked Rick again for his help. Now they had evidence that the affair between Sharon and Homberg did not end in August as Sharon had claimed.

The same statement cannot be both true and false at the same time under the same circumstances. Aristotle called this fact "the law of noncontradiction." He added another powerful principle called "the law of excluded middle." A statement is either true or false, but nothing in between. While philosophers may question the latter principle applied to statements about the future, Sharon's claims focused on the past. A contradiction loomed. She said the affair ended in August. But evidence of the affair continues after August. Sharon's problems soon involved more than these logical difficulties.

Her activities became another focus of the investigation. When Ruth disappeared on November 5, Sharon had coffee with her parents in Stoughton at 8:30 A.M. and they went shopping at the Farm & Fleet store about 12:30 P.M. Rick said he left her in bed when he went to work about 6:00 A.M. Her whereabouts between 6:00 A.M. and 8:30 A.M. on November 5 and her activities on November 4 became more important to clarify. When Drenkhahn talked with the manager of the local Plaza Hardware Store, he learned that on November 11, 1983, Sharon had rented a carpet-cleaning machine. The investigation gained renewed focus.

In January of 1984, Sharon moved into Ruth Homberg's office at Millfab and assumed many of Ruth's other duties. The transition grated on John White, a Homberg family friend hired by Homberg to work at Millfab in 1981. He told Ziegler that he first heard of Ruth's disappearance on November 7, 1983. He said that at Millfab in September, he saw Gary and Sharon kissing each other, and that later that month, Ruth talked with him about her unhappy situation. White also told Ziegler that he lent Gary Homberg his 1981 El Camino, newly purchased from the Millfab vehicle fleet in September of 1983. Gary asked to borrow it on November 4, about 1 P.M. White asked Homberg no questions. He retrieved his half-car half-pickup about 10:00 P.M. on November 5 at Millfab where Homberg presumably had parked it in the employee parking area.

White added that he put two and two together for himself. Homberg somehow got rid of Ruth and used his El Camino in the process. He did not keep his mathematical opinions to himself. Word got back to the Millfab president. White later told Ziegler that in February of 1984, Gary Homberg confronted him and demanded that he keep his opinions private.

Ziegler also found out from Homberg family friends Mr. and Mrs. Linke, who made an unannounced visit to the Homberg estate Saturday November 5 about 2 P.M., that White's El Camino sat in the driveway. No one appeared to be home. The Linkes telephoned the sheriff's department responding to the December 3 *Capital Times* newspaper request for more information. The case file grew steadily into 1984 with these telephone responses and their followups. Roxanne remained convinced that Gary had murdered her mother, and called regularly. She told Ziegler that she asked Homberg about her mother's jewelry box. She'd also noticed it missing from the bedroom vanity. Homberg told her that Ruth must have taken it with her when she left him. Armed with these bits and pieces, Ziegler planned his next visit with Mr. Homberg.

Homberg's standard blue three-piece business suit looked like an expertly tailored uniform, missing only the medals and decorations honoring past achievement and promising future performance. Ziegler said that he had some problems fitting together loose ends, and needed Homberg's help to locate Ruth. Where in Florida might she go? Where in Mexico? Did she have any friends in other countries? Where did she keep her passport? Did she have a credit card? And what did he find missing after she left? Homberg did not have anything to offer about friends, but she did have a current passport. He did not know where it might be. He said that she had taken more than $10,000 in cash from his den that, in his opinion, could take her a long way without credit. He did not mention the jewelry box. Ziegler did not ask. He did notice a bandage on Homberg's left little finger.

A series of calls located Dr. Zelm, a local chiropractor, who treated Homberg for the sore finger on February 10, 1984. He told Ziegler how Homberg complained about the finger bothering him for three months before his visit. Zelm said that he X-rayed the finger, and in keeping with the science of his craft, performed a spinal adjustment as treatment before submitting his bill. The injury did not appear to be work-related. Homberg did not say how he'd hurt the finger.

Despite some minor physical ailment preventing Homberg from flashing a diamond pinky ring on his left hand, he appeared financially well-heeled. On February 22, 1984, he paid off a $100,000 mortgage on his English Tudor property taken originally in 1982. By March 20, 1984, Sharon Jacobson Nordness moved out of the apartment she shared with her husband, Rick. The same day, March 20, Gary Homberg purchased a condo, 1015 Sunnyvale Lane, G, Foxwood Hills. On March 30, he remortgaged the Leslie Road property for $55,000. And on April 18, Sharon Nordness filed for a divorce from Rick Nordness. The money trail continued.

On June 19, 1984, Gary Homberg wrote a check for $13,000 to Sharon Jacobson Nordness. That same day, she deposited the check in her Valley Bank checking account. Later that day, she wrote a check for $12,977.50 to Zimbrick, Inc., a local Buick, Mercedes, and BMW auto dealership. Sharon had a new car. Ziegler and Drenkhahn had some solid leads. In December of that year, Homberg repaid an $80,000 loan from his in-laws, Art and Sally Nelson, plus interest. When Lt. Hendrickson looked over their growing timeline worksheet, he said what any good Norwegian knows. Money doesn't just grow on trees. And like any good Norwegian, Hendrickson wanted to know its source. If not on trees, money might grow on lumber. Ziegler and Drenkhahn had another thread to follow.

Money cannot buy happiness. Aristotle held that happiness comes as a byproduct of what he called *eudaimonia*, of living rightly, or in the words of the U.S. Army recruiting slogan, of "being all that you can be." Live right, Aristotle predicted, and happiness arrives as a side benefit. Aim at happiness, and the commodity can be neither produced nor enjoyed. Money existed as an enjoyable byproduct. Despite Homberg's money, or perhaps because of it, Sharon did not appear to be happy. She received her divorce on September 25, 1984, and changed her name back to Sharon Jacobson. The day after her divorce became final, she left Millfab and took a secretarial job at Gordon Flesch Co. in Madison. She moved out of the Foxwood Hills condo and into an apartment. Ziegler and Drenkhahn sensed that the affair had gone sour.

By 1985 business for Millfab had also taken a turn for the worse. Don Wahlin, 52% stockholder, at first blamed the Reagan recession that had cut into the building trades and decreased demand for the wood products his company produced. But as time passed, he wanted less abstract answers. He hired a certified public accountant to go over the company books and to suggest any cost-saving measures to save the company. The accountant found several irregularities that he reported to Wahlin to help explain some of the financial drain on company assets.

Wahlin learned that as company president, Homberg signed the payroll checks, including his own and Ruth's. The audit revealed that Homberg paid himself a $110,000 salary instead of the approved $45,000. He also overpaid Ruth, the company bookkeeper. The accountant's work showed that the additional salary came from overpayments for leased equipment. Homberg, the accountant reported, paid himself for equipment leased to the corporation after the lease agreement expired. Gary Homberg had an insatiable hunger for money.

His appetite finally brought him into court. On March 14, 1985, he received an appointment from circuit court to administer Ruth Homberg's estate. On November 14, 1985, at a hearing before Branch VII, Homberg submitted an application for a Finding of Disappearance and Absence, which the court granted. He could now control the remainder of Ruth's estate.

By March of 1985, detectives discovered that Homberg had a new romantic interest. On a business trip to Denver, he had met Jan McCusker, an attractive nurse. He continued to see her on subsequent trips. They dated through 1985. Sharon appeared to be out of the picture.

Information on Homberg's finances and romances continued to fill the case file, but Ziegler and Drenkhahn seemed no nearer to finding Ruth or discovering her body, or to proving their growing belief that Gary Homberg somehow murdered his wife. Both investigators continued to put in many hours and their superiors waited less patiently for the payoff. The search for Ruth had uncovered Gary Homberg's financial empire. Now they needed to develop and use this information to test their beliefs about Homberg's role in Ruth's fate.

Hendrickson and Ziegler developed the plan with Drenkhahn of the district attorney's office. In December of 1986 they brought Donald R. Murphy, an investigator from the Wisconsin State Department of Revenue, into the investigation. Drenkhahn and Murphy met Ziegler in his office to go over the now-huge Ruth Ann Homberg file. Everyone connected with the investigation hoped that Murphy's work would help uncomplicate the maze and simplify the navigating techniques. Documents shuffled between laps and desk, creating sister peaks to Ziegler's paper-capped mountain. The blizzard continued with Ziegler occasionally leaning back in his desk chair, cigar butt in hand, watching the confusion unfold.

Murphy, document quest still underway, looked up and explained to Ziegler that a routine audit of Mr. and Mrs. Homberg's state income tax returns starting in 1982 should be combined with a thorough audit of the Millfab books. Murphy might be able to find things that an ordinary CPA could miss. He specialized in uncovering embezzlements.

How, Drenkhahn asked, could Gary Homberg purchase a $250,000 English Tudor country estate, pay off mortgages, loans, property taxes, buy expensive jewelry, a condominium, give cash gifts to Sharon, and claim high business entertainment expenses all on a reported Millfab salary of $45,000? Ruth earned considerably less as company bookkeeper. Even given the scheme uncovered by Wahlin's CPA, the numbers did not compute. Gary Homberg had an additional unreported source of income. Presently, Murphy added, he planned to reconstruct the Homberg's financial lives and quietly examine the Millfab books. As it stood, it appeared that Homberg underreported income from 1982 on. The Department of Revenue might find more, including leads to locate Ruth.

Ziegler suggested that the financial irregularities and the disappearance might be connected. The obvious link: Gary served as Millfab president. Ruth served as company bookkeeper. Together Gary and Ruth Homberg served themselves from the Millfab buffet. Several hypotheses linking money and murder emerged from the ensuing discussion conducted on uncomfortable chairs and surrounded by sheaves of white paper. They agreed to split their investigation, Ziegler to head the search for the body, and Murphy to lead the financial probe.

Both tasks involved overlapping witnesses, evidence, and perhaps the same logical thread. They needed cooperative witnesses with more information. The new Sharon Jacobson appeared to be the best candidate. Ziegler would go to work on her as well. Drenkhahn would get the district attorney's office focused on a John Doe probe, the equivalent of a grand jury investigation. The last three years of investigative work searching for a missing person now lead through a maze of money.

In January of 1986, Don Wahlin's examination of Millfab accounts put Gary Homberg on notice. Since 1982, Wahlin had admired Homberg's optimism in the face of Millfab's growing financial adversity. It surprised him that a man with Homberg's talents would stay with what increasingly appeared to be a sinking ship. He felt that Homberg's 49% interest in the company, his positive attitude, and his image of success ensured that if anyone could turn the company around, Homberg could. But after the results of his

CPA's 1985 audit, he had some doubts. At Wahlin's request, the Millfab board of directors informed Homberg that his salary would be cut to $40,000 and that any more financial mismanagement would lead to his termination. Wahlin had not given up on Homberg.

For Mr. Homberg, the January news from his board of directors set the tone for the year. Ziegler, Drenkhahn, and Murphy planned to increase the pressure by involving the news media. They released information to the press, hungry for news about the investigation's progress, that Ruth Ann Homberg's disappearance had become suspicious primarily because she had not contacted her family for three years, despite daily contact with her parents and children before November 5, 1983. They knew that Gary Homberg would get a phone call for his reaction.

On August 13, 1986, the local papers printed Homberg's reply to their telephone interviews. He said that he remained at a loss to explain her disappearance.

"If somebody is dead, they're dead," Homberg said. "You can go on. But when you don't know, it's the worst." He added, "If she did leave me, then she certainly knows where I am."

Answering questions about his current feelings, he said, "It takes a good year-and-a-half to put yourself together after something like this. All I have to do is walk into my house and she's all around me. But I keep myself active and very busy. You put it on the back burner and go on with your life. You feel sorry for yourself." The article's author, Sharon Pitman, said, paraphrasing Homberg, "it's like death, he explained, it is the people left behind who suffer."

Mr. Gary Homberg did not plan to suffer long. He took immediate steps to get on with his life. He gave Wahlin a note scribbled in pencil announcing his resignation and a move to California. On September 1, 1986, Homberg and his new love, 20-year-old Michele Reiter, left for San Bernardino. On September 23, he listed his expansive residence for sale with Stark Realty for $250,000. By December 29, he had sold his 49% ownership of Millfab stock back to the company for $1,000.

Donald R. Murphy of the state department of revenue, nearing retirement after a distinguished career, took four months to analyze operations at Millfab. He came to know the flow of paper as well as he learned to understand the movement of materials. He tracked memos, payrolls, invoices, and receipts. He followed trucking schedules, raw wood deliveries, fabrication steps, and delivery destinations of the company's finished products. He compared raw material input and product output like a vigilant nurse measuring fluid consumption and production in a critically ill patient. He examined the company's unique money-saving attempts to produce power by incinerating wood scraps in its German-built high temperature furnace installed in 1979. By burning scraps to heat steam-generating boilers, all materials could be used efficiently. The boilers both heated the factory in the winter and supplied steam to run four wood-drying kilns. Murphy, quiet and unassuming, came to know both Millfab and Gary Homberg in more documented detail than any other investigator up to March 1987.

When Murphy, Ziegler and Drenkhahn showed Donald Wahlin a two-inch thick stack of faked checks, the former owner of Millfab looked dumbfounded. No wonder Homberg appeared to be so optimistic in the face of impending ruin for Millfab. This stack of Homberg fancywork came at least three months too late for Wahlin's interest in Millfab. On December 31, 1986, Wahlin had surrendered the company to its creditors, material suppliers who claimed $1.1 million in past-due payments. He had noticed that raw material consumption remained high and had increased since 1982, but even his CPR hadn't pinpointed the enormity of Homberg's scam.

The embezzlement, Murphy explained, operated as efficiently as the German furnace. Homberg started in 1982 by embezzling $37,310. He increased the amounts each year. In 1986 alone, Homberg sucked $239,866 from Millfab's operation. Murphy showed Wahlin a blank book of Millfab's supplier checks to illustrate the method. Writing the original check in the book made two copies on pressure-sensitive paper beneath. Murphy tore the top check out of the book and wrote his name on the "Pay to the Order Of" line. Homberg would tear out the top check, make it out to himself, and deposit it in his account. Murphy pocketed the illustration with his name on the payee line. Withdrawing a blank sheet of paper from his sport coat, Murphy then put the paper over the two pressure-sensitive checks remaining in the stack. Homberg, he said, then made out the copies to a legitimate lumber supplier. Murphy did so as Wahlin, Ziegler, Hendrickson, Drenkhahn, and Assistant District Attorney Judith Hawley looked on. Murphy then removed Millfab's in-house copy and said that Homberg posted this as a raw material purchase. The other copy, intended for the supplier, simply made its way into the metaphorical furnace. No supplier existed.

Homberg escaped detection, he said, primarily because at the end of the month, any raw materials purchased would have been milled into finished moldings and forwarded to purchasers. So lack of raw materials did not signal any particular problem in the operation. Murphy put Homberg's five-year take at more than $645,000. Wahlin appeared stunned.

"Now I know," he said, "why the business wasn't profitable."

Ruth Ann Homberg had to know about Gary's first two years of bilking Millfab. That much appeared to investigators as nearly certain. Gary Homberg worked in the same office where she served as the company bookkeeper. Clearly she dealt with the materials account on a daily basis. An elementary application of Mill's method of difference showed that Ruth did not play a necessary role in the scheme. The thefts not only continued but also escalated after her disappearance. But explanations of involvement, not some overly simplified notions of cause and effect, required testing here. Ruth's simple presence or absence could not establish explanatory relations on their own. To further complicate the testing picture, evidence of Gary's embezzlement did not automatically become evidence of murder. At least not without key missing pieces.

Sharon became Ziegler's potential source for those missing pieces. In 1986, Sharon Jacobson promised Ziegler that she would supply investigators with her diary. They also wanted her banking and telephone records. But by July of 1986, she changed her mind and refused. On July 25, 1986, her attorney, Daniel J. Collins, revoked previously granted authorizations for bank and phone records. Negotiation and cooperation ended. Both sides readied the field for battle.

In April of 1986, Sharon Jacobson, summoned before the District Attorney's secret John Doe probe, testified that she knew nothing of Ruth's disappearance. Ziegler already knew that she lied about her affair with Homberg and about her affections for Rick. He had no reason to believe that her lies stopped there. More pressures would be required to shake her testimony. Large doses of law, both logical and criminal, prepared the secret probe for Sharon Jacobson. It took investigators a full year to lay the logical foundation for the next two days in Sharon Jacobson's life. Inquisitors recalled her to the secret John Doe inquiry into the disappearance of Ruth Ann Homberg on April 22, 1987.

Sharon Jacobson spent an unpleasant day testifying in the grand jury probe. The setup for the underprepared bottle blonde rivaled a classic sting operation for catching the suspect in a criminal act. Bank deposits, phone records, surveillance reports, credit histories, and witness statements waited like mines to explode incautious lies. As the hours passed, contradictions piled up like war dead when each bit of painstaking investigative work rained doubt on her tales. It got rough when the inquisition's objective clarified for Sharon and her attorney. Sharon, the featured witness, became Sharon, the prime target for a murder charge. If she insisted on shielding Homberg, she could take the heat alone.

Contradictions aside, Sharon clung to her story that she knew nothing about Ruth's disappearance or about Gary Homberg's possible role. Shaking, pale, and exhausted, the weary witness claimed genuine ignorance of any crime, financial or otherwise.

"It's the honest-to-God truth," she said. "Honest to God."

But her honesty had been fatally injured by the logic of battle before the grand jury. Probers shook their heads, telling her that she had better return tomorrow with a story less dependent on divine corroboration.

Panic set in. Daniel J. Collins wasted no time negotiating with the Dane County District Attorney's office. On April 24, 1987, Sharon Jacobson returned to the witness chair carrying a blanket grant of immunity from prosecution for any and all crimes that her testimony revealed. Now she told a different story to the secret John Doe probe. Investigators had a smoking gun.

But they still lacked a body. Ziegler, Drenkhahn, and Hendrickson put a lot of thought into the search. The disappointing result did not come from lacking effort. Gary Homberg had from between about midnight on November 5, 1983, to about 7:00 A.M. to dispose of Ruth's body. White's El Camino might have played a role. One possibility, strongly favored by Rick Nordness, implicated Millfab's German furnace. According to White, no maintenance crews worked on the weekend of November 5 and 6. Homberg would have had the furnace to himself. White also said that regular ash cleaning occurred on November 10, 1983. If any evidence of Ruth's body remained at that date, it had long ago dissipated.

Fires seldom totally destroy a body. A typical house or structure fire burning between 1,200 degrees to 1,400 degrees Fahrenheit chars human arms after about 10 minutes. Even accelerant fires like Earl Thompson's seldom consume corpses. Experiments applying Mill's method of concomitant variation to human cadavers show that as time in the fire increases, the destruction increases. After about 15 minutes the legs, face, and arm bones show. At 20 minutes, the ribs and skull become exposed, and at 35 minutes the leg bones emerge from the reduced flesh.

Individual variations depend on the particular cluster of causes that happen to associate. The closer the body is to the source of heat, the greater the destruction. Any body raised above a fire source produces what investigators call the "candle effect." Melting body fat fuels the fire, increasing the temperature and therefore increasing the destruction. The more abundant the body fat, the higher the temperature and the greater the destruction. The Millfab furnace, however, would not desiccate a body the way a typical structure fire would.

Jon Heinrich, an air quality specialist for the state department of natural resources, had inspected Millfab's German-built furnace in 1979. He estimated that during typical operation, temperatures inside range from 1,800 to 2,200 degrees Fahrenheit. The furnace consumes the equivalent of 38 cords of wood per week. About every three weeks, maintenance workers remove one 33-gallon trash can filled with ash, all that remains of about 114 cords of wood consumed by the furnace. The effect on a single human body would be dramatic.

During legal cremation, human bodies enter a retort chamber heated to about 2,000 degrees for one and one half to three hours. After about two and one half hours, teeth, small pieces of bone, dental work and any jewelry remain. Usually funeral homes process these remains in a pulverizer, producing a fine dust to be stored in an urn or distributed according to family wishes. A body left at 2,000 degrees for four or five hours would not require a pulverizer. Even the teeth would probably shatter. Only minerals like gall or kidney stones might remain. Even if Ruth Homberg had gall or kidney stones and somehow they survived the furnace, they would probably go unrecognized among 33 gallons of ash collected and disposed of by maintenance workers on November 10, 1983. If Gary Homberg had put Ruth in the Millfab furnace, she was gone for good.

He also had time to bury Ruth anywhere on his four-acre Leslie Road estate, or on either of his other two properties totalling another 12 acres in the rural county. Mileage records for White's El Camino might have supplied distance estimates, but White had no reason to keep such records. Besides, the El Camino's role in Ruth's disappearance remained unconfirmed. On

April 9, 13, and 20, 1987, investigators earnestly searched these areas for her buried body.

Buried bodies leave various signs of their presence beneath the surface depending on surrounding conditions. In a shallow grave in soft ground, the body's decomposition produces a noticeable depression when surrounding earth fills the void once occupied by organs in the thoracic cavity. Or vegetation grows vigorously in areas newly supplied with nutrients compared with less-robust growth nearby. Often in deeper graves, differing layers of dirt become mixed, out of order. If the general area has uniform rich black topsoil, the grave's surface may mix sandy loam and gravel with the topsoil in the digging and burying process. Even so, finding a relatively small grave in a large area can be very difficult.

Infrared scanners to detect heat from decomposition, ground-penetrating sonar to detect human skeletal forms beneath the surface, and various probes to locate methane gas pockets produced by putrefaction supply technical support for discovering human remains. However, despite current technology, most buried human remains await discovery by hunters, campers, hikers, or construction workers when animal scavenging, erosion, or excavation exposes easily recognizable human bones such as skulls, femurs, or the innominates. Despite their limitations, all these technologies found a role in the search for Ruth Ann Homberg's body.

Helicopters with infrared scanners flew over the 16-acre area without success. Ground-penetrating sonar came up empty while covering much of the Leslie Road property. On the chance that the body had been buried in a metal container, metal detectors also scanned part of the area. Beverly DeGroot recalled that when she had looked out Ruth's bedroom window on November 14, 1983, she saw an area of bare ground near some trees. Probes in that area revealed nothing. Search dogs trained to identify the odor of human remains tracked the area without success. If Ruth's body lay in the area, a productive search required more restricted parameters. Short of bulldozing four acres and everything on it to look for mixed soil layers, every available technique had been tried without result.

The county budget could not afford another scientific search for her body. The case against Gary Homberg now depended on Sharon Jacobson, and on other evidence eliminating any possibility that Ruth remained alive. It also depended on how well Gary Homberg withstood the kind of pressure that eventually broke Sharon Jacobson. But Gary's personality handled pressure differently. With Ziegler and Drenkhahn looking on in 1987, Homberg had already passed a voluntary polygraph examination. The result neither surprised nor disappointed the investigators.

Erasistratus, an ancient Greek physician, observed that his patient's pulse rates increased when they told him lies. Since his observations in about 250 B.C., Mill's method of "concomitant variation" has been applied in attempts to correlate truth telling with various baseline physiological functions, and lying with their specific alterations. In the 1880s, Cesare Lombroso applied a mechanical device to measure changes in blood volume to discover physiological changes associated with lying. In 1921, John Larsen of the Berkeley California Police Department combined measurements of blood pressure, pulse and respiration, correlating their changes with deception. Later Leonarde Keeler added a galvanometer to measure the skin's electrical resistance and the "lie detector" emerged as a new scientific tool in the fight for truth and justice. They called the device a "polygraph" from "poly" meaning many, and "graph" meaning writing or picturing. Polygraphers interpret the four-line graphs and report any correlation establishing deception.

Many problems with "lie detectors" prevent their results from being considered as either scientific or legal evidence. The first problem is logical. The device at best measures whether a subject connected to its wires believes what he says. Believing it so, as it says in *Alice in Wonderland,* doesn't make it so. Unless, of course, absent signs of deception mean both that a subject believes what he says, and that what he says is true. The second problem is scientific. The underlying associations linking a liar's autonomic nervous system with deception lack any clear explanation. Many subjects known to be lying show no alterations in blood pressure, respiration, pulse rate, or galvanic skin response. Many others known to be telling the truth exhibit wild variations in response due to many other factors including obvious nervousness at being connected to the device in the first place.

The key problem with "lie detection" is practical. For investigators like Ziegler who believe in the reality of knowledge, a falsehood eventually contradicts an established fact. His job is to uncover those facts. The facts and the falsehoods together go to court and make their case against the liar. Sharon said she stopped seeing Homberg. They met a dozen times after. The signs of her deception did not require the wires of technology to detect.

Sometimes technology's wires cross. Sociopaths or other pathological liars become so accomplished at lying that deception becomes the normal response. Their deception escapes the lie detector's trap. The device has practical value in large part only to intimidate the insecure into telling what they know or truly believe. Gary Homberg did not at all appear insecure. The results confirmed for Ziegler, Drenkhahn, and Hendrickson their vision of the quarry.

Faster than a speeding bullet, Homberg resumed his old habits in California. He leased an expensive home under the name Gerhardt Reiter in Rialto where he lived with Michele Reiter. He ran daily operations as general manager for the Peterman Lumber Co. in Fontana, about 10 miles west of San Bernardino. His boss, C. A. "Pete" Peterman, paid him a salary of $100,000 per year. He continued to assemble other financial resources. In March, he contacted Valley Bank to close his and Ruth's accounts. He told Jan Schalow that "we have moved to California." He closed Ruth's checking account, her IRA, and three of his IAAs and collected cashier's checks for $19,011.43. He deposited the results, and his new payroll checks, in the Bank of Redlands in

California. On March 20, he attempted to close another of Ruth's accounts at another bank, but failed.

On Monday April 27, 1987, three days after Sharon Jacobson shared the new version of her story with the grand jury, San Bernardino County Deputies arrested Gary Homberg at the Peterman Lumber Co. They took him into custody and informed him that he faced extradition to Wisconsin. He had been formally charged with 48 counts of theft and four counts of filing false income tax returns. In his thick German accent, Homberg first claimed to be Gerhardt Reiter. Then he refused to give his home address. Then he gave investigators an address that didn't exist. When he saw district attorney's office investigator William Drenkhahn, Lt. Gary Hendrickson, and detective Merle Ziegler waiting at the San Bernardino County Sheriff's Office, he became less insistent that his arrest involved a simple case of mistaken identity. He waived the extradition proceeding and accompanied his captors on the long flight to the Dane County Regional Airport.

Court documents filed by the Dane County District Attorney's Office revealed that in addition to the 52 counts of criminal charges, they considered Homberg the primary suspect in his wife's possible murder. They described the murder investigation as "ongoing." References to a missing person investigation ceased. Some of Homberg's friends expressed shock.

Back in California, "Pete" Peterman, interviewed by Mike Miller of *The Capital Times,* said "I just don't believe it! They have to prove it first. He's a very upright guy. Any help he needs, he's got our backing 100%."

Peterman soon learned that Homberg apparently had no aversion to helping himself. When assistant district attorney Ann Sayles argued against bail reduction in May, she pointed out that when arrested, Homberg had the combination for the Peterman Lumber Co. safe. Company officials, including Peterman himself, had suffered another shock. Homberg had no authorization to have the combination. Some of the proof Peterman requested began to appear.

In one way, proving Homberg guilty of embezzlement became a tactic designed to buy Ziegler's murder investigation more time and to stir up the principals. In another way, the embezzlement and the murder remained linked through Homberg himself and his relationship with Sharon Jacobson. With these steps in place, proving the murder now depended on proving his embezzlement. After some legal maneuvering, that first step became easier than prosecutors initially had believed.

On May 1, 1987, the court set Homberg's bail at $300,000. Assistant District Attorney Judith Hawley argued for a ball set at $500,000. Since Homberg had friends and business associates around the world, gave police false information when initially arrested, and had access to large sums of cash, he might post bond and flee. She also referred to him as "the prime suspect" in a homicide investigation. Homberg's attorney Daniel McDonald argued that his client could not possibly raise $500,000, dismissing the prosecution's estimates of his wealth. He said that his client gave a false name and address when arrested in California because he did not want police to search his home. McDonald attempted to rebut the significance of Hawley's reference to his client as a "prime suspect" by pointing out that Homberg had been suspected from the start.

"There is a lot of suspicion that Gary Homberg is involved," McDonald said. He added, "There is no proof."

By May 6, Homberg had a new lawyer with a new story. Attorney James Connors offered a puzzling nonsequit, saying that his client refused to give his address to detectives because of a previous burglary at his home. He appeared before Circuit Court Judge Mark Frankel and requested a ball reduction to $250,000—$150,000 in cash and a $100,000 property bond—so that Homberg could return to California and resume work. Judith Hawley opposed the reduction for the district attorney's office and supported a high cash bond. She cited inconsistencies in Homberg's explanations for using a false name and refusing to give his address and a March 1986 financial statement showing Homberg's net worth at over $900,000. In reply, Conners pointed out Homberg's ties to the community and said that his ex-wife, Sara Homberg, offered to supply her home as a property bond. Conners directly attacked the relevance of referring to Homberg as "a prime suspect" in a murder case in posting bond.

"You don't hold people on suspicion these days," Connors argued.

"There is more than mere suspicion," Hawley responded, "There is evidence."

The embezzlement case appeared solid after Murphy's four months spent uncovering this evidence. For each of the 45 remaining counts, Murphy supplied assistant district attorney Sayles with documents proving not only that Homberg stole the money, but also how he took it.

Murphy traced the money from its source in the Millfab materials account through its role in Homberg's lifestyle. He collected the check carbons made out to suppliers, compared their specific amounts with deposits to Homberg's accounts, and examined supplier's books for Millfab payments. He documented materials ordered and delivered, comparing invoices with check carbons, to eliminate Millfab checks that corresponded with delivered materials. Each of the 45 checks signed by Gary Homberg was not paid to any Millfab supplier. Each of the 45 checks corresponded with amounts deposited in his personal accounts. From Homberg's bank accounts, Murphy could trace both misstatements of income on state tax returns and the money's use to support Homberg's self-indulgent lifestyle.

An analysis of Homberg's spending interested Ziegler because it tied into Sharon Jacobson. That linked the already solid embezzlement case to the less robust pending murder charge. Some of Homberg's checks went directly to Sharon Nordness. The condo rent and purchase, the IRA and checking deposits, and her new car all forged a solid link and served to bolster Sharon's new story about her relationship with Homberg and the events of November 5 and 6, 1983. But assistant district attorneys John Burr and Judy Schwaemle, who were busy assembling the murder case against Homberg from the 3,400 pages of documents, had doubts about placing the weight of their case on Sharon Jacobson's testimony alone. Their discomfort increased with the absence of Ruth's body. But Ziegler, Drenkhahn, and Hendrickson eventually supplied proof to replace Ruth's body that helped ease their distress.

Their original nagging anguish over the missing body had merit. If they followed their plan to charge Homberg with first-degree murder, theirs would be the first case in Wisconsin judicial history without a body to support the charge. Fewer than two dozen successful murder prosecutions without a body have entered the books in the United States. The first, in 1955, found Leonard Ewing Scott guilty of murdering his rich wife, socialite Evelyn Throsby Scott. The motive for his crime appeared as obvious to jurors as the search for her body appeared elusive to investigators. John Burr, with more than 20 years of experience prosecuting murder cases, pored over old transcripts of these missing-body murders. The more he and Judy Schwaemle pored, and the more they saw of Ziegler, Drenkhahn, and Hendrickson's work, the better they felt about the absence of Ruth's body.

Once Ziegler read the signs and formed his hypothesis that Ruth had been murdered, his conjecture required testing. Testing any hypothesis requires breaking it into its simplest parts. One part of being murdered is being dead. Another part is not dying by accident, naturally, or by suicide, but by homicide. Then the killer must be uncovered. Investigators may use the results of this analysis to predict by deduction what they might find, assuming each part of the hypothesis to be true. A dead person does not drive a car, travel, use credit, work, contact neighbors and family, or access bank or Social Security accounts. Ruth's death predicts the absence of such activity. The dead have no use for money. The living can't seem to exist without it.

Philosophers call this predictive process the hypothetico-deductive method, and some mistakenly equate it with the method of science. Ziegler knows better. His effort to explain what happened to Ruth Homberg, like the scientific enterprise to produce and defend different kinds of explanations, involves more logic than simple deduction. Many living people under certain circumstances may not drive a car, travel, use credit, work, contact neighbors and family, or use bank or Social Security accounts. But not Ruth. She never lived that way before. Her circumstances did not appear to allow it.

Such hypotheses do not appear spontaneously, allowing predictive deductions from their parts, which, if true, prove the conjecture. As explanatory stories, such hypotheses do not always have simple component parts detachable from specific contexts. The signs suggesting the hypothesis in the first place help focus the testing which often depends on the looser and less certain associations characteristic of induction in general and Mill's methods in particular. The weight of the evidence rests firmly on the explanatory hypothesis elevating the signs from coincidence to evidence in the first place. Ziegler's hypothesis that Gary murdered Ruth depends on her death being the best explanation of her disappearance in context, and on Homberg's actions being the best explanation of her death. In the absence of her body, Ziegler's test focused on Ruth's death. Before the significance of his tests could be assessed, he had to separate the mosquitoes from the marshland.

Ziegler's tests had built-in limits. His method produced evidence supporting the explanation of Ruth's disappearance as her death, but not an explanation of the death itself. Explaining her death as a murder involved different evidence. In that, he fell short of Murphy's work proving Homberg's $645,000 embezzlement from Millfab. And in that rested Burr and Schwaemle's initial discomfort. But in context, the thread of logic appeared and her murder made sense as the best overall explanation of her disappearance. Indirect evidence of her death had to replace the direct evidence that would have been supplied by her body.

On September 24, 1986, Ziegler ran his first credit check on Ruth Ann Homberg. Trans Union Credit reported no activity for anyone with Ruth's Social Security number. None of her bank or department store credit cards showed any activity after November 5, 1983. If Ruth lived, she lived without credit cards or checks and paid only cash after November 5.

According to Donald Murphy, Ruth's last Social Security account earnings were posted in 1983 from her last Millfab paycheck, which she did not cash or deposit. Gary Homberg deposited the check. Neither supplemental security income nor Social Security benefits had been credited to her account after November 5, 1983. No Federal Insurance Contribution Act (FICA) earnings appeared in the account after that date. No withdrawals appeared either.

Most people outside federal witness protection programs who assume new identities on their own retain the same Social Security account number to preserve their contributions. Ruth appeared financially astute enough to preserve her assets. The best explanation of absent account contributions seemed to be that she had not earned any reported income since 1983.

If she did not work to earn reportable income but had some other source of funds, her spending could be traced. Her bank accounts showed no activity other than Gary Homberg's meddling. She had neither made nor been paid any health, accident, or life insurance claims anywhere in the U.S. If she did not earn money, and did not spend money, how did she live? The best explanation in context seemed to be that she didn't.

Ziegler also had Dane County dispatchers Glen Bell and Mike Meyers run driver's license checks for Ruth A. Homberg, DOB January 9, 1939, in all 50 states and the District of Columbia. All 51 jurisdictions replied. Only one, Wisconsin, listed a driver's license issued to a Ruth A. Homberg, and that license had expired. Similar results came from inquiries to U.S. State Department passport representatives, postal officials, church and civic organizations, hospitals, voter registrars, and vital statistics record keepers. If Ruth still lived, she lived invisibly, instantly transformed on November 5, 1983, into a stealth person, a phantasm whose paper trail remained hidden from the radar of modern existence.

Even if Ruth could live unseen by governmental and financial entities, it seemed doubtful to Ziegler that she would remain invisible to her family. The strongest evidence confirming Ziegler's death hypothesis rested with Ruth's parents, Art and Sally Nelson, and her children, Rick, Rob, and Roxanne. Art and Sally Nelson had one child together, their daughter Ruth. They lived in the same county, the same town, and the same neighborhood with their daughter. They spoke with Ruth daily, went to lunches and dinners together, and shopped together regularly. They enjoyed an unusually close relationship nurtured by proximity. The Nelsons heard nothing from Ruth after November 5, 1983. She developed an equally close relationship with her own children. Yet she did not contact them nor had they been able to contact her since November 5, 1983. This lack of family contact was unusual. It would be usual if she were dead. It would be less usual if she were alive but living in a self-imposed exile from everyone and everything dear to her.

These results supplied no mechanical tests for murder: instead they supplied signs of Ruth's death that replaced her body. They could not simply apply Mill's methods of agreement, difference, concomitant variation, or residues to prove her death by the absence of records or the lack of family contact. Absence of proof is not proof of absence. However absence itself may be a sign. Mill's methods cannot directly prove her death, but they do help eliminate other alternatives. With all possible alternatives eliminated the best chance for the truth remains.

Many antecedent conditions can produce a trail of credit card receipts. Lost or stolen cards in the hands of unauthorized users can build up staggering bills. But by Mill's methods, no trail at all requires that all conditions sufficient to produce the trail remain absent, including Ruth. Stolen Social Security numbers produce new contributions to Social Security accounts, or more likely new withdrawals. Neither new contributions nor new withdrawals existed. Ziegler found no effects, financial or otherwise, requiring that Ruth remained alive. Her death explained these absences better than any alternative because Ziegler's work eliminated the competition.

Explaining these signs by Ruth's murder at Gary's hands required additional steps. But both her death and her murder could be supported by evidence even though investigators could not explain where Homberg hid the body, or even exactly how he killed her. Ziegler still had no idea what caused her death, or where to find her body.

Burr and Schwaemle both saw that Ziegler's elimination of alternatives to Ruth's death fit into a coherent picture explaining her disappearance as a murder. Their picture could overcome the missing body and absent cause of death. Establishing her manner of death as murder remained legally sufficient. Convicting her murderer required additional steps made more difficult by their dependence on Sharon Jacobson.

Convicting Gary Homberg of embezzling $645,000 from Millfab required only negotiations with his attorney. Choosing to forgo a trial, defense attorney James Connors hammered out an agreement with Anne Sayles of the district attorney's office dropping 44 of the theft charges. In exchange, Homberg pled no-contest on two counts of theft and two counts of filing false state income tax returns. On December 1, 1987, Judge Pekowsky found him guilty.

Homberg, in his thick German accent, assured the judge that he understood the charges and the implications of his plea.

"I'm here primarily because I want to get it behind me so that I can go on with my life, which I can't do right now," Homberg told the judge. He still faced a maximum $40,000 fine and up to 30 years in prison. The agreement included no stipulations for any recommended sentence. Pekowsky ordered a presentence investigation before the sentencing hearing scheduled for March 10, 1988.

At the March 10 hearing, Judge Pekowsky sentenced Gary Homberg to eight years in prison, five for theft and three for fraudulent tax returns. He ordered Homberg to pay a $5,000 fine and to make restitution on both the embezzlement and tax charges. Moments after Homberg heard the sentence he rode to the county jail where Merle Ziegler served a new arrest warrant charging him with the first-degree murder of his wife. Ziegler filed the complaint March 9, 1988, before Judge William Byrne. Assistant District Attorney John Burr, Judge Byrne, and Ziegler signed the document.

The complaint spun one paragraph of legalese followed by 22 pages of attached facts detailing the charge. The paragraph defined what Burr and Schwaemle had to prove beyond a reasonable doubt:

> "That the above-named complaining witness being duly sworn says that the above named defendant(s) in the county of Dane, State of Wisconsin, did, in the early morning hours of November 5, 1983, at the Township of Dunkirk, feloniously cause the death of Ruth Ann Homberg, date of birth January 9, 1939, a human being, with intent to kill that person; contrary to Section 940.01(1) of the Wisconsin Statutes, and upon conviction shall be sentenced to life imprisonment in the Wisconsin State Prison System."

The court appointed Dennis Burke from the public defender's office to handle Homberg's defense. Homberg claimed that he could not afford counsel, had no assets, and had become indigent. He couldn't have hired a better attorney at any price, even if he found his legal predicament telecast in black and white and defended by Perry Mason. He had in Burke an experienced defense attorney respected by his colleagues who loved the law and its history, sports, and his family. His plain-folks approach and sense of humor contrasted sharply with his new client's pompous, frowning demeanor. But Homberg had good reason to frown and Dennis Burke knew it when he entered a "not guilty" plea in April 1988.

As he studied the complaint, Burke formulated his defense strategy. He felt that the absence of Ruth's body did not count much against the state's case. He thought that the state could successfully prove that Ruth ceased to exist after November 5, 1983. He and his public defender's office version of Mason's fictional investigator Paul Drake attempted to gather information to show a jury that Ruth Homberg may have just taken off, and that Sharon Jacobson's incriminating story amounted to a web of lies. Burke and his investigator produced disappointing results.

Ruth emerged from his investigation as a likely candidate for both mother of the year and daughter of the century. Admired by everyone they contacted, she doted over her aging parents and continued to nurture her grown children. The most damaging activity in her background involved a penchant for attending church bazaars. The thought of Ruth designing and executing her own disappearance strained credulity. Even if she had, he found it unlikely that she would stay away from her father's funeral when he died on February 13, 1988, or her mother's when she died on April 4, 1988. Ruth was dead. Burke quietly pictured Sharon Jacobson as her likely killer.

His probe into Sharon Jacobson proved equally disappointing. None of her family, friends, or acquaintances painted her as anything close to an evil monster. Even Homberg himself from his state prison cell said nothing bad about her. She did not use drugs, drink to excess, or have casual affairs. In fact, she had remarried, and appeared to be on a more stable course in every area of her once-troubled life. She made a poor candidate for "Murderess of the Year 1983." Burke would earn his pay defending Gary Homberg.

His pretrial defense attacked the prosecution's lack of cooperation in supplying over 3,500 pages of accumulated investigative work. He filed for dismissal of the charges, claiming that his client's right to a speedy trial had been infringed. The sparring between Burke and Burr continued up to the trial, finally set for October 9, 1989. Before the trial began, Burr and Schwaemle had their own strategy problems to solve.

They spent much time second-guessing Burke's defense strategy. They both thought that the likely introduction of a Sharon-as-killer scenario could be refuted by times, places, distances, and witnesses. They disagreed about how to handle the absent body. Burr argued that they had no need to explain what Homberg did with the body, or even how he killed her. The jury could be shown indirectly that Homberg had several available means to dispose of her without introducing any particular hypothesis.

Schwaemle argued that failing to produce the true explanation, they ought to provide a range of possible explanations. Burr countered that doing so might provide Burke with something to attack and worse, provide grounds for reasonable doubt. They would lose control of their case. Expert witnesses would debate the finer points of cremation, the powers of heat sensing, gas probing, or ground penetrating technologies, and their focus on the case against Homberg would be lost. They agreed to ignore the issue until a telephone call four months before the trial invited them to reconsider.

Ted Heffner, a prisoner confined with Homberg, had information about the body. Heffner ran a tattoo parlor before serving his current 13-year sentence for assaulting a parlor patron who had the bad judgment to critique a masterpiece in the master's presence. When Burr visited him in prison, Heffner said that Gary Homberg admitted killing his wife and burying her body in a 55-gallon drum. Heffner knew about the white carpet, walk-in closet, dressing table, and marble floor in Homberg's English Tudor bedroom. Only Homberg could have given Heffner those details. Burr believed his story. After studying the case, and Sharon's evidence, he felt that the furnace supplied a false clue. Despite Heffner's reputation as a liar, he told a credible story. A month before the trial, he wrote Burke saying that the prosecution might call Ted Heffner as a witness.

Jury selection in Judge Gerald Nichol's court took all of October 9, 1989. Burr looked for common sense, uncommon among most people, while Burke hoped for plain folks, more likely troubled by the missing body than by the missing woman.

The next morning, jurors toured the former Homberg home on Leslie Road to get their bearings. By midmorning, Prosecutor John Burr made his opening statement. He presented the state's version of events powerfully and clearly, reading from a narrative written by Schwaemle. The opening told the story of a "self-made man, organized and meticulous almost to a fault" with an "obsession for what some people call the finer things in life," which drove him to embezzlement, adultery, and murder. The story detailed the inconsistencies in both his behavior and his statements after the disappearance. The story did not mention Heffner.

After the noon recess, Burke gave his opening remarks.

"My grandfather used to say that talk is cheap and good whiskey costs money," he said. He claimed that the state offered only cheap talk, and no evidence to bolster its claim that his client murdered his wife. "We're talking about good whiskey in this case."

He intended to focus on the lack of physical evidence.

"They tore up his yard, they turned the house upside down. They shook it, and they could find no evidence. They kept poking at the point of least resistance," he said, referring to Sharon Jacobson, "and finally it broke."

He implied that she told investigators what they wanted to hear not the truth.

"Pay close attention to Sharon Jacobson. She is the glue that holds this case together. Without her, the case falls apart."

As if to prepare the jury for bad news, he described his client.

"He's greedy, he's a thief, he's in jail because of his stealing. But this is not a case about financial dealings. This is a murder."

For the next two days, the prosecution presented a stream of witnesses, laying out Ruth's disappearance and Gary Homberg's duplicity. The Pokrandts, Beverly DeGroot, Deputy Anderson, and Ziegler gave their stories, as did 36 witnesses by the end of the line. All friends and family testified that they had close relationships with Ruth. All added that they had not seen her after November 5, 1983. If the witness attended Art or Sally Nelson's funeral, Burr asked if they saw Ruth there. None did. Witnesses also displayed Homberg's lies before the court.

Ziegler explained Homberg's changing assessments of how much money Ruth allegedly took from the house, and where she supposedly found it. Roxanne explained Homberg's story that Ruth must have taken her missing diamond ring, diamond bracelet, and watch when she left. But a year later, Gary Homberg took the three pieces of jewelry to GLW Designs in Madison.

He sold the bracelet on consignment for $4,200, had the one-carat diamond from the ring set in a necklace, and added diamond chips to the watch. In September of 1985, he gave Ms. McCusker from Denver the necklace made from Ruth's jewelry.

In testimony before the receivership hearing Homberg stated under oath that Ruth had no expensive jewelry, and that he made no profit from selling anything that she owned. He also testified that Ruth brought nothing into their marriage of any material value. Apparently he forgot about the deed to the four-acre Leslie Road property.

His very first statements to police exposed another lie. He told Deputy Anderson and dispatcher "Buck" Christianson of the Stoughton Police that he first became concerned when Ruth failed to meet him for a lunch appointment. But Kenlynn Pokrandt said that she and Ruth had plans to take Sally Nelson to lunch and attend a church bazaar in Stoughton that Saturday. Those plans did not include Gary. Burr and Schwaemle hoped that the path of reasoning required to develop the contradictions did not prove too convoluted for jurors to navigate. Two contrary statements can't both be true, but they could both be false. Jurors had to believe Kenlynn Pokrandt and the police, and disbelieve Gary Homberg. The chain of lies began to encircle Homberg with links forged by his own greed like Scrooge's vision of Jacob Marley's ghost.

By the end of the stream of witnesses, the signs of Ruth's death and Gary's lies became clear to those assembled. The jury's charge to read the signs and weigh the clues required a further exercise in reasoning. Prosecutors hoped to lead jurors along the trail blazed by investigators. By reading the signs, Ziegler, Hendrickson, Drenkhahn, and Murphy produced their hypothesis by abduction: that Ruth Homberg died November 5, 1983. Now, prosecutors hoped that the jury did the same.

By deducing implications from the hypothesis, investigators formulated their tests. If she died November 5, then all signs of life after that would be absent. They tested their hypothesis using Mill's methods on their predictions to eliminate the possibility that Ruth still lived. If Ruth still lived, observe the social and financial signs of her life. But no such signs existed. Tests eliminated the possibility of her being alive provided that the tests considered all the correct signs of life. Presenting the result deductively carried the most logical power. If Ruth still lived, signs of her life exist. But no signs of her life exist. Therefore, by a nonampliative inference called *Modus Tollens,* Ruth did not still live. So far, so good. But as Burke said in his opening statement, it all came down to Sharon Jacobson to explain what did happen to Ruth. She took the stand on the fourth day of the trial.

Good coverage of the trial in three local papers piqued public interest in the case. The courtroom could not hold all the spectators that showed up to hear Sharon's testimony. Many who lined up early had to be turned away. She sat in the witness chair almost directly across from Gary Homberg. Not once did she look at him. He stared at her impassively, just as he had stared at other witnesses as they tearfully recalled their memories of Ruth.

Schwaemle asked the questions and Sharon delivered her answers. Sharon described her fears both of Homberg and of being charged in Ruth's murder as reasons for lies to the John Doe probe in 1986 and to investigators earlier. She lied under oath, she said, to protect herself. For the same reason in 1987, she decided to tell the whole truth in Circuit Court Branch 9 in the matter of the State of Wisconsin vs. John Doe.

She testified that she stayed in bed after her husband Rick Nordness went to work about 6:00 A.M. Saturday, November 5, 1983. She dozed off and on and answered the phone about 7:00 A.M. Her lover Gary told her to meet him at the airport in half an hour. She asked him why. He replied "Just meet me there, I will tell you when you get there." She dressed quickly, drove to the Dane County Regional Airport, saw Homberg park Ruth's Buick Century in the long-term parking area, and picked him up. The ordinarily fastidious Homberg appeared tired and disheveled as he approached her car carrying Ruth Homberg's key chain.

From the passenger seat, he told her that "Ruthie is gone," that he had killed her. She asked what had happened and he told her that after returning from the Pokrandts', he and Ruth had an argument about their affair. Ruth, he said, threatened to call Don Wahlin. Sharon said that Homberg appeared extremely concerned about something that Ruth could tell Wahlin. She assumed that it concerned their affair. She did not know that Homberg embezzled funds from Millfab. Ruth never made the call, he said. He told Sharon to drive home on the interstate highway, then he said, "Now that you know that I killed Ruthie—you picked me up. You're an accessory. If I go to jail, you go to jail." Sharon testified in effect that if looks could kill, she would have joined Ruth immediately after receiving that dubious legal advice.

When Sharon asked how he killed her and where he put the body, Homberg replied that she did not need to know, and that the police would never find a body because "there is no body." He relayed his plan to call police, report Ruth missing, and portray the grieving husband. Sharon testified that she dropped Homberg at his Leslie Road estate about 8:30 A.M. and stopped at her parents' home to have coffee with them. Later she and her parents went shopping.

Judy Schwaemle then asked questions about what Sharon had seen and what the defendant said. Sharon said that she saw Homberg with Ruth's large marquis diamond ring after November 5, 1983. Ruth, she said, always wore the ring. Homberg told her that he removed the ring and planned to let some time pass before he sold it to "get something for myself." Sharon also said that back in July of 1983, Gary Homberg told her that a divorce from Ruth would be very difficult. He said that Ruth knew a couple of ways she could "nail me to the cross and I would go to jail." In September, she said he again talked of divorce being too costly.

Schwaemle wanted this "divorce too costly" testimony to introduce Homberg's previous statements to Sharon about murdering Ruth. Jacobson told Ziegler that in September of 1983, they discussed killing Ruth. She asked Homberg how he would get rid of her body. He replied, she said, that throwing her in the furnace wouldn't work because "there would be bones." Later the same month, Sharon and Homberg discussed putting sleeping pills in Ruth's espresso to learn how much it would take to put her to sleep. In October, Homberg asked Sharon to purchase sleeping pills, which she did. She said that he told her of his plan to put Ruth to sleep with pills, then carry her to the garage, start the car, shut the door, and make it look like suicide.

Getting this information across to the jury required some tact to avoid presenting Sharon as an equally incredible monster. She did not appear totally uninvolved. Her account of Homberg's statements to her in the car could be attacked on the ground that they appeared to be totally self-serving. On November 9, 1983, Sharon did take a comforter from Homberg's bedroom to the cleaners to remove what appeared to be blood. On November 11, she did rent the carpet cleaner.

Schwaemle asked, "Did he ever talk about committing the perfect crime?"

"It kind of intrigued him. It was a challenge. He thought he could do it," she replied.

Dennis Burke exploded. At a bench conference with Judge Nichol he objected that the "perfect crime" testimony did not appear in any witness statements that he had studied, prejudicially damaged his client, and on those grounds he moved for a mistrial. After a search for the appropriate statements in the record and a lengthy delay, Judge Gerald Nichol denied the motion but instructed jurors to disregard the prosecution's last question and the witness' answer. Both disappeared from the official record. Burke now faced eradicating both these comments and the impact of Sharon's testimony from the jurors' minds.

His cross-examination probed Sharon's testimony, attempting to paint her as a liar and a greedy manipulator, and offered faint suggestions that she might be a murderer. It seemed to some that the perfect murder testimony oddly enough may have helped rather than hurt the defense had it been admitted. Under his pressure, Sharon's story held up surprisingly well. After his questions, the prosecution rested its case. Ted Heffner stayed in jail. Burke presented the defense case Friday morning.

He called eight witnesses, but offered little new evidence. They each stated that Ruth Ann Homberg felt rejected and at the end of her emotional rope. Homberg did not testify. There was not that much to present. A promised defense witness who claimed to have seen Ruth Saturday afternoon November 5, 1983, failed to appear. In contrast to the procession of 36 prosecution witnesses lasting three days, the defense case lasted just over one hour. Closing arguments began that afternoon.

Judy Schwaemle closed for the state, summarizing their version of events. Gary Homberg killed Ruth sometime around 1:00 A.M. after an argument in their bedroom about Gary's affair with Sharon. He killed her when she threatened to call Don Wahlin and expose his embezzlement. She mentioned that Ruth had left everything behind—jewelry, cosmetics, and her last paycheck.

"She took nothing with her because she didn't go anywhere," Schwaemle said. "The fact is, Ruth Homberg is never going to walk through that door."

Burke stood up and eloquently attacked the prosecution's theory while defending his client. The logic of his case seemed to be that because all murderers are bad it does not follow that all bad men are murderers. He said that Ruth "was being eaten away by unhappiness and despair." She simply had enough of Gary and left.

"I can't tell you she is alive," he said. "I can't tell you she boarded a plane and hit the friendly skies. I don't know. I can tell you it's not inconceivable."

He went on to attack Sharon Jacobson, saying that she was "a very good liar. She's like a broken field runner. She follows her interference and when she sees a hole, she goes for it."

With that plea for reasonable doubt, Burke asked the jury to find his client not guilty.

John Burr rose to present the prosecution's final rebuttal. He emphasized the proof presented by the state's witnesses and countered the defense theory. At one point, he raised his hands and said, "The oldest weapon in the world I'm holding up right now." He did not mention the injury to Homberg's finger. He also held up a photo of Ruth and said, "Justice is not a murderer who successfully disposes of a body. Justice for her, ladies and gentlemen. Please." By 4:30 P.M. the jury had the case. After about five hours, the jury returned with its verdict.

At 9:55 P.M. Friday, October 13, 1989, Judge Nichol read the verdict: guilty. He offered Homberg concurrent sentences if he revealed the body's location. Either way, Homberg faced life in prison without parole. Homberg spoke in court for the first time. In his thick German accent, he complained that jurors did not question the credibility of investigators' reports.

"What did amaze me is that I and only I was at all times wrong," Homberg said.

To jurors he appeared as removed from reality as Col. Clink speaking to a group of Hogan's Heroes, proclaiming his own perfect record of preventing prisoner escapes from Stalag 13.

Homberg showed no remorse during the trial and now showed only bitterness at the verdict and its automatic sentence.

"I haven't killed Ruthie," Homberg said. "I haven't killed anyone else, ever. How can a person show remorse that hasn't done anything wrong?"

The unintended effect of his statements had listeners wondering whom else he had killed, and where he might have hidden other bodies.

The location of Ruth's body still bothers Ziegler, Hendrickson, Burr, Schwaemle, and everyone connected with the case. It could be anywhere on 16 acres of land. One of several construction projects involving cement at Millfab or on the Leslie Road property may hold the answer. At least one juror favored the furnace. The best explanation of the case predicts that Gary Homberg knows where her body rests. The best explanation of Homberg himself predicts that he'll never come clean. Those who searched in vain must endure the fallibility attached to the final set of logical alternatives with no single option confirmed by eliminating the competition. The residue of these alternatives clinging to the edge of possibility is all that officially remains of Ruth Ann Homberg. When asked where he think Homberg hid her body, Ziegler only says, "I wish I knew."

NOTES

1. References to Aristotle may be found in Richard McKeon, *Basic Works of Aristotle,* Random House, NY, NY. 1941.
2. Frisch, Otto, *What I Remember,* Cambridge University Press, Cambridge, MA. 1979.
3. Derek Gjertsen, *Science and Philosophy, Past and Present.* Penguin Books, 1989, pp. 95–96.

I never guess. It's a shocking habit-
destructive to the logical faculty. (Holmes)

chapter five

Explanation—the Majcher Case

Natural Signs and Statistical Inferences

> All the ideas of science come to it by the way of abduction. Abduction consists in studying the facts and devising a theory to explain them. Its only justification is that if we are ever to understand things at all, it must be that way.
>
> C. S. Peirce (5.145, 1903)

Death can never be explained easily. Stunned cries questioning "Why?" echo in a world forever diminished by a new absence. Disbelief and anguish sustain grief even longer when violent death comes randomly to the innocent. With no thread of logic apparent to placate the understanding and ease the pain of survivors' ignorance, and none to lead investigators to the perpetrator, life in civil society's Leviathan becomes nasty, brutish, and short. The deceptively simple "Why?" has many dimensions. The question has no simple answer. Absurdity teaches that death can never be explained completely.

When 21-year-old Patricia Majcher drove into her downtown Hamilton, ON, apartment building's parking garage after work about 9:30 P.M., she intended to park her car, enter the apartment she shared with two of her nine sisters, and have a quick snack. After eating, she would change clothes and leave again to visit her boyfriend, sick with the flu, that she had just managed to shake.

She died before she hit the concrete just beyond the rear bumper of her Pontiac Sunbird. She lay in a widening pool of steaming blood when another returning apartment-dweller discovered her body moments later. Explaining her death proved to be no simple matter for either family or investigators.

When a natural disaster like an earthquake occurs, scientists explain the phenomenon by analyzing the contributing physical conditions. They suspect moving tectonic plates, part of a larger geological theory explaining earthquakes in general whose actions fall under certain laws of nature. They apply that theory and those laws to this particular earthquake to tell its story. When an unnatural disaster like Patti's murder occurs, investigators explain the death by recognizing evidence to identify the victim, reconstruct the crime, and apprehend the person responsible. The senses of "explaining the earthquake" and "explaining the death" differ.

Death investigators do not have an available body of generalized "death theory" to explain particular cases in this theoretical sense. They cannot deduce an explanation for Patti Majcher's death from some generalized laws of nature. Her death isn't simply another instance covered under such laws and explained by their conditions. Instead, they reason backward analytically to identify the mechanics of the crime and link them with its perpetrator. In this sense the investigator's explanation becomes an identification of reasons and causes, a non-theoretical narrative of unique, personal, particular events in a parking garage that have few significant connections with other deaths through specified laws of nature.

Some believe that death investigation is not scientific, that explanations of particular deaths lack a theoretical basis in laws of nature both characteristic of and necessary for scientific explanations. But the role of natural laws in scientific explanations does not appear to be as clear as some philosophers of science make it sound. If Peirce is right, theoretical scientists behave like death investigators in Patti's parking garage when they attempt to explain a particular natural phenomenon or to uncover nature's secret laws in the first place.

The goal of scientific explanation since Galleo has been to expose nature's general covering laws. Early natural philosophers originated theoretical science by seeking to understand the universe as a whole rather than to settle for understanding one specific event like a single earthquake or one woman's death in Hamilton, ON. During the sixth-century B.C. the ancient Greek sage Thales proposed to explain the existence of the natural world by arguing that "everything is water." Other ancients, presumably unconvinced, challenged the explanation by posing counter arguments based on their own observations. With the exchange of reasoned arguments, the discipline called philosophy, literally "the love of wisdom," took its place at the center of human rational investigation. Until 1848, when William Whewell coined the term "scientist," natural science did business under the name "natural philosophy."

Developments in mathematics also shifted objects of scientific interest from particular natural events to increasingly abstract and more general scientific laws thought to cover all similar phenomena. Unnatural events with human agency such as Patti's murder did not fall within the scope of this early interest. Early physicists in the spirit of Thales crafted complex equations, first defining laws to describe planetary motion, then laws to capture the nature of motion itself. These eviscerated mathematical abstractions became the skeleton supporting the flesh of reality dictating methods for producing "scientific explanations." To explain a particular event scientifically, merely point to the relevant scientific law, and show that the phenomenon to be explained logically follows from it.

These abstract "covering laws" describe what must result when a single causal factor operates under a single law. However the forensic scientists and death investigators working around Patti's body must explain complex phenomena in areas where many different theoretical laws and sets of causes intersect. The goal of forensic science and medicine has been less to discover general laws and more to explain particular cases. Laws that help explain complex real cases like what happened to Patti Majcher between the driver's door and rear bumper of her Pontiac Sunbird are scarce. No general law tells us how to combine the effects of separate-yet-intersecting theoretical laws to derive an explanation. The deficiency does not require anything as complex as murder to illustrate.

Explaining something as simple as cooking a potato involves many combinations of causes falling under distinct laws of nature. Any cook knows that adding salt to water decreases a potato's cooking time. Cooking a potato at a higher altitude increases the cooking time.[1] We might attempt to formulate theoretical laws such as "adding salt to water while keeping the altitude constant decreases a potato's cooking time; increasing the altitude while keeping the saline content fixed increases a potato's cooking time." But neither of these laws explains what happens when we both add salt to the water and move to higher altitude to cook the potato.

The results of cooking at a higher altitude and increasing the salt cannot be explained by appeal to either of these abstract laws. A better law may eventually be discovered, but its discovery is not needed to explain what happens when cooking a specific potato in water with a specific saline content at a specific altitude. The explanation comes first. The law may or may not follow later. Theoretical scientists presumably reason from the phenomena to the laws, not the other way around. Although the goals of the theoretical scientist and the forensic scientist differ, the logic of their method appears similar. If death investigation is judged not to be science, at least death investigators working the Patricia Majcher homicide share a common method with practicing scientists.

Theoretical scientists do not simply apply the laws of nature and reason from them in a circle to discover the laws of nature. No laws of "law discovery" exist. Neither cooks nor forensic scientists apply mythical laws of nature to specific complex cases and merely read the results. There may be no relevant laws to apply. Reasoning backward analytically requires reading natural signs, formulating tentative explanations, and methodically testing them. Such explanations often have a precarious status, especially when associated inductively with others to construct laws by enumeration, forever held hostage to the contrary instance. The doubt a contrite fallibilism supplies often runs deep whether theorizing, cooking, or investigating Patti's murder.

These tentative explanations do not become "less scientific" because they fail to invoke established laws of nature, or "more scientific" because they appeal to covering laws. The "scientific" status of an explanation is independent of its connection with laws of nature. Philosopher Nancy Cartwright clearly distinguishes covering laws from explanations. Laws invisible in Patti Majcher's parking garage appear to be equally scarce commodities in explaining the death of Cartwright's camellias:

> "Last year I planted camellias in my garden. I know that camellias like rich soil so I planted them in composted manure. On the other hand, the manure was still warm and I also know that camellia roots can't take high temperatures. So I did not know what to expect. But when many of my camellias died, despite otherwise perfect care, I knew what went wrong. The camellias died because they were planted in hot soil.
>
> This is surely the right explanation to give. Of course, I cannot be absolutely certain that this explanation is the correct one. Some other factor may have been responsible, nitrogen deficiency or some genetic defect in the plants, a factor which I didn't notice, or may not even have known to be relevant. But this uncertainty is not peculiar to cases of explanation. It is just the uncertainty that besets all of our judgments about matters of fact. We must allow for oversight; still, since I made a reasonable effort to eliminate other menaces to my camellias, we may have some confidence that this is the right explanation.
>
> So, we have an explanation for the death of my camellias. But it is not an explanation from any true covering law. There is no law that says that camellias just like mine, planted in soil which is both hot and rich, die. To the contrary, they do not all die. Some thrive; and probably those that do, do so because of the richness of the soil they are planted in. We may insist that there must be some differentiating factor which brings the case under a covering law in soil which is rich and hot, camellias of one kind die; those of another thrive. I will not deny that there may be such a covering law. I merely repeat that our ability to give this humdrum explanation precedes our knowledge of that law.
>
> "In the Day of Judgment, when all laws are known, these may suffice to explain all phenomena. Nevertheless, in the meantime we do give explanations; and it is the job of science to tell us what kinds of explanations are admissible."[2]

The admissible explanations derive from a careful reading of the signs and follow a thread of logic common to the methods of both the sciences of life and the investigations of death. Explaining Patti Majcher's death required investigators to follow a thread of logic into the scientifically uncertain, lawless world of motiveless murder. The thread first appeared in the headlights of Stephanie Freeman's Monte Carlo at 9:35 P.M. March 11, 1988.

Stephanie turned off Main Street into the Century 21 Building drive, inserted her security card to open the electric garage door, and waited. Once activated, the lumbering door took about 30 seconds to complete its noisy trip from concrete entry floor to masonry ceiling. Past the door, the entry drive leads down a slope to the first parking level with two other levels further below. The moment she stepped on the gas to drive in, her headlights lit a male form simultaneously opening the panic bar exit to the garage door's right. He bent his head forward, looking both down and away. He appeared to have something tucked under his arm. Something from the darkness surrounding the form flashed light back toward her car.

She drove toward level one while the automatic door began its methodical descent. She turned the corner and began to swing into her parking spot when she saw the body on the concrete extending from Space 40 into the driveway like a carelessly parked car. She knew Patti. She saw steam rising from around her head and thought she might be breathing. She slammed on the brakes, opened her door, and ran toward Patti. Her feet froze on the cold concrete about eight feet from the body. Her single scream echoed through the three parking levels accompanied only by the steady hum of poorly placed 8-foot fluorescent light bars.

Numb and cold despite the wool blanket over her shoulders, Stephanie Freeman held a white foam cup of bad coffee in both hands while Staff Sergeant William North of the Hamilton-Wentworth Regional Police went over her story. She began to shiver uncontrollably. She could not identify the man she saw. She did not get a good look at him. She could not identify what he carried, or what might have reflected the light toward her car. She thought that he had a medium build, wavy dark hair over his ears, and wore a blue windbreaker. North knew that she could supply no more information here in the parking garage and that she needed medical attention. Whatever else she might remember could wait for the composite artist's interview.

Freeman had called police immediately after her scream; the communications center dispatched both the Hamilton-Wentworth Regional Police and the Royal Canadian Mounties. Each arrived at the Century 21 Building parking garage before 10:00 P.M. It was a short trip for the RCMP. They had offices on the second floor. Officers canvassed the immediate area in the center of downtown Hamilton searching for the possible suspect seen by Freeman. Others secured the scene, blocking both the garage's entry and exit doors off Main Street. Alternating blue and amber lights from parked patrol cars colored the concrete ground level of the tallest building in the metropolitan area. Two lights on a tripod illuminated the panic bar door as an ident officer on his knees dusted the surface for prints. The perpetrator's likely route from body to door received a thorough examination for footprints as detectives and ident techs walked slowly beside the path holding lights at oblique angles to the dusty concrete surface.

Illuminated by Hamilton-Wentworth Police floodlights, level one revealed every oil stain, spill, pit, and pockmark previously camouflaged by shadows. Freeman's Monte Carlo sat turned toward Space 45 between the Main Street ramp down to level one and the body behind the Sunbird parked in Space 40. Space 40 abutted a broad post about two feet from the wall. The support posts, looking like white doors to nowhere, appeared in pairs every four spaces. A pool of motor oil stained the concrete between the Sunbird and the body. Often tenants backed into their parking stalls leaving oil from uncooperative crankcases in two spots on the stall's surfaces. A/Sgt. Terry Hill noticed the footwear impressions immediately.

Their clear oiled outline led from the rear of Patti's car to her body and from her body toward the Main Street pedestrian exit door. From the rear of the car, Hill tracked the prints backward through a thin layer of concrete dust along the car's side leading behind the post next to the car. There the prints appeared to multiply in number without clear direction. Prints apparently from Patti's Reeboks appeared by the two-door Sunbird's driver's door then disappeared by the rear driver's side window. The prints left in the oil that Hill followed did not come from Patti's Reeboks.

Clear footprints left at a scene may supply class characteristics to identify the type of shoe leaving the print. While valuable, given thousands of shoes sold in any given market, class characteristics alone do not help identify the perpetrator. It may help to learn that the perpetrator wore Adidas running shoes, but not much if everyone else wears them, too. The less frequently the shoe type appears in a population, the stronger the evidence. But a clear shoe print may also be as good as a fingerprint to identify a suspect. Such prints reveal unique wear patterns, defects, or damage that identify one shoe of a given type and distinguish it from all others. For fingerprints to be of value the finger making the prints must be presented for comparison. Multiple individuating footprints become useless unless the shoe can be recovered for comparison. The prints on the concrete could help convict Patti's murderer if investigators could find the shoes that had left them.

The scene contained a wealth of additional detail. A thin layer of dust from nearby road construction coated the Pontiac's sides. The rear driver's side fender showed areas wiped clear of dust. Dust appeared on the victim's blue coat and pants. Bloodstains began by the trunk of the car, creating a pattern on the concrete behind the rear bumper leading to the pool of blood surrounding the body. Blood drops and smears appeared on the victim's shoes, head, face, and hands.

Bloodstain patterns supply vital signs to reconstruct events that produced the bleeding injury. A blood drop holds together by surface tension and falls as a ball when it drips. Projected blood pumped out by the heart from a transected artery initially spurts in greater volumes, then lessens with each fading heartbeat. The patterns left by dripped, projected, wiped, or castoff blood depend on the type of surface struck and the angle of impact. A hard smooth surface like a car bumper causes round drops to break apart less. A rough porous surface like a concrete floor causes the drops to break apart more, forming a sunburst pattern.

In general, the pointed end of a stain faces the direction of travel. A blood drop striking a surface at 90 degrees appears round with more sunburst irregularities on a rougher surface, less irregularities on a smoother one. As the angle decreases from 90 degrees to 0 degrees, the drop becomes elongated. From a given impact pattern, the angle can be calculated by understanding the mathematical relationship between the stain's shape and the impact angle.

In the 1890s, Dr. Eduard Piotrowski at the Institute of Forensic Medicine of the K. K. University in Vienna, faced a difficult homicide case. To evaluate the case, he needed to understand what bloodstains could reveal about the mechanism of head injuries. To satisfy his curiosity, he began important research which he published in 1895: *On the Origin, Shape, Direction and Distribution of Bloodstains Following Head Wounds Caused by Blows.* He attempted to reproduce patterns observed at the scene experimentally in the laboratory to explain the homicidal blows.[3]

Like Piotrowski, current researchers facing difficult cases experimentally produce bloodstains in different manners striking different surfaces under different conditions, and observe the result to derive their conclusions. The result is an explanation involving many intersecting and overlapping physical laws. The process parallels explaining the results of boiling potatoes under different conditions. Laws, if they come at all, come after the explanation of results in individual cases.

Descriptions and associations of many experimental results show that the sine of blood's impact angle equals the width of the stain divided by its length. This experimentally derived association explains nothing. As a law, with general regularity, it allows shortcut predictions, but requires an explanation to justify its acceptability. The justification develops from the physical properties of blood striking various surfaces under various conditions. With the angles of several stains determined, strings run from each will intersect at the point of origin. Given multiple points of origin and moving victims, the stains must be carefully grouped and the results cautiously choreographed.

Patti's movement from the driver's side door to the concrete behind her car could be accurately reconstructed. The scene appeared rich in dripped, projected, and wiped blood striking both smooth and rough surfaces. If officers searching the immediate area found a man with blood on his face, hands, arms, legs, or feet, the stains and voids should match the patterns left at the scene if the blood came from Patti. Matching the blood on the suspect with the blood at the scene also supplied individuating evidence. If necessary, it could be typed, or even proven to be from the victim through DNA analysis.

Hill noticed immediately that the victim had suffered a vicious cutting injury to the neck. She lay on her back at the end of the bloody trail, her left leg bent at the knee and her right leg straight. She wore white socks under the spattered white Reeboks, blue slacks, a white sweater wicking crimson stains from the neck wound, and a navy blue coat. Her key ring lay to the right of her head. The pool of blood extended from the tip of her brunette ponytail, lying on the concrete perpendicular to the top of her head, to the middle of her upper arms. Dried blood wiped across her face indicated that her attacker had turned her head to the left, finally leaving the chin up and slightly left of midline. Blood on her hands inconsistent with gravity indicated that her attacker also placed them over her stomach like a funeral director positioning a corpse in a casket. Her watch, necklace, and earrings remained in place. A Band-Aid covered the tip of her left index finger.

All of the Sunbird's doors were locked. She had not left a purse in the car, and none appeared in the parking garage. Reconstruction of the attack now depended on the results of the medical examiner's autopsy, combined with the scene analysis of footprints, bloodstains, and trace evidence like dust, hairs, fibers, or any unexplained material transferred to the navy blue coat, slacks, or shoes. Scene photography, measurement, and drawing continued through the early morning hours of March 12.

By the time the medical examiner removed the body, the odor of fresh blood warmed by floodlights permeated level one. The smell hit investigators as they entered and left like overpowering fumes from a department store fragrance counter. Sergeants Williams and North with Detective Steven Hrab and A/Sgt. Hill together with some of the 11 investigators assigned to the case met the medical examiner on level one, explained the ongoing pursuit of the suspect, detailed their preliminary findings, and described the overall scene. They arranged to attend the autopsy later that Saturday. By then, they would have more information about the victim and the results of the suspect search. The team would reconstruct the attack on Patti Majcher in her own parking garage and try to make sense of the apparently pointless carnage.

Patti's building, the Century 21, has 42 floors, 45 counting the three levels of underground parking. The structure rises between two major one-way streets, Main Street, running one way east, and King Street, here running one way west. Floors 38 to 42 house various business offices. Floors 5 to 37 house adult apartments, Floor 4, the laundry, floor 3, now vacant, held a defunct health club, and Floor 2 had RCMP offices, a business office, a photography studio, the Ontario Consulate, and a lawyer's office. Street level had a restaurant, another lawyer's office, a doughnut shop, a beauty salon, a flower shop, a Social Services office, and a realty office.

The building operates with three elevators, one exclusively for the offices, one exclusively for the apartments, and a shuttle elevator operational only during business hours. Both dedicated elevators stop only on garage Level 2. The shuttle goes only to parking Level 3. The shuttle deactivates at 10:00 P.M. to prevent unauthorized entry into the parking garage from the building. Tenants and businesses enjoy reserved parking during the day, but no reserved parking remains enforced after business hours.

The Main Street garage entry door opens with security cards issued to businesses, apartment tenants, and monthly parking patrons. A second overhead door serves as the exit and opens from the inside by a pressure plate. When opened, both doors first emit two piercing clunks, then grind and shudder like a horse-driven drawbridge slowly covering a castle's moat. Measurements determined that both doors take 35 to 40 seconds to open or close, accompanied by the same tune. Both overhead doors have adjacent pedestrian exit-only doors opened from the inside by pushing a panic bar. A stair exit-only door from the first parking level to Main Street receives scant use. Whoever greeted Patti beside her car after she locked its door, had access to Parking Space 40 on Level 1 in spite of any security measures at the Century 21 Building.

Patti Majcher had moved into her apartment four months before her final trip home. Unlike some victims of violence who appear to court senseless death through reckless living, Patti clearly exemplified the pure, blameless victim. In high school she did well both academically and socially, actively participated in church work with her family, and worked at several jobs to earn extra money. In her free time she produced amateur theater with a community group, currently working on a play called *Insane Asylum*. She neither smoked nor drank, even refusing tea and coffee. She enjoyed good friends, a loving family, and dated but developed no long-term romantic relationships, some said because of her high moral standards and disinterest in premarital sex. Her current boyfriend of five months appeared to be more serious, and some talk of marriage circulated among family and friends. Everyone who knew her, from her intimates to her employers and casual acquaintances, described her as vivacious, friendly, and considerate. Hamilton-Wentworth Regional Police investigators came to picture Patti Majcher as DaVinci's *Mona Lisa* and her death as a madman's slash across the canvas. Unlike a cut painting, no artists could restore her life.

By Saturday morning, her clothing hung on hangers to air-dry at the medical examiners office. The body lay on a stainless steel table across from the neatly arranged tools of the forensic pathologist's trade. Investigators stood a little further away than usual and did not speak. The morgue humor that helps depersonalize the victim for those who deal daily with death had taken the weekend off. Those who worked this Saturday exposed themselves to a very personal mortality. Only the camera motor interrupted the silence. After photographing the stain patterns, water washed the blood down the drain to expose the wounds more clearly.

Fingernail scratches appeared like wavy railroad tracks across Patti's forehead avulsing skin from right to left. The obvious trauma localized around the neck. An incised neck wound spared only a two-inch tag of muscle and the blood vessels on the left side. Everything else, the trachea, esophagus, cricoid cartilage, right jugular vein, carotid artery, intervertebral discs between C3 and C4, and the spinal cord, had been transected. The wound on the posterior side appeared irregular on the lower margins. The only other signs of injury appeared on the hands. A clean incised wound ran across the palmar surfaces of the fingers on both hands. The pathologist dictated findings into an overhead microphone concluding what had become painfully obvious to everyone present: The otherwise healthy victim died from a homicidally inflicted incised wound to the neck. No sexual assault occurred. The officially necessary understatements threatened to reduce even the most hardened investigator to tears.

The autopsy results, together with the scene analysis, allowed investigators to reconstruct the mechanics of the attack. Footprints, bloodstains, injuries and the body's position all supplied clues. Patti drove into Space 40, parked her car, and with her purse over her shoulder, locked the door. Her attacker approached from behind the pillar beside her car, reached over her head with his left arm, grabbing her hair with his hand and scratching her forehead. He pulled her head back with his left arm and put a knife to her throat with his right. She immediately put both hands to her throat attempting to grab the knife. The murderer pushed her forward and down, brushing her against the dusty car and forcing her toward the driveway. His knife cut her carotid artery by the time she reached the rear bumper where she immediately lost consciousness. Arterial spurts struck both car and concrete, leaving a telltale pattern. He pushed her beyond Space 40 into the driveway and attempted to sever the head with a sawlike motion. The noise of the garage door signaling an incoming vehicle interrupted his mutilations. He posed the body by turning the head, bending the left leg at the knee, and placing the hands on the stomach. He fled with her purse and the murder weapon. He waited by the panic-bar exit door until the overhead door had fully opened. When Stephanie Freeman entered, he opened the door and fled into the night.

It took investigators five weeks to track at least parts of his flight. Hikers in the popular Mt. Hamilton city park found her large black shoulder bag along the Bruce Trail one April Saturday afternoon less than a mile by foot from the parking garage. The bag and its contents had survived the effects of a bonfire. No money remained in the purse, on the ground, or among the ashes. A search of the area with a metal detector failed to discover the knife. Attempts to capture footwear impressions by the fire recovered the same pattern found in the parking garage. The purse and its contents could now be analyzed for trace evidence in the lab along with the clothing and fingernail scrapings. There appeared to be no shortage of physical evidence for follow up.

Other solid leads appeared quickly. Investigators learned that, at about 10:00 P.M. Friday March 11, a man covered with blood had entered Mother's Pizza Restaurant in a strip mall across Main Street from Century 21 and asked to use the restroom. He said that he had been in a fight, had a bloody nose, and needed to clean up. No one seemed to pay much attention to him. Alcohol, fists, and Friday nights often combined to produce bloody pub patrons. Beer also had its effect on the witnesses. Descriptions varied widely.

That same day, Patti left for her first job at a home lending institution where she worked from 9:00 A.M. to 3:00 P.M. She returned to her apartment about 4:00 P.M. changed into more informal clothes, and left for her second job as a waitress at the Village Inn, a restaurant in a middle to upper middle class area populated largely by university students. She worked from 5:00 P.M. until 9:00 P.M. and collected about $50 in tips on her shift.

On the way to her car she visited with her boss for a few minutes and they both left in separate cars heading the same direction through an alley to Marion Street. Both turned left on Marlon and headed toward King. At the stoplight at Marion and King, her boss saw a small beige car with two occupants stop beside Patti's Sunbird, make an erratic turn across two lanes of traffic, and travel in her direction when she turned left on King with the green arrow. After the light changed to green in his direction, her boss drove straight, arriving home about 9:40 P.M.

Investigators reconstructed and timed her journey home. The trip from the restaurant to the Century 21 garage takes eight minutes and six seconds, leaving as she did, stopping at the light, driving to the building, entering the garage with her security card, and parking in Space 40. If she left the restaurant about 9:15 P.M., she would arrive about 9:25 P.M. If Stephanie Freeman arrived about 9:30 P.M. the attacker had about 5 minutes to produce the scene that investigators spent days processing and months analyzing for clues to his identity.

The leads disappeared more slowly than they appeared. The process of successfully eliminating unsatisfactory alternatives proceeded until nothing remained. No available alternative explained Patti's death. The reasonable alternatives disappeared first, beginning with witness conflicts over the bloody pizza patron. Many witnesses finally agreed on details that perfectly described the RCMP officer visiting the restaurant during Friday's initial canvas of the area. After considerable legwork, investigators did locate a man who broke his nose in a fight and bled profusely. They interviewed both combatants and eliminated their connection with the parking garage across the street.

The actions of the beige car became more clearly innocent. About twice an hour at the corner of Marion and King, drivers wanting to turn left onto King find themselves in the wrong lane. The only way to negotiate the turn involves executing the same maneuver seen by Patti's boss. After the reasonable exclusions, not even unreasonable possibilities or mere coincidences escaped testing, despite the time and energy consumed. A vision of the slashed beauty highly motivated everyone connected with the case.

Wild allegations of underworld hits and overheard drug deals received official and complete, although skeptical, attention from the 11 investigators still officially assigned to the case. Reports of satanic rituals based on press reports of the victim's wholesome image, and hateful graffiti attacking everything religious from Mormons to Muslims occupied detectives for weeks. Her boyfriend, banking clients and restaurant customers each passed inspection along with apartment dwellers, former members of the third-floor health club, church members, and the building's business, Social Service, and parking tenants. All turned up nothing. The play she produced also required much legwork. In what turned out to be a cruel coincidence, one of *Insane Asylum*'s characters dies by having her throat slit.

The laboratory analyses also produced no leads. Trace evidence processed from the clothing held nothing unusual. Without something for comparison, its value decreased rapidly. Nothing helpful developed from the Adidas shoe prints. Individuation proved to be impossible without a shoe for comparison. The photos and casts merely occupied storage space in the evidence locker. The autopsy indicated that the weapon could be a long, sharp possibly curved knife but otherwise suggested no additional clues. It became increasingly clear that everything so far tested against the evidence had been eliminated. Nothing remained. And most frustrating to investigators, nothing remained to be done. No suspects to pursue, no laboratory tests to conduct, no scenes to reconstruct, no witnesses to interview, and no fresh leads to follow.

The logic of elimination dictates that correct explanations remain only if included among the candidates for testing. All reasonable suspects had been eliminated. Only unreasonable suspects remained. After six months of intense investigation, the remaining scenario involved a random killer, unconnected to his victim in any way other than through the murder itself. With none of the expected connections between victim and killer and none of the usual threads of logic to follow, random homicides become the most challenging deaths to investigate. It appeared that Patti's murder occurred merely by chance. With Patti on her path and the killer on his, the paths crossed at Space 40, Century 21 parking Level 1, about 9:30 P.M. March 11, 1988. Nothing could have predicted that Patti Majcher would be his victim. But even such unpredictable chance events contain a thread of logic allowing their reconstruction.

The plentiful signs from the scene, the victim's history, and the autopsy can supply a thread to follow when examined by eyes trained to identify the logic of weakness and evil. The first attempt came through efforts to discover links between Patti's death and other murders. Data from the Canadian case entered the FBI's Violent Criminal Apprehension Program (VICAP) computer program, a tool designed to analyze specific crimes of violence and perhaps link crimes occurring in different jurisdictions.

The idea behind VICAP originated when veteran Los Angeles Police Detective Pierce Brooks worked two homicides in 1958. He thought that elements from the two scenes linked both crimes, and attempted to learn if additional crimes with similar links appeared in other jurisdictions. He knew that no national resource center collected information to help hunters of transient killers. He also knew that police agencies tend to protect their own investigations and only reluctantly share painfully derived investigative leads. Brooks went to libraries, searching every major newspaper for stories describing crimes similar to the two he investigated.

VICAP developed as an attempt to improve on Brook's search for information by easing access and improving sources. Investigative agencies themselves submitted data for the computer, unfiltered by newspaper reporters, and in return hoped for leads from its analysis and comparison with other cases. The thread of logic may appear by linking a number of cases in a bigger picture. Knife attacks on women in parking garages. Step back to see the marshlands for the malaria.

By 1984 the National Center for the Analysis of Violent Crime (NCAVC) formed within the FBI with support from the National Institute of Justice. It incorporated innovative efforts to track crimes and criminals, including efforts to analyze such crimes and supply useful information to investigative agencies. Statistical signs reporting frequencies of similar crimes do not always become clues. The FBI's Behavioral Sciences Unit assists agencies reaching dead ends in random or serial homicide investigations. The Hamilton-Wentworth Regional Police completed a VICAP data entry form. No obvious links with other crimes throughout Canada or the U.S. appeared.

But experienced eyes trained by the Behavioral Sciences Unit now analyzed the signs collected and a glimpse of evil and the thread of its logic appeared, offering clues for investigators to follow and hope from the long wait to catch Patti's killer.

Criminal investigative analysis, popularly called "profiling," attempts to solve a crime by describing the perpetrator. The signs left at the scene, on the victim, statistical signs associated through any linked cases, and the profiler's own accumulated experience, allow the logical development of suspect information. In this process of reasoning backward analytically, the logic of profiling the criminal to solve the crime parallels the logic of diagnosing the illness to formulate the treatment plan. A picture of the suspect forms in what counts as the diagnostic stage, and investigative implications leading to his apprehension, develop in the replacement for medicine's treatment phase.

Investigative signs from the crime scene such as physical evidence patterns, body position, and weapons, together with data about the victim's background, habits, age, and the autopsy results, suggest a homicide type and style. The signs might suggest some measure of risk to the offender and the intent of the attack, based on the location chosen for the crime and the time spent controlling the victim. Considering victim selection, control, and setting, the crime may then be classified as an organized, well-planned event, as a disorganized spontaneous assault, or as having elements of each. From these tentative hypotheses, a profile of the killer slowly emerges. Suggestions for investigative follow-up derived from this tentative picture become test implications. The investigative results test the picture, reenter the loop as new signs, and help modify or confirm the chain of hypotheses sketching the perpetrator.

The reasoning assumes as a theoretical premise that the way a person thinks directs that person's behavior. Analysis proceeds from the observation of signs, to abductively produced hypotheses explaining the criminal's thinking, to deductive predictions of other likely signs or behaviors. The predictions give investigators a test either to strengthen or to modify the hypothesis. This logical testing-developing loop refines the hypothetical explanation through further predictions about other behaviors that supply additional investigative leads identifying the killer.

Sherlock Holmes demonstrates the profiler's logical practice when reasoning from signs to predictions describing Watson's actions:

> Watson: ". . . But you spoke just now of observation and deduction. Surely the one to some extent implies the other."
> Holmes: "Why, hardly . . . For example, observations show me that you have been to the Wigmore Street Post Office this morning, but deduction lets me know that when there you dispatched a telegram."
> Watson: "Right! But I confess that I don't see how you arrived at it."
> Holmes: "It is simplicity itself . . . so absurdly simple, that an explanation is superfluous: and yet it may serve to define the limits of observation and of deduction. Observation tells me that you have a little reddish mold adhering to your instep. Just opposite the Wigmore Street Office they have taken up the

pavement and thrown up some earth, which lies in such a way that it is difficult to avoid treading in it on entering. The earth is of this peculiar reddish tint which is found, as far as I know, nowhere else in the neighborhood. So much is observation. The rest is deduction."
Watson: "How, then, did you deduce the telegram?"
Holmes: "Why, of course I knew that you had not written a letter, since I sat opposite to you all morning. I see also in your open desk there that you have a sheet of stamps and a thick bundle of postcards. What could you go into the post office for, then, but to send a wire? Eliminate all other factors, and the one which remains must be the truth."

Unlike a profiler's reconstruction and deductive predictions, Holmes' predictions receive Watson's immediate confirmation. Both criminal investigative analysts and the Hamilton-Wentworth Regional Police did not enjoy that luxury. Also unlike the profiler, Holmes' predictions did not develop a model of some unknown person's *modus operandi* helping to identify Watson from among the hundreds of others at the Wigmore Street Post Office sending wires. The profiler's task carries greater uncertainty and more risk for error than Holmes' reasoning because complex hypotheses develop from many interchanging signs. Deductions from these hypotheses built from observations and experience are only as good as the hypotheses themselves.

Not all the profiler's hypotheses appear to be solid. With its apparent dependence on psychological theory, profiling appears to slip from the realm of scientific explanation to the realm of unfounded speculation. There appear to be no obvious, confirmed scientific laws of human behavior forming the bedrock for psychological theory. Each armchair psychologist or psychiatrist appears to be on an equal theoretical footing without the supporting foundation of scientific law. Without appeal to supporting laws, psychological theories become unscientific guesses, mere speculations, as Chief Justice Burger put it, "claiming too much in relation to what they really understand about the human personality and human behavior." (1970)

Yet criminal investigative analysis does not depend on psychological laws, or even its generalized theories, to produce its explanations in particular cases. Such laws may not exist. Such theories may evaporate. Eventually laws may be discovered. Someday theories may be confirmed. But explaining offender characteristics in a particular crime does not depend upon either discovering laws or confirming theories any more than explaining boiling potatoes or dying camellias depends upon first identifying requisite laws of nature or first deriving a generalized theory covering all such cases. Its goal is not to model all offenders, but to identify a particular individual. Its explanations concern characteristics of one person, not the properties of a class collected by theory and governed by law. The only required law covering that individual's action is a legal prohibition of murder, not a scientific generalization of behavior.

Associations of the particular explanations taken as signs may develop generalized theories, but not the other way around. The same order of things applies to either behavior or bloodstains. If dependence on scientific laws distinguishes a scientific explanation from a nonscientific one, then few if any scientific explanations of particular phenomena exist. Science then lives in its own abstract world of disembodied generalizations, disconnected from practical concerns. Yet whatever it is, science allegedly helps make sense of the world by supporting reliable predictions and developing a systematic understanding.

With apparently unsystematic leaps from body position, victimology, and forensic details to a criminal profile predicting a murderer's physical characteristics, habits, and both pre- and postoffense behaviors, criminal investigative analysis sounds more like sorcery than science. Sorcery does not qualify as science. Magic and miracles have no method. But profiling applies Holmes' method of reasoning backward analytically from the signs to their best explanation. Like Holmes' reasoning, the profiler's method incorporates the uncertainty characteristic of any abductive hypothesis or inductive association.

Simply having a method does not make something a science. Identifying a rationally defensible method, a logic, may not make profiling a science, but it does distinguish profiling from both sorcery and psychology, from magic and mere speculation. A method does not rely on unsupported guesses.

Holmes claims that he does not guess:

> "I never guess. It is a shocking habit—destructive to the logical faculty . . . [By guessing] You do not follow my train of thought or observe the small facts [signs] upon which large inferences may depend."

His larger inferences depend upon a complicated series of abductions, what Detective Richard E. Josephs calls "bets."

Holmes bets with some risk that Watson actually entered the post office, rather than merely walking past. Watson might have entered the post office for many reasons. Holmes formulates his hypotheses and eliminates those unsuitable for the facts. Watson confirms Holmes' remaining hypothesis. Holmes follows Peirce's advice for forming the best hypotheses from the available signs (see 7.220-320). The best hypotheses appear to be the simplest and most natural, the easiest and cheapest to test, and to make sense of all the signs. Holmes' bets about Watson's actions satisfy these conditions and the remaining hypothesis that Watson dispatched a telegram passes the tests. In that sense, even before Watson's merciful confirmation, Holmes can be sure of his explanation. As the fictional inspector Hercule Poirot puts it, "To be sure means that when the right solution is reached, everything falls into place. You perceive that in no other way could things have happened."

If the Hamilton-Wentworth Police were to solve the Majcher murder, the solution had to come by this method of studying the facts and devising a theory to explain them. A cooperative Watson, ready to confirm the carefully placed bets, could supply no guarantees of success. Sometimes criminal investigative analysis only prepares the mind and teaches patience while investigators wait for chance to reenter a case. The profiles constructed in the Majcher murder made sense of the senseless by finding its thread of logic and allowing investigators to follow the thread to the killer. Patience and chance both played a role. The thread began about seven months after the crime with another reconstruction of the murder.

The mechanical reconstruction based on physical signs at the scene supplied the basis for this reconstruction from the killer's point of view. Despite the philosophical difficulties of knowing what another person feels, sometimes reasoning from given signs tells us with some admitted uncertainty how another person thinks. A man with a testicular tumor the size of a volleyball lies dead in bed with the *Bible* in one hand and a copy of Mary Baker Eddy's *Principles of Christian Science* in the other. A driver with blood alcohol of .20 merges into freeway traffic on his way home. A group of construction workers yell suggestive remarks to a woman walking by the construction site. A heroin addict takes a needle from a garbage can, fills it with the drug of choice, and injects a leg vein. Some might say that all these signs show unreasonable thinking. Maybe from some evaluative sense of "unreasonable," yes—but from the deductive point of view, not illogical. If the premises can be identified from observing the signs, the logical thread can be pursued using the well-entrenched tools of formal logic.

Deduction does not discriminate among its premises. It represents pure tolerance, a diversity-embracing logical blindness that allows anything, no matter how repugnant from another point of view, as a starting point. "All women with brunette hair deserve to die. This woman has brunette hair. Therefore, this woman deserves to die." Deduction derives logical implications from premises without regard for the premises themselves. Garbage in, garbage out. The profiler's puzzle begins reconstructing the killer's premises by sorting through the killer's garbage. The assumptions may be unreasonable, crazy, flawed, false, or just nuts, but once discovered in artifacts both present and absent at the scene, they provide deductive implications of great investigative value.

Random killers may have aberrant beliefs, but no killing is illogical from the killer's point of view. The profiler uses the scene reconstruction to help identify the killer's premises and gain insight into his personality. People serviced by tabloid journalists may have more interest in personalities than ideas. But ideas and logic take the profiler to the relevant heart of the killer's personality.

Patti's killer had no way of knowing who might enter the Century 21 parking garage, or when the door might go up or come down. Friday evening at 9:30 P.M. in a high traffic area at the heart of a city with 500,000 inhabitants does not present many opportunities for secret rituals with concealed victims. He attacked her savagely and quickly, had no conversation with her, and controlled her immediately giving her no opportunity to assert herself. He did far more than necessary to control and kill her. In less than five minutes, he attacked, killed, mutilated, posed her body where she fell in an open area, and fled with her purse. He probably intended to take her head as a souvenir, but Stephanie Freeman's car interrupted his theft.

He arrived and retreated with his knife. He sought the cover of the parking garage to stalk a defenseless victim. Patti arrived as a target of opportunity. She probably never saw his face. The killing exhibited a disorganized, irrational frenzy—anger taken out on a depersonalized victim. Nothing a stranger could do parking her car precipitated his rage. Pent-up anger and fear dominate the killer's life and motivate his fantasy of control. His fantasy forms the pattern of the crime. Its discovery among the artifacts of the investigation predicts the solution.

Brightly lit photographs cover two small tables and several bulletin boards capture the scene in sequence. The video monitor displays well-lit concrete dust moving slowly across the screen, revealing marked and measured footprints like an android video of craters on the moon. Bright red bloodstain patterns appear, leading to the red-spotted white Reeboks, first one then the other. Navy blue against concrete jolts the vision to earth as the full body appears outlined in a crimson halo, an invader as unexpected as a brightly colored peacock on the cold lunar surface. The camera operator's occasional deep breaths intrude on the silence. No one speaks either on video or in the room.

Crime scene drawings supply measured references for the color accompaniment. Three coins spread over a six-foot stretch of concrete behind the post beside Space 40, and a green jelly bean lying under the body, now receive official attention. Consensus holds that the coins either came from her purse, open during the attack, or coincidentally appear from an irrelevant source. A candidate for a signature of the "jelly bean killer," the candy assumed its proper role when hikers discovered the purse. Green jelly beans numbered among Patti's few vices.

As experienced eyes moved again among the pictures on the tables, walls, and video, every sign indicated to Dr. Della Clifford that Patti had been the killer's first victim. A first-time killer lurked in the city of Hamilton with a newly developing M.O: Experience teaches killers and investigators alike. Random killers murder to satisfy their inner fantasy. When a killing fails to satisfy, changes occur. The most drastic change involves abandoning killing altogether as a means to satisfy their need. The first experience may be so unnerving that the thought of repeating it frightens the killer from ever trying again. Less dramatic changes involve improving techniques from experience, developing better means to lure victims, and more satisfying mechanisms of control, torture, and murder. A knife attack produced too much blood. Try manual strangulation. The victim fought too hard against strangulation. Try a gun. The gun made too much noise. Try a ligature.

Killers who do their homework and graduate from this school of bloody blows choose tools of death appropriate for different victims and alternate settings. When something works well, like anyone else, they then tend to stick with it until presented with some reason to change. The better they get, the harder they become to catch, and the more difficult linking their crimes becomes. The scene by Space 40 indicated to Clifford that this killer had rookie status. Victim selection, control time, location, risk of discovery, and weapon choice all suggested and supported the hypothesis. Perhaps the killing did not supply the required satisfaction. Obviously the killer did not carefully plan this attack. He did not present himself through his work to be honor roll material.

Like demonic homework hanging from a morgue refrigerator, the work decorating Della Clifford's office revealed the killer's anger, fear, and lack of careful planning. These characteristics permeated his existence, leaving their effects on his personal, social, and emotional life. The murder did not occur in isolation from his life as a whole. Clifford thought that he probably had prior outbursts of anger and therefore probably had both a criminal and a mental health history. The killer's name would appear on mental health, prison, or police arrest records. He may have been institutionalized either in a prison or a mental hospital.

Fear also takes hold in larger areas of daily life. At Space 40, he did not attempt to control or manipulate his victim with a clever ruse or even with fear. He took no chance that the victim might gain the upper hand. Clearly, then, he thought that she might have beaten him if given the chance. He lacked confidence in himself to handle that situation and probably other situations as well. That characteristic insecurity probably extended throughout his relationships, work, and living situations. Clifford thought that the murderer was unmarried, or divorced, lived alone or with one of his parents, and was unemployed. Any employment history would show frequent job changes in menial low-paying tasks. If he dated, he dated much younger women over whom he felt superior.

As a rookie killer, newly driven by his inner needs to this method for their satisfaction, Clifford put his age at between 20 and 30. She pictured him as a short, unkempt, physically inept man. His disorganized approach, lack of foresight, and dependence on chance, both to supply a victim and to facilitate escape, led Clifford to suppose that he enjoyed a solitary existence free from the obligations that relationships impose. He shunned the responsibility of owning or maintaining a car, and depended on others for most of his needs. He walked or took public transportation. He felt cheated by people who were better off, and felt that others owed him something. He probably had a criminal history of theft and assault. She bet that he committed robberies, snatching women's purses, probably in various parking garages.

Her view of his habits placed his living situation within walking distance of the Century 21 building. It did not strike Clifford as likely that he would board a bus carrying both purse and knife while blood spotted his pants and shoes. He had some measure of street smarts. He probably roamed the sidewalks of downtown Hamilton nightly, looking for someone or something to make him feel better about himself. He probably had a history of drug or alcohol abuse. He certainly had not read Aristotle on human happiness. If he had, he had not derived any benefit. If he read at all, he probably read whatever fueled his fantasies.

As an unhappy person searching for a quick shot of self-esteem, the killer felt the insecurity characteristic of a "wimp." His associates quickly put him in that category at an early age. Della Clifford came to see the attack and murder of Patti Majcher as the killer's grab at something to put him above others and to overcome his frustrating failures. He strove to prove to the world that he wasn't a wimp, thereby merely confirming that he was nothing else. Others may have stolen old ladies purses too, but he stole a young, athletic woman's purse. Others may have killed too, but he killed a woman out in the open. Others may have killed women in the open too, but he nearly got away with a souvenir no one else would have the stomach for: her head. His actions betrayed him for the wimp he remained.

As a classic moral coward, the killer could be expected to behave predictably under certain situations. Della Clifford developed a list. When confronted in a social context threatening his self-image and deepening his sense of inferiority and humiliation before an audience, she predicted that the killer would brag about doing something that no one else in the group had the guts to do. She predicted that he would eventually brag about killing Patti. He would reveal things that only the killer could know. An equally important prediction concerned the character of those in his audience whose respect and admiration he might seek. Forever compounding bad choices, his choice of an audience to supply him respect again would underscore his defective judgment. Either directly to police or indirectly to another associate, someone would snitch for their own gain, to get back at the killer, or to satisfy their own need for superiority.

Della Clifford's analysis depended on common-sense explanations developed from the signs hung from her walls, adorning her tables, and playing on her TV screen. The signs depicted the killer's garbage, flung incautiously aside like a cigarette butt tossed in the gutter. Patti Majcher merely joined his other garbage. The uncertainty of her developed hypotheses transferred to the predictions deduced from them. She could be wrong. Available descriptions of other random homicides predicted inductively that Patti's killer was a white male. Past associations correlating the statistical majority of violent crimes as intraracial could be wrong, too. Her killer could be a black female with big feet.

But there appeared to be no reason to think so, and plenty of reason to think not. Stephanie Freeman's description of the suspect leaving the Main Street entry supported the application of the white-male-theory to this particular case. Like any learning from experience, the signs must remain the teachers. The details, not the generalizations, indicate which, if any, associations come into play. The logic of the crime built from Clifford's common sense explanations fit the FBI's predictions of postoffense behavior, allowed predictions involving the physical evidence, and gave Detectives Hrab, Michael Hanmer, and Bruce Graham plenty to do.

FBI Special Agent Gregg McCrary from NCAVC predicted that after his escape from the scene, the killer walked to his private safe haven and cleaned the blood from his body, clothing, and weapon. He kept all items, the knife for a trophy and the clothing for economic necessity. He removed Patti's money from her purse, probably the $50 she collected in tips, and then developed his plan to dispose of the purse and eliminate incriminating clues. He would pick a familiar nearby area to destroy the evidence by burning the purse. His lack of success further supported that this activity was new to him. SSA McCrary thought that the offender might come to regret the crime only out of fear of discovery, remembering the clues that he may have left behind. The fear central to his life would show to those around him.

Both profiles gave renewed significance to the physical evidence. If correct, the killer would preserve his clothing and shoes. The knife would be his trophy. Unlike souvenirs hidden in drawers or closets, trophies appear more publicly displayed. They supply opportunities for bragging and boasting obvious even to the most inebriated sports bar patron. Blood may still cling to his trophy despite his washing efforts. The shoes may reveal both their pattern and traces of oil, dust and blood even after a year or more. The clothing may help match fibers from Patti's coat, dust from the car, or hair from her head. Hrab's problem now became where to find them. The profiles supplied some clues to follow and some predictions to test. The testing and pursuit gained some direction and investigators had both something to hope for and something to do.

When searching for a perpetrator, convicted felons provide a natural class of suspects. Jurists argue that past crimes do not provide evidence for current offenses. Investigators know better. Civil libertarians cry foul when newly paroled criminals routinely appear in police lineups. Yet supposing that an unsolved violent crime connects with an available violent felon supplies the simplest and most natural hypothesis to test. Each felon faces the elimination tests supplied by the evidence developed in the case. No shortage of felons hinders investigators. Usually too many match the crime. Hamilton-Wentworth investigators looked to the local parole board for help and early on the board supplied a host of promising candidates.

A month after Patti's murder, investigators continued work with the parole board, matching the criminal histories of parolees in the area with features of Patti's murder. Stephanie Freeman's description, improved by warmth and rest, helped generate a reasonable description of the killer. The composite drawing depicted a white male, 21 to 22 years old, 5-foot-7ish, 150 pounds, thin build, with dark brown or black curly or wavy hair, and dark eyes. On March 11, 1988, he wore a blue windbreaker, dark blue jeans, and running shoes. Investigators used this composite to test all the candidates supplied by criminal justice system records. Those who passed this initial test received individual attention. The entering class numbered about 350 white males fitting the composite. All brought varying backgrounds, some violent, some not.

Most of the violent offenders whose crimes included murder could be accounted for. Most do not participate in parole, winding up in maximum-security facilities like Kingston Penitentiary and Warkworth. Their release falls under a different bureaucratic category, depending on good behavior in prison and statutory release dates. Nonviolent offenders can be released from prison after serving as little as one-sixth of their sentences under the terms of what Canadians call "day parole." Eventually such prisoners return to the community anyway. The theory behind "day parole" involves a gradual integration of the offender into the community, supplying rehabilitative treatments and supervision while the parolee works, goes to school, or undergoes other treatments. They interact with the community by day, and return to halfway houses by night. About sixty five day parolees worked, studied, and lived in day parole facilities around Hamilton.

Of the hundreds of tape-recorded interviews conducted in April of 1988, one discussion with a day parolee who passed the composite test piqued the Hamilton-Wentworth investigators' interests. Except for the violence, the parolee's MO matched the Majcher murder. The interview involved a 21-year-old first-time offender released from Collins Bay medium security federal prison to day parole at St. Leonard's House on 24 Emerald Street South in Hamilton. St. Leonard's is just six blocks from Century 21.

His criminal history sustained the interest. Between February and March of 1986, 21-year-old Daniel Elliott Pietruk robbed women at knifepoint in the Eaton's Centre parking garage in Toronto while high on cocaine and alcohol. Pietruk admitted to many more than the four robberies resulting in the four convictions moving him to Collins Bay for his first five-year prison term. His criminal history began at age 16 and his crimes escalated in severity from burglary to robbery to armed robbery. No crime-free periods existed in his young life. At Collins Bay, he entered the Brentwood program, a drug and alcohol treatment counseling service provided inside the jail by the Windsor-based Brentwood Center. The program requires that participants honestly take responsibility for their lives, develop future plans for themselves and openly communicate with others. When eligible for day parole, Pietruk found himself at St. Leonard's House in Hamilton because of their emphasis on drug and alcohol rehabilitation. He arrived Wednesday, March 9, 1988.

Many others in the 350-member class of suspects also lurked in Hamilton Friday, March 11. Each of their tape-recorded interviews had to be evaluated with attention to their criminal histories, and particular attention to the fact that a criminal history records only those acts called to official attention. Many violent offenders may hide in otherwise benign criminal records. Each required individual investigation. And plenty of officially violent offenders supplied additional legwork. Many attacked women. Many used knives. Many prowled cars in parking garages. Some did it all. Finding many offenders capable of such a murder is depressing for obvious reasons; investigative depression deepens when each potential suspect is eliminated by physical considerations of time and place. If evidence could be developed to show who murdered Patti, then personal dispositions to kill became irrelevant. But now, such dispositions were all they had to go on.

As detectives Steven Hrab, Michael Hanmer, and Bruce Graham listened again to the tape recording of Pietruk's April interview conducted by Staff Sergeant North and Sergeant Vic Rees, they heard a bizarre disjointed account from a man who claimed to have "a disease." He wanted to stay in prison, and did not like day parole. He said that his jacket had been stolen the day after the murder. When asked by Staff Sgt. North for the running shoes that he wore to be checked for blood he said, "I'd be a fool to let you have anything of mine." He added that "I have bled wearing these shoes, other people have bled, females have bled while I was wearing those shoes, females have gotten harmed while wearing them because of me."

North told Pietruk three separate times on the tape, "We know you committed this murder." Never once did Daniel Pietruk deny his guilt. He failed the most elementary interrogation test possible. When asked to stand in a lineup, he refused. When asked for samples of his hair, he also refused.

He sounded cautious and paranoid, not an unusual tune for this class of citizen to play when being interviewed by police and questioned about a murder. But his comments about the shoes, the blood, and the jacket, and his reluctance to deny guilt all became signs that Pietruk had become a person of more than casual interest among his peers.

The investigation evaluating his taped interview showed that he had a late afternoon meeting with his parole officer, Kim Gillespie of the John Howard Society, on March 11. Questioned about his actions around the time of the murder, Pietruk said that he recalled only that he probably had eaten spinach salad at Toby's Restaurant in Jackson Square Mall about one block from Century 21. He appeared to have his time accounted for. A 9:00 P.M. curfew for new St. Leonard's residents apparently put him six blocks away from the Century 21 parking garage and Patti's murder at the time of her death.

The routine check of his story recorded another investigative disappointment. As a new member of the St. Leonard's drug and alcohol treatment program, Pietruk had to sign in and out using the house logbook. The book covering March 11, 1988 could not be found. His sign-in before the 9:00 P.M. curfew could not be confirmed. While conspiratorially inclined outsiders may attach great significance to this missing book, it did not surprise Hamilton-Wentworth Investigators. Logbooks to record the activities of convicted felons tend to disappear when entrusted to their safekeeping. Nothing yet appeared to rule Pietruk out as Patti's killer. His history of knife attacks in parking garages, his location on March 11 near Century 21, and the bizarre interview ruled him in. So, Hrab noted, did his description. Daniel Pietruk had wavy black hair, dark eyes, stood about 5-foot-5, and weighed about 150 pounds. He did unusually well in the initial composite screen test.

With Delia Clifford's and Gregg McCrary's profiles now in his hands, Hrab thought that Pietruk looked even better as a suspect. But other leads outside the scope of the parole board and criminal records had interrupted the pursuit. A twisted prankster had called police two months after the murder and used a fictitious name to identify himself under his real name as the killer. He then called to confess, using his own name. With time out to sort out that mess, investigators began their in-depth look at Daniel Pietruk by February of 1989. By this time, both Pietruk and his overseers at St. Leonard's House thought that he had been eliminated as a suspect in the Majcher murder. Both were wrong. Pietruk even took steps to ensure his elimination. But the steps backfired.

Even before Staff Sergeant North first interviewed Pietruk, the agitated new St. Leonard's parolee repeatedly told house staff that on Friday, March 11, he had spent time with a woman somewhere in the Mt. Hamilton City Park off the Bruce Trail. He could not recall her name or address, he said. He added that he'd thrown her belongings over the side of the mountain, certainly not an account to ease suspicions or to deflect official focus. But it raised no red flags for St. Leonard's counselors, routinely subjected to bizarre behavior and outrageous excuses on a daily basis.

He also shared the alibi with a woman he met Sunday, March 13, at a local AA meeting. His parole required continued drug and alcohol counseling through regular AA attendance. After she befriended him March 13, Pietruk asked Ann Johnson to tell police that she spent Friday, March 11 on Mt. Hamilton with him.

After one of those AA meetings, and after his strange request, Ann Johnson and a St. Leonard's counselor sat with Pietruk at a doughnut shop drinking coffee. Pietruk showed his companions a newly obtained driver's license, and proudly displayed his picture on the plastic card as if it were a portrait painted by a venerated master. Nurturing his self-esteem, both companions complemented the newly laminated form. His dark hair, short on top and longer in back, was neatly trimmed. Dark eyebrows rested above widely spaced Mediterranean eyes on either side of a broad nose. His lips floated above a rounded chin, facing the camera without expression.

By now the police artist's composite of Patti's killer, based on Stephanie Freeman's account, graced every store, shop, and restaurant in Hamilton. A copy hung in the doughnut shop beside the pay phone near the both where the three sat with their coffee. Johnson immediately noted the similarities between the license photo and the artist's composite. After making her therapeutically supportive comments, she teased Pietruk about the similarity, saying "Jees, Danny, are you sure you didn't do that?" She continued to smile. Pietruk was not amused, said nothing, and stared at his coffee without expression.

After 10 weeks at St. Leonard's, Pietruk's counselors also had little to smile about. On Friday, May 20, Pietruk and another parolee tried to sneak a prostitute into St. Leonard's through an upstairs window. He routinely drank and used cocaine in violation of his parole, and even took an unauthorized weekend trip to Toronto. These abuses became too much even for the lenient rehabilitative focus of the day-parole program. On June 8, 1988, Daniel Pietruk awaited his return to Collins Bay in the Hamilton-Wentworth Regional Police Detention Center. His counselors still noted in their reports that Pietruk had been eliminated as a suspect in Majcher's murder. The collected reports also referred to Pietruk as a "procrastinator." It became clear to Detective Hrab that for a procrastinator, Pietruk may have accomplished even more in his 10 weeks on day parole than the official record indicated.

Hrab, Hanmer, and Graham began to learn more about Pietruk from his prison paperwork. His official problems with drugs, alcohol, and behavior first appeared to authorities when his parents divorced. He left school and worked on and off, between incarcerations, as an upholstery assistant and stockboy. After the robbery convictions, he earned the label "procrastinator" through resisting prison system efforts to help him earn day parole.

When entering Collins Bay, he admitted that he had a serious drug and alcohol problem, and needed help. He saw a psychologist and enrolled in the prison's recovery program. After his first year at Collins Bay, prison officials pressed him toward day parole, and halfway house workers recruited him like colleges hounding a high school athlete. All he had to do was formulate a plan for his life outside prison. He did nothing. He did not want to leave Collins Bay. His reluctance to formulate a plan earned him a new label. Daniel Pietruk became a "perfectionist."

The mountain of psychological reports detailing countless interviews with Pietruk gave investigators more insight into his background. One psychologist felt that he had "a sincere desire to turn his life around" but that his "somewhat adolescent behavior" prevented any hope for success. The report described Pietruk as "rather easily irritated by individuals in positions of authority" and as being "inappropriately petulant, impulsive, and slothful."

The prescription for successful treatment outside prison required "hard-line supervision from someone who did not assume a position of authority over Pietruk." That sounded to investigators like demanding a painless root canal while prohibiting an anesthetic. Yet Pietruk, without a clear plan, became a St. Leonard's resident. A report preceding him to St. Leonard's described his knifepoint robberies as having "no actual violence involved."

The purpose of such psychological reports contrasted sharply with the goal of the profiles supplied by Clifford and McCrary. The purpose of the prison reports centered on the treatment of a troubled man, plagued by drugs and acting out through his crimes. They sought to explain Pietruk's difficulties and thereby supply plausible remedies, eventually returning him to civil society, a new and healed man. The profiles had no therapeutic goals. They sought to identify the criminal by explaining the crime. Their purpose centered on helping to discover who murdered Patti Majcher, and helping to develop evidence proving his guilt. Through the profiles' insights and their own investigative work, these psychological reports supplied a decidedly nontherapeutic perspective on Pietruk for investigators Hrab, Hanmer, and Graham. He fit the profile and the crime.

They had company seeing Pietruk as a strong suspect. By the time he sat in police detention awaiting return to Collins Bay, Ann Johnson also had her suspicions. She called Crimestoppers and reported them to the police. Her story found its way into the Majcher case file, which listed Johnson as "a credible witness." Once on to him, it didn't take long to put Pietruk and the profile together. His crimes exhibited escalating violence leading to a "first-kill" scenario. He lacked careful planning, revealed both anger and fear, and had both a drug problem and a criminal conviction for knifepoint parking garage robberies of women. He worked infrequently at menial jobs. He walked, took public transportation, or depended on others like Ann Johnson to get around.

He lived six blocks from the murder scene. He arrived two days before the murder. He fit Freeman's description.

The investigation had its leading suspect. Now investigators had to discover the evidence needed to test the explanation of these connections linking Pietruk to Patti's murder. Hrab, Hanmer, and Graham began the search for evidence based on the scene work.

The jacket, shoes, and knife became obvious targets of the province-wide investigation. With a suspect, the search parameters narrowed to Hamilton, Toronto, and the Collins Bay prison area in Kingston. The profiles indicated that the killer likely kept the knife as his trophy. However a first-time killer might do anything, especially one as disorganized as Patti's murderer. Pietruk said that he ate salads at Toby's in Jackson Square Mall. Many lies are merely half-truths. Investigators revisited the mall and again questioned mall workers.

Jackson Square, near Century 21, looks like every other North American mall. Shops sell kitchen doodads, the latest clothing, music, and T-shirts. The food court supplied a standard array of tables and strategically placed trash-cans. Surrounding food venders became a permanent county fair, preserved in plastic and illuminated by neon. The natural ambiance included sporadically placed planters holding flowers. Large ash trays filled with sand looked like they were tiny-tot sandboxes. Mall workers pushing steel carts patrol the area, clearing trays left by uncooperative food court patrons, wiping tables, cleaning the ash trays, and keeping trash out of the flowers.

Ella Williams served as the mall's official naturalist, periodically weeding and feeding the flowers and plants throughout Jackson Square. She also cleaned up after the mall patrons who used nature for trash disposal or to hide items shoplifted from mall stores.

Questioned by investigators, Williams reported that near the gourmet food section of the mall, she remembered finding a long kitchen knife in a planter box. She thought the blade might have been about six or eight inches long. She put the time of its discovery sometime after March of 1988. She attached no particular significance to the find at the time, and the knife joined the other trash she routinely added to one of the many Dumpsters servicing the mall. The chance of recovering the weapon by tracing the contents of a Dumpster unloaded a year earlier held little promise. But they had a witness who would swear to finding a knife in an area connected to the murder by proximity and to Pietruk by his own admission. They still lacked the murder weapon, but the eventual fate of the knife, as well as its origin, had a plausible explanation.

The jacket became more of a problem. Hrab and Hanmer's six-month oddessy again led to Toronto armed with the equivalent of a search warrant. When Pietruk left Hamilton and St. Leonard's for Collins Bay, his mother collected his belongings and brought them to Toronto to be stored at her home. Investigators hoped to find the blue windbreaker, bloody pants, or shoes. No jacket and no pants lay among Pietruk's belongings. They did recover a pair of Adidas running shoes. The soles matched the footprints left at the scene. Traces of blood remained on the shoes. They also found evidence of his recreational reading during his stay at St. Leonard's, a copy of *The Beauty Queen Killer,* describing itself as the true story of "a six-week cross-country spree of rape, torture, and murder." Investigators now had a little more insight into the fantasy life of the person they now believed to be Patti Majcher's murderer.

That insight became as important to gather as the physical evidence. The shoes remained the only hard evidence connecting Pietruk to the murder. The case required more. Pietruk's earlier questioning, while illuminating, had not broken him down, or elicited a confession. Identifying the killer's premises became an investigative priority. Such random killers often relive their murders through watching media coverage, reading books, revisiting scenes, or even through manipulating victims' families during their trials. An old profiler's adage says that "the murder ain't over until the killer says so." To play the game and win, investigators needed to learn how to get Pietruk to say "the murder's over." This brought the focus back to Collins Bay and Pietruk's life behind the walls of reform and rehabilitation.

When recommitted to the penitentiary, Pietruk reentered the Brentwood program. With defined rules requesting honesty and established goals of self-discovery, the program appeared to draw him into a mood of open communication. Depending on how much cynicism meets the facts, either he genuinely wanted to make a change in his life, or he found a new avenue for manipulation. Maybe he experienced the unraveling fear of discovery experienced by Dostoyevsky's Raskolnikov in *Crime and Punishment.* Regardless, he approached his Brentwood group of seven other inmates and admitted to them that he killed Patricia Majcher.

The limits of his newfound honesty reached only to these peers. The director of the Brentwood program at Collins Bay learned of his admission from one of the seven unusually cooperative group members. When Hamilton-Wentworth investigators Hrab, Williams, and Hanmer learned of the admission, the inmate whose honesty reached to administrative levels received an official visit.

The inmate said that Pietruk told the group that he grabbed Majcher from behind by her hair, cut her throat, and then "damned-near cut her head off." Pietruk told the inmate that after he killed her, he ran to a nearby Mother's Restaurant saying that he had been in a fight to explain the blood on his coat and face and asking to wash-up. He said that he hid the knife in Jackson Square Mall either in a flower box or an ashtray. He remembered digging it down. He took $50 from her purse, and got rid of the black bag off the Bruce Trail.

For the investigators from the Hamilton-Wentworth Regional Police, the inmate's story sewed things up. Newspaper reports mentioned nothing about these details of the crime. Unless he helped process the scene with A/Sgt. Hill, Pietruk knew these details because he killed Patti Majcher. That remained the only plausible explanation. The stories told by the other six inmate members of his Brentwood group matched in every detail. With corroboration, even from inmates, they had enough of a case to bring an arrest warrant to Collins Bay.

On August 16, 1989, Daniel Pietruk reached his mandatory release date for the Eaton Centre robbery convictions. At 8:44 A.M., he prepared to leave Collins Bay only to meet Sergeants Hrab, Hanmer, and Graham, armed with their arrest warrant charging him with murdering Patricia Majcher. Handcuffed, he rode once again from Kingston back to Hamilton.

At the central police station's custody area, after mugshots, prints, and as part of the processing routine, he removed his jacket and shoes before entering Cell 10. Hrab and Hanmer watched as Pietruk ceremoniously untied his shoes, and placed them neatly on the floor. With a thumb and forefinger, he picked up each shoelace, gently laying it on top of the tongue, crossing one lace over the other. He positioned the shoes just so, slightly away from the wall. Pierce would say, "the sign resembles the signmaker." Hrab and Hanmer merely exchanged a suggestive glance and said nothing.

The next day Pietruk arrived at the Terminal Towers courthouse in handcuffs and leg-irons, wearing a T-shirt, jeans, and running shoes, covering his head with a denim jacket to hide his face from waiting photographers. He made a series of appearances in August and September 1989, with his attorney requesting delays so that she could study the case against him and assemble a defense. He faced a charge of second-degree murder, the crown prosecution opting not to undertake the burden of proof required to establish premeditation. He admitted to entering the Century 21 parking garage to prowl cars for valuables, and maybe to do a robbery or two, if the opportunity arose.

His attorney, fearing prejudicial publicity, successfully petitioned the court to limit press coverage of any judicial proceedings, particularly restricting publication of the evidence against her client. Publicly, investigators merely said that their 17-month investigation finally came together. Public Information Officer Staff Sergeant Gary Clue described the timing of the arrest as the culmination of painstaking legwork rather than the discovery of some new evidence, or a special favor granted by chance developments. Reminiscent of Hercule Poirot, Clue said, "I don't think anything fell out of the sky. All the pieces of the puzzle finally made a picture."

Investigators never presented the picture to any jury. After negotiations and delays, Daniel Pietruk finally pled guilty to the second-degree murder of Patricia Majcher. On October 1, 1990, he received a life sentence. Under terms of the sentence, he becomes eligible for parole in 12 years. With no trial, no witness testimony, no physical evidence presented, and no publicity, Pietruk, day-parole policy, and the difficult craft of psychological assessment flee the light of public scrutiny like a maggot into the darkness.

When prisoners leave confinement early, public policy discussions about what constitute acceptable risks to society given their release, and how to assess the degree of certainty that a prisoner has been rehabilitated, lack the details that an individual case in a specific context provides. Baseless generalizations denigrate the public discussion. No general laws appear to cover all offenders. Each offender, like each crime, has some unique element distinguishing it from any other.

Many investigators, hardened by the long grind and legwork required to track random killers, view rehabilitation and its programs skeptically. Even if Pietruk became a well-adjusted, fully functioning human being behind bars most question early release. Some question any release. Recidivism remains rampant. Even children catch on. One child on a tour of the FBI in Washington, DC, when shown photographs of their 10 most-wanted fugitives, simply asked, "Why didn't you just keep them when you took their pictures?"

According to some, like profiling and treatment, punishment and rehabilitation have different goals. Punishment may well have no deterrent effect, and may not improve a person at all. It may prove costly and inconvenient. Punishment should be unpleasant, not the equivalent of a personality makeover at a psychological spa. Any makeover must be earned and sought from the depths of an individual's soul. The seeking may be a byproduct of punishment or it may not. But no one can compel another to do the right thing or to become a good person. Force only fosters insincerity.

For whatever reason, Daniel Pietruk wanted to remain in Collins Bay. Instead he received day-parole. For whatever reason, Daniel Pietruk chose to come clean to fellow inmates, then to the sentencing judge. After 17 months of intense investigation, everything fell into place. The reconstruction of the crime was as complete as possible. In no other way could things have happened.

To explain the senseless tragedy of Patti's murder, opponents of the absurd invoke a covering law for victims implying that Patti merely happened to be at the wrong place at the wrong time. Defenders of the absurd disagree. Patti, locking her car door at Space 40 after her restaurant shift, stood exactly where she belonged. It was Daniel Pietruk who happened to be at the wrong place at the wrong time.

NOTES

1. Cartwright, Nancy. "The Truth Doesn't Explain Much." *American Philosophical Quarterly*. Vol. 17, no. 2, April 1980.
2. *Ibid*, 1980.
3. Herbert Leon McDonnel rediscovered Piotrowski's work and reestablished it among the literature about bloodstain patterns.

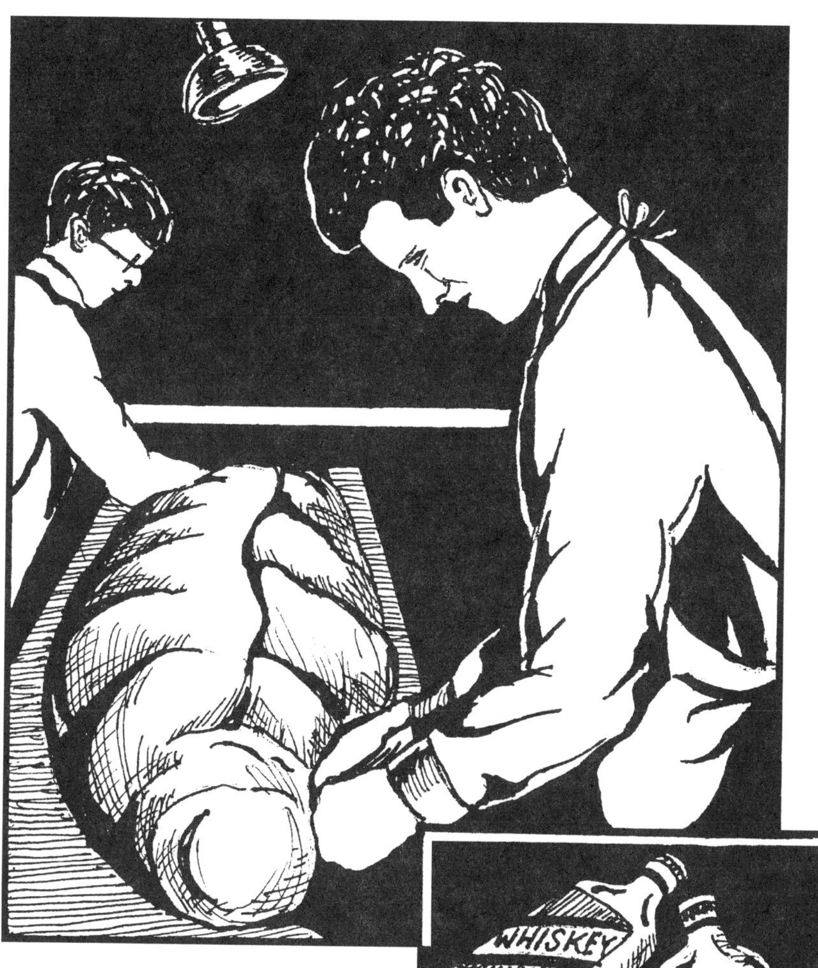

The student must be taught to observe.

chapter six

Diagnosis—The Ridgeley Case

Natural Signs and Logics of Discovery

> Never trust to general impressions . . . but concentrate upon the details.
>
> Sherlock Holmes

The microtome he'd used to slice his samples of heart muscle sat beside the pile of previously prepared slides stored in cardboard folders like a child's penny collection. Each folder had a case number with a brief description of the terminal event that turned someone's heart into a histological curiosity. Dr. Richard Thorley Shepherd, Dick Shepherd to anyone who knows him, sat on a stool peering through a Leitz microscope at a slide prepared by Dereck Tremain, histologist and laboratory director for Guy's Hospital Department of Forensic Medicine. Forensic pathologists, like their clinical counterparts, also spend considerable time peering through microscopes.

London's Guy's Hospital rises on the south side of St. Thomas Street near the London Bridge Station. The original buildings flanking two large courtyards still survive. A bronze statue of Thomas Guy stands in front of the main entrance pediment, which is supported by six Ionic columns. A modern concrete skyscraper rises above the courtyards to the southeast dwarfing the historic brick and stone structures. The Department of Forensic Medicine makes its home in an old yellow brick building to the west of the oldest structures.

Guy's buildings reflect the rich history of the distinguished physicians, professors, and students passing through the institution since 1722. Among the notables, John Keats studied medicine at Guy's. Each new medical advance discovered by professors and learned by students, like each new building, dwarfs earlier visions of grandeur. The litany of discoveries at Guy's over the last 280 years forecasts that today's latest breakthroughs will become tomorrow's artifacts of ignorance. Rudyard Kipling (1865–1936) put this plight of medical research into poetry:

"Wonderful little, when all is said,
Wonderful little our fathers knew.
Half their remedies cured you dead—
Most of their teaching was quite untrue . . ."

Guy's Hospital trained its share of clinical pathologists to examine the effects of these novel remedies, offered to patients over the centuries to save life and restore health.

Their descendents work in improved labs but continue to correlate pathological findings with clinical data from both living and dead patients to uncover signs of therapeutic success as well as indications of medical failure. In this age of daily scientific development and changing organ transplant protocols, they check the chart to learn if a slide represents life or death, a recipient or a donor, the hopeful or the hopeless.

Every death presented to a clinical pathologist in a research and teaching hospital is assumed to be natural. Even gross medical negligence may be seen as a natural complication of disease and pass undetected under the microscope's limited view. Signing death certificates for uncooperative patients refusing to respond to innovation becomes the primary responsibility of the attending physician. The clinical pathologist's focus narrows to an examination of the original diagnosis and the mechanism of death, rather than an explanation of its cause or manner. The goal remains to improve treatments and advance the clinical care of patients, to examine the latest discoveries and gauge their effects, for better or worse.

Shepherd's forensic cases, like those represented in the cardboard folders beside him, come to Guy's Hospital with sketchy, dubious, or absent clinical histories. In many cases, the identity of the decedent and the time of death also remain mysteries to be solved. He often begins with no consulting physician's diagnosis of the condition, no record documenting its etiology. Unlike his more isolated clinical counterparts, Shepherd must present his discoveries in open court before a critical public.

When testifying at a London coroner's inquest, he gives evidence to guide the coroner's ruling on the manner of death in cases requiring a public hearing under the uniquely British Coroner's Court System. Sudden, unexpected, or traumatic deaths fill coroners' courts' dockets. Shepherd's diagnoses of these deaths, although offered in court, do serve the living.

Discovering unsafe products and practices, exposing congenital conditions or family predispositions, or alerting the public to present dangers—whether they be infectious or criminal—all inform the living to improve health and safety. Like his clinical counterparts, Shepherd remains a physician.

The problem of producing and supporting a diagnosis in a sudden, unexpected death brings him to the Leitz and the medical research lab with Tremain. There he joins his clinical colleagues, attempting to improve the chances for accurate medical diagnosis, and explain the mysterious deaths defining his practice as a forensic pathologist. Explaining the sudden collapse and death of people in apparent good health with no relevant medical histories is one of forensic medicine's greatest challenges.

When someone in apparent good health suddenly drops dead, a preliminary diagnosis may postulate some cardiac problem resulting in a heart attack called a myocardial infarct, or simply an "MI." Often autopsy findings confirm the diagnosis, and the evidence supports classifying the manner of death as natural. Significant atherosclerosis of the coronary arteries, hypertrophy, or thickening, of the left ventricular wall, a generally enlarged heart, or scar tissue from previous infarcts all count in favor of the diagnosis. But with minimal findings in these areas, and no necrotic tissue from previous infarcts visible under the microscope, both supporting and modifying the original diagnosis becomes more difficult.

When properly stained, dead (necrotic) areas of heart muscle, damaged during prior heart attacks, appear under the microscope as black islands in a red sea of normal tissue. When the first and only heart attack proves fatal, no necrotic tissue appears. In a sense, all the tissue dies at the same time leaving no signs to distinguish areas of infarct necrosis from areas of otherwise healthy heart muscle.

Each cardboard folder next to the microscope contains heart tissues from sudden deaths with no microscopic evidence of prior infarct, and with MI as the best remaining explanation after Shepherd's investigation ruled out the competing alternatives. He and Tremain developed a staining technique to identify areas of infarct to confirm the diagnosis of a single fatal MI with no prior history. The colored signs staining the areas of tissue that had been invisible to the older technique pointed in a new direction.

Through the Leitz microscope, known areas of infarct appear dark purple, or dark blue. Normal cells stain magenta and collagen becomes green. As Shepherd places the last slide from the cardboard folders on the microscope's stage, he sees areas of dark purple revealing previously invisible areas of fatal infarct. Supporting or refuting a diagnosis of a single fatal MI now appears to be possible histologically, at least with tissues taken from the recently dead.

The Department of Forensic Medicine at Guy's Hospital had supplied another research step forward in the ancient effort to explain a sudden death scientifically and to improve the understanding of those still alive. Now the technique would face further animal and human testing on many fronts in Guy's medical school and beyond.

The days of an isolated intellect pursuing solitary research are long gone. Since its official establishment in 1948, The Department of Forensic Medicine—with its focus on mystery, crime, and death—appeared to rest uneasily in a research and teaching hospital, with its focus since 1722 firmly fixed on understanding, healing, and life. But mystery and understanding, crime and healing, death and life become indistinguishably intertwined. As C. S. Peirce put it, "Speaking in a broad, rough way, it may be said that the sciences have grown out of the useful arts, or out of arts supposed to be useful." (MS 1.226) The department of forensic medicine in the yellow-brick building at Guy's testifies to this interrelation of science and the useful arts, a department where practical problems often occasioned scientific discovery.

Problems of failed treatments and diagnostic uncertainty emerged in the eighteenth century's age of plagues and poisons, inflicting growing pains on the useful art of medicine that stimulated scientific progress, and occasioned further discovery. When a physician's previously successful treatments had little or no practical effect on new patients with similar symptoms, science entered to help discover why. Both physicians and researchers sought explanations. Perhaps their teachings or their techniques needed modification. Or perhaps their tools of diagnosis required sharpening. Like sand irritating an oyster to produce a pearl, crime entered the clinical hospital setting and stimulated new layers of scientific research. The research leads to new discoveries to support more accurate diagnoses.

Many deaths that had routinely passed as natural from bubonic plague turned out to be homicides caused by such poisons as arsenic or mercury. The initially obvious and familiar symptoms of vomiting and abdominal pain offered identical support for competing diagnoses of plague or poison. Tests initially performed to confirm a diagnosis of each alternative eventually discovered additional signs which, when added to the original symptoms, helped to justify the development of one explanation and the abandonment of another. Plague deaths and heavy metal poisonings turned out to present distinct signs, unique to each process, for the observant physician to detect. These signs appeared macroscopically, through observing the activities and demeanor of the afflicted, or microscopically, through examining the characteristics of stomach contents, blood, and tissue.

The discovery and observation of these increasingly detailed and specialized signs, recognized through solutions to such practical problems as distinguishing unfortunate disease from deliberate poison, form the heart of medical diagnosis. Following the logic of this diagnostic process opens one window to the mystery of scientific discovery.

In the eighteenth century, Scottish philosopher David Hume enshrined experience as the foundation of both science and discovery when he said that experience creates habits of mind through repetitious associations that we come to trust. Instinct for seeing a solution or making a discovery becomes akin to creative intuition, and develops only through repetitive individual experience. Solutions, once derived, can be tested by logical methods, but the original derivation depends on mysterious extralogical creative powers fueled by associated experience.

C. S. Peirce did not accept an account of science or scientific discovery emphasizing past experience alone. He recognized that we often correctly distrust our experience and must decide when it applies and when it does not. New experiences enter as poisons among plagues to confuse and confound. As Peirce says, "The medical men . . . deserve special mention for the reason that they have had since Galen a logical tradition of their own." Diagnosis must somehow distinguish among all the contingencies that occurred before some defect or disease took hold in order to isolate its likely cause. Peirce continues, "working against reasoning '*post hoc, ergo, propter hoc*' . . . (literally, after that, therefore, because of that) we must first decide for what character we propose to examine the sample (of potential causes), and only after that decision, examine the sample." (MS1.95–97; see MS696)

Performing tests to develop more detailed signs of disease or poison depends on first recognizing both the need for the distinction and the details suggesting the causal relevance of those tests. The slides of heart tissue stained by Tremain and examined by Shepherd did not collect in their cardboard folders by accident. They earned their place under the Leitz through a series of earlier abductive decisions founded on careful observations.

Developing the skill of observation required to recognize relevant signs and distinguish them from unrelated coincidences underlies much of the teaching in medical schools such as Guy's. According to Dr. Joseph Bell of Edinburgh, the logic of diagnosis depends on the careful observation of trifles:

> "Try to learn the features of a disease or injury . . . as precisely as you know the features, the gait, the tricks of manner of your most intimate friend. Him, even in a crowd, you can recognize at once. It may be a crowd of men dressed all alike, and each having his full complement of eyes, nose, hair and limbs. In every essential they resemble one another; only in trifles do they differ—and yet, by knowing these trifles well, you make your recognition or your diagnosis with ease. . . . The great broad characteristics which at a glance can be recognized as indicative of heart disease or consumption, chronic drunkenness or long-continued loss of blood, are the common property of the veriest tyro in medicine, while to masters of their art there are myriads of signs eloquent and instructive, but which need the educated eye to discover. . . . The importance of the infinitely little is incalculable."[1]

Similarities between the methods of medical diagnosis and the reasoned solution of criminal mysteries, chronicled by Sir Arthur Conan Doyle, soon cemented departments of forensic medicine to medical schools, both on the continent and in the U.K. Science felt the impact of practical concerns and public policy issues at the same time that medical science began to affect the resolution of legal matters.

Investigations into deaths that happened to have judicial implications gained additional medical interest and formal research in forensic medicine assumed its proper position in prestigious English research and teaching hospitals like Guy's. Shepherd took his place among the distinguished company of former Home Office, Metropolitan Police, and Crown Coroner's consulting forensic pathologists such as Sir Bernard Spillsburg and Professor Keith Simpson.

Unlike their clinical counterparts, such figures gained both popular and medical recognition for their abilities to read the signs and diagnose a medical mystery, discovering its solution. Their diagnoses in high profile death cases become front-page news. Spillsburg entered the medico-legal limelight in 1918 for his part in solving the murder of Cora Crippen. In the spirit of *America's Most Wanted,* the public followed Scotland Yard Chief Inspector Walter Dew's pursuit of her killer. Hawley Harvey Crippen, and his lover, Ethyl DeNuve, crossed the Atlantic from England to America on the luxury liner *Montrose* followed by Dew. The public eavesdropped via a new device called "the wireless."

At the equally well-publicized trial, Spillsburg identified Crippen's murdered wife Cora from a piece of abdominal tissue recovered from a shallow grave in Crippen's basement. The remains, which showed one of Cora's old surgical scars, were laced with hyoscine. Crippen, convicted of the killing, eventually hanged for his wife's murder. Spillsbury's testimony in the Crippen case brought the diagnostic powers of forensic medicine to popular attention in the English-speaking world, a position already enjoyed by the discipline in both Germany and France, as well as centuries earlier in China.

The popular fascination with the medical diagnosis of maniacal murder continued in England through the widely publicized cases of Professor Keith Simpson. In 1949, Simpson identified Mrs. Durand-Deacon, a stout 69-year-old widow, who was shot, then dissolved in a sulfuric acid bath by John George Haigh. Although admitting guilt, Haigh boasted that he could not be convicted of murder because prosecutors could produce no body.

Forensic medicine again rose to the challenge and captured public attention when Simpson identified Mrs. Durand-Deacon from an undissolved gallstone, protected from the acid by a layer of fat, and the remains of her dentures, impervious to the effects of the acid. The testimony occasioned much publicly discussed medical research on the effects of sulfuric acid on human bone, tissue, and fat, as well as on synthetic denture materials. The problem of scientific victim identification thereby occupied a previously empty slot in the English-speaking public's curiosity.

Shepherd, like Simpson who also was a member of the department of forensic medicine at Guy's, has had his share of front-page cases. The identification of victims in a military air crash in Newfoundland, and the bombing of Pan Am Flight 103 over Lockerbee, Scotland, became high-profile cases. All forensic pathologists at one time or another face investigations capturing the public's fascination with personalities, or their appetite for the garish, ghoulish, and gruesome. Their diagnoses made, tested, and presented, both physician and medical opinion then weather cross-examination in both a court of law and the court of public opinion.

Medical investigators like Shepherd apply the same methods to produce and defend their medical diagnoses in these high-profile cases as they apply to any less publicized death. Method, not personality, localizes their professional interest in discovery. Most often, diagnoses of death's cause and manner neither visit court nor entertain the public. Death usually carries a more private pain that leaves public opinion far behind.

A forensic pathologist's medical opinion advances no cures. Death has no cure. Hilaire Belloc (1870–1953) wrote cynically about the physician's curative prowess in the face of death:

"... Physicians of the utmost fame
Were called at once; but when they came
They answered, as they took their fees,
'There is no cure for this disease'..."

Only puzzles about its significance, meaning, cause, manner, and mechanism float in death's wake. In most commonly encountered cases, the death investigator's discoveries addressing these puzzles appear neither to interest nor to enlighten the living.

Forensic pathologists offer their explanations and opinions as discoveries based on diagnoses of their patient's own peculiar symptoms, the signs left at the scene of death, any available medical or social history, and the post mortem examination of whatever remains of the decedent. No treatments offered. None accepted. Sometimes confirming research bolsters difficult diagnoses, a welcome ally in a hostile world of uncertain expert opinion, unscientific public pressures, or solitary decision.

The dark purple under the Leitz lens occasioned a modest hope among the staff of Guy's department of forensic medicine. The Rhodamine B and light green method might open another avenue of confirmation for a well-traveled diagnosis, usually offered in cases unlikely to make the headlines, but more likely to be of practical value to grieving families and to other researchers developing preventative medical treatments. A new sign had been uncovered. The logic described by Peirce and exercised by Bell had another instance.

The test's basis rested in recognizing the relevance of certain biochemical changes in the heart muscle during an infarct that reacted to the new staining technique differently than the surrounding tissue unaffected by the "heart attack." The technique, if sound, could help to identify the cardiac role in a death, whether the manner of death turned out to be natural, or otherwise.

The importance of discovering a death's cause often depends on the larger context raising questions about its manner. Many low-profile deaths in questionable contexts prove to be the most interesting from the medical point of view. In such cases, the forensic pathologist's diagnosis of the death's cause and evidence developed to explain its manner may challenge a lay view of the nonmedical signs taken by themselves. Signs unavailable to the best observers require an educated eye for discovery.

The more confirmations available to the pathologist, the better the chance of eliminating incorrect diagnoses in favor of the remaining best explanation. In medicine, tests to diagnose and confirm do not easily separate. Their mutual dependence on the recognition of apparent trifles relates them like sound to music.

For the forensic pathologist on call, the sound of the telephone has no soothing musical effect. A persistent double-ring supplied by the British phone system interrupted Shepherd at home in Sutton after another long day in London. The call from Police Constable Clay of the Slough Branch of the Metropolitan Police cautiously and precisely reported that "the apparently lifeless body of a man has been found in a flat."

PC Clay pretended no medical qualifications. Death's mystery, if it was a death, remained for Shephered to unravel. Some long days have no end. Shepherd's life of research, teaching, and his role as consulting pathologist for the Metropolitan Police took him to Slough. He left home behind to make his observations and perhaps, eventually, to put another murder under his microscope.

In Slough, his headlights illuminated four police cars, two lighting trucks, and several local fire district officers who gathered around a two-story flat-roof stucco building. Two uniformed bobbies waited at the curb, directed him to park, and opened his door. Detective Superintendent John Childerley walked slowly toward him as he removed his medical bag, camera, and video equipment from the car. In the age of modern medicine, Dr. Shepherd remained one of the few physicians who still made house calls. Members of the Department of Forensic Medicine continue an ancient tradition with little company from their contemporaries.

Childerley, taking Shepherd's video equipment under his umbrella, supplied an official account of events up to his arrival. The occupant of Flat 2B, one Charles Ridgeley, age 62 years, had not been seen by his neighbors since before the Christmas holiday. According to each of the other residents of the four-plex dwelling, Ridgeley lived alone in 28 and, except for sporadic visitors, kept largely to himself. Two days ago about midnight, an angry commotion awakened the tenants of Flat 2A, a Mr. and Mrs. Dillington, who heard pounding on the door of 2B, cursing, and loud demands for immediate entry. After a time, the two men beating on the door had left in disgust.

The next day on the way to the market, Mrs. Dillington had met Mrs. Edna Colson, who lives in 1B with her husband Steven. As they stood on the corner waiting for the bus, both women discussed their displeasure with a foul smell lingering around the building and resolved to lodge a complaint with the building's resident manager. After several phone calls, the manager, an occupant of Flat 1A, finally agreed to track down the pungent and disquieting odor. According to both women, the task seemed to be more trouble for Mr. Clyde Saunder than enduring the situation, or moving one's nose to the pub down the street.

Childerley continued recounting events as both he and Shepherd walked slowly toward the building from the curb, sharing the umbrella. Saunder, he said, called police because after cleaning the hallways between flats on each level, emptying and cleaning the dustbins, and washing the sidewalks, he noticed that the persistent smell appeared to be coming from 2B. He thought that Ridgeley had left for the Christmas holiday to visit relatives in Liverpool, and did not want to use his passkey to enter the flat without official company. If the sewer had backed up in 2B, he said, he wanted to fix the problem before Ridgeley's return. He did not want to be accused of removing Ridgeley's personal property from the flat.

Childerley explained that Saunder's concern apparently rested with his multiple convictions for burglary and two counts of armed robbery, for which he'd done time at Broadmore. Ridgeley also had his own reputation. As an accomplished burglar himself, he'd done time for both his thievery and for receiving stolen goods. According to police informants, Ridgeley now did business as a local fence for merchandise secured by younger aspirants to his former trade. Saunder and Ridgeley did time together in Broadmore. If there really is no honor among thieves, then at least fear motivates the exercise of caution.

When Clay arrived late in the day, he accompanied Saunder to 2B. Clay entered with the passkey, and Saunder remained outside in the open-air hallway. The light switch failed to illuminate the darkened flat. The temperature in the entry equaled the 40-degree Fahrenheit temperature outside. From his vantage point at the front door, Clay saw blood drips going both into the kitchen and into the lounge behind a closed door. He used his flashlight to work his way among the clothing, kitchen implements, bedding, and newspapers scattered on the floor. His efforts to open the lounge door met with resistance. He forced the door open enough to gain entry, and saw Ridgeley on the floor, head against the door, a former career criminal now functioning as an inelegant doorstop. He saw more blood drips, and a knife on the floor near the body. Ridgeley lay in a sticky brown pool. Blood appeared by the knife. Overcome by the odor, he unlocked and opened the sliding glass window to ventilate the room. He backtracked, secured the scene, and reported his discovery.

Shepherd and Childerley walked alongside the building, and up the back stairway leading to both 2A and 2B. Shepherd noticed on his way up that the first-floor locking mailbox labeled "2B" appeared to be full. Saunder, looking like a ferret with a cigarette, stood with Clay and several other officers just past the open doorway leading into Ridgeley's flat. One of the officers standing with Saunder reported that, because Ridgeley was delinquent in payment, the electric power to 2B had been cut off by the utility at the end of December, which meant that the flat had been without power for the better part of a month. The police remained outside. In Shepherd's experience, that remained as reliable a sign of the body's advanced state of decay as the aroma intruding on the most oblivious observer. He opened his case, drew on a pair of surgical gloves, picked up his flashlight, and entered 2B.

The two lighting trucks stationed outside the building directed their powerful lights into the flat through its sliding glass windows. The lights mounted on lifts raised by cranes from the vehicles below shined through the kitchen windows to the south, and the lounge or living room windows to the east. Areas of darkness appeared at odd angles to the small windows despite wattage sufficient to illuminate an entire outdoor playfield. The flat looked like the inside of a shipwreck illuminated in its watery grave miles beneath the surface. Shepherd's flashlight explored the areas of darkness as he slowly made his way past the entry and began to examine each area of the flat. The truck's engines supplied a steady accompaniment for his movements.

What appeared to be blood dripped along the hallway, past the entry from the kitchen to the lounge. The secondary spatter indicated at least two trails leading in opposite directions, one that led from the kitchen to the lounge, and another that returned to the kitchen. One of the trails led into the bathroom through the door between the other two rooms.

Each room appeared more disorderly than the last. The kitchen cupboards remained open, their contents haphazardly strewn over counters, table, and floor. Two chairs, companions to the chrome and linoleum table, lay overturned in the middle of the room. Blood first appeared beneath the chrome border circling the table, forming sunburst drips on the floor. The sink contained both the indistinguishable remains of uneaten meals as well as the unwashed implements of their creation and consumption. No refrigerator occupied the area. Blood led from the middle of the kitchen floor toward the entry and into the bathroom.

The flashlight shone into a layer of opaque water in a once-white tub, and a padded chair sat in the middle of the floor between the tub and the sink. Water dripped from the sink tap, staining the bowl rust-brown beneath the spigot. What looked like underwear floated in the tub like soggy corn flakes in rancid milk. The water level appeared to have dropped about an inch since the wash had entered its indefinite soak-cycle. Blood drips collected beneath the chair's edge, then returned to the hallway, leading toward the half-open lounge door.

The lounge served both as the flat's living room and bedroom. If an unreported tornado had ever touched down just outside London, it had struck Ridgeley's lounge. Clothing, bedding, and back issues of the daily newspaper mixed with every imaginable accoutrement of daily life. The debris occupied unlikely positions under windowsills, over furniture, and on the floor. Shepherd edged past Ridgeley who now lay on his right side with his left hand suspended in midair, a sign of his trip from stomach to side when Clay forced the door open. The second truck's powerful lights starkly illuminated the room's contents. To the sound of the stereo diesel engines powering the lights, Shepherd knelt to examine the area around the body, and then the body itself.

Ridgeley lay in a foul pool of sticky fluid, the byproduct of putrefaction and autolysis, natural processes that account for animal decomposition. Putrefaction begins when circulation ceases. Gastrointestinal bacteria and other microscopic residents of the body use the newly depressurized veins and arteries as escape tunnels, visiting tissues along their routes like rats visiting homes through a neighborhood sewer pipe. Microbial action produces the methane gases and fermentation associated with the bloating and greenish discoloration accompanying decomposition. When the fermentation pressures increase, fluids purge from body openings, usually the mouth, nose, and anus, following the path of least resistance toward the outside world.

Unlike putrefaction, autolysis begins as a chemical process, a breakdown of cells due to the action of intracellular enzymes. Organs with the most enzymes autolyze fastest, those with the least autolyze more slowly. In advanced decomposition resulting in skeletonization, often only the prostate in the male and the uterus in the female remain as identifiable organs. Each organ boasts the least circulation and lowest enzymes levels to explain its longer resistance to the effects of both processes.

Both putrefaction and autolysis depend on environmental factors and individual circumstances as they follow their course in decomposition. Cold ambient temperatures slow or even halt both components of decomposition, but other factors also play a significant role. A warm environment, heavy clothing, obesity, or infections accelerate the processes, while tight clothing or a metal, stone, or concrete surface that conducts heat away from the body retards decomposition. Medications such as antibiotics also have a role to play. The fluid surrounding Ridgeley, and the general ambiance hanging over the Slough four-plex, resulted from the putrefactive process associated with his decomposition.

Just beside the door, in front of the shrinking putrefactive pool, Shepherd saw what appeared to be bits of partly digested food, deposited as antemortem emesis. Ridgeley had vomited before he died. Shepherd also saw two empty whiskey bottles lying on their sides. About five feet behind both the bottles and the body, a knife lay over some newspapers. Several coins joined the knife. Shepherd noted that the knife appeared to be a bread knife, about 12 inches long with a red wooden handle about four inches long and a saw-tooth blade eight inches long. Drops of blood added a reddish discoloration to parts of the blade and to the newsprint underneath. By the adjacent couch, evidently serving as Ridgeley's bed, several plates with unidentifiable remains coating their surfaces lay under more newspapers. Apparently the tornado's path led from the kitchen. The blood trail from the plates to the knife disappeared at the edge of the fluid now serving as Ridgeley's mattress.

The body wore a short-sleeved undershirt, slacks, and socks. The face remained indistinguishable, contorted by the force of gravity pressing skin against wood. The right cheek assumed the flat contour of the floor from its prolonged contact during decomposition. Black-tinged leathery skin covered a thin build, a sign that the body had undergone some mummification.

Mummification usually occurs in dry climates when the body dehydrates rapidly. Other factors may combine with dehydration to produce the effect. Periods of dry heat followed by cooling after a loss of fluids could result in early mummification of fingers, face, and extremities. Ridgeley's hands, head, and arms appeared dry and brown. Shepherd could see no obvious signs of injury, but that assessment would have to wait for better viewing conditions at the nearby Wexham Park Hospital morgue.

As he pushed the arm to roll the body further toward its back, a mass of white maggots raced from the light toward the cover of darkness within the body. The common house fly, *calliphoridae,* may supply valuable information about time of death. Such insects often become the first visitors, immediately laying eggs in the warm moist areas of the body such as the eyes, nose, mouth or anus, sometimes even before death. They also favor areas of injury such as stab wounds, or other sites of trauma.

As the eggs hatch, they form maggots that eventually pupate, encasing themselves in temporary homes where they grow into flies. When they hatch, they leave the pupae cases behind like abandoned trailers, and move on to lay their own eggs, beginning the cycle anew. Finding signs of the larval stage, maggot stage, pupae stage, or empty pupae cases can help investigators determine how long the body has been a host to its unwelcome visitors.

Forensic entomologists interpret such signs with their specialized knowledge of insects and their life cycles in specific regions. The time intervals between each development stage, called an instar, the environmental conditions, and the season each play a role in any post mortem interval estimate. Both signs left by decomposition and signs of insect activity often interrelate when both resource-hungry processes feed each other's needs like eager sadists beating willing masochists.

The maggot masses, racing to consume the scarce resources supplied by the host, generate high temperatures that make their life cycle relatively independent of ambient temperature. The maggot mass expands and contracts to cool or warm its own environment, and this warming affects temperature-dependent putrefactive and autolytic processes. Thus, decomposition may proceed in a relatively cool environment with the presence of maggots to keep the body's temperature elevated. Other areas of the body, more dependent on ambient conditions, may decompose differently given additional factors. While completing the body's tip to its back, Shepherd felt its warmth in the cool room as the maggots fled from his view.

Beneath the body, several pupae cases appeared. More mixed among the tornado's distribution of cloth and paper near the corpse. With the screenless window wide open to help dissipate the stench of death, any flies had long since made their escape. Shepherd walked back to the hallway, retrieved his video equipment and camera, and photographed the contents of 2B. He collected a sample of the pupae cases, and brought in a large plastic sheet to wrap the body.

Aided by two reluctant police constables on either end of the plastic package, Ridgeley left 2B for the last time, entered a police wagon, and rode to Wexham Hospital for his autopsy.

As a consulting pathologist for the Metropolitan Police, Shepherd did autopsies both at Guy's and elsewhere. Depending upon the coroner's district, he examined most bodies either in a central autopsy facility or in a hospital under contract with the coroner serving the area of the body's discovery. When he arrived at Wexham Hospital's morgue, the plastic package lay on a stainless steel table awaiting his attentions. Childerley, the Coroner's investigator, crime scene officers, and several other police officers each stood behind the body. The evidence containers, cameras, and autopsy staff awaited Shepherd's instructions. Childerley reported to Shepherd the results of his subsequent investigation, conducted after their last meeting under the umbrella, as both dressed in surgical scrubs.

He said that Ridgeley had visited his regular local pub December 22, and had drunk more than usual to celebrate Christmas with his cronies. He often had difficulty walking and keeping his balance, especially after a long night of drinking, so two friends loaded him in a cab, paid his fare, and directed the driver to the nearby flat. Earlier in the evening, Ridgeley told them that he planned to visit his family in Liverpool over the Christmas holiday, so no one missed him when he failed to show up at the regular times for his usual drinks. Everyone thought that he was on his trip.

Childerley contacted the cab company and managed to identify the driver who delivered Ridgeley to his flat. The cabby said that he helped Ridgeley find his keys and open the locked door to 2B about midnight. He watched him stagger in and heard the door lock behind him. That's the last anyone saw of Ridgeley, described by his friends as about 5-foot-11 and 62 years old.

None of Ridgeley's friends could identify him now. As he opened the plastic sheet, Shepherd noted that the body's appearance had not improved over the Christmas holiday. However, identification did not depend on visual features. The body on the plastic also measured 5-foot-11. The coroner's investigator held Ridgeley's criminal record, including his fingerprint cards. Shepherd injected a small amount of embalming fluid under the epidermis of the wizened right thumb, returning the wrinkled tissue to a smoother form to help reconstitute the fingerprint pattern. He linked the newly smoothed thumb, and pressed clear tape over the surface, sticking the print transferred on the tape face up under a clear plastic sheet. The thumbprint from the body matched the thumbprint from the criminal history. Now both suggestive circumstances and confirming fingerprints identified the body as Charles Ridgeley, age 62 years.

Shepherd removed the plastic shroud and examined the body under a bright surgical light hung from an overhead arm. More maggots scurried for cover. He saw dried blood present around the forehead, right eye and nose, but the leathery skin presented no obvious injuries to explain the blood's source. Extensive maggot infestation appeared around the mouth, face and neck with apparent post mortem maggot injury to the front of the neck. After close examination, the attendant removed the clothing with a scissors. No other signs of trauma appeared on the now-naked body. Extensive early decomposition, partial liquefaction, and some mummification each contributed to the strong odor overtaking everyone in the room except Ridgeley himself.

Opening the body did little to improve the room's overpowering atmosphere. Shepherd removed and examined each of the body's organs in turn. After reflecting the scalp, he saw a 4.5 cm laceration of the right parietal region, passing 2 cm lateral to the midline toward the side of the skull. This, he thought, supplied the source for the blood observed earlier. The skull had no fractures, and the brain, while softened by decomposition, showed no signs of either intra- or extra-cerebral bleeding.

Other organs revealed few surprises. The mouth contained fluids of decomposition and many maggots, but no injury to the lips appeared. The pharynx, larynx and trachea remained clear with no signs of injury to surrounding tissues. The lungs showed overall edema, but the pleural spaces were clear. The stomach contained a little fluid from the autolytic mucosa, but remained otherwise empty. The rest of the digestive organs, kidneys, liver, bladder, and generative and endocrine organs, while normal, were distended or liquefied by the biology and chemistry of decomposition. The heart provided Shepherd with his foremost diagnostic clue.

He found moderate aortic and coronary atheroma; the walls of the arteries had both hardened and narrowed with plaque. The heart itself weighed 630 grams, enlarged by any standard. He found the familiar concentric hypertrophy of the left ventricle, an increase in the heart's size measuring how hard the heart had worked to pump blood through the narrowing arteries. He saw no signs of previous MI, often visible macroscopically in severe cases as scar tissue among otherwise healthy cells. He collected no samples of blood for toxicological analysis, but removed several sections of heart muscle for later examination.

As he retrieved the heart from the overhead scale and placed it onto the cutting board for sectioning, he explained to Childerley that he had discovered the solution to the mystery of Ridgeley's death. The investigators waited for the pathologist to explain his discovery, dissolve the mystery, and rescue them from this smell that they would wear in their hair and taste in their mouths for the next several days, despite liberal applications of shampoo and toothpaste.

Shepherd began with his result: "Charles Ridgeley died due to natural causes." No one said anything.

He saw in the investigators' eyes the need for answers to a series of obvious questions about the decedent's criminal history, the witnesses' description of angry pounding on his door, the ransacked rooms, the bloody trail in the flat, and the knife. The building manager, who had a key to the flat and knew Ridgeley from prison, had appeared nervous and uncomfortable at the scene.

Saunder now remained occupied with police at the station as they explored his unsatisfactory answers to their detailed questions about his activities and relationship with Ridgeley. Even from his vantage point back at the hospital morgue, Shepherd could tell that Saunder had been given the role of chief suspect in a homicide. After a moment of silence to allow his conclusion to sink in, he explained his diagnosis of Ridgeley's death. He began with the scene.

Shepherd recalled that when Clay entered 2B, the body lay against the closed lounge door. Clay said that he had to push the body away from the door to enter the lounge since the door opened inward. So Ridgeley remained alive with the door closed, at least alive enough to crawl toward it and to die as a door stop.

"The question," Shepherd asked rhetorically, "is how did Ridgeley come to die before the closed door?"

He retreated to December 22, beginning at the pub.

"Ridgeley drank a great deal according to witnesses, and a cabby delivered him to 2B, leaving him quite drunk in his flat," Shepherd continued. "The blood trail between kitchen and lounge through the bathroom resulted from a laceration on his forehead. He fell in the kitchen and hit his head on the table. The blood trail began there. Drunk, he went into the bathroom and lounge, back to the kitchen, and ended up in the lounge, still bleeding."

"How do you know he wasn't hit by someone who had a key to the flat?" asked Childerley on behalf of the assembled group.

"Of course I can't say absolutely that he was not pushed by someone into the kitchen table," Shepherd replied. "But the autopsy shows that he was not hit in the head. The laceration bled profusely, but no other indications of a blow to the head appeared on the skull or in the brain. And nothing in 2B indicates the presence of someone other than Ridgeley himself. Mere possibilities without any evidence to suggest their further pursuit don't count for much."

Shepherd continued to explain his findings. He described how Ridgeley bled in the lounge, dripping blood as he staggered around the room. Ridgeley closed the door at some point among his many movements in the lounge. He then fell to his knees and vomited, emptying his stomach. The vomiting helped induce either a cardiac arrhythmia, an irregular heart beat leading to fibrillation, a mere quiver of the heart muscle rather than a full beat to sustain circulation, or an MI, a heart attack.

"Take your pick," Shepherd concluded. "Either one is a natural or accidental death."

Shepherd's diagnosis of the death methodically united each element of the case and tied them together in a larger picture showing the cause and manner of Charles Ridgeley's death. His process of discovery broadly parallels an act of creation in either the sciences or the arts.

Creative discovery has often been described as the province of inspired genius rather than methodical labor. This version of discovery, like those adapting Hume's views to their own ends, holds that after the mystical act of creation, justifications produced by ordinary mortals serve to confirm the insights of these creative geniuses whose discoveries pave the road of human progress. Logic and method have long been thought to apply to these justifications and confirmations of new discoveries, but to be absent from the process of creation and discovery itself.

Medical diagnoses, like Shepherd's explanation of Ridgeley's death, show that the logics of discovery and confirmation relate much more intimately than such a simple divorce supports. The act of creation may involve more of the methods of forensic science than any distant philosophical observer might expect. The medical researchers at Guy's reach discoveries as part of a process of investigation, modification, and reformulation. Solutions to puzzles do not appear *ex nihlo* (from nothing), but develop methodically over time, often in the wake of earlier failures.

Shepherd's diagnosis of Ridgeley's death emerges as part of this methodical process. His discovery of its cause and manner, like many discoveries, did not involve the creation of something completely new. In science, as long as the realists have their way, some discoveries like Kepler's discovery of Mars' elliptical orbit, or Harvey's discovery of the circulation of blood, paint an explanatory picture that helps humans understand the way things actually work, independently of accepted theories or popular beliefs. Such acts of creation result from an engagement with the relevant parts of the world, or as Peirce would say, from learning to read the signs.

Peirce spent much of his working life as a scientist with the Coast and Geological Survey but dedicated himself as a philosopher to understanding the logic of science. He spent the last 14 years of his life detailing "a method of thinking based on a logical and nonpsychological study of the essential nature of signs." He thought that logic extended to the creation of hypotheses and did not begin with their testing. For him, a sign is "something by knowing which we know something more." A sign is a pragmatic instruction to read and interpret.

Reading signs depends on appreciating the small points, the details that appear to those schooled in observation but disappear to the novice, the incautious, or the hasty. Observation, according to Joseph Bell, can be taught to medical students who must learn to discover the cause of a disease:

> "The recognition [of disease] depends in great measure on the accurate and rapid appreciation of small points in which the disease differs from the healthy state. In fact, the student must be taught to observe. To interest him in this kind of work we teachers find it useful to show the student how much a trained use of observation can discover in ordinary matters such as the previous history, nationality and occupation of a patient. The patient, too, is likely to be impressed by your ability to cure him in the future if he sees that you, at a glance, know much of his past. And the whole trick is much easier than it appears at first." [2]

The trick in Shepherd's diagnosis of Ridgeley's death relied on the signs he observed in Flat 2B, including the drops of blood, decomposition, maggots, and his examination of the body's internal organs. Like most acts of scientific creation, his had to address the common beliefs developed by those whose attention to detail did not extend much beyond the most obvious signs already familiar to them. His discovery, like most discoveries once made and communicated, becomes both obvious and simple. Holmes would even describe Shepherd's discovery as "elementary."

"What about the knife, and the apparent ransacking? Saunder may have searched the flat for money," Childerley said.

Shepherd provided this account. The blood on the knife had been dripped on the blade as the knife lay on the floor. He found no injuries on the body that were consistent with such a knife used as a weapon. A bread knife, with its flexible saw-tooth blade would not make an effective weapon in any case. Used as a weapon, the blade would probably bend. The knife remained unbent. Other kitchen items appeared in the lounge, helping Shepherd conclude that the knife's presence in the lounge remained coincidental.

"I saw no signs of ransacking," he continued. "Ridgeley did not keep house the way you or I might."

He explained that the items on the floor in each room had been there a while and appeared in layers deposited over time, not thrown from other places in a single destructive event. The dates on the newspapers closest to the floor were earliest, those piled on top, must recent. Food on plates that intermixed among the layers had also been there for some time.

The cool temperatures in the flat after the power had been shut off, the maggot infestation, and the state of decomposition all indicated to Shepherd that Ridgeley probably died shortly after he returned to his flat early on December 23. The latest date on a newspaper was December 22. The mail had not been picked up since then.

"The angry pounding on his door may signal unrelated criminal activity," Shepherd said. "But I'm betting that no pounding, angry or otherwise, could have awakened Ridgeley early that morning."

"So," Childerley asked, "what do your autopsy findings say?"

Shepherd summarized the results of his examination. He explained that Ridgeley had hypertensive heart disease. The heart enlarged by backpressure and no longer an effective pump, worked poorly to supply the brain with oxygen. He probably had unsteadiness and could fall even without the added effect of alcoholic drink. His medical problems alone could have resulted in death at any time.

Shepherd then explained how circumstances probably lead to Ridgeley's death on December 23.

"The drink, the fall, the blood loss, and the heart disease all worked together in what we call a cascade effect, a kind of medical version of Murphy's Law," Shepherd said.

He explained how the underlying heart disease already impaired circulatory function. Adding the strain of drunkenness and vomiting likely overtaxed the deficient heart muscle. The blood loss from the laceration probably had the least effect on his death, Shepherd thought, but pointed most clearly to the unsteadiness associated with both drunkenness and hypertensive heart disease.

"In any event," he said, "the blood does not point to a knife-wielding killer ransacking the place for ill-gotten gain. Nor would the head injury contribute greatly to his death."

"Whatever you discover about Ridgeley's criminal enterprise or his associations with Saunder, they do not appear to play a role in his death,"

Shepherd added. "I give the cause of death as hypertensive heart disease. The manner of his death is natural, not accidental."

The assembled officers appeared both relieved and thankful to be leaving the Wexham Hospital Morgue. Just another death due to simple natural causes, another ordinary Sunday night in Slough. They would be able to lean on Saunder a bit more, and perhaps solve a few burglaries as a side benefit to the evening's adventure.

With the precision of Sherlock Holmes, Dr. Dick Shepherd had unraveled another official mystery. The police working with Shepherd had developed a great confidence in his abilities and trusted his medical conclusions. He thought like they did; he just knew more about getting information from unpleasant corpses. They preferred to handle the likes of Saunder, leaving the dead to physicians such as Shepherd.

Physicians to the living as well as to the dead often present their diagnoses as deductive discoveries, derived from their specialized knowledge of covering medical laws, and their collective experience with inductively associated symptoms. Patients with hypertensive heart disease are unsteady on their feet. Ridgeley had hypertensive heart disease, so he was unsteady on his feet. As components of discovery, not relevant to presentation, they omit mentioning the underlying abductions.

The abductions select the applicable symptoms and medical principles from among the many available to explain their patient's complaint or death. The signs indicated that Ridgeley was probably drunk, and unsteady for that reason. Reasons appeared suggesting that he might have been pushed or hit on the head. He bled in the flat, and blood loss can lead to fainting, another source for unsteadiness. Shepherd explained Ridgeley's death by reasoning through this complex interconnected web of circumstances, each leaving a trail of signs to be interpreted.

Presenting discoveries to explain an individual patient's history, nationality, occupation, and complaint without acknowledging the intermediary signs displayed by the patient himself, render the process of discovery invisible. Shepherd relied on signs from the decedent and the scene, as well as the dead man's history, to develop his explanation of Ridgeley's death. His initial announcement that Ridgeley died of natural causes appeared to the assembled police as an ingenious, even mysterious discovery.

Medicine exercises the logic discovery on daily basis through diagnosis. Abstract scientific laws of death and decomposition that apply directly to the body in 2B do not exist. Peirce holds that humans discover complex entities like diseases by meeting them through their signs. He says that "our knowledge of the majority of general conceptions comes about in a manner altogether analogous to our knowledge of an individual person . . ." Pierce then criticizes Claude Bernard (1813–1878) who claimed that a disease is not a thing, but amounts merely to a set of symptoms. Pierce countered that diseases are "just as much a thing as the ocean is a thing . . . [and had Bernard understood this,] . . . He might have set himself to work very usefully to obtain some further acquaintance with that thing." (Ms. 316). Diagnosticians who fail to recognize signs as indicators remain doomed to dwell in the realm of symptoms, forever separated from the domain of cures.

The logic of signs lies at the heart of instinct, scientific method, Bell's diagnoses, and Doyle's "reasoning backward analytically." Peirce's logic provides both a heart and a soul for Shepherd's discoveries. What we discover through this logic are not merely signs. According to Peirce, Bernard failed to see that. Signs point from somewhere, drawing our attention to another thing somewhere else. "London 65 miles." The signpost differs from the city. Colored stains on a microscope slide of heart tissue point toward or away from an infarct. They do not embody a heart attack. Signs require an object signified and an interpreter. Abductive interpretation, for Peirce, extends beyond Hume's more passive associations of experience.

Shepherd did not abstractly associate a collection of signs in Flat 2B and think that by themselves they amounted to anything. The events leading to Ridgeley's death, the object of the investigation Sunday night in Slough, remained highly individual things pointed to by a complex collection of signs. Any signs of death in general remain remote, abstract, and uninteresting in this mystery. Even if Shepherd knew all the general signs of death, they alone would not help him explain how Ridgeley came to die in 2B. Signs "in general" do not point anywhere, or to any particular object or event. He would still need a method of selection among the signs available in 2B to discover the explanation of Ridgeley's death on December 23.

The art of death investigation assumes the anti-Galilean stance of medical diagnosis, focusing on the individual sign rather than the general feature. The Galilean-style scientist eliminates unique elements as superfluous, accidental accessories on the way to discovering general laws or principles. The art of detection emphasizes minute details to discover explanations of individual cases.

The goal of Galilean discovery remains universality, while the goal of forensic discovery remains singularity. In the Galilean approach to science, collected discoveries amass general covering laws or thematic features. In the forensic approach, the discoveries chronicle explanations of unique singular events such as Charles Ridgeley's death. One investigation appears impersonal, generic, and remote—the universal nature of motion, the process of autolysis, or the stages of putrefaction. The other investigation appears personal, individual, and unique. The motion of Mars, the autolysis of Ridgeley's heart, or the process of putrefaction in 2B over the Christmas holiday—one remains sanitized by generality while the other carries the odor of decomposition.

Both activities count as discovery nonetheless. Perhaps both grow from the same practical roots, branching in different directions. Certainly both branches flourished at Guy's Hospital, even in the department of forensic medicine. They came together often in the department's laboratory.

The microtome run by Tremain sectioned the final samples of heart tissue from Ridgeley, Charles, CSH31s. He prepared the tissue for sectioning by fixing the samples in paraffin blocks that form cassettes designed to fit onto the microtome. The sharp microtome blade shaves off thin layers of the embedded tissue, similar to a woodworker's plane shaving a plank. Tremain then floated the sections in a warm water tray where he transferred them onto glass slides. The slides then received stains according to the type of tissue and the desired histological goal.

He prepared these slides with the Rhodamine B and Light Green Method for myocardial infarct. Both Shepherd and Tremain wanted to learn what role, if any, advanced early decomposition played in the biochemistry of detecting a single fatal MI with their staining method. They tested for both the presence of a positive result to account for Ridgeley's death, and for any false-positive result as an artifact of the autolytic process. One objective became to explain a singular event, the other, to examine a general principle covering any test of similarly decomposed tissues using the as yet untested method.

Logic held that if their analysis of the biochemistry involved in a single fatal MI was correct, the autolytic process should have no effect on the staining. The enzymes softening the heart tissue in autolysis differed from the chemical changes in any newly necrotic tissue localizing the infarct among surrounding healthy tissue. Autolysis would affect both the newly necrotic and the surrounding tissues equally. The distinguishing chemicals should remain as long as the tissue remained capable of accepting a stain. The same limitations that applied to any method testing decomposed tissue samples applied to their method. Some tissues are just too far gone to yield any signs at all, regardless of technique. The scientific discovery of either a singular fact or a general principle becomes impossible with those samples. They offer no signs for interpretation. With such tissues, those scientific methods reach their logical limits.

In assessing the logic of scientific method in general and discovery in particular, mainstream philosophers have long denied the informativeness of logic and logical inference, content to relegate the discipline of logic to deduction, and scientific method to the deduction of particulars from general laws or features covering individual cases. That position leaves untouched the task of explaining those uses of logic that apparently yield new information, which methodically unmask new discoveries and perhaps even lead to an accumulation of the general laws alleged to cover composite cases, and license traditional scientific deductions in the first place.

Peirce attempted to provide such an account, focusing on abduction as the centerpiece of scientific method and the heart of scientific discovery. Unlike Peirce, in the tradition of Bell and Doyle's fictional Sherlock Holmes, Shepherd remained content simply to exercise the activity in the absence of such an account, and to fly in the face of much philosophical tradition.

As he peered into the microscope, the cardboard slide folder labeled "Ridgeley, Charles, CSH31s" beside him, Shepherd saw areas of magenta mixed with areas of dark green through the eyepiece of the Leitz. As he scanned the slide he saw no areas of dark purple or dark blue. None of the heart tissue slides from the folder differed. All appeared devoid of the dark purple or blue coloring, the signs characteristic of a single fatal MI in this test. He noted his conclusions cautiously on a yellow notepad beside the microscope.

He reasoned that they would need to conduct further tests examining the effect of decomposition on the staining technique. He suggested that they proceed through research on the interrelated biochemistry of infarct necrosis and autolysis.

His observations through the Leitz, although inconclusive, remained consistent with his bets explaining Ridgeley's death by a cardiac arrhythmia rather than an MI. They also remained consistent with all the previous cases of single fatal MI examined with the technique. But mere correlation alone, the basis of inductive association and experience, would not settle the matter. Science rests, after all, on justified explanations. Confirming an explanation of the interrelated processes of infarct and decomposition would eventually help settle the matter and allow a proper interpretation of the signs revealed by the staining technique. The research, with frequent interruption by unrelated mysteries, would take time.

Research continues at Guy's Hospital much as it has for 280 years, focused on the details, the signs and what they reveal. Discoveries continue to emerge following the same deliberate route through the signs. Perhaps only geniuses like Kepler or Einstein solve the most difficult problems and make truly great scientific discoveries. But to concede this does not concede that their reasons for developing the solutions and formulating the discoveries belie rational methods.

In forensic medicine, the same methods apply to the famous and to the obscure, the singular or the general. Discoveries concerning Ridgeley's death, or the histological detection of single fatal infarcts, point as additional signs to an underlying reverence for life. The staff of Guy's Hospital's department of forensic medicine favors a principle capturing this reverence once stated by Gladstone. He said: "Show me the manner in which a nation cares for its dead, and I will measure with mathematical exactness the tender mercies of its people, their respect for the laws of the land, and their loyalty to high ideals."

The worthiness of this underlying principle surpasses the noteworthiness of any famous decedent whose death might become an occasion for scientific discovery. Slides made from the well-known at Guy's rest on shelves in uniform cardboard folders indistinguishably mixed among all the others, waiting together for eventual observation and future discovery.

NOTES

1. Joseph Bell, 1893, "Mr. Sherlock Holmes," Introduction to the *Fourth Edition of A Study in Scarlet.*
2. Trevor Hall 1978:83, quoting Joseph Bell.

See the value of imagination.

chapter seven

Confirmation—The Selsner-Martin Case

Logical Testing

> The only point in the case which deserved mention was the curious analytical reasoning from effects to causes, by which I succeeded in unraveling it.
>
> Sherlock Holmes

Officers Lucerno and Jackson expressed little surprise when the voice from their patrol car radio invited them to a domestic dispute at 1325 East Wheelwright. They merely groaned. The dilapidated house in an old Tacoma working-class neighborhood had become familiar territory over the last 18 months. Ever since Betty Selsner and Carlo Martin took up residence in the faded two-story wood-frame building, Lucerno and Jackson averaged two calls to the place each Saturday. Invariably the first call would come in the morning, and the second around dinner. But this Saturday, Selsner and Martin must have gotten a late start. The first call came in at 1:05 P.M.

Betty Selsner and Carlo Martin took drinking and fighting seriously. These favorite activities went together. When things got out of hand, either the most annoyed neighbor or the least drunken combatant called police. A trip to the emergency room and a day or two in jail merely sent them to their respective corners for minor repairs. When the bell rang, both fighters came out for another round of both drinks and punches. Except this time.

When Lucerno and Jackson parked in front of the residence, they saw Carlo on his back in the dirt off the front porch. He had broken through the wooden railing, his arms straight out at the same angle as a kid making a snow angel. His heels stayed on the edge of the porch's tongue-and-groove flooring. His sleeveless undershirt had a big hole in the chest. So did Carlo. He looked like a white watermelon opened in the middle for viewing. This time Carlo would stay down for the count.

By the time detectives Sid Morland and Art Tipfield arrived, Betty's split lip and bloody nose had received medical attention and she was sobbing on the upstairs bed. She could not communicate. When she tried to speak, she either spewed slurred venom, nodded silently on the edge of consciousness, or cried quietly. She wore only a torn slip, which hung off her shoulders like a faded, flaccid windsock. The blood that had dripped from her face as she hung her head over her lap formed a round spot on her stomach, helping the windsock resemble a battle-weary flag.

Her thin arms carried a record of previous injury. Large bruises of various hues colored her forearms like tie-dyed tattoos. A sparrowlike face carried the reminders of what looked like 10 rounds with the world welterweight champion. She reeked of alcohol. Empty vodka bottles in various denominations littered the bedroom along with clothing from the better part of two neglected wardrobes—one male, one female.

The carnage continued from the bedroom down the stairs to the living room, ending with Carlo off the front porch. Broken glass carpeted both hallway and stairs. Fragmented frames hung from the walls, their pieces held together only by wire looped over nails driven into plaster. Chunks of fractured wall sat like flagstones along the path to ground level. Splintered lath appeared where greater force had been applied. Blood drips marked the plaster and glass trail down the stairs like pigeon droppings on a path in the park.

The television immediately to the right at the bottom of the stairs no longer had a screen. Glass from a large mirror over the fireplace lay on the mantel and hearth. Only the couch remained upright. Glass from that window, which overlooked the porch, covered its cushions. Broken bits of mullion and chunks of ancient glazing compound joined the glass. Large shards remained in the window frame, rising like stalagmites from the floor of a cave.

The front door, to the left of the couch and directly across from the foot of the stairs, hung open into the room, broken from its hinges but still attached to part of its frame. Blood decorated the first floor debris like sprinkles on Christmas cookies. An old double-barrel shotgun joined the destruction on the floor. Its wooden stock suffered a large crack from the missing shoulder plate to the back of its union with metal. Both barrels had fired, and both muzzles aimed toward the porch.

The bloody trail led through the door to the outside of the broken living room window. Glass from the jelly-jar porch light lay on the black rubber doormat that bid visitors a simple "welcome to our home." Detectives Morland and Tipfield knelt between the broken window and the body. A set of car keys and a single bedroom slipper lay below the window. Carlo had taken both barrels in the chest.

His undershirt, pushed up by his protruding belly, hung out over his light green boxer shorts. The other bedroom slipper hung precariously from the toes of his left foot. Scabs and bruises dotted his legs like lichens on tree branches. In addition to the gaping hole in the middle of his chest, blood coated his hands and scratches covered his forearms. A silver St. Christopher medal on a plain steel chain draped over his prominent Adam's apple and hung in the dirt. The three-day beard, usually an accurate timekeeper for his binges, held bits of broken glass and sheet rock. Blood coated his swollen lips and ran from his bulbous nose. Long gray wisps of hair lay over his head, failing to conceal its bald surface. His eyes remained open and stared into the clouds floating over the porch roof.

Lillian Herman stood with Officer Jackson behind the bald head and beyond the walkway to the porch next to the yellow crime scene tape that now blocked access to the house from the sidewalk. Lucerno and the paramedic who treated Betty Selsner's bloody lip and nose remained upstairs with the inebriated patient. Jackson questioned Mrs. Herman, the complainant, and took notes for his report.

She called police, she said, after an unusually loud morning row between Carlo and Betty. She had awakened about 7:00 A.M. to their fighting, but they had quieted down again for a couple hours. When they resumed, the noise steadily escalated. By about 12:45 P.M. she heard breaking glass and screams of pain. That continued until she heard loud thuds, like hammering. She couldn't just listen anymore. She feared that Betty would be hurt. She heard Carlo yelling indistinguishably just after she hung up with the police. Then she heard a loud roar. She couldn't tell if it was one or two together. She immediately looked out her window, and saw Carlo lying in the dirt off the porch. She did not see Betty. She waited inside her front door until she saw the squad car arrive.

After questioning Lillian Herman, Officer Jackson radioed records for a criminal history check on Carlo Martin and Betty Selsner. He knew that both had distinguished careers as barroom pugilists and domestic brawlers. After a brief search, the records officer reported that besides the expected drunk and disorderly convictions for both, Betty had several weapons charges, including one conviction for assault with a deadly weapon. Two years earlier, she had shot Carlo in the foot with a .22 rifle. Jackson thought that she probably had aimed for his head when she pulled the triggers of both the .22 and the shotgun. This time, her aim had improved.

Detectives Morland and Tipfield carefully inspected both Carlo and the scene. Tipfield walked behind the yellow boundary and talked to Jackson, then rejoined Morland on the porch. They both walked upstairs and arrested Betty Selsner on suspicion of murder. Otherwise leaving the scene intact, they found her some clothing, helped her put on a pair of her shoes, led her down the stairs through the living room, and sat her in the back of a squad car. After the short ride downtown, she sat on a small metal cot in Cell 15 and resumed the position she had occupied on her own disheveled bed.

The death appeared to have a straightforward explanation. In a drunken brawl, Betty Selsner blew away her common-law husband, Carlo Martin. The recorded history of their drunken brawling in Washington state alone covered 14 pages. Betty had prior weapons charges and had shot Carlo before. On that basis, the detectives felt that the prosecutor would probably file for second-degree murder, and bargain down to manslaughter to save the expense of a trial. Any first-time public defender could produce a years-of-physical-and-alcohol-abuse argument to explain her actions that would jeopardize a second-degree murder conviction. Drunks will be drunks. The case against Betty Selsner, like most domestic homicides, appeared to be closed almost as soon as the shots had opened Carlo's thoracic cavity. The investigators had seen it all many times before. This case presented no mystery to detectives Morland and Tipfield.

Mysteries depend on things not always being what they seem. Investigators learn that contrary to the often-quoted saying attributable to Plato, things usually are just exactly as they appear. The revealing tank top, tight skirt and high heels do advertise the prostitute as she leans suggestively toward a car window to negotiate both service and price. The six stocking-capped figures in the '82 Buick low-rider cruising a suburban street at 2:15 A.M. do telegraph trouble. Mysteries result when for whatever reason, investigators can't penetrate the fog cloaking the appearances. Killers may help conceal their enterprise by hiding beneath the cover that respectability affords, killers such as Ted Bundy, the young Republican law student crisis-line-volunteer. But no fog shrouded Carlo Martin or protected Betty Selsner.

Learning how things "really are" in a death like Carlo Martin's depends on reading the signs at the scene, interpreting any relevant patterns, and incorporating the results of any autopsy. The learning process continues through testing proposed explanations developed from these signs. An explanation that merely completes a coherent picture and that simply appears "likely" to the casual observer may not be the best explanation when all of the available signs are considered. Such an explanation stakes no claim on either being the true explanation, or the best one under the circumstances. Peirce cautioned against confusing "likelihood" as "preconceived belief" with "probable truth." Merely coherent pictures do not make probable explanations when they ignore relevant signs. "You know my method," Sherlock Holmes says. "It is founded upon the observance of trifles."

Sometimes reading the signs to develop probable explanations depends upon applying both specialized knowledge and unique experience. Such signs may appear clearly to one person yet may remain invisible to another. That exposes one source of mystery. No mystery could develop if both Sherlock Holmes and Dr. Watson both overlooked and forever dismissed what happened to be significant signs. But usually Holmes sees things that Watson misses. When that happens, tests to confirm one reading of the signs and to eliminate alternatives become the center of the investigative method applied to solve the mystery.

The first step involves discovering a mystery where none had been recognized before. Unless Watson loses faith in his original preconceptions, Holmes' insights lose their power to inform. Like most, Watson resists abandoning his preconceptions because he holds them for good reasons. In the same manner, Morland and Tipfield held to their assessment of Carlo's death for good reasons. Holmes must overcome Watson's good reasons with better reasons to justify setting those preconceptions aside. Any assault on the two detectives' explanation of Carlo's death occasions a similar conflict between their reasonable belief in the original account and the new reasons offered to undermine their confidence.

In the investigative arena, that clash of reasons can generate further conflict between those who supposedly have specialized knowledge and those skeptical of such prowess. The specialist must supply better reasons to abandon the obvious than the skeptic's reasons to hold onto it. Resolving the clash, common in science, depends on confirming one explanation and thereby eliminating the competition. The mystery in Betty Selsner's case developed and the conflict began when Pierce County's first and newly appointed medical examiner received a call informing him of Carlo Martin's untimely death.

By the time Jacob Lasorta, MD, spoke with the police dispatcher, Betty Selsner had sobered up enough in her jail cell to explain to detectives Morland and Tipfield that she remembered nothing. She could neither confirm nor deny that she had shot Carlo. She now merely sat on her bed in Cell 15 crying with more purpose. Lasorta then spoke with Morland and Tipfield and heard them describe a case that held no great mystery for them. As the new chief medical examiner in an office recently established to replace an old coroner's system, Lasorta's role remained unfamiliar to detectives accustomed to the older ways of doing business with death.

The medical examiner viewed each new case as a training exercise for both the M.E.'s office and for the police who now worked within a new death investigation system. He expected police or any agency responding to a death to call the medical examiner's office early in the investigation. Neither he nor his investigators served as a mere removal service, cleaning up after a death by transporting and storing the decedent until a funeral home could be selected. They had legal jurisdiction over the body and the biological evidence at any death scene and were expected to present that evidence in court should the need arise. They had the experience and training to interpret the signs of injury and to correlate them with signs at the scene, and they applied that forensic medical knowledge to help explain any sudden, unexpected, unattended, or violent deaths.

The specialty of forensic medicine extends well beyond the clinical inspection of human organ systems into the surrounding circumstances and environments that contribute to injury and death. Sometimes that extension precipitates conflicts between medical examiners offices and police agencies, who often are suspicious of any intrusions into their crime scenes or potential threats to their authority. Lasorta hoped that a training program would head off such potential turf problems by emphasizing a team approach, one expert helping another in a mutual quest for the truth. Any team forms slowly over time, with each team member gradually earning the respect of the others as they work together.

Most M.E.'s offices are organized to serve this integral role in the investigative process. Medical examiners do not serve under the police, the prosecutor, or any other investigative agency. Their independence from such official bureaucracies enhances their ability to follow the facts wherever they lead, whether the path enjoys official popularity or not. They do not serve law enforcement by collecting the evidence to support established police theories. Like Sherlock Holmes, medical examiners value their independent observations.

Holmes says, "I have trained myself to notice what I see." Like Holmes, Lasorta read the signs for himself, following where they led. After talking with detectives Morland and Tipfield, he accompanied his investigator to 1325 East Wheelwright to do just that.

Both Morland and Tipfield appeared annoyed at having to return to a scene they saw no need to revisit. They had reports to write and paperwork to complete. With the suspect in custody, they had no reason to waste their time showing some bookish MD life in the big city, or worse, to have some noncommissioned personnel peer over their shoulders and into their homicide investigations. When Lasorta and his investigator arrived, the detectives sized them up and immediately asked if they needed help removing the body. The body could wait, Lasorta said. It wasn't going anywhere on its own.

In response to Lasorta's questions, the detectives impatiently reviewed the case for the medical examiner and his investigator as if sidestepping intrusive newspaper reporters. No need for Ident, they explained, since the woman obviously shot the man with both barrels. They explained that with her record, a manslaughter plea became a virtual certainty. With questions answered, they invited the medical examiner to look around, and to let them know when he and his helper had completed their tour. Both detectives leaned against their unmarked car parked at the curb, and took out their cigarettes. They glanced at their watches between puffs. Lasorta and the investigator walked slowly toward the house, taking in the sights on the front porch and beyond through the open door.

Blood had dripped across the porch, from the door over the welcome mat to the window. The dripping formed a more extensive pattern by the window, where another pattern appeared. Between the window and the body, a mist of blood in tiny drops covered the porch flooring. Lasorta saw the same pattern repeated on the siding just beneath the windowsill. Small drops also coated the long shards of glass and broken wood, a fractured mess that once had been the living room window.

Following the mist toward the body, he saw that the undershirt had been scorched around the gaping wound in the victim's chest. The wounds, while big, formed tight circular patterns, slightly overlapping, accented by black fouling and burning around the edges. He looked through the window into the living room and saw the weapon lying on the floor about eight feet away, its muzzle pointing toward the body on the porch.

They walked through the opening once secured by the broken door, touching nothing. They followed the blood, which repeated the dripping pattern seen on the porch leading to the window. Both knelt to examine the battered shotgun lying on the floor. The weapon rested over bits of broken glass and several pieces, both large and small, lay on top of the battered stock. The blood mist reappeared just inside the gun's barrels. Bits of plaster filled the grooves on both hammers and appeared in the deep scratches and cracks covering what remained of the stock. White sandlike material and other as yet unidentified substances appeared to be ground into the gun's butt. Two triggers protruded from the underside, exposed beneath the gun through the fractured stubs of the now-absent trigger guard.

Following the line from the gun toward the body, Lasorta observed the glass, wood, and glazing compound on the couch under the window. Flecks of old white paint, probably lead-based given the age of the house, also appeared on the glass and over the couch. From the living room floor before the window, both representatives from the medical examiner's office followed a trail of dripped blood, broken glass, and fractured plaster up the stairs toward the bedroom.

Below a large hole in the wall in about the middle of the stairs, Lasorta bent to examine a broken bit of metal mixed with shredded lath and chunks of plaster. The trigger guard had made it only halfway down the steps. On the second-floor landing, covered with more glass, the shotgun's butt plate stuck through a group photo beneath a tear in the picture. Bits of black wooden frame still clung to the edges of the photo. Blood continued along the landing, through the narrow hallway and into the bedroom.

The trail led to more broken glass beside the rumpled bed. A broken bottle and what looked to be the remains of one or two broken tumblers had ragged edges coated in blood. Other blood drips appeared over the exposed mattress, and puddled beside the bed on the floor. A closet door opened beside a small dresser that once stood against the wall across from the bed. It now leaned against a chair overturned near a radiator, spilling the contents of four drawers onto the floor. Inside the closet, the scattered contents of a box of shotgun shells covered the debris of dirty clothes and bent hangers littering the floor.

Above the radiator, a broken bedroom window had a streak of blood running down the sharp edge of a piece of glass left in the window's upper half. The lower half remained intact. Glass collected between the lower pane and the outside screen, which was bent and rusty but unbroken. It looked to Lasorta like almost everything in the room not attached to the walls, including most of the empty liquor bottles, had put in a brief appearance as a projectile of some sort. And almost everything breakable had been broken in a battle royal that apparently began in the bedroom and ended with the body on the porch. Neither Lasorta nor his investigator said anything as they walked into each of the other rooms in the house beginning upstairs.

The upstairs bathroom's tub, toilet, and sink had once been white but now appeared to share shades of gray and brown. The hex-tile floor stuck to their feet as they entered to check the room for any medications. Bottles of both aspirin and Pepto-Bismol gave the room its only bright color. Dirty underwear soaked in three inches of brown water that coated the inside of the tub, and a pair of pantyhose hung from the shower curtain rod. The second upstairs bedroom remained vacant except for several empty beer cans, two liquor bottles, and a coating of dried vomit over the oak flooring in the corner of the room.

Downstairs, the kitchen continued the theme of despair and neglect that decorated the rest of the house. Dirty dishes were scattered on the floor, in the sink and on the stove, as were half-full pots and pans. The investigator opened the refrigerator and found a half-gallon of milk, now solid, several cans of beer, and a package of what once may have been hamburger. The cupboards held few secrets. Bottles of vodka appeared randomly placed among the drawers, doors and recesses of the rest of the room.

The kitchen door leading to the overgrown backyard remained locked from the inside. The door to the basement, also locked, had a nail in the middle supporting a broom and dustpan, both with the price tags still in place. The door from the kitchen to the tiny dining area off the living room remained closed. Opening the door, the medical examiner walked into the dining room, through the living room and out the front door. The detectives remained leaning against their car smoking freshly lit cigarettes.

Lasorta walked to their car and asked them about Betty Selsner's injuries. Morland and Tipfield described her split lip, bloody nose, and bruises. Lasorta wanted to know about her feet. The detectives thought that her feet had been uninjured, but they could not swear to it, although she had sat barefoot on the bed. Officer Lucerno had stayed with her when the medic treated her injuries. When they both went upstairs to arrest her, they had supplied her with footwear and clothing for the trip to the squad car.

"Why do you ask?" Morland wondered out loud to Lasorta.

"Because," he replied, "you have arrested an innocent woman for a crime that she did not commit." He spoke quietly, respectfully, and with conviction. The surprised expression on the detectives' faces supplied a clear sign that the mystery of Carlo Martin's death had just begun.

Lasorta's matter-of-fact announcement presented the detectives with their first surprising observation of the day. They now struggled to make sense of it. Either the new medical examiner had a screw loose somewhere, or he had seen something that they had missed. Their bets overwhelmingly favored the former. The detectives saw no signs that anyone other than Carlo and Betty had been in the house. The shotgun lay in the living room, and the body lay on the porch. The annoyed neighbor, Lillian Herman, did not supply a reasonable alternative suspect. Betty had the credentials, the motive, the opportunity, and she sat in jail. She had to be behind the trigger. No observation recorded by the medical examiner could overcome the unassailable facts of this open-and-shut domestic homicide case.

Just what counts as an observation, and how observing differs from perceiving or just plain seeing, are questions that have occupied philosophers for centuries. Philosopher of science Karl Popper describes an observation as "a planned and prepared perception." Peirce supplies an account of just how he thinks such planning and preparation works to transform mere seeing into informed observing:

> "Looking out my window this lovely spring morning I see an azalea in full bloom. No, no! I do not see that; though that is the only way I can describe what I see. That is a proposition, a sentence, a fact; but what I perceive is not a proposition, a sentence (or a) fact, but only an image, which I make intelligible in part by means of a statement of fact. This statement is abstract; but what I see is concrete. I perform an abduction when I so much as express in a sentence anything I see. The truth is that the whole fabric of our knowledge is one malted felt of pure hypothesis confirmed and refined by (testing through) induction. Not the smallest advance can be made in knowledge beyond the stage of vacant staring, without making an abduction at every step." (Ms.692)

The abductive process Peirce describes as observation accounts for Holmes peering and poking among the details of a mystery. "It has long been an axiom of mine that the little things are infinitely the most important," he says. He begins his observation by reading, recording, connecting, and distinguishing signs. He then develops a broader interpretive explanation to connect the observed facts and to discover the most likely causes of any observed effects. He next deduces the consequences of his hypothesis, predicting the discovery of additional observations. He finally tests the hypothesis and the consequences it predicts by searching for the observations it entails. This search, in the broad sense, supplies experimental tests of the emerging explanation. This process accounted for Lasorta's explanation of Carlo's death, which in turn entailed that Betty did not shoot her common-law husband.

In opposition to this conclusion, the two detectives stood by their explanation and its prediction of Betty's guilt. They thought that the medical examiner would have to develop some extraordinary evidence to support his wild statement. But with the new pecking order established by law, they had to work with him and his investigators in the future, so it struck them as a good idea to establish their superior investigative skills early in the relationship. They could bring him along, and eventually he could prove to be of some use to them when he stuck to medicine. They decided to let the M.E. dig himself a hole, and watch him crawl in.

By now, Lasorta had mobilized the forces of his office and persuaded Morland and Tipfield to request Ident officers to process the scene. Carlo's hands and feet enjoyed the cover of paper bags tied with string. After extensive photography and laborious sketching, bits of the scene found their way into various containers for travel to the state crime lab. The weapon, bits of glass, wood, paint, and drops of blood from the bedroom, hallway, living room, and porch all made the trip downtown.

During this flurry of activity while Carlo traveled from the porch to the medical examiner's van, Morland and Tipfield asked Lasorta why he put so much effort into processing such a simple scene. After all, didn't he see that he merely collected evidence to prove Betty guilty of Carlo's homicide?

Lasorta used the opportunity to clarify the role his office played in death investigation. His office functioned, he said, to exonerate the innocent as well as to implicate the guilty. The medical examiner could help detectives determine if a crime had been committed in the first place, as well as help supply information to evaluate any suspects that detectives eventually developed. To do so, he said, it helped to assume that each death he investigated presented evidence of a homicide. Again, Morland and Tipfield appeared surprised.

Holmes announces that "A mixture of imagination and reality . . . is the basis of my art." Hypothetically assuming a death to be a homicide supplied the most questions to ask and allowed the most answers to develop. The assumption supplied a plan to prepare for making observations. Was the decedent alone? Were the windows open, or closed? Was the door locked or unlocked? Were the lights and appliances on or off? Such questions extended from the scene to the body itself.

Only some of the many questions about the body depended on expert medical assessments. Questions about clothing or position required no special medical credentials. But if the questions remained unasked, answers later might be hard to come by. Such planning for observations at a scene did not mean that every death must be processed mechanically as a homicide with equally exhaustive detail and disregard for time or expense. But each must receive equal attention to detail. There's a difference. The difference involves Karl Popper's notion of preparation for perception.

Even when deaths appear to have obvious explanations, asking the right questions supplies a lasting benefit. Mangled bodies appear in a small airplane crushed against a hillside. Crash deaths. An accident. But, Lasorta added, did the pilot have a heart attack? Was the pilot drunk, or on drugs? Did the plane malfunction? Was the wreck intentional? Did someone poison the pilot's coffee? Was the pilot despondent about a personal problem?

The assumption of homicide to plan the questions, he explained, did not depend on the death actually being one, or on the investigators initially believing that the death had been caused by another. If it was, the questions both asked and answered would uncover and develop the evidence. If it was not, the questions helped to rule out homicide, and to develop the best alternative through a process of elimination.

"You have explained what you saw here by saying that Betty Selsner shot Carlo Martin?" Lasorta said. "Let's see how the evidence develops to support that scenario."

The way Lasorta spoke, neither detective felt either mocked or threatened. Yet both remained confident that their explanation could withstand anything that developed from the scene, or from the body.

The medical examiner invited both detectives to the autopsy Sunday morning. Reluctantly, both accepted. Their paperwork would have to wait a little longer. Working with the new medical examiner appeared to involve a major commitment of time, the further allocation of increasingly scarce technical resources, and an added drain on limited personal energy. With these involvements in mind, the detectives rang the service bell next to the garage door at the medical examiner's office at 6:00 A.M. the next morning.

Carlo Martin lay on a stainless steel gurney, looking much as he appeared on the porch but with both arms at his sides. He had just been posed for a series of photographs that would never decorate any hallway. Lasorta removed the bags from Carlo's hands and noticed that the fingers, coated with dried blood, had many small cuts. Three lacerations accented the knuckles of his right hand and blue covered the knuckles of the left. Flecks of white material appeared in the lacerations.

Each tear avulsed or pushed the skin from the thumb toward the little fingers like a shovel pushes snow down a sidewalk. A thick coating of soot extended from the palmar surface of both hands, up the wrists, and along the lateral side of the forearms. Lasorta removed the flecks, placing them into small envelopes labeled with the autopsy number, case number, and location of discovery. He swabbed the fouled hands and arms for gunshot residue, and removed Carlo's undershirt.

The tight cluster of shot, the presence of burning and fouling, and the circular appearance of the wound, with minimal scalloping of margins, all predicted the distance between the muzzle and chest. From the present signs, Lasorta estimated that the muzzle discharged no more than two feet from the undershirt covering the chest. Test firing the weapon could duplicate the patterns on the shirt and determine the exact distance if necessary.

The autopsy assistant's Y-incision carefully avoided the round chest wounds that straddled the midline. Lasorta dissected the wounds and recovered two wads, one from each shell, and noted the many pellets lodged in the thoracic cavity. The shotshell cases from the battered double-barrel weapon were plastic with a brass head holding a center-fire propellant charge. They remained in the weapon's chambers.

These shotshell cases contained the powder charge, wads, and shot. The wads, disks, or sleeves, which usually are made of felt, paper, or plastic, hold the powder and shot in position. Four wads usually complete the task, one securing the powder, one filling the space between the powder and shot, and one holding the shot. The overshot wad leaves the barrel with the shot when the weapon fires.

The double blast striking Carlo Martin literally shredded the heart muscle and the aorta. Some of the pellets raised black bumps under the skin on his back on both sides of the spinal column. They looked like well-endowed blackheads just out of either hand's comfortable reach. A sample of the pellets removed from the wounds each measured .095 inches and weighed 81 milligrams. The shotshell cases in the gun said "7 1/2 shot," which meant that Lasorta could expect that about 350 such pellets entered the body from each blast.

Besides the two wads and 700 shot pellets, no foreign material appeared in the wounds, on the shirt, or around the wounds' margins. That did not surprise Lasorta. It did surprise the two detectives watching the autopsy from the edge of the room. With the help of scientific method, the detectives' explanation of Carlo Martin's death received its first Holmes-style test.

While completing the autopsy, weighing the organs, and noting the fatty liver consistent with the decedent's use of alcohol, Lasorta asked Morland and Tipfield to state their version of the shooting scenario. The detectives obliged while Lasorta removed his gloves, tossed them into the biohazard waste receptacle, then scrubbed his hands. His assistant, meanwhile, collected and reinstalled the parts removed from Carlo's thoracic cavity with the help of a large plastic bag.

The detectives leaned against the wall and Morland did the talking. He contended that Betty fired the gun from the living room while Carlo faced the living room window from the porch.

The investigative problem becomes to confirm that account. Such confirmations often emerge in scientific investigations through what has been called "the hypothetico-deductive method." The method applies deductive logic to the original hypothesis to derive a prediction that the hypothesis already supports. The evidence illuminated by the hypothesis, like a pathway lit with a flashlight's beam, either confirms or disconfirms the prediction. Lasorta now trained the light of hypothetico-deduction onto the two detectives' jointly held hypothesis.

Lasorta spoke as if consulting a medical colleague about a problematic diagnosis. "If Betty shot Carlo from the living room through the window," he said, "then bits of glass pepper the wounds. No glass can be found in the wounds. Therefore, Betty did not shoot Carlo from the living room through the window."

The deduction represents a valid form of reasoning called modus toliens, Latin for "the method of taking away." The hypothesis remains committed to all the circumstances which would make it true, among them the effects of shooting both barrels of a shotgun through a glass window. When those effects do not appear, the explanation committed to them becomes "taken away" by the evidence. Reluctant to give up so easily, detectives Morland and Tipfield presented a possible counter.

Morland shifted his weight uncomfortably onto his other foot, abandoning the support provided by the wall. The window, he said, broke before the shots were fired. She broke the window with the gun barrel then shot Carlo with both shells. So no glass would be found in the wounds because the shots hit no glass on their way to the target. Tipfield looked pleased with Morland's reply. They stood their ground. They would teach the new medical examiner a lesson in homicide investigation. But the detectives' hastily accepted addition modified their original hypothesis and added to their first scenario.

Such additions become subject to the same method of confirmation. They transport to the scenario specific commitments about the condition of the window, the rooms, the wounds, and the minor injuries that tag along for the ride like water in a tidal wave. If the conditions do not appear, then the "method of taking away" removes the additions requiring their presence. The amended scenario then carries the credibility of a deadbeat dad's claim that the child-support check must be lost in the mail.

Testing the amended scenario applies an additional valid deduction called modus ponnens, Latin for "the method of putting in place." If the living room window breaks from an impact, then it fractures due to blows delivered either from inside, in the living room, or from outside, on the porch. With broken glass as evidence, the window has indeed broken from an impact, not from a hot fire raging in the building. Therefore, it was broken either by a blow delivered from within the living room, or from out on the porch. Like a chain, more conditions then appear to be put in place. Building the chain, putting in place and taking away, requires observation, Popper's planned and prepared perceptions, Holmes' sense of noticing what he sees.

When a blow strikes one side of a window, the glass bends in the direction of the force until it begins to crack. The first cracks appear on the side opposite the striking force. The edges of the broken glass bear stress marks that testify to the side first cracked, opposite the side first struck. The stress marks formed arches perpendicular to the side first cracked which curve nearly parallel to the side first struck. If the window was broken by a blow from the living room, then the radial crack stress marks form a right angle on the porch side of the glass.

Lasorta observed during his visit to the scene that the window glass stress marks formed a right angle to the living room side. The window broke from a blow originating on the porch. Modus tollens delivered the disconfirming blow to the detectives' amended scenario. However the window broke, it broke from a blow delivered outside the living room. Betty did not break it with the shotgun barrel from inside.

When faced with the medical examiner's logic, again explained as if at a conference among colleagues, another modification suggested itself to the increasingly uncomfortable detectives. After all, nothing Lasorta had noticed about the glass proved that Betty did not fire the fatal shots. The medical examiner's tests of the wounds only showed that she did not fire them through an intact window, and that the window did not break from inside.

"Suppose," Morland said, "that the window broke from blows to both sides. Carlo hit it from the outside, and Betty hit it from the inside." Tipfield looked less pleased than he did after Morland's earlier modification. Morland's amendment now carried the ring of a retreat.

When more than one blow breaks glass, a new fracture line ends at an existing crack. Glass found at the scene would have opposing stress marks pointing two directions along radial fractures produced from opposite sides of the window. Lasorta noted that the outside of the glass wore a dried dirty layer, while the inside had a greasy film coating its surface. No fractures exhibited opposing stress marks.

Almost all the broken glass appeared on the couch inside the living room. He observed that at least two blows struck the window, both from outside.

Several fracture lines ended at existing breaks in the glass still attached to the window frame by bits of wooden mullion and chunks of glazing compound. Morland's new amendment to the detectives' previously amended scenario could be swept away with the glass it failed to explain.

Lasorta's planned approach to the signs at the scene had already included a consideration of these possibilities. The options now suggested by Morland and backed by Tipfield to support their hastily accepted conclusion of Betty's guilt were formed without regard for the pattern of signs available for observation. The options had already suggested themselves to Lasorta through the signs he observed on the porch and in the living room. Further signs suggested the necessary modifications to account for the developing picture of Carlo and Betty's fatal battle.

Holmes advised investigators, "Never trust to general impressions, but concentrate upon the details." The details not only suggest the hypotheses to be considered, but supply the means to test the competition, eliminate inadequate alternatives, and confirm the eventual victor. The mechanisms of creation and discovery intertwine through observation with the process of testing and confirmation.

When Peirce insists that tests accompany abductions, he describes an intimate relationship between the signs, the proposed conjectures they suggest, and the method of their confirmation. "Tests" do not always take two weeks, require the services of a laboratory, or involve specialized scientific knowledge. In Carlo and Betty's living room, Lasorta performed brief tests of hypothetico-deduction on shards of glass. To this living room laboratory he brought his eyes, with their preparation for observation, his attention to detail, and the deductive equipment of modus tollens and modus ponnens. Like the sons of Serendippo's king, Lasorta prepared to use his abductive conjectures supported by tests to confirm the innocence of the detectives' unjustly accused prisoner.

In a twist of roles and an exchange of circumstance, Carlo and Betty could serve as an inverse image of Claus and Sunny von Bulow. The von Bulows lived in luxury. The Martin-Selsners lived in squalor. The von Bulows had millions. The Martin-Selsners had nothing. But did Claus twice attempt to murder his rich socialite wife, Sunny, by administering insulin injections? Not if the evidence shows that a suicidal overmedicated Sunny injected herself, and that other family members contrived the scene to support Claus' guilt. Did Betty at least twice attempt to murder Carlo, finally succeeding with a double shotgun blast to his chest? Not if the signs at the scene say otherwise.

"Singularity is almost invariably a clue," Holmes announces of such signs. "The more featureless and commonplace a crime is, the more difficult it is to bring home." The von Bulow case appeared to be quite uncommon. Many of its features stimulated public controversy, engaged high-priced lawyers, and spawned books and movies. Holmes says that "what is out of the common is usually a guide rather than a hindrance." Public opinion may still be divided about Claus' role in Sunny's coma, although legal opinion confirms Claus' innocence. But few would ever notice Betty's case long enough to form even the most superficial opinion of her guilt or innocence. To the public, the features of her case and Carlo's death remained all but invisible.

Carlo would not be publicly missed from his social circles. Cab rides to the liquor store had little social or cultural impact. Neither belonged to a fancy country club or traveled in important social circles. Betty didn't even visit the local beauty parlor. She had no influential friends or family to intervene on her behalf, and no money to pay for the rights privilege often purchases. Interested relatives did not clamor for a share of Carlo's fortune. Neither existed. Most family members could not be located to be notified of his death. Those who were notified expressed little surprise and less interest. The signs at the scene held the only uncommon surprises. They supplied the singularity in the case against Betty that formed its defining features and carried with them the clues to unravel its mystery.

Betty Selsner's apparent point of common ground with Claus von Bulow depended on confirming Lasorta's explanation of Carlo's death. Unlike von Bulow, she remained unaware of her own guilt or innocence. Betty sat accused with only the new medical examiner between her and more trouble leading to even more jail time. Fortunately for Betty Selsner, Dr. Lasorta's reconstruction of the events leading to Carlo's death on the porch clearly distinguished the evidence of wounds, glass, gunshot residues, and blood from the coincidences of personality and privilege.

"It is only the colorless, uneventful case which is hopeless," according to Holmes. Selsner's case, despite public disinterest and the detectives' belief in her guilt, was far from hopeless.

Betty herself could supply neither protests of innocence nor confessions of guilt because in her alcoholic stupor she simply had no memories to support either of these traditional avenues usually open to persons accused of crimes. But she did carry signs of value to the investigation, and Lasorta wanted to see them. He already had developed his own predictions of what he would find, formed by deductions from his evolving explanation of Carlo's death. Examining Betty could either support or refute these predictions, and help confirm or modify his embryonic hypotheses.

Still dressed in blue scrubs, he made his predictions clear to the two detectives standing uneasily across from him by the stainless steel sink.

"Betty," Lasorta said, "will have no deep cuts on the bottoms of her feet, and no pattern conclusions or abrasions on her chest or shoulder consistent with the butt of the shotgun. She will have no gunshot residue on her hands, face, or slip. Any glass particles found on her skin, hair, or clothing, except those on footwear supplied for her trip to the squad car, will be distinct from the glass fragments found by the living room window."

Lasorta smiled and offered Morland and Tipfield a friendly wager, openly risking his predictions and acknowledging his fallibilism. Neither detective took the bet. They apparently no longer liked their odds. They accompanied the now smartly dressed medical examiner to the jail, and entered

Cell 15 with him to make their Sunday afternoon observations and test his risky predictions.

Betty Selsner exhibited no contusions or abrasions consistent with the "kick" of an old double-barrel shotgun fired by a thin-skinned alcoholic woman. Lab techs who met the medical examiner and detectives in the cell collected glass from Betty's hair, swabbed her hands, and retrieved her slip. These tests would take a week to complete. But Lasorta announced that he now had developed enough evidence to give birth to his hypothesis explaining Carlo's death and Betty's role, and to confirm its conclusions.

As county medical examiner, Lasorta told detectives Morland and Tipfield that he would rule the manner of Carlo's death to be accidental. The surprising announcement received a skeptical greeting from the two detectives standing with the medical examiner and a recently arrived deputy prosecutor who represented the country's prosecuting attorney.

Lasorta mustered reasons to confirm his diagnosis of the situation. The cogency of his reasons and the investigative interest of the case had nothing to do with social status, money, prominence, or the worthiness of its principals. Betty bore the guilt of no crime here, he said, because the evidence showed that no crime had been committed, not because the circumstances showed that she was admired or reviled, rich or poor, a saint or a sinner, or guilty of previous or distinct crimes.

Skeptical of both the powers of science in general and the medical examiner's reconstruction in particular, detectives Morland and Tipfield, joined by the deputy prosecutor, supplied an anxious audience for Lasorta's case. They waited more patiently than before in the city homicide office conference room Monday morning, one week and two days after Carlo's death, for an explanation of this new obstacle erected by the medical examiner in their simple domestic homicide.

When Lasorta arrived and entered the conference room, he described the scenario suggested by the signs at the scene and confirmed by the evidence the signs illuminated. He presented his analysis to two experienced detectives and a prosecuting attorney who had seen and heard just about everything at least once before. His litany was accompanied by strong coffee and smoke from the detectives' glowing cigarettes.

Morland and Tipfield assumed the roles of Sir Arthur Conan Doyle's fictional Inspectors Gregory and Lestrade, who begin each case as incredulous opinionated opponents, only to end as admiring supportive converts, wondering at the simplicity of the mystery and the obviousness of Sherlock Holmes' resolution. As Holmes says to Watson, "Inspector Gregory, to whom the case has been committed, is an extremely competent officer. Were he but gifted with imagination he might rise to great heights in his profession." Commenting on his method, Holmes adds, "See the value of imagination. It is the one quality which Gregory lacks. We imagined what might have happened, acted upon the supposition and find ourselves justified. Let us proceed."

Lasorta began with the signs in the bedroom, uncertain about the extent of Morland and Tipfield's imaginative powers.

In their typical fashion, protective of their time and impatient for the bottom line, the detectives wanted to hear the scenario without the distracting details. Lasorta countered that those inconvenient details both suggested and confirmed the scenario. Sooner or later, the details would supply the confirmation of this reconstruction of the final battle between Carlo and Betty.

According to Lasorta's reconstruction, Carlo retrieved the old shotgun from the closet during the bedroom battle. Shells of the same type found in the weapon littered the closet floor. An oily rag sat in the closet's corner. Carlo grabbed his key ring, probably from the dresser, putting it through his left third and fourth fingers. With Betty disabled on the bed, his rage focused on everything else in his path.

His path led downstairs, probably on the way to the car, and the shotgun served as his tool of destruction along the way. He clubbed the walls with the gun's stock, bashing the gun against the pictures on route. The butt plate broke off on one attack against the plaster, the trigger guard fractured with another blow that penetrated the wall.

In the living room, Carlo continued breaking everything in sight, swinging the gun like a Little League batter possessed by the devil. Finally smashing the front door, he staggered out onto the porch, bashed the porch light like a high and outside pitch, and as a final act of destruction, turned to face the as-yet-undamaged living room window. Holding the shotgun in both hands by the barrel, he bashed into the window at least twice, the final time catching the exposed triggers on the window's broken wooden mullions and vertical shards of glass.

As he pulled the reluctant gun by the barrel to free it from the window's grasp, both triggers pressed against the opposite force of splintered wood and glass, discharging the weapon. The gun fired into Carlo's chest, flying from his bloody hands like a missile from its launching pad. It landed in the center of the living room, both barrels facing toward Carlo and the shattered window. Carlo traveled in the opposite direction, an unwitting example illustrating Newton's useful myths of motion. The keys fell to the porch floor.

The detectives smoked in silence. The prosecutor began to nod early in Lasorta's narrative.

"All of the reconstruction's points," the medical examiner said, "can be supported or refuted by the evidence developed at the scene, from the autopsy, and through our examination of Betty Selsner."

"The physical evidence," Lasorta added, "involves Edmond Locard's basic principle of forensic science stating that 'every contact leaves a trace.' "

Locard's principle led Lasorta to the bothersome details, abhorred by Morland and Tipfield, which served to confirm the scenario through a series of predictions leading to various experimental tests.

Lasorta began his series of predictions and observations with Betty in the bedroom.

"Betty did not walk through the hallway or down the stairs before or after Carlo received both barrels in the chest," he began. "Her bare feet remained uncut. If she had walked down the hallway, or even very far in the bedroom, the broken glass covering the floor would have cut the bottoms of her feet. Her feet had no such cuts. Even if she smashed the glass in the hall, along the stairs, and in the living room on her way down, she would have had to return through the broken glass in the living room, up the stairs, through the hall, and back into the bedroom. You found her sitting on the bed in the upstairs bedroom after you found Carlo on the porch. Again, no cuts on her bare feet, no slippers or shoes with glass from those sources imbedded in their soles, and no sign that Betty moved from the bedroom."

"Wherever the battle began," he said, "the fighting between Carlo and Betty remained in the bedroom."

"The glass also tells the same story according to the results supplied by the crime lab," he said.

Lasorta reported that the fragments recovered from Betty had both a distinct density and a different refractive index from the glass found in the hallway, or in the living room. If the glass fragments had a common source in the living room, then the density and refractive indices would match. Since they did not match, they did not have a common source.

"The lab techs visiting the jail cell recovered two differing glass samples from Betty's hair," Lasorta continued.

He explained that one sample had the same refractive index and density as the glass from a picture over the bed, and the other the same index as glass from the bedroom window. Additional fragments were consistent with broken vodka bottles also present in the bedroom.

Matching densities and refractive indices do not necessarily mean that the corresponding glass fragments have a common source. But the source of all the glass found on Betty remained consistent with glass found in the bedroom and inconsistent with glass found anywhere else.

The detectives remained suspicious of such vague talk about consistency. They wanted simple answers to simple questions. Did the glass found on Betty come from the bedroom, or not? They had spent too much time with lawyers and too little time with scientists to be comfortable with such cautious comments.

Lasorta explained the procedure and significance of the tests performed by the crime lab to determine both the density and the refractive index of glass fragments. Density is defined as mass per unit volume. Density determinations involve floating the unknown fragment with a control fragment of known density in a solution of bromoform and bromobenzene, adjusting the levels of each fluid until the chips remain suspended in the liquid. When both chips are suspended, their densities equal the density of the suspending solution.

Once investigators learn a fragment's density, another immersion test determines its refractive index. Refractive index is defined as the ratio of the speed of light in a vacuum to the speed of light through the material in question. Like density, it defines a physical property to help characterize the object in question. The unknown fragment enters a liquid medium with a known refractive index, varied by the scientist until the fragment, outlined by so-called Becke lines, disappears from view. The Becke lines disappear when the fluid and the fragment reach the so-called match point. At that point, the fragment and the fluid have identical refractive indices. When two different fragments have identical match points, they have identical refractive indices.

Both tests supply class characteristics of the fragments, but do not identify a common source. The density of a single sheet of window glass may not be homogeneous throughout. While two glass fragments from the same sources may have a slightly different density and refractive index, two fragments from different sources generally do not have the same values for each. For that reason, the tests function to exclude by extreme dissimilarity rather than to include by exact identification.

If two glass fragments come from the same confined source such as a windowpane or a tumbler, then they have an identical density and refractive index. Distinct densities and refractive indices supply evidence to "take away" the hypothesis of common origin. The glass taken from Betty differed from any glass found in the hall, stairs, or living room. While its source could not be identified by such tests, the fragments from Betty had the same density and refractive index as glass found in the bedroom. Absent any other possible sources, the bet that the glass came from the bedroom should win the pot. But confirming Lasorta's case did not rest solely on the laboratory's glass analysis. A larger picture began to emerge, covering the canvas with bold strokes painted in blood.

"Betty bled in the bedroom," the medical examiner continued. "Blood dripped from her face and onto her slip as she sat by the bed. The paramedic's run sheet states that they took some time to stop the bleeding from her lip and nose. If she walked downstairs after her injury, then she dripped her blood along the way."

"My original bet that she did not drip her blood was confirmed by typing the stains," he said. "Betty has Type A blood and Carlo has Type O blood. No Type A blood dripped along the route to the porch. Only Type O blood dripped on the floor, or cast off on the walls. So Betty did not walk downstairs dripping her blood. Betty's injuries, the glass, and the blood all help confirm my scenario of Carlo's death."

Now detective Tipfield began to nod occasionally along with the deputy prosecutor.

"Blood from the living room, the weapon, the window, and the porch also work to confirm this shooting scenario," Lasorta said. He continued talking with the tact of a skilled teacher who allows students some pleasure of discovery on their own along a guided path.

He explained that the blood stains on the walls and floors came from blood thrown off an object in motion, like a bleeding arm moving long various arcs toward each surface. These cast-off bloodstains combined with blood dripped into blood, probably from Carlo's nose or lip, that collected on the floor when he stopped for a breather, or where the cast-off patterns and blows indicated multiple strikes with the gun stock.

Detective Morland managed his first slight nod of assent toward the medical examiner during this explanation.

Lasorta continued, saying that the gun itself also carried stains that supported the shooting-as-accident reconstruction. When the gun fired into Carlo's chest, blood from the impact traveled toward the source of energy. This blow-back spatter appeared faintly on the section of the shotgun's barrel apparently out of Carlo's reach. But blow-back spatter coated the dusty outside surface of the window glass like paprika on a potato. The gun also had a faint coating of blood inside the barrel, drawn into the weapon as the hot gasses from the exploding powder cooled. Along the barrel that Carlo held with his bleeding hands, blood appeared wiped toward the muzzle. He had already bled on the barrel and his hands still bled when the shots rocketed the weapon through his grip.

The soft-spoken doctor continued to incorporate into his narrative the laboratory results recently delivered to his office by the crime lab.

"The lab found one partial fingerprint in blood on the barrel identifiable as Carlo's. The surface had been too smeared to be of much use developing other prints," Lasorta said.

The gunshot residue tests came out exactly as the signs of fouling on Carlo and their absence on Betty suggested. Carlo's hands, arms, and chest showed the presence of both burned and unburned powder residues along with traces of barium and antimony. But Betty had no residues present on her hands, face, arms, or slip.

The country's new chief medical examiner continued his account, mixing the interrelated processes of discovery and confirmation, of observation, hypothesis, prediction, and further observation.

Firing the old gun in the lab revealed a considerable leak in the breech, allowing abundant residue discharge toward any shooter. Lasorta reasoned that if Betty had fired the gun, she would have been covered with residue. She exhibited no residue. So she did not fire the weapon.

"Additionally, if Betty fired a double blast from the shotgun, she would have some sign of the gun's kick on her shoulder or chest," the medical examiner said. "She had no such signs, further evidence that she did not fire the shots at Carlo."

The mounting confirmations began to sound like the overkill of twin close-range blasts into Carlo's chest. Paint residue appeared on the triggers from the window's wooden mullions. The broken stock carried traces of glass, plaster, and paint from sources in the upstairs hallway, stairway, and living room. Blood that had dripped on the porch in front of the window appeared consistent with Carlo's standing there to deliver his two blows toward the living room. His slippers carried glass from his travels imbedded in their soles, and some rode along on his three-day stubble. Lasorta summarized the first conclusion developed from these results, applying the powerful method of putting in place, modus ponnens.

"If the glass fragments, bloodspatter patterns, injuries, and gunshot residues are not consistent with Betty shooting Carlo, then Betty is innocent," Lasorta said. "All this physical evidence is inconsistent with Betty shooting Carlo. So Betty is innocent of shooting Carlo."

Modus ponnens, like any valid form of deductive reasoning, depends on putting true statements in place to ensure a true result. When falsehood enters, all bets are off, regardless of valid form. The foundation of the chain remains the signs suggesting the hypotheses, and the signs observed as their confirmation. Even given his sound reasoning to exonerate Betty, the medical examiner's case required a second conclusion developed from the evidence, additional support to show that Carlo's death had been accidental.

"Now if Betty didn't shoot Carlo," he continued, "the problem becomes to explain his death. The evidence that clears Betty also helps confirm the accident scenario."

But a parallel logical problem develops for any reasoning that moves directly from the fact that Betty did not shoot Carlo to the conclusion that Carlo accidentally shot himself. Certainly if Carlo accidentally shot himself, then Betty did not shoot Carlo. But from the added fact that Betty did not shoot Carlo, deduction does not allow the inference, on those grounds alone, that Carlo therefore accidentally shot himself. Such logical problems involve errors in reasoning from one fact to another called fallacies.

This particular deductive fallacy has been named "affirming the consequent," moving in formal error from the discovery of the consequent condition of an "if-then" statement to its antecedent condition. Carlo accidentally shooting himself is an antecedent condition sufficient for the consequent condition that Betty did not shoot him. But the consequent condition alone, that Betty did not shoot Carlo, does not lead deductively to the antecedent condition that Carlo accidentally shot himself.

Some philosophers of science believe that all reasoning from effects to their probable causes suffers from this deductive defect, called the fallacy of affirming the consequent. Philosopher Morris R. Cohen quips that "Logic books are divided into two parts: In the first part on deduction, the fallacies are described, and in the second part on induction, they are committed." Other philosophers such as Baas VanFrassen add that all "inferences to the best explanation," or what Peirce calls abductions, merely commit the fallacy of affirming the consequent. As fallacies, they pack no rational punch.

But the likes of Peirce and Dr. Bell, through Doyle's Sherlock Holmes, do not constrain abduction to this mechanical shadow version of "inference to the best explanation," moving directly from effect to cause thereby committing a formal deductive fallacy. Holding that "if Carlo's death is an accident, then paint from the window's mullions appears on the trigger; the paint is there, so Carlo's death is accidental," commits the fallacy of affirming the consequent. But abduction as described by Peirce and exercised by Bell and countless investigators of violent death is not this type of mechanical inference based on simple deductive rules.

Neither Peirce nor Holmes separates the problem of developing a correct method of inference from the problem of practicing the right method for data recognition, collection, and evaluation. As Holmes says, "It is of the highest importance in the art of detection to be able to recognize out of a number of facts which are incidental and which vital." He emphasizes the importance of observation in this intertwined process of discovery and confirmation that he calls reasoning backward analytically: "The world is full of obvious things which nobody by any chance ever observes."

What makes an explanation of an effect "the best" involves its development from observed signs in a process of abduction, hypothetical deductive prediction, and inductive testing. The process embraces an explanatory fallibilism that coats the inferences with an obscurity often dependent on the physical context surrounding the required explanation, and the various abilities of particular investigators. Such an individualized context belies the rigid formalization and generic abstraction at the heart of deduction. It limits the overly simple account of reasoning from effects to causes that invokes a formal fallacy to account for the inference.

But the contingent context does not block a reasoned defense of the solution to a mystery. It only underscores the obvious: Profound mysteries remain until their solutions can be produced. With the solution in sight, and a clear eye focused on confirming tests that apply hypothetico-deduction, the original mystery becomes elementary. That lasting elimination of mystery appears to be at least a part of what makes an explanation "the best."

Lasorta might have developed his explanation dissolving the mystery of Carlo's death by eliminating the available competing alternatives. As Sherlock Holmes observes, "One should always look for a possible alternative and provide against it. It is the first rule of criminal investigation." Seeing just what counts as "the competing alternatives" for serious consideration illuminates the limitations of a purely mechanical, deductive approach to the explanation of given effects.

An imaginative defense attorney once argued that his client did not commit a murder because milliseconds before the bullet that his client fired struck the decedent, the victim died of a heart attack. That remains a possible alternative explanation, and nothing developed in the autopsy could rule it out, at least not before Dr. Shepherd and Dereck Tremain developed their rhodamine B and light green method for staining heart tissue. But it also remains an improbable explanation. No signs observed anywhere in the case suggested the heart-attack death scenario. The attorney's ad hoc explanation developed through a purely adversarial interest in defending his client, not from any signs at the scene, in the decedent's history, or observed at the autopsy.

An imagination uninformed by observation introduces as many avenues for error as an imagination absent altogether. Like Morland and Tipfield's amended shooting scenarios proposed to preserve their original conviction that Betty shot Carlo, the available signs at the defense attorney's shooting scene also said otherwise by their absence. This absence of signs often serves to eliminate competing alternatives by failing to license their development in the first place. In Sir Arthur Conan Doyle's *The Lion's Mane,* Inspector Bardle explains some dark red lines on the victim's back as the result of contact with a red-hot wire net. His explanation merely accounts for one unique detail and ignores the boundaries supplied by the larger context of signs from both the body and the scene. No source of wire. No source of heat. No blistered or burned skin. No traces left by any such contact.

Lasorta did not need to eliminate the possibility that Carlo had been shot by an invisible intruder, or that he had been zapped by a death ray from a Klingon star cruiser. No signs at the scene suggested either hypothesis. The possibility that signs had been overlooked, were absent, or became invisible, formed a measure of the reasonable uncertainty attached to any explanation formed by fallible humans. The available signs at 1325 East Wheelwright did suggest that Carlo had been shot by accident.

"Consider," Lasorta said, "the paint on the shotgun's triggers, the blood, the gunshot residues, and the wounds, together with the larger pattern of destruction in the house."

He began his tidal wave of inference using the observed signs to confirm his account.

"If Carlo intended to shoot himself, blood from his hands would be on the trigger, or the gun would be with him on the porch," Lasorta said. "Neither obtains. So Carlo did not intend to kill himself. Also the range of the shots is inconsistent with suicide. If Carlo fired the shots suicidally, the muzzle would contact his body. The muzzle did not contact the body, so he did not fire the shots suicidally."

Morland, now in the spirit of the discussion, raised a question. A puzzled look shadowed his brow.

"How do you know," he asked, "that Carlo didn't break the window with the first blow, then merely hook the triggers over the wood with the second, and blow himself away on purpose?"

"The answer, of course," replied Lasorta smiling, "is that we do not know, cannot know, and never will know for sure. But the larger pattern of his destruction, the fact that he carried the car keys along with him, and his past history, all count against suicide."

"All we can do here, from our perspective, is place our bets," Lasorta added. "Since I'm signing the death certificate, I'll bet that he never even knew that the gun had two shells in its chambers, or if he did, he forgot that fact on the Saturday he used it like an oversized truncheon to smash his way onto the front porch."

Lasorta explained that Carlo pulled the gun toward him, thereby pushing its triggers against the broken window mullion, firing the weapon.

"We can see the paint, the blood and the fouling residues," Lasorta said. "We can't see his intentions as mental events."

The law holds that intent can be measured by objective actions, by steps taken, not by invisible mental activities. If outside observers gauge Carlo's intent by his drunken smashing and trashing behavior on his way to the porch, then he intended to continue the process by smashing the living room window. The larger pattern of the scene helps measure Carlo's intent in this legal sense. Lasorta saw no signs that appeared to disrupt these inductive associations, nothing to fray the weave of the scene's overall fabric.

Peirce would say that the measure of legal intent involves the process of abduction inherent in any perception that goes beyond blank staring. The logic of human knowledge in general and of science in particular exhibits a structure similar to the logic of this Holmes-style investigation described by Lasorta to his audience of three in the overly warm and smoky homicide conference room.

The investigation of Carlo's death involved nothing less than commitments to the nature of human knowledge, the logic of its discovery and confirmation, and an awareness of the limitations that each process brings to our state of knowing and believing. It exercised the moral integrity required to follow the evidence where it led, and to distinguish the relevant features of a case from those irrelevant forces that nevertheless enslave popular interest, cheapen the human spirit, and undermine the human intellect.

After exercising these commitments, meeting the limitations, and applying his intellect to Carlo's death, Jacob Lasorta, MD, returned to the medical examiner's office. Meanwhile his investigators had delivered five new cases, resting on the stainless steel trays used to store the medical mysteries that he applied his skills to help solve. Many mysteries were to follow. The bulk of them received little attention outside the medical examiner's office.

Detectives Morland and Tipfield returned to duty with a developing sense for appreciating the details, and a less black-and-white approach to their cases. They developed a working relationship with the medical examiner's office that led to the successful resolution of many investigations over the next several years.

Betty Selsner, released from jail, continued her drinking and fighting ways. Over the next four years she returned to jail 13 times for drunk and disorderly charges, serving three weeks here, and two months there, for offenses ranging from public drunkenness to drunk-and-disorderly, and resisting arrest.

Four years and five months after Carlo's death, a medical examiner's investigator responded to a dead-body-found call, visiting a fifth-floor room of a once-majestic hotel turned flophouse. One of the fifth-floor residents noticed an unusually offensive odor. A patrol officer, accompanied by the dwelling's manager, had opened the door of Room 514 to find blood stains dripped, wiped, and splashed everywhere. Betty Selsner, dressed only in a soiled slip, lay in a foul pool, bordered by dried blood and crusty vomit, beside her dark-stained and unmade bed. Broken bottles helped furnish the otherwise sparsely appointed room. Both putrefactive and autolytic processes swelled her body, tightening the slip around her arms, chest, and legs. She had been dead at least three weeks.

Her death, despite the appearance of Room 514, was natural. She died of a massive GI bleed, a side effect of chronic alcoholism. She was 56 years old. *Soli Deo Gloria.*

The fight or flight response.

chapter eight

Proof—The Melrow Case

Causal Explanation and Formal Deduction

> Those rules of deduction laid down in that article of mine . . . are invaluable to me in practical work.
>
> Sherlock Holmes

By the time Dick Shepherd met Detective Superintendent Wesley Levine at the Guy's Hospital morgue, 80-year-old Stephen Melrow had been dead for 12 hours. Melrow lay on the gurney that he'd ridden from the ER to the refrigerator about 9:30 P.M. the night before. He wore only EKG leads on his chest. Death had separated Melrow from even his false teeth. His full upper and lower dentures remained in Metropolitan Police custody along with his clothing.

From his frail appearance, Melrow would not have been out of place in any hospital morgue, awaiting collection by some local mortuary. Levine's presence and the request for Shepherd's services appeared to be the death's only unusual features. Levine greeted Shepherd by explaining police interest in an elderly man on a gurney in a hospital morgue.

While Shepherd changed into blue scrubs, Levine said that Melrow had left home about 7:30 P.M. to visit his local pub and play checkers with a friend. As he walked down a busy sidewalk near London Bridge Station, witnesses saw two boys approach Melrow from the opposite direction. One boy grabbed him and spun him around, holding his arms behind his back, while the other stole his wallet. As the boys ran, Melrow walked about 50 feet, sat down on a raised concrete flower bed, and suddenly collapsed backward, striking his head on the container's opposite edge.

While witnesses rushed to help Melrow and perform CPR, two other boys on bicycles followed the robbers' retreat to a nearby building and called police. Melrow's muggers, who still carried their victim's wallet, were identified by the bicyclists and arrested by the officers. An ambulance rushed

Melrow to nearby Guy's Hospital where he remained unconscious and died two hours later. The muggers faced charges of robbery and assault. Levine appeared with Shepherd to learn from the pathologist if his suspects would also face charges in Melrow's death.

Witnesses to Melrow's mugging consistently said that the boys struck no blows. They said that the muggers used no weapons and inflicted no apparent injuries. Any additional charges in this case completely depended on the results of Shepherd's autopsy. Levine explained that the two boys' solicitors had already engaged a forensic pathologist from Charing Cross and Westminster Medical School to perform a second autopsy should Shepherd's results prove contrary to defense interests. Levine now watched as Shepherd bent over the body and began his external exam to document visible trauma.

An area of bruising measuring 1.5 cm in diameter appeared on the right upper chest. Small pin-point petechial hemorrhages dotted the eyelids. The edentulous mouth showed no injury to lips or gums, and no airway obstructions appeared. Both arms had several purple ecchymoses, patches similar to small bruises or large petechiae, common to elderly skin and aging capillaries. After photographing the body's anterior surfaces, Shepherd examined its posterior aspects.

Turning the body, Shepherd observed a superficial horizontal laceration on the left side of the head, 2.5 cm to the left of the occipital protuberance, the natural high-point on the landscape of the posterior skull. After examining every inch of the body's surface, he found no other external signs of violence or trauma. After more photographs, attendants moved the body from the gurney to the autopsy table, placing a rubber block under the back of its neck.

Making a "Y" incision and reflecting the skin on the chest revealed diffuse bleeding over the sternum and discreet areas of bruising above the inner margin of the third rib and over regions of the fifth and seventh ribs in the mid-clavicular line, an imaginary border from the middle of the collarbone down the ribs dividing each side of the ribcage in half. Reflecting the scalp exposed a cluster of small patchy hemorrhages up to 0.5 cm in diameter in the right temporalis muscle overlying the right side of the skull. Shepherd found no corresponding external mark on the right temple.

The skull had no fractures, but he saw recent anterior fractures of the right third, fourth and fifth ribs, and the left third through seventh ribs. The left ribs had fractured from their attachment to the sternum. While Levine watched, Shepherd removed the internal organs for examination and histological section.

The pharynx and larynx, in the language of forensic pathology, appeared "unremarkable" to Shepherd. But the contrary designation, "remarkable," does not exclusively capture the signs needing a pathologist's interpretation. Depending on the case, an unremarkable pathological finding might be quite unusual, and require extensive explanation.

A violent homicide with unremarkable organ systems and no apparent signs of trauma would be quite unusual. Each absent sign would require some explanation. An 80-year-old male with "unremarkable" organ systems would, with only apparent paradox, be quite remarkable. It would be unusual to live 80 years without some significant pathological changes. Shepherd found that Melrow's cardiopulmonary system appeared consistent with his age and lifestyle, a finding both pathologically remarkable and logically usual.

On their way to the scale in Shepherd's hands, both lungs looked like soiled sponges. With moderate pressure, the tissue released foamy gray bubbles. Unremarkable lungs appear more firm, less wet, and do not release such bubbles. Both lungs were grossly edematous, uniformly swollen with fluid, and had marked generalized emphysematous changes.

A pulmonary emphysema appears as an increase in alveolar size and a decrease in their number. The enlargement of the remaining spaces destroys the alveoli's surface, accounting for the tissue's spongy appearance and its inefficiency in oxygenating the blood. A collapse of the smaller airways traps expiration gases, decreasing the efficiency of respiration and increasing breathlessness during exertion.

The lungs also showed Shepherd a mild chronic inflammatory thickening of the airways, consistent with symptoms of chronic bronchitis. He recorded their weight, sectioned the tissues for microscopic examination, and turned his attention to Melrow's cardiovascular system, the respiratory system's now-silent partner.

The aorta showed moderate atheroma, a deposit of lipids, or fats, on the inner walls of large- and medium-sized arteries. They commonly appear in middle age, and when the deposits constrict the arteries, the flow of blood becomes impaired. When the supply of oxygenated blood to the heart muscle decreases, ischemic heart disease, a mechanical obstruction of the blood supply to the heart, results.

Shepherd examined the coronary arteries, the vessels supplying blood to the heart muscle, or myocardium. The left marginal or end branch of the circumflex artery showed severe atheroma, narrowing or stenosing the opening by three-quarters of its diameter. Only one-quarter remained patent, or open, to supply blood to the heart muscle. He weighed the heart on the scale, recording its 365 gram measurement in his notes.

He saw no evidence of recent or old scarring from infarction on the myocardium itself. Histological examination may show areas of infarct as yet invisible to the unaided eye. He dissected the heart further and noted that the valves and pericardium appeared "unremarkable." He removed sections of the myocardium, and placed the heart in a container of formalin to preserve the specimen for any subsequent examination.

Only the esophagus presented additional findings. It showed a marked dilation or enlargement, containing a large quantity of partially digested food. This common condition, known as a hiatal hernia, presents a protrusion or rupture of part of the stomach through the esophageal hiatus of the diaphragm. It can cause symptoms of indigestion, and in some cases can affect the mechanical function of the diaphragm, one of the muscles that controls respiration.

Shepherd removed the remaining organ systems, examined, sectioned, and described them as "unremarkable." Removing his gloves and scrubbing his hands at the sink, he offered his conclusions to Levine, who stood patiently behind Shepherd, protected from the fluids associated with an autopsy and its immediate aftermath. Levine waited to learn why Melrow died.

Shepherd told Levine that he found signs pointing to significant long-standing respiratory and cardiac disease. These, he explained, had been exacerbated by a large hiatal hernia. He explained that all Melrow's injuries appeared to be minor, and that they had neither caused nor contributed to his death. The fractured ribs and chest bruising resulted from heroic CPR efforts to revive Melrow after his collapse. The laceration on the back of the left side of his head and the externally undefined deep bruise on the temple appeared to be minor trauma associated with his backward fall into the planter. Shepherd explained that Melrow had died from the effects of ischemic heart disease, chronic bronchitis, and emphysema.

In the language of forensic medicine, these effects, which developed gradually over Melrow's lifetime, caused Melrow's death. But "causes" seldom occur as single factors invariably leading to specifically predictable effects. "Cause" itself remains a simple concept only in the abstract worlds of pedagogical fantasy and judicial determination. Levine needed Shepherd to address the complex causal role that the mugging played in Melrow's death. That final feature of potential causal significance occurred suddenly at the end of his 80-year lifetime. Levine's quest for a causal explanation of Melrow's death raises what philosophers call a "complex question."

Complex questions fail to isolate a single component requiring explanation from among many interconnected processes contributing to distinct but related effects. Levine's question, "Why did Stephen Melrow die?" represents such a complex question. The context in which the question arises influences the answer: Medical, personal, and legal contexts produce different kinds of explanations.

In a clinical medical context, the question often involves "cause" in the sense of physical mechanisms: a medical reason explains why someone dies of ischemic heart disease. The ultimate reason, either hypoxic or anoxic encephalopathy, involves a mechanism affecting the oxygen supply to the brain. In a personal context, however, a question like, "why did Stephen Melrow die?" may be noncausal if it calls for answers to questions such as "Why did Melrow have to die, as opposed to being taken ill?" "Why do his relatives have to suffer this loss?" or "Why did Melrow have to die, as opposed to his checker partner, or someone more evil than Stephen Melrow?"

Events such as Melrow's dying become complex because they have many parts. Parts include the tragedy of his death and the loss by friends and family, as well as distinct types of "causes" for it, like going to the pub to play checkers, walking near London Bridge Station, not taking a cab, being

80 years old, having serious heart disease, and meeting two muggers. Seeking explanations of the entire event at once, either causal or noncausal, becomes an unguided hike through a briar patch of misdirection. Forensic contexts require the discovery of questions that identify and isolate single aspects of an event to be explained.

To analyze an event, investigators separate its component parts, and ask questions one at a time. This analysis involves breaking a complex event into its component parts much like chemical analysis involves breaking down chemical compounds into their basic elements. In death investigations, causal explanations develop by analyzing complex events and asking specific causal questions to explain signs representing given effects. Nature mixes them up in a tangle of signs. Reasoning backward analytically must separate them, sorting the relevant signs from the irrelevant according to context.

Aristotle recognized these interconnecting features of the natural world when he analyzed "cause" into four distinct kinds of characteristics things possess. He did not mean by "cause" simply "something that brings something else about." Aristotle used each kind of characteristic to categorize objects and events, to explain what they are like, to account for what they are, and to understand how they work, develop, and change. Such an evaluation would help Shepherd scientifically settle the complex causal question posed by Levine, and help determine the signs of Melrow's death relevant to the forensic context.

In a sense, Aristotle's account of the concept of "cause" became an early account of scientific explanation. His analysis of causal explanation depended on his other systematically developed philosophical views. As a student of Plato, Aristotle adopted some of his master's positions, and adapted others to fit his own theories. While the exact relationship of their philosophical opinions occasions much scholarly debate, a general sketch suggests key differences in their alternative approaches to science.

Where Plato saw reality as abstract and mathematical, Aristotle viewed the world as concrete and visceral. Each vision has enjoyed both followers and detractors over the centuries. One practical difference between their positions appeared through explanations developed for natural processes, the subject of natural philosophy, later dubbed "natural science" by William Whewell in 1840.

Followers of Plato tended to focus on transcendent mathematical form, often discounting particular appearances in a quest for the solid underlying reality of formal laws. Those walking along Aristotle's path maintained a more imminental focus, seeking explanations relating both formal laws and unique concrete particulars. Aristotle systematically related these abstract and concrete features in his account of "cause."

In Aristotle's system, all nature remained alive in that it progressed through purposeful development. He called that development the "natural form," a natural potential in things that became actual in physical matter the way that an acorn might, under the right natural conditions, develop into a mighty oak tree, or that under the right conditions, plaque might deposit on healthy arterial walls.

Given his teleological, or goal-oriented view of the natural world, Aristotle asked four kinds of questions to discover the "right natural conditions" explaining a present natural effect: What materials were involved?; What forms were actualized?; What end was sought?; and What initiated the process? In common sense fashion, the four questions gather information about the effect's material composition, its blueprint or structure, its natural goal or tendency, and its mechanism of movement. The answers to these four questions distinguished, respectively, what he called material, formal, final, and efficient causes, distinct components of the natural process of change from the merely potential to the materially actual.

Shepherd and Levine, standing in the Guy's Hospital morgue beside Melrow's "materially actual" remains, faced a complex causal question about the "right natural conditions" explaining the "cause" of his death. They did so by untangling four diverse Aristotlean-style questions. The questions do not neatly translate from Aristotle's views into the language of forensic medicine. But the distinct forensic notions of a particular death's cause, manner, and mechanism owe an intellectual debt to Aristotle's efforts to understand scientific explanation as a complex logical process. Like the medical and legal components explaining a death, his analysis of "cause" involved separable yet logically interrelated factors discovered through recognizing the effects to be explained in a specific context.

Melrow's death, like any particular complex event evident through its effects, has many causal components in each of Aristotle's senses: material, formal, final and efficient causes explaining the deposit of lipids on artery walls, the disruption of the lungs, and even formal components explaining the cause of the causes themselves.[1] Each different type of cause, from genetic, biochemical and physiological, to environmental, social and psychological, carries some underlying specialized theory developed for explanatory support. For Aristotle, given such explanatory principles, particular matters of fact could be proven by deduction, explained as particular instances of the explanatory rule, through what he called a valid syllogism.

Applying any theory of scientific explanation, including Aristotle's, depends on isolating the puzzling natural process that requires explanation, and identifying the corresponding theory to apply as the general explanatory principle to deduce the particular effect. But no general scientific theories explain the diverse causal interactions of interest to Shepherd and Levine in crafting a specific causal explanation of Melrow's death. Explanatory theories and principles abound. Selecting those appropriate to apply and assessing their interaction becomes an exercise in Peirce's abduction.

Shepherd and Levine now focused on identifying the specific causal role that Melrow's muggers played in his death, and developing a scientific causal explanation of his death addressing that role. Shepherd sat deeply in thought as Levine explained that the time between Melrow's assault and his collapse had been less than 10 minutes, and that the distance between the point of attack and the flower bed had been less than 50 feet.

Shepherd pointed to a basic causal principle of physiology associating increased stress with increased heart rate. Beyond the mere association of these effects, the principle supplies an explanatory connection. When the heart rate increases, the work that the heart does also increases. With these increased demands on Melrow's diseased cardiovascular system, collapse and sudden death might easily follow an episode of stress. The mugging presented an episode of stress, and therefore, Shepherd said, could be related causally to his death.

Shepherd's meditation had given Levine his answer. The muggers faced an additional charge of manslaughter in Melrow's death. In preparation for their trial in Crown Court, the accused's solicitors decided to arm the defending barrister with the thinking of another forensic pathologist from Charing Cross and Westminster Medical School, Dr. Rowland Baine.

At 2:00 P.M., Baine reviewed Shepherd's autopsy and performed a second postmortem examination. He examined Shepherd's freshly typed report, the police photos, the clothing, the dentures, the body, and the organs. Later he would review the histology. Based on these observations, he developed his interpretation of the pathological findings, and formed his own conclusions about the causal factors involved in Melrow's death.

In addition to the bruising and laceration recorded in Shepherd's report, Baine found a bruise measuring 2 cm by 1.5 cm on the upper right abdomen. He confirmed all of Shepherd's other findings. In his report, he described the heart as being of normal size, with its coronary arteries showing severe atherosclerosis. He recorded a 75% narrowing of the anterior descending artery and a branch of the circumflex artery, a slight thickening of the left ventricular wall, and irregular small areas of myocardial scarring caused by chronic myocardial ischaemia. He found no signs of myocardial infarction or coronary artery thrombosis, a blockage of the artery caused by a dislodged bit of plaque, or a blood clot pumped through the circulatory system from another area of the body. His observations appeared to conform with Shepherd's.

Like Shepherd, Baine concluded that Melrow died of ischemic heart disease with chronic bronchitis and emphysema as contributing causal factors. He found the injuries to be minor, and said that they did not contribute to causing death, but showed that Melrow had been exposed to physical and emotional stresses before he died. He emphasized that Melrow's cardiovascular problems remained longstanding, and that they could have caused sudden death at any time, with or without precipitating factors, such as the stress of a mugging. He found no acute cardial lesion, like a thrombosis, nor an infarction.

Unlike Shepherd, Baine said that either a thrombosis or an infarction could be related causally to an acutely stressful episode. Their absence indicated, in his opinion, a limited, even negligible, causal role for the stress of the mugging. Melrow could have died at any moment, mugging or not, stress or not. Baine concluded that in his opinion, the medical findings established no direct causal link between the assault and Melrow's death. Shepherd, on the other hand, concluded that the same findings supported a direct causal link between the stressful assault and the death.

Holmes explained one basis for reaching such logically opposed conclusions from the same observations. When Watson says, "I can see nothing," Holmes replies, "On the contrary, Watson, you see everything. You fail, however, to reason from what you see. You are too timid in drawing your inferences." (See " The Adventure of the Blue Carbuncle," in *Complete Works,* Vol. 1, p. 244.) In another case, Watson again attempts to explain such divergent results by saying, "You have evidently seen more in these rooms than was visible to me." Holmes retorts, "No, but I fancy that I may have deduced a little more. I imagine that you saw what I did." (See "The Adventure of the Speckled Band," in *Complete Works,* Vol. 1, p. 257.) Part of seeing a sign involves recognizing its significance and building it into an inference. Dismissing signs and what follows deductively from them as irrelevant along one path, and including them as relevant along another, may result in contradictory conclusions drawn from the same observations.

The principle of noncontradiction, first detailed by Aristotle, holds that the same statement cannot be both true and false at the same time, in the same way, within the identical context. Either the mugging did or did not causally contribute to Melrow's death. Both statements cannot be true. The causal conclusion accepted by the court would determine both the manner of Melrow's death, natural or homicide, and the fate of the muggers now charged with manslaughter. The issue before the Crown Court turned on the scientific proofs each distinguished pathologist could provide to support these contradictory conclusions about the causal role of the mugging in Melrow's death.

Court convened three months after Melrow's double autopsy. After hearing testimony from police, the bicyclists, and the other witnesses to the mugging, the court focused on resolving the contradictory conclusions developed from the two pathologists' conflicting proofs.

Ordinarily "proving something" involves demonstrating its truth. In this ordinary sense, a deduction supplies the strongest kind of proof. Deductions clearly expose and demonstrate the relationship of the steps leading to the results that depend on them. With proper steps, the result stands. But improper steps vitiate the results. Shepherd took the stand first to present the steps leading to his conclusion.

From the stand, he developed his opinion that the medical evidence, the scene, and the history supported a direct link between the assault and the death. He began by explaining that the heart muscle requires oxygen to function. If insufficient oxygen reaches the heart, the muscle either dies or beats irregularly. Either effect, alone or together, colloquially termed a "heart attack," can lead to sudden death.

Formulating the next steps, he explained that oxygen reaches the heart via the blood supplied through three small blood vessels called the coronary arteries. The blood becomes oxygenated in the lungs, where mechanical respiration draws air into the alveoli and the blood's CO_2 exchanges for O_2. As the heart works harder, it demands more oxygen; respiration increases while more blood flows through these arteries to the heart. Partial or complete blockage of one or more of these vessels due to deposits of plaque leads to a decreased ability to supply the heart with oxygen required during periods of increased work. Mechanical interference with respiration also decreases the efficiency with which the blood becomes oxygenated.

Anyone with blocked coronary arteries, emphysema, chronic bronchitis, and a hiatal hernia may appear normal prior to a "heart attack," since at a normal work load, the heart has an adequate supply of oxygenated blood. When the heart works harder, the artery blockage prevents extra blood with its accompanying oxygen from reaching the muscle, and either the heart muscle dies or it develops an irregular beat. The inefficient oxygen exchange in the lungs and the mechanical obstruction of the diaphragm further decrease the available oxygen, making matters even worse for the heart.

He explained that the human body responds to stress caused by fear, pain, anger, or other strong emotions, by releasing a hormone called adrenalin produced by the adrenal gland. Adrenalin causes an increase in both heart rate and blood pressure. It shuts down inessential blood vessels such as the bowel, while opening those of the legs and arms in what's called the "fight or flight" response. This increases both blood pressure and heart rate, causing the heart to work harder and to require more oxygen.

Stress, he explained, can therefore be a precipitating causal factor in the development of a "heart attack," causing sudden death in someone with significant narrowing of one or more coronary arteries. The attack does not occur simultaneously with the stress since adrenalin continues to cause effects for some time after the stress leading to its release ceases. So, he emphasized, the collapse and death may follow the stress by some minutes. He then summarized his causal reasoning relating Melrow's death to the attack.

Shepherd first said that witnesses saw Melrow walk a short distance after the assault, then sit down before collapsing backward into a flower bed and striking the back of his head. Given the mechanism of a stressful assault, the proximity in time and place of the assault and collapse, the narrowing of his coronary arteries, the impairment of his lungs, and the mechanical restriction that his hiatal hernia placed on respiration, a direct causal link follows between the assault and the death. In short, Shepherd explained, Melrow appeared fine before the attack, working within his coronary and respiratory limitations. The attack put him beyond his capacities and he died as a result.

A vigorous cross-examination attempted to shake Shepherd's testimony. The causal role of stress in Shepherd's proof bore the brunt of the defense's assault. Defense barristers contended that while Shepherd's reasoning appeared formally solid, one of the steps contained a flaw that contaminated his conclusion. His causal deduction from general theoretical principles therefore failed to implicate the accused in Melrow's death.

Defense questions first explored general issues of sudden unexpected death, then focused on one of Professor Keith Simpson's cases at Guy's from 1959. A 19-year-old dockworker died after a fistfight with coworkers. His injuries appeared minor. Simpson's autopsy revealed a severe endomyocardial fibroelastosis of the heart, a congenital thickening of the left ventricular wall by collagenous and elastic fibrous tissue with malformation of the cardiac valves. The coroner ruled the manner of his death to be "misadventure," not manslaughter, even though the victim died suddenly during a "stressful attack."

Through questioning, the defense attempted to draw parallels between Melrow's pre-existing medical condition, which made him vulnerable to sudden death, and the 19-year-old dockworker's sudden death during a minor altercation. Both could have died suddenly at any time, with or without the attacks. The stress appeared to be coincidental rather than causal. Therefore, the attacks played no causal role in either death. Shepherd's deduction solving the mystery of Melrow's death, they suggested, contained a flawed causal step.

When Holmes deduces a mystery's solution, he proves it to the satisfaction of both Watson and the dull-witted inspector Lestrade. But his proof is built to withstand anyone's critical evaluation, including those brighter than his usual sidekicks. When he presents a deduction rather than his usual abduction, Holmes follows the correct deductive pattern that logicians call "valid form."

Aristotle was the first to classify systematically various valid deductive forms of reasoning that he called syllogisms. One such pattern, for example, holds that from "All F are G," and "All G are H," therefore, by form alone, it follows that "All F are H," regardless of what F, G, and H represent. Modern logicians recognize many complex valid forms generated by following valid deductive rules of inference. These "valid" rules countenance certain steps from one statement to another. Any result, or conclusion, that can be linked to given statements taken as assumptions by valid applications of such rules, represents a "formally valid inference" from those assumptions. For example, given an assumption of "If P, then Q" and "P," by form alone, validly infer "Q," again regardless of what P and Q represent.

Such valid deductive patterns, studied by logicians at a high level of abstraction, demonstrate a concern for form without regard for content. Formal validity's practical punch derives from its marriage with content. Passing the test of formal validity tells only half the story about a deductive proof's power. Holmes' deductions withstand careful scrutiny because they have both valid form and indisputably true content: The bridge of inference extends validly from correct assumptions across the abyss of error to the safety of a true result.

When such a deductive proof puts true statements into valid form, logicians describe the reasoning as "sound." Sound reasoning represents the strongest possible proof: True assumptions, plus valid form, guarantee true conclusions.

All deductions, sound or unsound, begin with certain "givens." Logicians call these givens "assumptions" to denote their logical status in the proof. Assumptions remain unjustified by stated reasons in a given proof, and are simply regarded as given truths upon which to build one's reasoning. If a parent hands a child a handgun, allowing him playfully to point it at a friend and pull the trigger, the friend may assume that "the gun is not loaded." Calling this an "assumption" assesses its status as "given," or "taken for granted."

Assumptions however, may be justified by other reasoning in different contexts. The friend may have watched the parent unload the gun yesterday. But assumptions lurk everywhere: The friend may also assume that "no one loaded the gun since yesterday." He may be fatally mistaken.

Some assumptions in proofs of scientific explanations derive from other sound deductions. But many proofs contain weak, uncertain, or even false assumptions as their starting points. Detecting such assumptions becomes a vital skill in assessing the soundness of a proof. Assumptions that turn out to be false, or inadequate for the proof's explanatory context, collapse the bridge of inference leading to the conclusion.

Holmes, following Peirce, derives the assumptions in his deductions from careful observations, risky abductions, or confirming inductive tests, as well as through other hypothetico-deductive processes. Despite their dependence on the support provided by such "givens," deductions present powerful proofs because accepting those givens entails embracing any conclusion validly derived from them. But the "givens" remain open to logical challenge.

Holmes' deductive success rests in his powerful ability to develop true statements abductively from which he extracts his deductive result. His independently derived abductions always best explain the signs that suggest them, and withstand the challenge of his confirming inductive tests.

Logically challenging the assumptions of a deduction involves understanding both the logical method that helped develop them, whether deductive, inductive, or abductive, and the specific context surrounding the deductive proof itself. Both involve knowing where various logical methods apply and where they do not in order to separate sound from unsound reasoning and to sort knowledge from error.

Throughout its examination of Shepherd, the defense probed his proof for error, attempting to characterize Melrow's mugging as coincidentally, not causally, related to his death. They acknowledged the validity of Shepherd's reasoning, but attacked its soundness. The flawed step, according to the defense, involved this mistaken attribution of a causal role to a coincidental event. Like the 19-year-old dockworker, Melrow could have died at any time. The crown prosecutor attempted to blunt the attack. In response to his next set of questions, Shepherd defended the soundness of his argument by assessing the logical foundations of the comparison.

With not uncommon courtroom serendipity, Shepherd happened to know the 1959 case from a study he'd made of Professor Simpson's original case notes, which rest on his office shelf at Guy's. On page 174 of these notes, he said, Simpson sketched the case's scenario and his autopsy findings.

A yellowed newspaper clipping reporting the case appeared taped to the opposite page. The case, he said, helped to support his findings, not to refute them.

The dockworker regularly engaged in heavy labor, putting increased work loads on his heart, and frequently participated in on-the-job fist fights. In that sense, he did nothing out of his routine when he died suddenly. A good case could be made supporting the explanation that his death and the fight remained coincidental events. He might have died during an episode of heavy labor, or during any one of the many other fights he seemed to enjoy. The case, however, according to Shepherd, did not parallel Melrow's death. The signs and circumstances differed relevantly.

Shepherd said that reading these signs and deciphering the circumstances pointed to each case's unique features. While the cases share a classification as sudden, unexpected deaths, the causal features differ. Not all sudden, unexpected deaths shared every feature. The dockworker's causal path appeared consistent with his normal pattern, following a blueprint of activity established through his history. He operated according to his habits when he died. His habits unknowingly extended his heart beyond its physiological limits.

Melrow's planned causal path had been interrupted by the muggers' external movements. These movements in turn caused the stress that initiated the cascade of physical events leading to his death. Melrow operated within his heart's limits by acting according to his habits. An external force disrupted those limits, and therefore played a causal role.

The proximity of the mugging and the death in both space and time further supported this causal role and counted against a mere coincidental association. Shepherd explained that the general physiology of stress has been both well documented and scientifically accepted. When Melrow's planned activity, his physiological condition, and the interruption of the muggers with their goal of securing his wallet join together with the physiology of stress, the conclusion causally relating the mugging and the death follows as a matter of logic.

Shepherd's causal reasoning, the type often applied in courtroom explanations of a death's cause, appears to trade on several intertwining notions of cause, reminiscent of Aristotle's analysis. In each sense of "cause," the relation between cause and effect remains explanatory. The cause in some sense explains the given effect.

The abductive logic of particular signs and their interpretation allows Shepherd to distinguish relevant observations from irrelevant artifacts, and to separate the crucial evidence from mere coincidence in the specific context before the court. He left the stand after exercising the opportunity to defend the soundness of his proof by supporting the explanatory power of its assumptions.

The defense then called Baine to present to the court its version of the death's causal story. Baine developed his conclusion that the medical evidence, the scene, and the decedent's medical history supported no direct link between the assault and the death. He began by focusing on the natures of ischemic heart disease, chronic bronchitis and emphysema. He explained how mechanical arterial blockage prevents adequate blood supply to the heart and how pulmonary compromise disrupts the adequate oxygenation of the blood. Death, he emphasized, could result at any time with or without precipitating factors such as the stress of an attack.

The prosecution, noting the omission of any causal account of the stress from a documented attack, asked Baine on cross-examination if he thought that confrontations with muggers might cause stress reactions, such as those characterized by the "fight or flight" response. Baine said yes.

He then asked Baine if such stress and the classic "fight or flight" response might have increased Melrow's heart rate, respiration, and his body's demand for oxygen.

When Baine replied that it might have, the crown prosecutor asked if such an increase might cause either anoxia of the myocardium, or an irregular heart beat. Again, Baine replied yes.

The prosecutor then asked if either anoxia of the myocardium, or an irregular heart beat might in turn cause collapse. Yes, Baine replied, it might.

He finally asked Baine if such a collapse in a person with Melrow's medical history might prove fatal. It probably would, Baine said.

The prosecutor had no further questions. His causal point had been made as clearly as he could make it. Now determining the true causal role of the attack in Melrow's death was up to the jury.

Before deliberating to reach their decisions, juries often endure hours of conflicting expert testimony. They may ultimately decide which authority to believe for very odd reasons. Sometimes one expert just "looks smarter" than the other, or one witness appears "nice" and the other fails to measure up. Juries universally appreciate clear, powerful testimony, and often believe the most forceful witness, even if that expert has overstated the case, while the less forceful authority carefully testifies within the limitations of appropriate scientific certainty.

Jurors facing the responsibility of making a decision with important consequences often seek certainty in a quest akin to Descartes' illusive search for a rational method to supply certain knowledge. The jury hearing the Melrow case faced what appeared to be two conflicting geometrical proofs, each apparently departing from different postulates. Both pathologists appeared capable, competent, and honest. Certainly each of their contradictory conclusions followed from their respective premises like a geometrical proof.

The uncertainty rested in the truth of the given premises, the assumptions akin to geometrical postulates. It focused on the relevance of including or omitting the "fight or flight" principle in the causal sequence. Regardless of their own mysterious methods, it remains the job of juries to sort out such conflicting proofs and to pick the winner.

The jury retired, deliberated, and returned, finding the defendants guilty of manslaughter in Melrow's death. The boys were assigned to juvenile corrections for not less than three, nor more than five years.The method the jurors applied to reach their decision remains unknown to prosecution, defense, scientific experts, and investigators. Regardless of the method they actually applied, Aristotle would have held out "logical method" as the only avenue to gain knowledge of the natural world, and the only possible path to reach the truth, no matter how complex.[2]

NOTES

1. Detecting a formal cause of death might involve sorting out the potential abstract structures or blueprints defining anything from the natural development of tissues such as genetic codes, physical laws, or biological dispositions, to the decedent's plan of action, such as walking to a pub to play checkers.

   Discovering such plans may also involve discovering a final cause of death, the natural goal or purpose accompanying the various formal potentials involved, whether those of the decedent or others involved in the death. Some have argued that this loosely approximates what the forensic pathologist means by manner of death.

   Aristotle's notion of a material cause loosely involves answers to general questions supplying an understanding of and a familiarity with living tissues, including heart, lung, skeletal muscle, and bone.

   Sorting out the efficient cause of death might loosely translate into uncovering what the clinical pathologist calls the mechanism of death, added to what the forensic pathologist calls the cause of death.

   In each instance, it remains helpful to view Aristotle's contribution to an analysis of "cause" as a theory of explanation. Peirce often appears simply to leave it at that.
2. Yet like the potential for error in a jury's method of reaching a decision, Aristotle's account of scientific method appears to have limitations. His metaphysics of science arguably failed to account for the quantitative, mechanistic, abstract conceptions of nature associated with the mathematical covering laws developed by Copernicus (1473–1543), Galileo (1564–1642), and Newton (1642–1727). Yet it remains a powerful testament to a philosophical struggle with the nature of scientific causal explanation.

   Its main defect as an account of scientific explanation appeared less as the inability to account for covering laws and more as a failure to detail the logical methods of discovery and confirmation required by the four kinds of causal principles that it described. Peirce's account of the logic of signs provides one suggestive remedy, and a practical avenue for scientists like Shepherd and investigators like Levine to follow in identifying the "right natural conditions" to explain a suspicious death.

   Followers of Aristotle's deductive logic who ignore his meditations on "cause" may offer theories of logic confined to deduction, as if no other inferences carry much weight. The formal validity of a proof remains empty in a practical context without plausible, if not true assumptions from which the deductions proceed. Often the difficult decisions faced by a jury depend on a method for sorting out such assumptions. Yet no rational power withstands the attack of a sound deductive proof.

The ancient philosopher Epictetus applied the power of deductive proof to defend the ancient assumption that whatever we mean by "logical method," logic remains a useful and necessary cognitive tool:

> When one of his audience said, "convince me that logic is useful, he said, Would you have me demonstrate it?"
> "Yes."
> "Well, then, must I not use a demonstrative argument?"
> And, when the other agreed, he said, "How then shall you know if I impose upon you?"
> And when the man had no answer, he said, "You see how you yourself admit that logic is necessary, if without it, you are not even able to learn this much—whether it is necessary or not."

—Discourses of Epictetus

There is nothing more deceptive
than an obvious fact.

chapter nine

Error—The Baby Beldon Case

Fallacious Appeals to Medical Authority

Some facts should be suppressed, or at least a just sense of proportion should be observed in treating them.

Sherlock Holmes

Children cleaned, oiled, and serviced heavy machines in the textile factories of 19th-century England, literally greasing the wheels of the industrial revolution. Their size allowed them to scurry like rabbits in the dark warren of gears and wheels that turned a profit for upper-class industrialists. Twelve hours a day, six days a week, they toiled amid the dust and grime of civilization's technological progress. Too often fatigue, malnutrition, heat, and noise mixed with spinning blades and grinding cogs to exact the price of progress: many children lost limbs; others, perhaps more fortunate, lost their lives.

Nineteenth-century English law protected domestic animals from mistreatment, but no such laws guarded children. They endured like the commodities of free trade, living as the property of parents and at the pleasure of employers. Circumstances appeared to differ little for children in other parts of the world. They remained a cheap source of labor, a fungible, renewable resource in the battle to win the industrial revolution.

Eventually they became more widely recognized as casualties in the revolt. In England, John Stuart Mill developed a "scientific ethic" that he called "utilitarianism" to help face the rising social evils spawned by technology. With the trappings of mathematical calculation and psychological assessment, the theory appealed to a public enamored with science and its methods. Ultimately Mill and his followers used the theory to affect social policy and enact child labor laws. In the United States, others took the lead to establish restricted working hours, defined safety conditions, and regulated wages. The effort focused on preventing young casualties while ensuring continued technological and economic progress into the next century.

Gradually, such labor laws spread among civilized societies and children began to experience civil protection from employer exploitation. They now enjoyed both parental and societal shields from physical harm. The greatest traumatic danger to a child's health had now been prevented as a matter of social policy, or so many continued to believe through the 1960s. Social health policy and medical research turned from trauma to focus on eradicating childhood diseases.

Several recalcitrant and poorly understood "syndromes" however, slowed landmark progress in childhood disease diagnosis, treatment, and prevention. Some frequently observed signs and symptoms, associated as a syndrome, began to form an image of one disease that resisted unequivocal explanation.

In 1930, Dr. David Sherwood discussed "Chronic Subdural Hematoma in Infants" in the *American Journal of Diseases of Children.* The affliction usually appeared in infants during their first year. He describes the signs as:

> "A serosanguineous xanthochromic encapsulated fluid . . . found under the dura, which condition in infants often causes enlargement of the head, vomiting, irritability, hemorrhages in the eyegrounds, downward displacement of the eyes, and symptoms of the central nervous system, the most prominent being convulsions."

The condition, he says, has been community referred to as "pachymeningitis interna hemorrhagica," a name signifying an infective process for which there appeared to be no supporting medical evidence. Its etiology remained a mystery.[2]

In 1946, John Caffey, MD, a pediatric radiologist, described multiple spiral fractures in the long bones of infants who also suffered from such subdural hematomas. Was this part of the same syndrome? The fractures he described appeared unusual: metaphaseal fragmentation, traumatic cortical thickening, and different stages of healing. He remained puzzled. He said:

> "In not a single case was there a history of injury to which the skeletal lesions could reasonably be attributed and in no case was there clinical or roentgen evidence of generalized or localized skeletal disease which would predispose to pathological fractures."[3]

He proposed his surprising but still tentative conclusion: "The fractures appear to be of traumatic origin but the traumatic episodes and the causal mechanism remains obscure."[4]

In 1962, C. H. Kempe, MD, intentionally coined the provocative term "the battered child syndrome" in a paper with that title. For years parents had lied about absent "traumatic episodes."[5] They beat, stretched, twisted, and pummeled their children. The dark ghosts on X-ray films revealed children caught among the gears and wheels of dysfunctional families and psychotic caregivers. Child abuse became a public health issue. Trauma regained its place with disease as a major threat to the well-being of children everywhere. Emergency rooms and pediatric physicians became the first line of defense in a renewed fight against battering the young.

Now when a child appears in an emergency room, the story explaining the visit often receives as much attention as the presenting symptoms themselves. Stories that fail to match symptoms become matters for official investigation. Some symptoms, including fractures, contusions, burns, blunt-force trauma, or signs of neglect, merit even greater attention. That increased attention also turns toward the story explaining the injury or the reason for a trip to the hospital. When a child in apparent good health dies suddenly, suspicions heighten measurably. The unexpected tragedy and its attendant signs require detailed medical and legal analysis beginning with the first call for help.

Molly Beldon, seven months, had drifted beyond anyone's help. She lay dead in the Pediatric ICU of St. Mary Catherine's Children's Hospital in Cincinnati for reasons that appeared both suspicious and unclear. Physicians had notified detectives about their young patient even before her death. Dr. Hal Darlen and Dr. Phil Templen suspected that Molly died from anoxic encephalopathy, a lack of oxygen to the brain, in her case as a result of the brain's swelling. She also had retinal hemorrhages, a rupture of blood vessels in the first of the retina's three major sections, visible in both eyes. The signs of ischemic encephalopathy, cerebral edema, and retinal hemorrhage suggested abuse. The doctors' preliminary diagnosis focused on "shaken baby syndrome."

Police detectives Jim Waller and Randy Stevens waited with the baby's mother, Sharon Beldon, in the ICU waiting room. Molly Beldon had been pronounced dead at 7:15 P.M., less than three hours after her move from the emergency room. Detectives and physicians had begun to piece together the chain of events leading to the baby's death in an attempt to understand the signs their young patient presented.

Sharon Beldon told admitting physicians Darlen and Templen that she had picked up Molly from the Caring Bear Daycare at about 3:30 P.M. She said that when she arrived, Molly lay sleeping on a couch covered with a blanket. She lay on her stomach with her face toward the back cushion. The blanket had rolled over her face in a lump between her mouth and the seat. Sharon said that when she picked Molly up, the baby felt stiff, looked blue, and her eyes had rolled back in her head. Molly's breathing sounded raspy and labored. She shook her child in an attempt to wake her, but the child did not react. Molly merely continued breathing, the pupils of her open eyes hiding behind her upper lids. Sharon said that she yelled at the daycare center operator, Ellen Boudet, that she would drive Molly to the St. Mary Catherine's Hospital ER for help.

When they arrived, Molly's treatment began in Trauma Room 2. Both physicians explained to Sharon that Molly's condition appeared grave. Stabilized, with her life supported by a respirator, she was transferred to ICU.

While sitting with detectives in the ICU waiting room, Sharon Beldon said that she first brought Molly to Caring Bear Daycare one week ago when she began taking classes at a nearby vocational school. She wanted to become a legal secretary. She dropped Molly off at about 8:00 A.M. and had picked her up about 3:15 or 3:30 P.M. after her classes. She explained that her husband, Ryan, returned from his construction job about 4:00 P.M. to care for Molly while she worked as a waitress from 5:00 P.M. to 9:00 P.M. in a small neighborhood restaurant. She explained that they had chosen Caring Bear Daycare because its cost fell within their current financial constraints.

Sharon had lost her ability to communicate further when Dr. Templen told her that Molly lay dead in Room 564. First hysterical, she now sat sobbing uncontrollably on a waiting room sofa, recently joined by her tearful husband. An arm over her shoulder, he tried awkwardly to control his grief by consoling hers.

Their only child's death appeared completely unexpected and totally devastating for the hard working couple who now faced an empty and uncertain future. Whatever else lay ahead, they would now begin to endure the rigors of an official inquiry into their child's unexpected death in room 564 of the St. Mary Catherine ICU.

A full investigation into Molly's death began for detectives on two fronts: both with the Beldons, and at the Caring Bear Daycare. Mrs. Ellen Boudet had called the hospital after Sharon's frantic departure to advise them of her client's pending arrival. Several hours after her call, she sat on the couch in her modest home-turned-day care facing detectives Waller and Stevens. She ran the day care, licensed by the state for up to 12 children, with her husband, Pierre, her teenage daughter, Tricia Gavin, and one employee, Sally Ostrude. She said that she, Tricia, and Sally tended the children. Pierre took care of things around the house, but did not actively help with child care.

From the look of the house, Pierre did not take his assigned task very seriously. Weeds had overtaken the small front yard, and paint peeled from the building's sooty exterior. Water leaked from both the kitchen and bathroom faucets, and the toilet emitted a continuous whine, like a man with the flu. Cracks and gouges appeared on most visible interior walls. Down a set of stairs, a well-worn easy chair faced a large television. The sounds and colors of daytime entertainment enthusiastically played to an absent audience. The colorful accessories necessary to entertain eight to 10 children covered the floors like debris from a tornado's visit to a trailer park.

On a typical day during this past week, Ellen said that she'd tended 10 children, ranging from six weeks to eight years in age. She said that Molly first came one week ago. She or Sally fed her soy formula as necessary, but administered no medications. From her one week's experience, Ellen described Molly as a fussy baby, who cried a lot and would not sleep in a crib. She or Tricia would often carry Molly around while tending to other children and rock her until she became sleepy. They would then put her down on the couch for her naps, covering her with a blanket. When she slept, they left her alone.

Whenever she awakened, she cried. Sharon, she said, had told her that Molly had been treated by their pediatrician for an ear infection. Ellen attributed Molly's crying both to the ear infection and to the first separation of mother and child.

Ellen explained that this separation did not appear to be particularly easy for either Sharon or Molly. Sharon called everyday about noon to see how Molly felt, and to inquire about her activities. Several times, Sharon told Ellen that she worried about how Molly felt, how fussy she was, how much she cried, and about her ear infection. She had called at 11:45 A.M. on the day Molly died.

When Sharon called, Ellen told her that Molly appeared to be somewhat congested, but that otherwise she continued doing well, at least by the standards of behavior set during her first week of day care. That day, according to Ellen, Molly remained as fussy as ever. She said that Sally carried her around until she became drowsy, and then laid her on the couch for her nap. Ellen said that she became occupied with other children inside while Sally played with the older children in the back yard. Ellen reported that Pierre had dedicated his day to defrosting the kitchen freezer. He apparently checked the progress of the melting process from his headquarters in front of the downstairs television.

Tricia, who watched TV downstairs with Pierre, responded when Molly cried the first time, picked her up and patted her back until she again became sleepy. She lay on the couch after Tricia put her down until Sharon arrived, found Molly blue, and rushed her to the hospital. Tricia had apparently been the last person to attend to Molly before Sharon arrived.

Tricia said that in her opinion, Molly didn't like her much. She said that Molly cried all the time, especially whenever she held her, had a funny cough, and hacked like she was constantly trying to spit up. At 14, Tricia had developed very little in the way of a maternal instinct. She appeared content to stare at the TV, attempting to blot out the presence of her stepfather. According to the detective's investigation, she had not always been so successful.

Child Protective Services (CPS) recorded a complaint that Tricia Gavin had filed, accusing Pierre Boudet of beating her with his belt, slapping her face with his hand, and applying additional unspecified psychological abuse. Tricia had been given counseling and placed with her natural father. Eventually, Pierre had been exonerated officially. She returned only recently to the Boudet household to assume her position in front of the television. Other CPS records proved equally interesting to detectives Waller and Stevens.

No less than four complaints remained on file charging Ellen Boudet, doing business as Caring Bear Daycare, with rough treatment of the children. According to one report, she allegedly spanked a five-year-old for wetting his pants. In another, a parent charged that she allowed their baby to wear a soiled diaper for a whole day. Two other reports appeared further to chronicle the increasing frustration Ellen endured while attempting to care for eight to 10 children every day for the last three years.

In each case, the complaints had been resolved, the day care's license remained intact, and the business continued to operate, at least until now. Ellen Boudet contacted her clients and informed them that the Caring Bear Daycare would close until the issues in Molly's death had been resolved, and until, once again, an investigation had lifted the clouds of suspicion from her childcare operation.

From their investigation of the Caring Bear Daycare, detectives Waller and Stevens had some relevant signs to follow, and some important information to report to the medical examiner. The medical findings appeared crucial to discover when the abuse might have occurred, and therefore who should become the primary suspects. The medical thread began with the two St. Mary Catherine's physicians, Drs. Hai Darlen and Phil Templen, both of whom focused on their diagnosis and treatment of Molly's condition in their report to detectives.

The two physicians initially felt that Molly had either suffered a blow to the head, endured some form of suffocation, or had an extremely virulent infection, possibly meningitis. They explained that lab tests conducted on samples of blood, cerebral spinal fluid, urine, and tracheal aspirate showed no growth of pathological organisms. Therefore, they ruled out infection. That left either a blow to the head, suffocation, or possibly "shaken baby syndrome," a violent shaking of an infant that causes its brain to collide with the sides of the skull, producing swelling, called edema, and hemorrhages.

Having ruled out infections, each of the physicians' remaining options to explain Molly's death had criminal implications. As clinical care givers, the physicians shared these discoveries with her parents. The physicians knew that the detectives had found Sharon and Ryan to be adequate new parents, adjusting as well as could be expected to the physical, emotional, and economic stresses of a new baby. They appeared loving and concerned for their child, exhibiting signs of grief appropriate for the enormity of their loss. As a sign of their concern, they appeared crushed by the criminal implications suggested by the physicians.

They first blamed themselves for placing Molly in an unsafe environment. Sharon beat herself with the heavy club of hindsight. She now saw the warning signs at Caring Bear that her need for economical day care had hidden from her earlier. The unkempt yard, the clutter, the teenager with an attitude, the blaring TV, the short three years in business, and even the low price that initially attracted them, became blows of self-torture. Predictably, the scope of hindsight widened and the blows changed direction.

Soon their anger turned outward toward Ellen Boudet and the Caring Bear Daycare. They became convinced that Molly had been murdered by evil, or at least slovenly, caregivers. Their worst fears were confirmed with news of the CPS complaints against both Pierre and the Caring Bear Daycare. The grieving parents followed the case closely as detectives continued to pursue its medical thread from a clinical setting in the ER and ICU through the Pierce County medical examiner's office.

Dr. Oscar Viccore had copies of Molly's medical records from her brief stay at St. Mary Catherine's. Detectives Warren and Stevens attended the autopsy, and informed Viccore of their interviews with both the parents and the day care providers. Viccore listened carefully. He then began his examination.

The little body wrapped tightly in white rode the full-size gurney like a marshmallow on a railroad car. Facing such diminutive dead patients was a more somber task than his usual encounters. The detectives watched from behind the glass observation window as Viccore unwrapped the white package and shined the overhead light toward the gurney.

The body showed signs of medical intervention. He noted multiple needle punctures and related subcutaneous bleeding over the right and left subclavian and left femoral regions, common sites for IVs and other blood work. An IV catheter in the right femoral area, and a urinary catheter both remained in place, their empty tubes now leading nowhere. Rigor mortis appeared uniformly developed, and livor mortis appeared on the body's posterior except where pressure from contact with the gurney held the settling blood away. He slowly moved the light from head to toe, first observing the body's anterior surfaces.

The eyes remained clear with no conjunctival petechial hemorrhages, a bleeding found in the thin mucous membrane covering the front of the eye and lining the eyelids. The ears, nose, mouth, tongue, and neck appeared unremarkable. A small bruise appeared over the mid sternal region, and diaper rashes covered the perineal area. He turned the body to examine the posterior more closely.

He saw scattered deep skin petechiae on the back and around the anus. No bruising, abrasion, or anal injuries appeared. The arms and legs showed no signs of note, and no evidence of trauma. Viccore made notes while the body visited X-ray, returning with images of its interior. The radiographs showed normal skeletal development, with no fractures, either fresh or healing. Armed with X-rays, he then wheeled the gurney into the autopsy area to begin the internal examination.

The Y-incision revealed severe edema of the underlying tissue, but no bruises. An abnormal collection of pale straw-colored fluid appeared in the pleural and peritoneal cavities. Diffuse hemorrhages permeated both the anterior mediastinal soft tissue and the superior thyroid. He made vertical incisions on both sides of the posterior trunk and found scattered tiny areas of petechial hemorrhage in both the subcutaneous and the muscular tissue. Turning the body, he incised the buttocks, finding neither subcutaneous nor deep muscular bruises.

Pursuing his diagnosis, he examined and described each of the body's internal organs. The skull remained unfractured, with no epidural or subdural hemorrhage present. He examined the leptomeninges, finding them thin and delicate with no purulent exudates, the necessary byproducts of a meningitis infection. Rule out meningitis. Other findings in the brain proved more interesting.

He found severe hemorrhagic congestion of the subarachnoid vessels in the cerebellum. The swollen brain weighed more than 1,000 grams, almost twice the average for a normal child at her stage of development. He found severe anoxic changes in the cerebrum, brainstem and cerebellum. The optic nerve appeared unremarkable, as did the ears.

The neck and spinal cord showed no signs of injury or other abnormality. The upper airway remained clear. The lungs exhibited occasional petechiae, and both remained congested and swollen. The epicardium showed several petechial hemorrhages, but otherwise the heart appeared normal. Except for intermittent petechial hemorrhages and anoxic changes, the other organs appeared normal. He removed sections of each organ for histological examination.

So far, the autopsy both suggested several explanations for Molly's death, and ruled out others. Refusing to make any premature diagnosis, Viccore signed the contributing cause of death on the death certificate as "pending microscopics." The official cause and manner of death would have to wait.

The reality of forensic science and death investigation frequently requires the exercise of patience. Often the interval between death and diagnosis serves to cement prior judgments and to fix initial perceptions among those unaccustomed to this necessary activity. Grieving parents, seeking closure for a tragic segment of life, and ER physicians, accustomed to lab results stat (immediately), understandably find waiting a difficult skill to cultivate.

When the impatiently awaited microscopic and lab results finally do arrive, they often meet resistance supplied by explanations developed without their benefit for reasons more emotional than scientific. In such cases, lab results fight these fires of preconception, ignited by impatience and fueled by untested speculations, as effectively as a full bladder facing a forest fire. The results of Viccore's histological examination by now faced the flames fanned by the ER physicians' diagnosis of shaken baby syndrome. But they showed that the diagnosis was more smoke than fire.

Under his microscope, Viccore observed severe anoxic changes in the brain tissue. He found focal hemorrhage in the interstitial tissues of the heart, with no ischemic changes noted. The lungs showed severe diffuse acute fibrinopurulent bronchopheumonia. Aspirated vomit appeared in the bronchi. Fibrin clots and areas of hemorrhage also dotted the slides of lung tissue. He saw inflammatory infiltrates with a prominent thickening of the alveolar septae. Treated with a special stain to reveal the presence of bacteria, the final slide of lung tissue showed some gram positive cocci, a sign confirming the presence of unwelcome invaders.

The other organs examined under the microscope presented evidence of both congestion and hemorrhage. The right eye showed red cells infiltrating several layers, but absent in the optic nerve sheath. The left eye also showed no optic nerve hemorrhage, with the bleeding confined to one layer. After studying the slides and recording his observations, Viccore finished his autopsy report and completed the death certificate.

He found the cause of death to be anoxic encephalopathy and cerebral edema. This in turn had been produced by acute fibrinopurulent bronchopneumonia and probable systemic infection, or sepsis, with mechanical asphyxia secondary to suffocation. He found the manner of her death to be accidental: Molly Beldon, congested with pneumonia and weakened by an infection, suffocated on the couch when laid face down against the blanket and cushion.

He wrote his opinion after assessing the circumstances, medical history, and police investigation of her death. He said that her condition and position resulted in a respiratory arrest, diminishing oxygen supply to the brain. This in turn developed a bleeding disorder, a disseminated intravascular coagulopathy, due to anoxic effects on the blood's clotting mechanism. The pathology, history, and scene all pointed toward an accidental death.

Classifying a death as an accident did not rule out further determinations of legal responsibility. Many accidents carry legal, even criminal, implications. Those unfamiliar with a medical examiner's language stating manner of death often confuse "accident" with "no one responsible" as easily as they confuse "homicide" with "murder." Viccore's report clearly ruled out homicide and ruled in accident, with its attendant legal subcategories open to further interpretation.

He sent copies of his report to Drs. Darlen and Templen, to detectives Waller and Stevens, and spoke with the parents, Sharon and Ryan Beldon. The detectives completed their reports, and both the police and CPS investigations closed. Caring Bear Daycare reopened the clouds of doubt apparently blown clear. But the difficulties Viccore's report presented for both the treating physicians and the baby's parents indicated that the controversy, far from being over, had just begun. The Beldons had hired an attorney.

Morgan Brown specializes in personal injury and wrongful death litigation. He asked for and received copies of all the official documents pertaining to Molly Beldon's death. He found himself in the position of trying to persuade the Pierce County prosecutor's office to file charges in what he, the Beldons, and both treating physicians believed to be the criminally wrongful abuse death of a seven-month-old child. The prosecutor's office investigated the matter, and after review, declined to file any criminal charges "at this time," a deputy prosecutor said.

In the interim, Brown advised the Beldons to pursue civil action against the Caring Bear Daycare, Ellen Boudet proprietor, seeking damages in the wrongful death of their daughter. The same arguments developed to support any prosecutor's criminal case could now bolster the civil case against Caring Bear Daycare. The opinions of treating physicians Darlen and Templen formed the heart of the legal case against Ellen Boudet and supplied the first step in Brown's proof of her wrongful death.

Both physicians remained disturbed by Viccore's findings and unconvinced by the reasoning presented in his autopsy report. They believed that he had committed serious errors in his analysis of the case. On that basis, Brown filed his civil suit. Dr. Templen would present the medical evidence as the plaintiffs' first witness in Beldon vs. Caring Bear Daycare. The matter would be resolved by a jury, selected to hear the opposing arguments and to rescue the truth from the clutches of error.

Truth remains one of the most difficult abstractions for philosophers to clarify. If not equally difficult, the concept of error in science runs a close second. Error in the forensic sciences, as in the theoretical sciences, is not a simple notion. Not all errors involve mistakes of the same type. Whatever account philosophers of science give, error does not reduce simply to believing something that isn't true.

Error could also be believing something that is true for the wrong reasons. Scientific error involves some sort of mistaken procedure that, regardless of outcome, contains certain specific flaws. Those flaws usually invalidate the procedure, ensuring that it fails to reach a successful outcome apart from chance circumstance. Scientists develop and modify procedures to improve the chance of reaching correct results. Flawed methods block this methodical advance toward true understanding. Erroneous methods advance science little beyond results obtained through random guesses.

Holmes eschews random guesses, claiming that: "I never guess. It is a shocking habit—destructive to the logical faculty . . . [when you guess randomly,] . . . You do not follow my train of thought or observe the small facts upon which the large inferences may depend."[6] However not all guesses are random guesses. Holmes' powers of observation, or as Watson says, his "extraordinary genius for minutiae," and his attendant ability to develop compelling solutions to criminal mysteries, depend upon a complicated series of abductions that Peirce would call methodical guesses.

Peirce says, "We must conquer the truth by guessing, or not at all."[7] Holmes' success as an investigator depends on rejecting random guesses as "destructive to the logical faculty" while embracing Peirce's methodological guesses as the heart of scientific methodology. Holmes in fact follows Peirce's recommendations for hypothesis selection and development. He follows guesses, or hypotheses, that remain simple and natural, easy, and cheap to test, and yet that contribute to explaining all the relevant facts.

According to Peirce, such methodical guesses must always be considered as questions to be answered by the tests that they logically entail. Scientific detection depends on a guessing-testing-guessing chain leading to defensible explanations of mysterious phenomena. That chain and its evidential links distinguishes an informed guess, characteristic of scientific methods applied to produce correct explanations, from a random guess, oblivious to the "small facts upon which large inferences depend." While methodical, the practice of applying this informed guessing procedure to a mystery does not ensure a correct solution.

If applying the forensic sciences to a death aims to produce, evaluate, and defend correct explanations of its circumstances, that task risks involving mistaken procedures in several ways. Errors could enter through incorrect observation, misinterpretation, or the incorrect applications of tools, techniques, or experience. This broad class of errors involves mistakes in protocol. These may result either from inadequate background knowledge, whether inexperience or ignorance, from flaws in the protocols themselves, or in the worst case, from dishonest manipulations to support preconceived results.

Errors also may enter into the production and evaluation of such explanations through mistaken inferring from given premises to the expert's conclusions. But not many real errors in death investigations result from mistakes in protocol or reasoning alone. Ordinary errors usually combine these defects, and seldom separate neatly for easy identification. None the less, errors usually can be identified and untangled by discovering the misapplication of specific procedures, other flaws in the protocols, or fallacies in the reasoning from their results. Discovering such error often results in defending a competing explanation, free from the demonstrated defect, as a better alternative.

Representing Ellen Boudet as the Caring Bear Daycare, attorney Jane Friniti conducted her investigation and came to believe that any errors in the explanation of Molly Beldon's death rested with doctors Darlen and Templen. She prepared for her defense of the Caring Bear Daycare by consulting with Pierce County's chief medical examiner, whose autopsy findings became the focal point for Brown's attack. Viccore's conclusions faced Templen's alternative in civil court.

The trial began over a year after Molly Beldon's death, and nine months after Brown filed the wrongful death suit. Jane Friniti waited anxiously as Dr. Templen took the stand. She had carefully prepared for this clash of medical opinion, pitting the official incumbent explanation against a brash challenger.

Following Brown's lead, Templen presented his credentials for the court, recounting his multiple degrees and his vast experience in pediatric critical care. Friniti rose and asked him how many of his critically ill or injured patents had died. He replied that he lacked precise numbers or percentages, but that he treated critical cases that resulted in death for about one-quarter of his patients. She asked him to recount his experience in postmortem studies, clinical pathology, and forensic pathology. None, he replied. Friniti agreed to support qualifying Templen as an expert in pediatric critical care. He could offer opinions to the court as an expert in that field.

Such expert opinions often carry great weight with juries. Once qualified, scientific experts act to inform the judge and jury, drawing inferences from the evidence based on a body of experience and knowledge lying beyond the reach of both the average judge and typical juror. In theory, experts offer opinions based on successful scientific arguments, offered rationally to support a particular conclusion. The success of such reasoning depends on the successful application of the three basic logical components of scientific method.

When deductive reasoning has valid form and proceeds from true assumptions, the conclusion must be true. Successful abductive, or inductive arguments support conclusions that appear more likely true than false but allow room for some small doubt. Such reasoning mixes together rationally to support the expert's opinion. Successful arguments of this sort ideally persuade jurors to accept the expert's scientific results.

Given successful arguments, there may, in fact, be unreasonable people among the jurors who refuse to accept correct conclusions. They may remain unpersuaded. This, of course, does not trouble a scientist whose sole interest may be to establish the truth or the probability of the result, and not simply to influence people's beliefs. A sound deductive argument has a true conclusion whether or not anyone in a jury box believes it. Truth, whatever theory philosophers defend explaining its nature, remains independent of people's actual beliefs. Unlike an election, the numbers don't count in determinations of scientific truth.

But unlike ordinary scientific reasoning, expert scientific testimony offered by forensic scientists in court aims to establish both the truth or probability of a conclusion and to influence each juror's beliefs. The numbers do count in a jury's verdict. Ideally, jurors believe the conclusions of successful scientific reasoning, and refuse to be persuaded by unsuccessful efforts. Ideally, a successful argument persuades both rationally and psychologically. But incorrect arguments may appear to be successful. Such arguments persuade psychologically but fail rationally. Juries may be unduly persuaded by errors thinly disguised as cogent expert opinion.

Often the persuasiveness of such testimony derives from psychologically persuasive errors in reasoning called fallacies. Usually, but not always, fallacious arguments have true premises, so they initially appear convincing. Recognizing fallacious arguments and exposing their errors exposes their efforts to persuade without successful justifications. Over the centuries, philosophers have named some common fallacies. Others become so complex and convoluted that it is difficult to isolate a single error, or even to name one error as primary.

To show how complex reasoning fails to carry the rational burden of proof exposes the fallacy. Simply reasoning from false assumptions does not, by itself, involve a fallacy. The error must be found in the reasoning, not simply in the premises or the protocol, for the error to be a proper fallacy.[8]

With Templen qualified as an expert, Friniti recognized that Brown's use of Templen to support his case risked committing a fallacy. Unnoticed, the error might improperly persuade the jurors. Yet may sway jurors, recognized or not.

Templen qualified as an expert in pediatric critical care, but not as an expert in forensic pathology or forensic medicine. Friniti carefully drew attention to the limitations of his authority to underscore any effort by Brown to commit what philosophers have called the ad vercundiam fallacy.

Ad vercundiam literally means "toward diffidence, or lack of trust." Certainly not all authorities can be trusted. But this specific error involves an illegitimate appeal to authority, an expert in one area offering an opinion in a superficially related but actually distinct field. An orthopedist and a gynecologist both practice medicine, but a gynecologist's medical opinion about treating a compound-complex femoral fracture carries little weight against an orthopedist's judgment. They operate in different spheres of authority. Friniti knew that jurors tend to lump medical experts together simply because they all have a medical education. Certainly on the face of it, a gynecologist's opinion about the fracture merits more consideration than a gardener's assessment.

But spheres of authority rarely divide like textbook examples of the ad vercundiam fallacy. Not all appeals to apparently divergent expert medical authority commit fallacies. Forensic pathologists may disagree among themselves about a specific bullet wound, but appeals to their competing opinions in a homicide case do not in themselves involve fallacies. Other reasons for their disagreement must be explored and offered to the jury, supplying additional information necessary to reach a verdict in the case.

In Beldon vs. Caring Bear Daycare, Templen's area of pediatric critical care included experience in the diagnosis of fatal injury and disease. It would be a mistake to dismiss his testimony as utterly illegitimate. Clearly his area of expertise was relevant to Molly's death.

Friniti determined to note the signs that Templen recognized, and the medical explanations he developed from them. The case would be argued at the level of the evidence offered for apparently conflicting authoritative opinions. Friniti knew that this strategy placed a great weight on the jury. Friniti's task remained to sort Templen's various opinions as they developed from Brown's questions, and to expose their errors to the jury.

Brown asked Templen simply to describe the steps he took to develop his diagnosis of Molly's condition when she arrived in the ER. Templen stated that he and Darlen first had ruled out infection as a potential cause of the child's symptoms. Cultures taken of blood, cerebral spinal fluid, urine, and tracheal aspirate showed no growth of pathological organisms. A chest X-ray taken on admission to St. Mary Catherine's showed none of the usual signs of pneumonia.

Brown then asked Templen how he would account for any postmortem findings of pneumonia, if no signs of the infection initially appeared.

Templen replied that the pneumonia could be explained by the severe shock and coagulopathy that the child suffered following an injury. He described this as neurogenic pulmonary edema. These changes had been caused both by clinical therapy in the ER and ICU, and by the ischemic hypoxial disease process. This meant, he explained, a mechanical limitation of oxygen supply to the body affecting all oxygen-dependent metabolic processes.

When Brown asked about any other explanations of the pneumonia, Templen replied that neither he nor his colleagues knew of any infectious pneumonia which could rapidly cause the death of a previously healthy infant.

Templen continued to explain the clinical signs which might be mistaken as signs of infection. He said that an elevated white blood cell count with a normal differential cell count signified a stress response. Stress, in turn, would precipitate some fever, due to a hypermetabolic state. So, he concluded, both elevated white cells and fever could be explained by stress.

Brown asked what might have provoked such a stress response. Friniti objected to the question. She urged that it called for a conclusion outside the witnesses' area of expertise and called for unwarranted speculation.

Brown offered to rephrase the question. He asked Templen what additional signs he had observed that might help support a diagnosis of the stress response.

Templen answered that the child also had extensive retinal hemorrhages, and that such bleeding commonly appeared in infants suffering from shaken baby syndrome. Generally, a severe shaking, which causes the brain to collide with the interior of the skull, produces severe cerebral edema and hemorrhage. Also an elevated white cell count and fever could result from the stress. The doctors had observed in Molly both cerebral edema and hemorrhage as well as the signs of white cell elevation and fever associated stress. So, Templen inferred, from his perspective as a clinician, Molly Beldon was shaken, and suffered injury from shaken baby syndrome.

Brown asked if he had received and read a copy of the medical examiner's autopsy report. Templen replied that he had.

Brown then asked for his clinical opinion about the injuries leading to the child's death. Templen replied that an infant of Molly's age could have been shaken, then suffocated, but recovered enough to breathe on her own. When placed in a position on her stomach that inhibited respiration, hypoxia resulted. This, he said, would explain all the clinical as well as the postmortem findings detailed by the medical examiner. It explained the severe cerebral edema, retinal hemorrhages, profound metabolic acidosis, severe cardiovascular insufficiency, and the profound coagulopathy. These signs could not be explained by an infection, he added.

Brown asked him for his opinion about the infant's cause of death. Templen answered that he agreed with the medical examiner's conclusion that Molly Beldon died of mechanical asphyxia secondary to suffocation. However, in Templen's opinion, suffocation itself became the primary factor which precipitated the course of events leading to death. He added that the pulmonary signs found post mortem resulted from attempts at resuscitation and clinical interventions following a lethal injury. Brown had no more questions.

Templen made a good witness. He appeared well-dressed and professional, held his hands still, exhibited neither distracting nor annoying mannerisms, and talked appropriately to the jury. He attempted to explain medical terminology simply and clearly. Friniti saw several jurors nod with understanding as Templen explained his findings. He appeared sincere, honest, and concerned. He sounded confident and his opinions looked as solid as any advanced by Sherlock Holmes himself.

Like Holmes, Templen worked as a dedicated and persevering professional, anxious to uncover the truth. Unlike Holmes, he lacked the broadening influence of educated thinking. The very intensity of his investigations produced errors. Templen narrowed his vision by holding the object of his research too closely. He saw several points clearly, but his narrow focus blurred his view of the bigger picture.

The difficult task of shaking his testimony appeared to depend on reaching to the depths of his medical analysis. Friniti would have to expose its foundation of error, and show his failure to account for relevant facts beyond his limited field of vision. Such a task would not be accomplished by a superficial assessment of his testimony's logical fallacies alone.

Like most fallacies, the errors in reasoning presented through Templen's testimony did not fit into neat textbook categories. One suggestive error came close to matching a formal error in reasoning called "affirming the consequent."

Templen appeared to argue that severe shaking (antecedent condition) causes cerebral edema, hemorrhage, and stress reactions (consequent conditions); they observed these effects (consequent affirmed); therefore, Molly had suffered a severe shaking (conclude antecedent condition).

This argument remains formally invalid: Just because shaking causes those effects, it does not follow from their presence alone that all the other causes of those effects have been excluded. A bullet in the brain may be sufficient to cause death, but the presence of death does not formally guarantee the presence of a bullet in the brain. The conclusion does not follow formally from the given premises.

The inference offered by Templen gains its psychological power to persuade because it suggests a missing abductive connection between the observed effects and their probable causes. The issue is not formal, but explanatory. Templen's testimony affirms that shaken baby syndrome supplies the best explanation of both the clinical and postmortem data. Undermining this testimony involves understanding the medical explanations linking the observed effects, as signs, to this probable cause.

The formal fallacy, apparent to Friniti in Templen's testimony, served as a sign pointing to the deeper logical problems supporting this diagnosis. These problems would best be exposed and presented to the jury by calling Dr. Viccore, the Pierce County medical examiner, to testify. He took the stand after Templen.

Friniti asked Viccore to summarize the information he had regarding Molly Beldon's physical condition before her death.

Viccore said that contrary to Sharon Beldon's memory of Molly's perfect health, the baby had been sick for two weeks before her death. She visited her pediatrician for the treatment of an ear infection. His medical charts indicated that he prescribed antibiotics and sulfa medications, which she took for 10 days prior to her death in the St. Mary Catherine's Hospital ICU.

Friniti then asked what effect such medications would have on laboratory tests for signs of systemic infection. Viccore replied that cultures of blood, CSF, urine, and tracheal aspirate would show no growth of pathological organisms because both the antibiotics and sulfa medications would still be at high enough levels to prevent their development.

She then asked Viccore to account for the post mortem appearance of pneumonia in the infant's lungs.

He described his microscopic finding of acute fibrinopurulent necrotizing bronchopneumonia in sections of lung tissue. The microscopic signs of this condition differ markedly from those characteristic in RDS, or respiratory distress syndrome.

Friniti asked why bacteria did not appear in the lung sections stained for microscopic evaluation.

Viccore explained that routine sections of organs with bacterial infection will not usually reveal the bacteria. A special gram stain must be applied. When prepared with such a stain, her lung tissue did show some gram positive cocci. Contrary to Templen's belief, bacteria did appear in the lungs.

Friniti asked if such bacterial infection could result in sudden death. Brown objected that this called for a conclusion outside the witnesses' area of experience, but the judge overruled the objection.

Viccore replied that he had seen such cases. Ten years ago, he had performed an autopsy on a child who had a tonsillectomy on a Thursday and died before a planned discharge on Friday. The child presented no obvious symptoms of infection, but the autopsy revealed an acute bilateral bronchopneumonia as the cause of death.

While statistically uncommon, the signs Molly Beldon's case presented pointed toward a similar diagnosis. Friniti had to use Viccore's testimony to overcome the current predisposition to favor child abuse as the usual explanation of a child's unusual death accompanied by hemorrhage, or bleeding. Friniti continued to follow the medical signs, allowing Viccore the chance to explain them to the jury.

Friniti asked Viccore about finding an elevated white count with a normal differential cell count. Viccore explained that leukocytosis of 52,000 could not be explained by a stress response alone. The normal differential count could be explained by previous antibiotic therapy, administered for 10 days prior to her death to treat an ear infection.

Anticipating a question that may have formed in some jurors' minds, Friniti asked Viccore why the antibiotics in Molly's system, even if given for another type of infection, did not prevent the development of pneumonia.

He answered that many organisms destroyed by broad spectrum antibiotics may be controlled only through their continued administration. When dosage levels fall, as they did when Molly finished her course of treatment for the ear infection, the undestroyed organisms continue to grow. The body's immune response continues to fight the infection. With a fast-growing and virulent invasion, the congestion continues to develop, even though the infection has been slowed by the drugs.

Friniti then moved toward the most familiar sign of child abuse, known perhaps even by jurors without any knowledge of anatomy or physiology. She directed Viccore's attention to the bleeding described by Templen as characteristic of shaken baby syndrome. She first covered retinal hemorrhages, then allowed Viccore's reply to cover Templen's mention of subcutaneous and muscular hemorrhage, which he could not explain as an artifact of therapeutic intervention, or by a natural disease process. Templen's testimony pointed jurors from those signs toward a beating as their only possible explanation.

Viccore looked toward the jury and said that he did not believe that Molly Beldon had been shaken. He added that if she had been, the shaking had nothing to do with her death. He explained that in a typical shaken baby syndrome case, retinal hemorrhages form a partnership with subdural or subarachnoid hemorrhages like a sign with its signpost. He cited the early literature, mentioning observations made by Sherwood, Caffey, and Kempe. Molly Beldon had no intracerebral bleeding. Thus, the retinal hemorrhage had another explanation.

He described the mechanism of the retinal hemorrhages as the result of intracranial pressure from a cerebral edema, a swelling that blocked venous return and eventually caused anoxic encephalopathy. The edema, he said, had been caused by asphyxiation from suffocation. The resulting lack of oxygen had a disastrous ripple-effect on the synergistic relationships managed by the cardiopulmonary system. One obvious sign of such anoxic trouble appeared when the blood's clotting mechanisms became imbalanced.

Bruises, the collegial term for bleeding under the skin, result when blood vessels rupture through external pressure or direct impact. Blood infiltrates into areas adjacent to the point of impact in an irregular fashion, squeezed into the surrounding tissue both by the force of impact and by leaking from the ruptured vessel. Clotting soon blocks the ruptures, leaving the irregular bloody infiltrate as a sign of the original blow. However, he explained, the subcutaneous and muscular hemorrhages seen on Molly Beldon provided different signs pointing toward another explanation.

These hemorrhages appeared rounded, discrete, and noninfiltrating. The blood had not been forced from torn vessels by a rupturing blow. This type of bleeding appeared as a result of coagulopathy, not as a consequence of trauma. Coagulopathy, he explained, refers to a disease process affecting the blood's clotting properties. Molly suffered from a hemorrhagic syndrome following from the activation of clotting factors and fibrinolytic enzymes thoughout the small blood vessels.

In this hemorrhagic syndrome, fibrin, a component in clotting, deposits in the vessels consuming platelets and clotting factors. Fibrin degrades and biochemical changes prevent clot formation. As a result, the vessels "leak blood" and the surrounding tissues, unable to obtain oxygenated blood, die. The coagulopathy resulted initially from a cascade of events beginning with anoxia, Molly's inability to get enough oxygen through normal respiration.

Friniti now asked Viccore whether suffocation due to injury might be the primary factor in Molly's death, and whether the signs of coagulopathy and pneumonia that he described could have resulted from attempts at resuscitation and critical care following the injury.

The signs from the scene, history, and autopsy all point toward an infective pneumonia compromising her breathing, Viccore said. She had been fussy and cried frequently. This could be explained by her new day care setting and missing her mother, but when joined by her cough and wheezing, as well as the cocci found in postmortem lung tissue, it becomes a sign of illness. When placed on her stomach for a nap, the position further compromised her breathing, resulting in a positional asphyxia. Placing a healthy infant in such a position would not normally be considered either unusual, or dangerous.

Friniti asked if Viccore knew of any other signs to support this opinion. He replied that a pulmonary pathologist reviewed the microscopic sections of lung tissue, and determined that the pneumonia had been long-standing, and not the consequence of postincubation resuscitative attempts.

Friniti feigned puzzlement to bring the jury along, then asked why, if the pneumonia had been long-standing, did the ER chest X-ray fail to disclose its presence?

Viccore replied that about 70% of infant pneumonia cases present signs of congestion on X-rays, while 30% do not. Without a lateral view, and if the child remains dehydrated, no signs of pneumonia will appear on the X-ray film. Molly did not have a lateral picture taken, and had not been well-hydrated while feverish, fussy, and restless. For these reasons, signs of her pneumonia would not necessarily appear to the ER physicians on an A-P X-ray.

Friniti then asked if any finding in Viccore's postmortem examination supported the opinion that her death resulted from injury due to abuse.

"No, none," he replied. He repeated that her death, in his opinion, resulted when congested by infectious pneumonia, she could not effectively oxygenate her blood due to her position on the couch.

Brown hammered at Viccore's testimony concerning the order of events leading to Molly's death. He could not shake Viccore's position that long-standing pneumonia and positional asphyxia led to cerebral edema and coagulopathy resulting in her death by anoxic encephalopathy. He could not shake Viccore's opinion that Molly's death had been accidental.

Brown's case for abuse would have to rest on the strength of Templen's testimony, and rely on his second expert witness, Dr. Rudolf Boone, M.D., a traveling forensic pathologist and psychiatrist from San Francisco specializing in child abuse cases. The second player in Brown's proof confidently crossed his legs in the witness chair as he settled in for his performance.

At Brown's prompting, Boone testified that he had never seen a clearer case of child abuse. He said that he had read both Viccore's autopsy report and the hospital records. He had interviewed Ellen, Tricia, Sally, and Pierre. Boone testified that nothing in the evidence could rule out abuse as the manner of Molly's asphyxia. He spoke to the jury with assured authority, mimicking the way Sherlock Holmes might confidently reveal a mystery's solution to the dull-witted Watson. In his opinion, Boone said, Molly's suffocation resulted from an injury caused by physical abuse.

Friniti objected but the judge overruled her objection. Boone could offer the court his expert opinions on the case. She knew that his testimony involved a fallacy called ad ignorantiam, a Latin phrase literally meaning "toward ignorance."

The error involves offering appeals to ignorance as reasons to support a given conclusion. Arguing that Molly had died by abuse because it has not been disproven, (we do not know that she did not die by abuse), or because one does not know how it could be disproven (we cannot go back in time to see what did not happen to her), commits the ad ignorantiam fallacy. But absence of proof against the abuse scenario does not alone prove its truth. Alternative explanations can better account for the signs. Friniti would have to take Boone through his questionable diagnostic methods to reveal his basic ignorance of the case and his misreading of its signs.

Boone had offered firm, unequivocal testimony in simple terms. But he represented an unfortunately common courtroom presence, the "hired gun" forensic expert who appear on the stand to persuade jurors by authority, regardless of method. Friniti knew Boone by reputation as such an authority figure. She suspected that his investigation of Molly's death amounted to no more than a short conference with Brown, a cursory reading of the case reports, and a brief interview with the principals. He relied on his tactical abilities, persuasive powers, and status as an often-unchallenged child abuse expert to carry the burden of his proof. Such tactical tricks and dubious persuasive techniques have been well documented since the meeting of western science and the law in ancient Athens.

The traveling Sophists in Socrates' time became the first known western "experts" to sell their services for a fee. Socrates enjoyed poking holes in their arguments, challenging their premises, and, by asking questions, showing audiences that the Sophists did not really know what they pretended to. They seemed to display an insufferable ego, preventing them from ever saying "I don't know." After all, they were paid to know. But wisdom, Socrates said, involves both knowing when you know, and when you do not. Integrity measures one's willingness to confess a relevant ignorance in public.

Alan R. Moritz, MD, restated Socrates' point in an address to the 35th Annual Meeting of the American Society of Clinical Pathologists in 1956.[9] If forensic experts fail to recognize when they do not know, and develop an aversion to challenges, tests, and followup investigation, then they become dangerous "pretenders to wisdom." Perhaps years of unchallenged experience leads to this infallible "Sherlock Holmes" mentality. Moritz says:

> "This Sherlock Holmes-type of expert may see certain bruises in the skin of the neck and conclude without doubt that they were produced by the thumb and forefinger of the right hand of the strangler. He may see an excoriation of the anus and maintain unequivocally and without benefit of other elements of scientific proof that the assailant was a sodomist. He ignores the essential component for proof of the correctness of any such scientific deduction, namely, the nonoccurrence of such lesions or changes in control cases. Such a pathologist usually has the happy faculty of failing to remember the many similar bruises of necks that were known to have been produced by mechanisms other than

pressure by the thumb and fingers. He fails to remember the many anal and rectal excoriations that were caused by injuries other than sodomy. Such a pathologist is a delight to newspaper reporters owing to the fact that he makes good copy."[10]

Socrates follows such popular know-it-all experts, asking one small question about something that bothers him, or raising a point that he does not understand. Then the expert's ignorance emerges for all to see. The expert has no answers, and usually has not even considered the proper questions. Such an expert operates without benefit of logical method, building conclusions on the shifting sands of prejudice and preconception.

Ideally, the adversarial legal system provides the forum to expose weak or unreliable testimony. Realistically, such hired guns often get away without facing a Socratic-style courtroom test exposing their cavalier approach to cases. But Boone did not escape the rigors of a spirited cross examination focused on his methods.

Friniti, prepared for her encounter both by her interview with Viccore and her knowledge of medical method, attempted to orchestrate Boone's self-destruction on the stand. She planned to expose the traveling expert's lack of preparation, faulty medical understanding of the case, diagnostic ignorance, and illogical dismissal of important evidence that counted against his opinion. Friniti began by asking Boone how he arrived at his conclusion that Molly's death resulted clearly from injury due to abuse.

Boone described his reasoning, looking confidently toward the jury as he spoke. He said that Molly either received blows from her parents, or from someone at the Caring Bear Daycare. Since neither parent delivered any blows, he concluded that they had to have come from someone at the daycare.

Friniti asked Boone if he knew that her parents and everyone associated with the Caring Bear Daycare denied ever striking Molly.

Boone replied that while all principals denied striking the child, he found that circumstance hardly surprising. In his experience, those guilty of beating a child rarely confess their transgressions. Friniti then asked why he chose to disbelieve Ellen, Tricia, Sally, and Pierre, and to believe Sharon and Ryan.

Boone said that previous CPS complaints and charges against Ellen and her daycare painted a pattern of abuse that extended to explain Molly's death. Molly's parents had no such history and appeared to be loving and caring parents.

Friniti found two immediate problems with Boone's reasoning. The first involves a form of fallacy called "false dilemma." Boone presented a proof proposing only two alternatives, "Molly struck by parents," or "Molly struck by day care workers." Deductively, he failed to consider the obvious possibilities that both Molly's parents and the day care workers struck the child, or neither delivered any blows. Boone ignored alternatives that also appeared to account for other signs that the case presented.

Perhaps both the parents and the day care workers told the truth about Molly's care. Maybe they both lied, and each struck the infant separately. But if evaluating a proposed explanation entails that certain options be considered, it is an error to omit their consideration. Friniti did not let the error pass.

She asked Boone if his experience included cases of abuse from multiple sources, say, by both parents and babysitters. He replied yes. She also asked if in his experience he had ever seen a case of abuse involving neither parents nor day care workers as the agents of injury. Again, he replied yes. She then asked if he had considered these alternatives in Molly's case. No, he replied. In his opinion, the evidence indicated that the blows had been delivered by day care providers.

But his reasoning to show that Molly had been struck by Caring Bear staff also committed an error in reasoning. He alleged a pattern of abuse by appealing to CPS complaints filed against the day care. But he ignored the fact that all charges against the daycare had been investigated, disproven, and dismissed. To support a pattern of abuse extending to Molly's death in the face of contrary evidence by ignoring that evidence also involves an error in reasoning.

Friniti asked Boone if he knew that all CPS complaints against Caring Bear Daycare had been dismissed. He said no. She then asked if one such complaint painted a "pattern of abuse." Did two? Did three? Boone replied that it depended on the nature of the complaints.

Friniti asked Boone to describe the complaints against the day care that formed the pattern he found.

Brown objected, but the judge overruled the objection. Boone had testified to a pattern of abuse and counsel could explore both the pattern and its basis.

Boone admitted that he remained unfamiliar with the specific charges against the day care. He did not know exactly how many complaints had been filed, their dates, or their natures. Boone's pattern began to fragment.

Friniti asked if a mother's complaint that her child had endured a soiled diaper for four hours constituted a pattern of abuse that could help explain Molly's death.

Boone replied that neglect and abuse associated more often than not. Boone no longer looked confidently at the jury. He stared in anger at Friniti. She could sense that the hired gun himself had begun to lose self-confidence and his testimony had lost its credibility.

Expert testimony free from error persuades more credibility than reasoning sprinkled with mistakes. Scientific errors may go unnoticed without astute prosecutors or defense attorneys to point them out. The courtroom forum to expose errors, both serious and minor, depends on the attorney's ability to recognize them as they develop.

Their role of exposing errors in expert testimony may explain why attorneys remain as popular among physicians as Socrates became among the ancient Athenians. Exposing an expert's errors, however minor, in open court undermines the trust and confidence placed in the expert, destroying the effectiveness of the testimony. Friniti now had Boone both angry and defensive. She moved on to explore his medical opinions.

Friniti asked Boone to describe the medical evidence supporting his opinion that Molly died by injury. He explained that both the retinal and muscular hemorrhages indicated blows and shaken baby syndrome.

Friniti asked Boone to describe to the jury the nature of any hemorrhages that result from blows. He described them as irregular in shape, the result of ruptured vessels due to compression. She then asked Boone if the hemorrhages on Molly's body appeared irregular in shape.

Boone replied that all hemorrhages due to blows appear irregular.

Friniti suspected that Boone had examined neither the retinal nor the muscular hemorrhages, but formed his opinion about their cause based on Brown's claims. He had relied on his general impressions from Caring Bear Daycare's past CPS complaints. Boone had ignored the evidence supplied by Viccore's autopsy.

Boone shared a tendency exhibited by police investigators in almost all of the Sherlock Holmes stories. Both seem to ignore "trifles" and adopt explanations that account for a few obvious facts. But as Holmes says, "There is nothing more deceptive than an obvious fact."[11] After accounting for the obvious facts, Boone refused to consider any discovery that did not support his own favored explanation. He had, in Holmes' words, committed the error of "twist[ing] facts to suit theories, instead of theories to suit facts."[12]

He also had committed the fallacy of "ignoring the question," answering a different question than Friniti asked about Molly's hemorrhages.

Friniti said that she did not ask about all hemorrhages from injury, but about Molly's hemorrhages. Without a pause, she asked Boone if would describe for the jury the nature of hemorrhages resulting from coagulopathy. Boone described the rounded, discrete, noninfiltrating hemorrhages earlier described by Viccore for the jury as characteristic of Molly's hemorrhages.

When Friniti asked Boone if he thought that Molly's hemorrhages had resulted from coagulopathy, he angrily replied, "Look, the question isn't what I think. The question is what it's going to take to satisfy a reasonable person about these issues. And I don't think there's anything that can satisfy you."

By inference, Boone called Friniti "unreasonable." If he dismissed coagulopathy as a false explanation of Molly's hemorrhages because Friniti appears "unreasonable," Boone would commit the ad hominem fallacy. Ad hominem literally means "to the human." Boone offers negative claims about Friniti to count against the conclusion that she supports. If Friniti is "unreasonable" as Boone infers, this status does not relevantly refute coagulopathy as an explanation of the hemorrhages. Even "unreasonable" attorneys can defend true conclusions.

Friniti asked Boone if he had read Viccore's autopsy report. He replied that he had. He said that in his opinion, the report dismissed abuse as an explanation for Molly's death because overworked medical examiners habitually try to avoid the tremendous effort that such cases involve. Coagulopathy presented, in his opinion, merely a convenient labor-saving explanation.

Friniti failed to see how any labor had been saved through Viccore's detailed diagnosis. Boone merely offered a circumstantial form of the ad hominem fallacy: since busy medical examiners' have heavy case loads, reject coagulopathy as an explanation of Molly's hemorrhages. General workloads remain clearly irrelevant to the merits or demerits of a specific diagnosis. The proper critical interest focuses on the evidence offered to develop and support the explanation and to propose and assess alternatives.[13] Boone himself had attempted the only visible labor-saving shortcut past the evidence, so Friniti made his brief trip as unpleasant as she could.

She developed the medical evidence for Boone's comment, focusing on coagulopathy, and on the specific tests Viccore had done to show that the noninfiltrating hemorrhages pointed away from blows. Their round discrete shape pointed to coagulopathy, not trauma. Her questions lead Boone to agree that none of the hemorrhages described in the infant's autopsy appeared consistent with impact injury. Through these questions, she also managed to show the jury another of Boone's tricks.

In his testimony, he used "hemorrhage" interchangeably with "contusion" and "bruising" and confused the two distinct mechanisms competing to explain Molly's retinal bleeding. The equivocal use of terms involves using the same word, "hemorrhage," to mean at least two different things, "bleeding from a blow" and "bleeding from coagulopathy." Boone had to admit that Molly's bleeding, if as described by Viccore, resulted from coagulopathy, not trauma. Friniti then closed in on Boone's other reasons for supporting abuse by day care providers as the cause of Molly's death.

Boone testified that Molly had been fine before she arrived at Caring Bear the morning of her death, that she subsequently died, and that therefore the cause of her death lay among the debris of the daycare. Friniti exposed this shortcut as a clear instance of the false cause fallacy.

This error involves stating simply that one event comes before another; therefore, the preceding event causes the latter's occurrence. While causes do precede effects, this fact alone does not establish a causal connection. Again, Boone preferred sidestepping the relevant evidence and relied on his preconceived beliefs about the Caring Bear Daycare.

Friniti tried to show the jury that Boone's entire testimony assumed Ellen's day care to be guilty of abuse, and interpreted the evidence in light of that assumption. The fact that CPS complaints had been filed against Caring Bear Daycare had colored his entire view of the case. He had committed the most serious error that a forensic expert can commit: He had assumed as truth the results of his investigation in order to prove their truth. This fallacy, called begging the question, involves arguing in a circle. Friniti had now closed the circle around Boone.

Boone admitted that his impressions of abuse, when faced with the clinical and histological evidence of prior infection, could be mistaken. In an effort to save face, he looked toward the jury box and added that it remained up to each juror to decide the truth about Molly's death. But Boone merely appeared to pass the buck to a jury unaware of their role as receivers. Brown attempted to intercept it in his closing statement and hand the decision more smoothly to the jurors.

As he stood facing the jury box, Brown recounted the emotional devastation suffered by Sharon and Ryan Beldon. They left their only child in good health with a licensed daycare provider only to find Molly unattended, dying on a couch. Two respected pediatric critical care physicians and an expert in child abuse testified that Molly had been shaken and suffocated; that she recovered enough to breath on her own, but that when placed carelessly and irresponsibly on the couch, her breathing had been inhibited by the blanket.

Brown implied that the blanket had been intentionally stuffed over her mouth to make an abusive death appear accidental. He also appealed to the Pierce County medical examiner's finding that Molly died by "mechanical asphyxia secondary to suffocation." This had not been a natural death due to a disease process, he said.

He emphasized that Molly had been injured, and that the injury had been inflicted by the day care workers. Without making a formal accusation, he implied that either Tricia or Pierre had produced the injury. Regardless, he said, Ellen had the license and therefore bore the responsibility for what happened to Molly.

He asked the jury to award damages of $3 million the Beldons; $2 million in compensatory damages for loss of life: and $1 million in punitive damages for wrongful death. While he spoke, he held a 8 x 10 color picture of Molly, dressed in pink and wearing a big toothless smile, her blue eyes looking toward the jury throughout his speech. He would be a tough act to follow.

Friniti took the stage and faced both the challenge and the jury. She began by saying that mere impression and vague innuendo do not constitute a proof of wrongful death. Nor do they support allegations that Ellen Boudet bears the responsibility for this tragic and complex event. Molly did not die of a disease, but the disease in her lungs helped explain both the mechanism of her death and its tragic manner. Friniti said that the evidence showed how Molly died accidentally through no negligence or error on anyone's part. The medical examiner's investigation and the resulting physical evidence showed that the only error entered the case through the testimony of doctors Templen and Boone.

Contrary to their testimony, the evidence showed that Molly had not been healthy when taken to day care. She had an ear infection, and had developed pneumonia. She had been congested, and had difficulty breathing. The medical evidence showed traces of this longstanding virulent infection in both lungs. As a result, she remained fussy and uncomfortable when placed in a crib. Normally, placing a fussy child on her stomach to sleep poses no unusual danger. Tragically in Molly's case, her position on the couch compromised her breathing and continued a cascade of events leading to her death.

The medical evidence showed no signs of abuse or injury as elements of these events. It was, she said, the type of accident for which no one shouldered the weight of responsibility. The mistaken testimony of doctors Templen and Boone certainly left room for reasonable doubt. She pointed out their errors not to disparage them personally, but to clear a path to the truth about Molly's death. There are no unimportant errors in death investigations.

Looking at each juror, walking along the jury box, Friniti said that since everyone makes errors, it is important to recognize them, and to allow for their correction. Reaching conclusions established by the weight of the relevant available evidence always leaves open the possibility that new evidence may be discovered, and that these conclusions may be modified. New microscopic evidence of coagulopathy fit with pneumonia and suffocation but not with trauma and abuse. What evidence, she asked rhetorically, indicated that Molly had been intentionally suffocated? None she said, answering her own question.

Pausing, changing direction, and remaining focused on the jury, Friniti said that when the weight of the relevant available evidence does not justify one conclusion over an alternative, we must settle for informed ignorance. But in this case, she said, no evidence showed that Molly suffered either criminal abuse or deliberate injury. In fact, the weight of the evidence showed that she suffered from a natural disease that compromised her ability to breathe. This pneumonia lead to her suffocation.

Furthermore, Friniti continued, no additional evidence indicated that she had been criminally suffocated. Reasonable doubt of wrongful death clearly existed. She asked the jury to find that Ellen Boudet had no role in Molly's death. Her death remained the kind of accident for which no responsibility, criminal or moral, could be assigned.

After Brown's and Friniti's closing statements, the jury received instructions from the judge. They could, she said, award damages without deciding that Molly suffered intentional abuse.

They deliberated for six hours before returning with their verdict. The jury awarded punitive damages in the amount of $250,000 to the Beldons in the wrongful death of their daughter, Molly. They found that her death, while accidental, had been the responsibility of Ellen Boudet, doing business as the Caring Bear Daycare.

The house that once held the Caring Bear Daycare now hosts a computer retail and repair business. The front yard has been paved with black asphalt to accommodate patron parking. Bicycles in various sizes lean against the building. A large poster invites its customers to participate in the information revolution. Inside, a cluster of kids peer into a colored screen, rotating in shifts to operate the keyboard.

NOTES

1. David Sherwood, MD, "Chronic Subdural Hematoma in Infants," *American Journal of Diseases of Children*, Vol. 39, No. 5, May 1930, p. 980.
2. Ibid., p. 980.
3. John Caffey, MD, "Multiple Fractures in the Long Bones of Children Suffering from Chronic Subdural Hematoma," *Am. J. Roent.*, No. 56, 1946, pp. 163–173.
4. Ibid.

5. C. H. Kempe, F. N. Silverman, B. F. Steele, W. Droegemueller, and H. K. Silver, "The Battered and Child Syndrome," *JAMA*, 181: 105–112, 1962.
6. Sir Arthur Conan Doyle, *The Sign of Four*, in *The Complete Sherlock Holmes*, Vol. 1, p. 89; Doubleday & Co. Inc., Garden City, NY., N.D.
7. C. S. Peirce, Ms. 692.
8. Common informal reasoning errors are often divided into two groups: fallacies of ambiguity and fallacles of relevance. Fallacies of ambiguity involve errors in reasoning resulting from ignoring the ambiguities of ordinary language: ambiguous words, phrases, or sentences. These fallacles include equivocation, accent, composition, and division. Fallacies of relevance involve errors in reasoning that result from no rational connection between the premises and conclusions: the premises are not evidence for the conclusion. Particularly common fallacies of relevance include ad baculum, ad misericordiam, ad populum, ad ignorantiam, false cause, ignoring the question, complex question, and begging the question. Formal fallacies involve deductive errors, confusing valid with invalid argument forms.
9. Alan A, Moritz, MD "Classical Mistakes in Forensic Pathology," Proceedings of the 35th Annual Meeting of the American Society of Clinical Pathologists, 1956, pp. 382–1395.
10. Moritz, pp. 1389–1390.
11. Sir Arthur Conan Doyle, *The Boscombe Valley Mystery*, in *The Complete Sherlock Holmes*, Vol. 1, p. 202; Doubleday & Co. Inc., Garden City, NY., N.D.
12. Sir Arthur Conan Doyle, *A Scandal in Bohemia*, in *The Complete Sherlock Holmes*, Vol. 1, p. 161; Doubleday & Co. Inc., Garden City, NY., N.D.
13. Unlike a hospital autopsy, the focus of the medicolegal autopsy differs. With the different focus comes additional work. Moritz describes the mistake of remaining unaware of an autopsy's objective:
14. It should be realized that the medicolegal autopsy is often expected to provide information that would not be looked for in an ordinary hospital case . . . An examination that would be entirely adequate by ordinary medical standards may be so inadequate from a medicolegal standpoint that a murder may not be recognized, or an innocent person may be charged with a murder that was not committed." Moritz, p. 1383.

No master looks good unless confronted with a bad student.

chapter ten

Disagreement—The Darcy Case: An Open Verdict

Opinion, Uncertainty, and Conflicting Conclusions

> Circumstantial evidence is a very tricky thing . . . ; it may point very straight to one thing, but if you shift your own point of view a little, you may find it pointing in an equally uncompromising manner to something entirely different.
>
> Sherlock Holmes

With a slap of the gavel, Her Majesty's Coroner closed the inquest into the death of Sharri Tempelton Darcy and hammered home his conclusion of an "open verdict." An open verdict satisfies no one. It's an official admission that the evidence points nowhere with sufficient clarity to support one manner of death over another. The coroner said that to record a verdict of either suicide or homicide, he had to be satisfied that the evidence pointed to one or the other beyond a reasonable doubt. Despite the assembled facts and expert conclusions, he was not satisfied, so recorded the open verdict. Usually not everyone agrees with such an assessment of the corpus delicti. Sharri Darcy's case proved to be no exception to that rule.

The circumstances of Sharri's death developed passionate support for two explanations dividing family, polarizing investigators, and inflaming spectators. Public opinion clearly favored explaining her death as a murder. Officials split evenly between murder and suicide. Most family believed in what the coroner called "wrongful killing," but fringe relations embraced suicide. According to advocates for each alternative, the body of evidence provided both unequivocal and compelling support for only one view—theirs. The coroner's open verdict satisfied these raging passions as effectively as a Christmas kiss to a hormonal teen from a doting grandparent.

Everyone, including Detective Inspector John Kennington, left the law courts at Beaconsfield frustrated, on edge, and dissatisfied. All wondered how such a clear case had become so confused. But in every other respect Kennington stood alone. He disagreed with both of the favored explanations of Sharri's mysterious death. He thought that the so-called "lady in the lake" had a different story to tell, one that had begun long before her life had ended. After all, the statuesque blue-eyed blond had lived 27 years before Mrs. Esther Therson saw her immaculately manicured hands projecting just above the surface of Plimpson Pond.

On Sunday morning, Mrs. Therson walked with her dog Maggie along Plimpson's shoreline. They would drive to the lay-by parking area just off the main highway by the pond, park the car, and walk down the public access path toward the water. A play area and a public toilet lay to the right and a few small trees stuck up among the underbrush to the left. Along the water, they would follow the hard gravel surface for two-and-one-half miles around the pond, returning full-circle to the path leading to the parking area. Maggie would run ahead, frolic among the sparse vegetation, and occasionally bound into the shallow water to chase a duck or to retrieve a stick.

Three months before the coroner's unpopular inquest verdict, on such a Sunday morning, Maggie immediately ran down the path toward the water, stopped, and began barking. Esther followed, and saw the hands. Long red fingernails extended like claws from pale white fingers. The palms faced upward. As she approached the beach, she saw a woman lying face down in the shallow water, feet toward the shore, wrists tied behind her back with a red battery jumper cable, and ankles bound with yellow nylon rope. She wore tight fitting jeans, a red sweater, a black vest, and black high heels with spikes that broke the surface like miniature periscopes. Maggie barked and Esther screamed.

Two canoeists, unloading their vessel from a car-top carrier, heard the commotion and ran from the lay-by to investigate. One returned to the car and drove to notify local police, while the other helped Esther gently lift the body from the water. They noticed a blue scarf tied around the mouth as a gag. One shoe fell from a lifeless foot during the move. They carefully placed the body face down on the shore, just as they had found it in the water. CPR was out of the question. The woman was beyond human help. Maggie sat quietly beside her mistress, who waited with the canoeist for his friend to return with the police.

When the police arrived, they blocked off the parking area, the access path, and the shoreline around the pond. With the scene secured, Chief Inspector Donald Chilgress took charge of the investigation, assisted by Detective Inspector John Kennington. They assigned officers to interview potential witnesses, and to investigate the vehicles parked in the highway lay-by which doubled as a parking area for the pond.

Meanwhile, scores of crime officers worked along the path between the parking area and the body. Before the group approached the body, Chilgress made sure that the home office consulting pathologist, Dr. David Benjamin, received his Sunday morning wake-up call and a legitimate excuse to miss Sunday morning church services.

Benjamin arrived within an hour. By then, the coroner's officer had supplied Chilgress with a tentative identification, and the investigation had shifted into high gear. Chilgress reported the results of their first hour's work to the attentive pathologist as both stood in the parking area between the highway and the pond.

He told Benjamin that the vehicles parked in the lay-by included a black Vauxhall four-door sedan registered to Sharri Tempelton Darcy, blond female, age 27. A blond-female between 20 and 30 lay dead by the shore near the pond. No keys appeared in the Vauxhall. The driver's side seat had been fully reclined. Both front doors remained ajar. A male's gray jacket, size extra large, had been stuffed under the passenger's seat. Three empty black plastic trash bags with grass clipping residues, a cigarette lighter, and a woman's watch accompanied the jacket on the floor of the front seat.

Chilgress explained to Benjamin that between the car and the body, scenes of crime officers first discovered a single stiletto heel mark beside a small tree on the left side of the path to the water. No other footprints appeared in the area, not even those of Esther or the canoeist who helped retrieve the body. The only other marks visible on the hard ground, he said, showed the toenails of Maggie's paws as she apparently ran toward the water, then stopped.

While searching toward the pond shortly beyond the heel-mark, police found a plastic auto towrope package, which had held a yellow cord designed to rescue vehicles from mechanical distress and drag them toward help. The yellow rope from the empty package now secured the dead woman's ankles. Their search continued past the shoreline into the shallow water beside the spot where Esther said she'd found the body. In about six inches of water, officers recovered a black jumper cable, one lead tied on itself to form a slipknot. When the immediate area had been processed, the body could be approached and inspected more closely.

Benjamin and Chilgress walked toward the dead woman followed by Kennington. Both policemen stood while the pathologist knelt beside the ankles to examine the yellow cord. His eyes worked their way from the feet toward the head.

The towrope merely encircled the ankles but had not been tied. The hands were loosely held behind the back by a red plastic-covered battery jumper cable which formed two large loops around the wrists. He saw that a wide blue scarf covered the mouth, one end crossing over the other. The fabric overlapped her neck and lay flat against its left side, again without a knot. Benjamin noted that none of this binding would have secured a struggling victim. Each restraint could easily be applied and removed without help from another person. He turned the body and examined its front.

The face appeared purplish-red and bloody purge exited from the nostrils. Rigor had fully developed, and the body felt cold. Benjamin measured the temperature of the pond water, thinking that the body had not been immersed long enough to reach the 13.5-degree C water reading. He placed the approximate time of death at between 8 and 12 hours earlier, but would not commit himself to an exact time. Further examination required transporting the body to a nearby hospital morgue for the autopsy. Both Chilgress and Kennington accompanied Benjamin and the body to Wexham Hospital for the postmortem examination.

The body lay on a colorless hospital gurney, a blaze of yellow, red, and blue, like a spring bouquet on a gravestone. Water pooled on the gurney from the wet clothing and dripped occasionally to the dark slate floor. Benjamin slipped her wrists free from the red jumper cables without difficulty, slid the blue scarf off her mouth and neck, and pulled the yellow towrope past her feet. Each item was carefully preserved.

Benjamin then listed her clothing as he removed each article: one right stiletto-heeled silver-decorated black shoe; a pair of form-fitting blue jeans with zippers on the cuffs and mud on the knees and thighs; a black vest; a dark red sweater; a white lace-trimmed brassiere which he found pulled up over the breasts and unhooked at the back. The hooks remained undamaged. The decedent wore no underpants. He found no jewelry. She had nothing in her pockets. He resumed his head-to-toe inspection under the powerful examination light.

Her face appeared suffused and bluish-red with distended neck veins. Small petechial hemorrhages dotted its surface, increasing in their frequency over the eyelids. He saw several darker red spots, possibly blemishes, on her forehead. Extensive subconjunctival hemorrhages supplied a red coloring to the now dull gray-blue eyes. Her teeth had left their impression on the sides of her tongue without bruises or lacerations. No injuries to the teeth, mouth, or lips appeared.

A ligature mark completely encircled the neck with a bruise marking a knot four inches below her left ear. The width of the mark and the shape of the bruise exactly accommodated the size of the black jumper cable and the configuration of its slip knot.

A single scratch began on her right cheek, appeared again below the ligature mark, and completed its arc just below her right breast. Benjamin noted a small bruise on the back of her left hand between her thumb and index finger. Ten long fingernails painted bright red remained completely undamaged. He found two bruises on the outer aspects of both the right and the left thigh. Her pubic hair had been dyed blond and cut short. He found her vagina rugose and wrinkled, with scanty thick sticky mucoid exudate, but he saw no obvious seminal fluid. He found the anus slightly patulous but uninjured.

The legs had been shaved from the pubic region to the toes. All 10 toes enjoyed the attention of bright red nail polish. The sole of the right foot had traces of mud, but the left sole did not. Benjamin jotted some notes, lay his clipboard aside, and began his examination of the internal organs.

The skull bore no injuries. Its inner aspect showed patchy yellow stains. The brain appeared swollen, engorged, and cyanosed. The cerebral vessels remained normal. The meninges were congested but unstained.

Benjamin found the thyroid gland congested and cyanosed. The hyoid bone, thyroid cartilages, and cricoid remained intact. A small hemorrhage appeared in the right sterno-mastoid muscle under the ligature mark, but no other evidence of injury to the neck appeared.

The pleural cavities, ribs, and sternum appeared normal. The trachea and bronchi contained frothy watery fluid and the lungs appeared bulky and doughy from acute emphysema and inhaled fluid.

The pericardium showed petechial hemorrhages, but otherwise the heart appeared healthy. The swollen liver had been displaced downward by the heavy lungs. The spleen was deeply congested and plum-colored. He found some mostly digested food in the stomach, but identified bacon among its contents. Otherwise, he found all organs to be unremarkable.

He collected blood, stomach contents, liver, cut and plucked head and pubic hair, and swabs from the anus and vagina. He preserved the ligatures and gag as well as her clothing. While removing his rubber gloves and scrubbing his hands, he gave Chilgress and Kennington his preliminary results: He said that Sharri Tempelton Darcy did not die a natural death. She drowned.

Both Chief Inspector Chilgress and Detective Inspector Kennington appeared puzzled. How, they wondered out loud, did she come to drown? Did her attacker hold her underwater? Did he choke her with the jumper cable, then push her into the pond? Chilgress asked the pathologist for his view about the manner of her death. Benjamin obliged without hesitation, his authoritative voice carrying an air of certainty unusual for a forensic pathologist. This clear voice remained especially endearing to the barristers who called him as their witness in crown court.

Benjamin appealed to his observations at the scene and his postmortem examination to craft his reply. He said that prior to drowning, an attempted ligature strangulation occurred using the black jump lead with its slipknot. The ligature marks and bruises on the body showed that it had been pulled from the front toward the left side to apply pressure to the neck. The body showed no signs of physical assault, exhibiting neither injuries of attack nor wounds of defense. The unusually long and painted fingernails remained in perfect condition, belying any struggle. The ligatures around the wrists and ankles could not restrain an unwilling, fit young woman of 27. Both the red jumper lead and the yellow towrope clung loosely around her extremities, and he said that they had possibly been applied by the decedent herself.

Benjamin concluded by saying that Darcy appeared otherwise healthy, with no apparent underlying disease, and that therefore, in his opinion, she had committed suicide.

Chilgress looked at the pathologist for a full 10 seconds before he said that he found it hard to believe she would tie herself up and drown herself. Kennington found it so hard to believe that it never even had occurred to him as a reasonable explanation. Both Chilgress and Kennington had seen exactly the same things as Benjamin. Yet they seemed to be moving toward different conclusions along distinct explanatory paths. Benjamin, never at a loss for words, had a reply ready to address Chilgress' doubt.

He told the policemen that in the last three months, he had attended three female suicidal drownings. All three had first attempted to strangle themselves with a ligature. He said that one had even applied a gag. In his estimation, the gag had been applied to stifle involuntary screams and insure uninterrupted success. All three women chose outdoor locations, two in a lake, and one in a farm's pond. Each location had some personal significance for the victim, he said. He recommended that police investigate the meaning that Plimpson Pond held for the decedent.

Ignoring his investigative recommendation, Kennington immediately asked about the position of her brassiere, the scratches on her face and lower chest, and the bruises on her thighs and left hand. He wondered to himself whether three homicides had passed undetected, masquerading as suicidal drownings.

Undeterred, Benjamin replied that the scratches appeared to be postmortem artifacts, consistent with her being pulled out of the water. The small bruises on her thighs and left hand had no significance since her clothing remained undamaged and her fingernails remained intact. He added that she may have bruised her hand while pulling on the black cable. He explained that her brassiere had been detached and pulled over her breasts when her body had been lifted from the water and placed face down on the shore.

Chilgress asked Benjamin how he reconstructed the events leading to her death given the evidence at the scene and his autopsy.

The pathologist replied that he had no doubt that Darcy drove her car to the pond, walked willingly to the water's edge, applied the gag and the ligatures, and drowned herself. He said that he saw her death as a suicide almost immediately when he observed the body lying on the shore. The loose fitting ligatures, the intact nails and clothing, and the absence of injury all confirmed his suspicions. She had not been attacked.

Once he had eliminated assault and attack, he said that suicide remained the only possible option. He also could support his reconstruction with a current study explaining suicide by drowning as an increasingly common option for distressed females choosing to end their lives.

According to the study, a dramatic mechanism for ending life becomes an extreme form of the Munchausen Syndrome, a form of self-mutilation to gain attention and sympathy. The syndrome takes many forms including soliciting attention by abusing or killing one's own children, or mutilating or killing oneself. He explained to Chilgress and Kennington that the syndrome was named for Baron Munchausen, a knight who received great public adulation when he returned from the Holy Crusades mangled and battered. It turned out that he mutilated himself to buy the attention.

In Benjamin's opinion, Sharri Darcy probably suffered from an extreme form of the same syndrome. That would account for the odd binding of hands and feet. She sought sympathy and attention by pretending to be a murder victim.

It became clear to Chilgress that Benjamin had made up his mind. Sharri Darcy died a suicide. From his own experience, Chilgress knew that no additional evidence could sway the pathologist from this conclusion. He assigned Kennington to develop background on the victim, and to assemble the laboratory findings. Chilgress had clear misgivings about calling her death a suicide.

Kennington also had a hard time swallowing Benjamin's conclusion: The so-called reconstruction stuck hard in his throat. It glossed over details and dismissed many observations as coincidental artifacts. It also failed to explain rather obvious puzzles. If she drove to the pond, where were her car keys? Where was her purse, her money, her identification? An exhaustive search of the pond and its surroundings uncovered nothing except a pail of grass clippings behind the toilet. Why were both driver and passenger doors ajar? How, he wondered, had the black jumper cable found its way from her neck into the water with her hands still held behind her back by the red cable? Had she first attempted to strangle herself, discarded the black cable, then bound herself with the red one?

Without a doubt Benjamin could craft answers. He had a reputation as a crafty witness: she tossed her keys in the pond; someone visiting the lay-by coincidentally took her purse; an unrelated prowler opened the passenger side car door. The possible answers would gush like a severed artery. Perhaps he would even cite supporting statistical studies. But confirming either his answers or any alternatives posed serious difficulties. Kennington and the police needed to discover more evidence to help sort the options. The case soon gained additional information from the evidence taken to the lab.

Metropolitan police criminalists found only Sharri Tempelton Darcy's fingerprints on the plastic towrope bag. A partial print of her left index finger also appeared on the black jumper cable. The red cable had been too smeared and no identifiable prints could be recovered. The jumper cables and the towrope had come from the trunk of her black Vauxhall.

The car had been towed from the lay-by to the police garage. When started in the garage, police found that the shift linkage on the four speed manual transmission had been bent and its selector would not engage any gear. The engine ran, but the car remained inoperative. Sharri had driven to the lay-by, but could not drive away. Chilgress began to think that she had experienced car trouble, opened her trunk to get a towrope, and been attacked by whomever had come to her aid. The attacker had used the jumper cables from her trunk. His view began to jell. Kennington still had questions and continued to search for more evidence.

He sought to reconstruct her last day and discover why she went to Plimpson Pond. He wanted to piece together what she did there, and how she ended up face down in the shallow water. He needed witnesses from the parking area, friends, family, and perhaps even other forensic experts. He began his quest by advertising on the BBC's *Crimewatch,* requesting that witnesses who saw anything that Saturday in the lay-by parking area near Plimpson Pond contact police. Meanwhile, he interviewed Sharri's housemate, Sandra Kelley.

Sandra answered an ad Sharri had placed when she was looking for someone to share a house owned by her dad. Sharri worked as a secretary for a firm specializing in international trade and Sandra worked as a receptionist in a dental office. They got along well in the six months they'd shared the house, but she did not consider herself to be Sharri's close friend. They each enjoyed different activities, and moved in different social circles. Sharri's smoking proved to be their only major conflict. Sharri never went far without her cigarettes. Sandra did not smoke.

Sandra said that Sharri was very friendly, extroverted, and affectionate. She loved going out with men. She had a succession of boyfriends since they lived in the same house, four or five she thought, maybe even six. When they talked about men, Sharri invariably brought up her fear of contracting AIDS. She talked about swearing off men for a year to concentrate on her career. But according to Sandra, Sharri never seemed to make the break. She either had a new boyfriend, or returned to one of the older models.

Kennington asked Sandra to recount her contact with Sharri the Saturday she died at Plimpson Pond. She said that during the afternoon, Sharri mowed the lawn, and bagged the clippings in three black plastic trash bags. When Sandra last saw her she wore a baggy gray sweatshirt, dark sweat pants and white athletic shoes. Sharri said that she had plans for the evening, and awaited a phone call from a friend. Sandra left to visit her parents, and never saw her housemate again.

Kennington wondered about Sharri's moods. Sandra said that she appeared to have bouts of depression, usually either about events at work, or her relationships with men. Whenever she felt in such a mood, Sandra said that Sharri always took out her diary, lay on her bed, and wrote until she felt better. Kennington knew that the diary would be required reading. He found this personal record in the top drawer of her bedside table.

Kennington felt uncomfortable paging through a handwritten volume recording the intimate thoughts of a woman he had seen taken apart by a pathologist. The entries appeared sporadic, following her moods more than the calendar. His discomfort increased as he got the general sexual gist of many entries.

As a happily married man, sex had long since ceased to be a driving force in his matrimonial relationship, let alone a preoccupation of his fantasy life. He and his wife built a partnership that included sex as a byproduct, one of many ways to express their mutual respect, affection, and joy in each others company. More often than not, they simply enjoyed working around the house together and let it go at that. Kennington's fantasy life more often focused on solving difficult cases, driving spectacular motorcars, or enjoying a family vacation devoid of travel tension, conflict, and strife.

Sharri would have found Kennington a total bore. The feeling would have been mutual. She appeared focused on alternate avenues to sexual gratification, and on the men who could drive her there. This physical component apparently motivated her selection of males for relationships. The diary recorded both her frustrations with the men she chose and the sexual adventures they shared. If the diary were literally true and not mere fantasy, she acted out her sexual dreams with many willing male partners. If her writing could be believed, Sharri clearly enjoyed the secret thrill of bondage and the physical rigors of carnal athletics.

The diary listed her partners merely by numbers. He could find no legend matching these numbers with the names used in other discussions. In several entries Kennington noted a concern for contracting AIDS because of her multiple sex partners. Bouts of despair correlated with this concern, as well as with dumping men who began to treat her badly, or being tossed over by men when they followed newer conquests.

According to the diary, sex certainly did not exhaust her interest in life. Her joys included a close relationship with her parents. She wrote extensively about her appreciation for their support, both emotional and financial. Her mother seemingly acted as her personal confidant.

On the last page of the diary, Kennington found a note labeled "Plan." Sharri listed her financial obligations for the upcoming months, including paying up her auto insurance for the next year, and a list of preparations to make for her parent's 30th wedding anniversary celebration three months in the future. The diary did not appear to Kennington as the record of a suicidal schizophrenic. He would consult with her mother to deepen his developing impressions of this woman he met as she lay face down on the hard shore of Plimpson Pond.

Sharri's mother had passed her good looks on to her. She appeared tired and sad, but dignified as she answered Kennington's questions. He phrased them delicately. She responded openly and in his opinion, honestly. She said that she and her daughter spoke frankly about her sexual relationships with men, and her fear of contracting AIDS. She said that Sharri had one particular male friend, Roger, who she knew her daughter had resumed seeing recently. He lived somewhere in the area near the lay-by beside Plimpson Pond. She did not know the exact address or location, nor did she remember his last name. Kennington wondered privately which number Roger had in Sharri's diary.

She added that her daughter might have driven her car to see Roger Saturday night, had car trouble, stopped at the lay-by, and sought help. Sharri's mother believed that while seeking aid, her daughter had been attacked and murdered. Chilgress and Mrs. Darcy saw things the same way. Kennington wanted to know more about the car.

Mrs. Darcy said that Sharri had been extremely particular about her Vauxhall. She had it serviced regularly, washed and waxed it weekly, and always kept it clean and orderly. Her father had given her jumper cables and a towrope, which she kept beside the spare tire in the trunk. She always knew where things were, and rarely misplaced anything.

Her mother said that in general Sharri behaved in a compulsively tidy fashion. Several of her daughter's housemates had to move because of an irreconcilable clash of neat with sloppy housekeeping styles. In keeping with this neatness, her mother said that Sharri never would put trash bags that had contained grass clippings in the passenger area of her car. She often dumped her clippings on her father's compost pile rather than pay to have them collected. She thought that leaving them in bags by the street was both uneconomical and unsightly.

Kennington asked about any health problems. Mrs. Darcy said that Sharri had low blood pressure and fainted on occasion. She smoked too much, but other than infrequent bouts of insomnia, her daughter remained quite healthy. She said that she had given Sharri a bottle of 20 Seconal, sleeping tablets to assist with this occasional problem.

Kennington had already found the bottle in Sharri's dresser drawer. It still contained 20 tablets. That number of Seconal could probably kill her entire household. He asked if Sharri had ever spoken about suicide.

No, never, her mother replied. She said that her daughter had ordinary problems, but had resolved to meet them head-on. She planned to better her career by returning to school, and to improve her choice of men by leaving them alone for a while. She added that her daughter always seemed to pick men who turned out to have other women in their lives. None proved to be faithful. They always abandoned her or she left them. Sharri could not seem to find a man to be a companion, lover, and true friend.

As an outsider, Kennington could see why, but he said nothing. He resolved to find Roger and meet at least one of the men in Sharri's life, perhaps one identifiable from his number in her diary.

Roger's full name turned out to be Roger Pembroke. He lived about three miles from Plimpson Pond in a small country-style cottage. He told Kennington that he spoke with Sharri late Saturday afternoon when they made plans to meet for a drink. He said that she called him about 7:00 P.M., saying that "something came up," and that she would have to cancel. He told her that he was tired anyway and would stay home. If her schedule permitted, she could stop by his cottage later in the evening. Roger explained that when Sharri said "something came up," she meant some other man.

Roger told Kennington that he and Sharri had been lovers, but that they now dated other people. They remained in touch and dated each other occasionally. Roger said that Sharri neither telephoned again, nor visited him that Saturday night. He never heard from her after the 7:00 P.M. call. He had no idea why she went to Plimpson Pond or with whom. Kennington's most promising lead ultimately petered out. Roger was a wrong number.

Other leads soon surfaced. Several calls came in as a result of the BBC's *Crimewatch* appeal. Ruth Stanforth said that she drove into the lay-by near Plimpson Pond about 7:00 P.M. because her four-year-old daughter had to go to the toilet. She saw a large trailer truck, a dark green, expensive-looking car, maybe a Mercedes or a Jaguar, and a black car. She took her daughter through the gate and saw a blond woman carrying a black plastic bag, leaving a trail of grass clippings on the path. She also saw a middle-aged man dressed in an expensive suit. No one else appeared in the area. She said that she could not be sure if the trailer truck was occupied or not.

An extensive search for the man in the smart suit driving the expensive green car proved fruitless. Too many expensive green cars connect with too many men wearing tailored suits. Without something more to limit the search, progress remained impossible.

The trailer truck Ruth Stanforth saw belonged to Harry Demmick, who parked his rig at the lay-by and walked to his nearby farm home. He pulled in about 5:00 P.M. on that Saturday and did not return to his truck until the following Monday morning. Another truck driver heard the *Crimewatch* request and phoned with his story.

Donald Farren drove a transport truck and like his neighbor, Harry Demmick, parked it at the lay-by. He said that he parked between 1:30 and 2:00 A.M. Sunday morning and saw several empty trailers and a black Vauxhall. His first reaction dismissed the car as an enclave for a courting couple. As he drove past to park, he noticed that it was empty and that the front doors had not properly closed. The driver's side seat reclined completely like someone had slept there. He then supposed that the car had run out of fuel. He walked past the Vauxhall, but saw no one around, so continued to walk home.

Kennington found several people who corroborated accounts already developed. But no other witnesses supplied additional information. No one else saw a green, expensive car. Further *Crimewatch* requests for drivers of expensive green cars dressed in fancy suits who visited Plimpson Pond went unanswered.

In the face of the impasse, Chilgress decided to collect expert opinions in an attempt to develop more evidence. He began with the diary.

Dr. Michael Buck worked as a consultant psychiatrist for a local hospital. He reviewed the diary, knew nothing else about the case, and expressed his opinion based solely on its entries. He looked specifically, according to Chilgress' instructions, for any hint of psychological abnormality that might predispose Sharri to commit suicide. He found none. Sharri made plans for the future, both personal and professional. She left no signs in her diary of being suicidal. Her concern about AIDS struck him as normal for a sexually active young single woman enjoying multiple partners.

Buck said that statistically, suicides tend to be older, divorced, or widowed rather than socially integrated people like Sharri. He could find nothing in her diary that suggested a cry for attention consistent with binding herself and flopping into Plimpson Pond to drown. Chilgress' homicide view enjoyed apparent support. Both Chilgress and Buck found suicide an improbable explanation of her death. But Benjamin disagreed.

Benjamin also reviewed the diary and found the details of bondage and the series of sexual partners indicative of a cry for attention expressed as a need for constant sensual gratification and the approval of others. In his view, she realized that she could not stop indulging her sexual compulsions, and would eventually contract the AIDS virus despite her better judgment. Her suicide became both an ultimate cry for attention, and an act of despair based on genuine self-knowledge. Benjamin would not back down—Sharri died a suicide. Armed with Buck's opinion, neither would Chilgress—Sharri died a murder victim. The line of disagreement appeared more clearly drawn.

Forensic experts and investigators commonly disagree during developing investigations or in courts of law. Often experts and investigators see the same thing, make the same observations, but interpret what they see differently. They reason from the same observations to develop differing interpretations. They see the same thing, but don't believe the same thing.[1]

Yet ordinary seeing does not amount to observing. Observing carries with it experience, knowledge, beliefs, values, theoretical commitments, and the goals for looking in the first place. Seeing simply describes a physical state, a photochemical excitation producing a neurological experience. In this sense, two people may see the same thing in that they experience similar photochemical excitations, but they may not see the same thing in that they bring to their experience different backgrounds. What a pathologist sees as a subarachnoid hemorrhage, a lawyer sees as just so much coloring. They do not observe the same thing. In the latter sense, seeing is a kind of believing.

A surgeon seeing a patient with an elevated temperature, who complains of severe right side abdominal pain, observes the signs of an acute appendicitis. The patient likely faces an appendectomy. The same patient visiting a chiropractor receives a spinal adjustment, while a visit to the Christian Science Reading Room introduces the sufferer to the inspiration of Mary Baker Eddy. In all but the latter case, a bill remains a certainty. Like bills, these observational beliefs based on the observers' backgrounds cannot be avoided. Observations are not made in some kind of intellectual vacuum.

Pierce would identify the ability to observe as the ability to read signs. Part of that skill involves recognizing the difference between what the sign shows and what the reader's personal background imposes. Reading signs involves exercising what he called the logic of abduction. Critical judgment becomes necessary. Good surgeons know that not every patient with an elevated temperature and right-side abdominal pain has an appendicitis. Look for a bullet wound; add to the context of observation; look for other signs, and make appropriate adjustments. Recognize limitations. Refer the patient to an appropriate expert. Follow the evidence.

The disagreement over the evidence in Sharri's death festered, given divergent readings of the signs at the scene, on the body, and even in the diary. Further observations merely added to the debate and did nothing to stem the infection. Chilgress contacted an expert on knots to take a look at the jumper cables, towrope, and scarf.

Former metropolitan police inspector Burton Hammston studied knots for over 40 years. He authored several technical articles and worked with both the British Museum and the National Maritime Museum. He told Chilgress that an ordinary overhand knot on the black jump lead formed a sliding noose. Without continued pressure, the loose knot would slide back and release the neck. It remained tight only with the continued application of force.

He found that the red jump lead formed a double loop with a front turn making two loops of the rope around the left wrist and a single loop over the right. When one side loosens, the other side tightens, not an ideal method for restraining a captive. He said that these bonds could be tied to oneself either by configuring the cable behind the back, or by stepping through the makeshift handcuffs from the front.

He found no knots at all on the towrope. It merely wrapped rather loosely around the ankles. The nylon material would not tighten further in the water, and would not constrain anyone for long.

The blue scarf had a single knot, like the first step in tying a shoelace. It kept its position through the friction of the cloth against itself.

Hammston told Chilgress that none of the materials offered any signs indicating whether the same hand had tied all three ligatures. The uncommon material suggested to him an impromptu rather than a premeditated action. He found the total absence of knots very unusual. Sharri had been too fit and strong a woman to be cowed by such haphazard restraints.

Chilgress figured that Sharri must have been initially incapacitated by her assaliant, making the restraints at most mere insurance, or at least, superfluous. Her blood showed no presence of drugs or alcohol, only moderate levels of nicotine. She had been HIV negative. He asked Benjamin for an opinion about possible mechanisms for incapacitating the woman, making the holding power of the restraints irrelevant.

Benjamin had his own ideas explaining the weaknesses of the cable, rope, and scarf to control and subdue a vigorous woman. He concluded that Sharri applied them to herself with suicidal flourish. He did not keep his conclusions to himself.

After again expressing these opinions, he told Chilgress that hypothetically, the ligature around her neck might have compromised her respiration by mechanically compressing both the carotid sinus and the vagus nerve. The effect mimics the result of a sleeper-hold. The constriction depresses respiration and heartbeat, dramatically drops blood pressure, and to the untrained, the recipient of the force appears to be dead. In severe cases, unless corrective action begins immediately, the person may not recover.

Benjamin added that Sharri had not been dead when she ended up with her mouth and nose underwater. He reminded Chilgress that she had drowned. Benjamin would stick to his view despite a storm of controversy or any future twists in the evidence. He would hold it through the coroner's inquest the way Dorothy held Toto through the Kansas twister.

Benjamin's view, with his reticence to let it go, carried weight. But so did other views expressed by reputable experts. Dr. Buck, the psychiatrist, had his view about what the diary revealed. Burton Hammston, the knot expert, offered an interpretation of the restraints. All three had unique abilities, backgrounds, and experiences to apply to the case.

Chilgress and Kennington struggled to read the burgeoning signs. The three experts' views became additional signs among the multitudes generated from the scene, the autopsy, and the witnesses. If the physical and testimonial evidence supplied signs pointing toward an explanation of Sharri's death, the three experts' views merely obscured the route to a solution. The experts displayed confusing, if not conflicting, signs.

Chilgress and Kennington struggled to integrate their divergent elements and read the full story that this evidence had to tell. Consolidating diverse expert views had never been an easy task for either inspector. Yet Chilgress functioned better as a consensus builder. That skill helped him become chief inspector. Kennington felt that building a consensus resembled navigating a ship by following its wake. That feeling would ensure that he remained a detective inspector for the duration of his career. Despite their differences in approach, each policeman knew that subjective factors affect how experts make observations and how they read the signs before them.

Observing occurs in a specific context that includes more than the scene marked off by yellow tape around Plimpson Pond. It also includes more than a particular observer's background knowledge, personal experience, theoretical commitments, long- and short-term goals, and even more than the observer's moral character. While all become part of the unseen landscape, the context includes the expectations these invisible additions create in the observer. Peirce's abductions require their careful recognition and critical assessment.

Both Chilgress and Kennington knew that such expectations affect what the observer sees, and that the failure to recognize them leads to trouble. It happened to them before. On August 6, 1985, police surrounded an Essex farmhouse after receiving a call from Jeremy Bamber, the adopted son of the residents. He told police that his 61-year-old father called him to say that his sister Sheila had gone crazy with a rifle. During his father's call, Jeremy said that the line went dead. Police arrived, broke in, and discovered five dead: Neville Bamber, his wife June, their adopted daughter Sheila, and her twin sons Daniel and Nicholas. Neville had two black eyes and numerous cuts. Sheila held the murder weapon, a .22 semi-automatic rifle, in one hand, and a Bible in the other.

Before they arrived, police expected to find a domestic homicide/suicide, and that expectation filtered their view of the scene. They failed to observe the significance of Neville's injuries. He had been in a fight with the killer. Their expectation became a source of error which they eventually corrected. Jeremy had fought with his father and committed the murders using a silencer which he took off the rifle before placing it in Sheila's hand.[2]

While perhaps practically unavoidable, expectations may be either appropriate, or inappropriate. The forensic pathologist, psychiatrist, or knot expert applies unique background knowledge and experience to read signs and extract explanations inaccessible to the ordinary observer. Each may impose appropriate expectations. A sudden collapse leads the pathologist to expect natural cardiac causes. Chronic insomnia leads the psychiatrist to expect depression. A ship's line leads the knot expert to expect a sailor's knot. Often the difference between appropriate and inappropriate expectations involves being aware of their role, and being willing to investigate their relevance in order to approve or reject them.

But inappropriate expectations[3] impose a layer of indefensible preconception tainting the result. Little if any investigation follows their imposition. They remain unchallenged and unexamined. Trusting uncritical experts often can be dangerous. Expert opinions must be as cautiously approached as creamy potato salad at an August church picnic.

An expert's additions to the case must be defensible by scientifically supportable, logically coherent reasons. Such reasons can be very nontechnical and may include discovering expectations accessible to the lay investigator yet hidden from the unselfconscious expert. The reasoning relies on a scientific method less imbued with theoretical or technical sophistication and closer to common sense than so-called pure science.[4] Any implicit expectations imposed by an expert that may influence the outcome of the case must endure this careful scrutiny. Such affected expertise may narrow the field of vision so far that the solution disappears.

In Edgar Allen Poe's *The Murders In the Rue Morgue,* the police fail to solve the mystery because they fail to evaluate their assumption that the murderer was a man. Given this initially reasonable expectation, they refused to adjust it in the face of conflicting signs. As a result, they failed to identify and interpret the available clues. The victim had been killed by a runaway gorilla who climbed up a tall building's drainpipe. The case involved neither homicide nor murder. They looked but they did not see.

The problem of what to look for, of how to direct the inquiry, of how to sort the clues from the coincidences, and of how to identify what "truth" to seek—all of these problems concerned both Peirce and Doyle's Holmes. In the face of conflicting solutions to each, Holmes functioned as a kind of consensus builder, perhaps one winning Kennington's approval. According to Holmes, "when you follow two separate chains of thought . . . you will find some point of intersection which should approximate the truth."[5]

Somehow, the conflict pitting defenders of a suicide theory to explain Sharri's death against proponents of a homicide scenario had to be resolved. To find a point of intersection in his own cases, Holmes first constructed a possible story suggested by all the signs. He then proved this possible story analogous to the actual one. Kennington felt that the Darcy investigation had bogged down in the first step. Both possible stories failed in many different ways to consider all the signs. Expectations entered to alter the evidence. Kennington, with his own expectations, knew that he would be lucky to accomplish the first step.

He unwittingly followed Holmes' advice, twisting the evidence this way and that for a different perspective, and in a sense converged the conflicting accounts to create another possible story.

Kennington reexamined scene photographs, lab reports, property inventories, and autopsy records. He reviewed statements reporting facts and submissions conveying opinion. He began thinking about what did not appear: her car keys and her cigarettes.

Police searched in the pond for days, but recovered no keys. Of course that did not guarantee that they weren't hiding in the pond. Kennington had periodically spent hours looking for his own car keys and failed to find them. Luckily his wife exercised her own superior investigative skills during these memory lapses, and made the recovery, usually right where he already had searched. Still, he bet that Sharri's keys did not land in the pond. Certainly, her cigarettes had not.

The keys would sink, but a pack of cigarettes would float. None appeared in the water, under it, or in the area around the pond. She had a reputation as a heavy smoker, never far from her cigarettes. The pond area's trash bin had been emptied about 5:00 P.M. and no empty packs decorated the area. Kennington bet that someone else took her cigarettes away. He also bet that the keys and the smokes traveled together, wherever they went.

He then considered what did appear, beginning with the body. Her bra was unhooked, and pulled up over her breasts. The scratch began on her right cheek and appeared again below the ligature mark, then reappeared below her right breast. Benjamin insisted that the scratch and the unhooked brassiere represented postmortem artifacts caused by moving the body from the water to the shore. Yet Mrs. Therson and the canoeist both insisted that they lifted the body carefully and did not drag it on the bottom or the shore. They both agreed that the body did not bend, and remained stiff throughout its short journey. Rigor had been almost completely developed. It did not seem likely that moving the body had unhooked the brassiere. Kennington bet that the position of the bra had a much different explanation.

Benjamin described the scratches as "clearly postmortem" since he saw no evidence of bleeding. Yet prolonged immersion of a minor perimortem scratch in the 13-degree C water could leave the same effect. Kennington, while no forensic pathologist, noted that the skin along the small scratch slightly evulsed, or piled up, from head to toe, not from toe to head. To be postmortem, the scratch required scraping the body toward the middle of the pond where her head pointed, not toward the shore and her feet. Given Therson's story, if any dragging inadvertently occurred, it moved in the opposite direction. So Kennington thought that the scratch also had another explanation.

The bruises on the outer sides of her thighs interested Kennington as much as they disinterested Benjamin. While the pathologist dismissed them as coincidental, Kennington saw them as evidential. They appeared in an area consistent with her legs being spread apart and forced against two hard surfaces. He thought about her car, the position of the seat, and the condition of the shift linkage. He considered the door's arm rest and the shift lever as possible surfaces to cause the bruises. He noted that both front doors remained ajar when the car had been discovered.

He remembered the days of his own youth when he considered gymnastics to involve the positioning of a willing female partner in a parked car. He recalled bending the linkage on his own father's vehicle after a particularly stimulating date. The bruises, whether coincidental or not, initially pointed him in this direction.

Perhaps Benjamin had been right about the bruise on her left hand as one result of her pulling on the black jump lead. A latent print from her left hand had appeared on the cable. Certainly Benjamin was right about the absence of a struggle. The condition of both her fingernails and her body spoke loudly against any unwelcomed attack and subsequent resistance. So did the loose bonds.

Kennington considered the scarf and the black jump lead. He had investigated a half-dozen autoerotic deaths involving ligatures gone sadly wrong. Four had been males, but two were females. In each case, a ligature had been applied to heighten sexual stimulation during masturbation. To prevent unsightly bruising, some type of protective layer had been placed between the ligature and neck. In each case, the self-tightened ligature had caused the loss of consciousness. Then some Rube Goldberg safety device designed to release the bond in the event of unconsciousness failed, resulting in an eventual call to the police and an embarrassing public inquest. The position of the scarf suggested both a gag and protection for the neck. But Sharri's hands remained behind her back, and the ligature had been removed. That pointed away from an autoerotic adventure gone bad.

Kennington had seen several cases of ligature stimulation that did not involve autoerotic activity. Collars or other ligatures would be self-applied and controlled to heighten orgasm during sex with a partner. The activity often accompanied varying degrees of bondage or differing levels of sadomasochism. The lack of knots on her bonds suggested a feigned restraint, as Benjamin suggested. But given her history, Kennington did not buy Benjamin's explanations.

Unlike Benjamin, Buck found no suicidal tendencies in her diary. Neither did Kennington. He did find evidence of a sexually adventurous young woman, fond of men and apparently addicted to their company. Yet Benjamin's autopsy discovered no seminal fluid in her vagina. But he did find some mucoid exudate, one product of sexual stimulation. Again, immersion in the water may have disrupted such evidence and destroyed any telling signs of recent vaginal or anal intercourse. Although no condom or its wrapper appeared, one might have been used. While unlikely, given her fears about AIDS, it remained a possibility. Perhaps the condom accompanied the keys and the cigarettes. In that event, Sharri had not been alone at Plimpson Pond.

Chilgress maintained that Sharri had been surprised, disabled, bound, and put in the water by her murderer. Kennington supposed that she had willingly participated in her bondage, been inadvertently disabled, and placed in the water by her unwitting killer. Kennington reserved surprise as a reaction for whomever dumped her in the pond.

Both Benjamin and Chilgress had been right in certain respects. According to Kennington, Sharri had acted to put her life in danger as Benjamin suggested. She did not act alone, as Chilgress suggested. Her death emerged from Kennington's meditation not as a suicide, not as a murder, but as a homicide explained as an accident. In his view, the criminality of the death began with the negligence of her unidentified partner.

His rough reconstruction had Sharri engaged in a sexual encounter at the pond where she agreed to meet her mystery date. She'd planned to visit Roger later, so chose the spot with that in mind. Rather than dump the grass clippings at her parents, she opted to save time, and dump them behind the toilet near the play area where she had been seen by Ruth Stanforth and her daughter. Perhaps her date was late. Perhaps he drove the green car.

They may have talked, smoked, and initiated sex in the car. Perhaps their passions took over, the trunk opened, the jump leads and towrope emerged, and her fatal adventure began.

Kennington had examined the play area. Perhaps the bruises occurred when her legs pressed against the edges of the child's slide. Maybe the mud on her knees and thighs originated there. Possibly it came from nearer the water. The lab couldn't tell. Her bra was pushed up, and someone's fingernail made the scratch moving down her body from head to toe, two movements in opposite directions. Perhaps she pulled the ligature too hard. The vagus nerve involvement favored by Chilgress and described hypothetically by Benjamin rendered her unconscious.

Her mystery partner found no respiration, no heartbeat, panicked, and carried her to the water. He stopped to prop her by the tree leaning her heel into the hard ground. Or perhaps before becoming unconscious, she walked on the soles of her shoes, as women who find themselves walking off a paved surface in high heels often do. Maybe she lost her balance, plunging a heel into the ground. Or maybe she started out standing in or near the water. The hard ground made it difficult to tell.

In any event, Kennington figured that her partner thought she was dead and either put her in the water, or left her there face down. He panicked. So far, maybe negligence. But when he left her, failed to report her death, and attempted to cover his tracks, his actions become more clearly criminal. He removed evidence of his presence, somehow taking her keys, cigarettes, and the condom which Kennington admitted perhaps existed only in his imagination. Her mystery partner hurriedly stuffed the grass bags in the car. They joined Sharri's watch and lighter that already rested on the front floor. The jacket was probably a coincidental artifact with no relevance to her death and no connection to her mystery partner. Or maybe it belonged to him.

Admittedly Kennington's scenario postulating this mystery partner involved a stretch of the imagination. It had lots of "perhapses," "maybes," "possibilities," and outright guesses. It rested on many assumptions about the diary and suppositions about the missing evidence. He spent his time attempting to confirm or disconfirm this hypothetical account. He got nowhere.

Holmes' second step, confirmation, proved to be extremely difficult. The same set of facts admitted other possible scenarios. Yet the investigation had to establish the most probable explanation beyond a reasonable doubt. Possible was just not good enough. Kennington's mystery partner required an identity, which the investigation attempted to supply.

Investigators worked around the clock, uncovering Sharri's friends, lovers, former friends, former lovers, social acquaintances, business associates, neighbors, and relatives. Kennington thought that this large group probably included everyone listed merely by number in her diary. He and Chilgress remained convinced that she had not killed herself and Benjamin remained committed to his suicide scenario. Chilgress still believed that she had been murdered, but Kennington stuck to his accident theory. The lack of confirming results merely increased unsupported speculation, and both perpetuated and aggravated the existing disagreement.

According to Benjamin, an unrelated prowler had taken the absent keys and missing cigarettes. Chilgress thought that the murderer had removed them, while Kennington believed that her panicky partner kept the items. Supporting evidence remained elusive. But not because of lacking investigative effort.

Criminalists attempted to lift prints from the car, the watch, the bags, the lighter, and even from the body. Laser light sources failed to reveal hoped-for latent prints on her breasts. Such efforts, desperate moves in any case, require luck in the best of circumstances. But exposure to the pond water virtually eliminated any hope. Nothing of note appeared on any of the other surfaces. While criminalists analyzed the physical evidence, other investigators conducted the interviews.

By the time of the inquest three months after Sharri's death, all the physical evidence had been processed, and well over 500 witnesses had been identified and questioned. But only relevant facts interested Her Majesty's Coroner. Consequently, only a relatively small group of witnesses were called to the Beaconsfield law courts to present evidence when the hearing began.

Testimony came from Esther Therson, the canoeists, Sandra Kelley, Mrs. Darcy, Roger Pembroke, Ruth Stanforth, and the truck drivers, Harry Demmick and Donald Farren. Relevant facts and opinions were delivered by Dr. Michael Buck, Burton Hammston, and of course, Dr. Benjamin. Chief Inspector Chilgress presented the results of the police investigation, including a summary of the roadblocks reached by following the available signs. Clearly they did not represent a unified front. It remained up to the coroner to untangle the disagreement according to law.

The coroner heard the case and the evidence, which appeared before his court like a now-it's-a-chalice/now-it's-two-faces pattern recognition puzzle. The conflicting opinions spilled over into three day-long sessions. Before he closed the proceedings on their last frustrating day, the exasperated coroner explained the legal significance of the facts and opinions that he had heard. He began by reiterating the inquest's limited objectives.

A coroner's inquest attempts to establish facts, including the identity of the decedent, and when, where and how the death occurred. He reminded those assembled that it was not in any sense a trial. The witnesses merely aided the coroner's attempt to answer these factual questions officially for the record. He summarized the facts accepted by his court before he explained his verdict.

The official record now said that Sharri left the house that she shared with Sandra Kelley sometime around 6:00 P.M. on Saturday. No one knew exactly where she went, but apparently she ate some food, including bacon. She planned to meet Roger Pembroke, but phoned him about 7:00 P.M. and said that "something came up." She also probably planned to dispose of the grass clippings from her mowing earlier that afternoon.

She was seen by Ruth Stanforth and her daughter at Plimpson Pond early that evening, perhaps near 7:00 P.M. Mrs. Stanforth also said that she saw an expensive green car and a man dressed in a suit at the lay-by near the pond. No one else saw this, and no such car or man had been discovered. After that, no witnesses saw Sharri until Esther Therson discovered her body Sunday morning.

Mrs. Therson, with help, removed the body from the pond and placed it on the shore.

Benjamin testified that drowning caused her death. Prior to drowning, an attempted strangulation occurred using a black jumper cable.

Hammston described the loose fitting ligatures and expressed his opinion that the selection of materials suggested an unplanned action. He found the absence of knots remarkable.

The pathologist testified that the clothing, body, and bonds suggest that the decedent took her own life.

Based on her diary, Buck expressed the opinion that Sharri had not been suicidal, but on the same basis, Benjamin said that she had been.

Mrs. Darcy testified that her daughter did not embrace suicide, and that such an action would be completely out of character. She added that her daughter might have had low blood pressure and had been subject to fainting spells.

Chief inspector Chilgress suggested that she may have been assaulted, but that the police have been unable to identify an assailant, or produce any conclusive evidence that connects another person with her death.

With these facts entered into evidence, the coroner said that he could now officially rule that the decedent, identified as Sharri Tempelton Darcy, age 27, had been found dead Sunday in Plimpson Pond. He was satisfied that drowning caused her death. Her death, therefore, had been unnatural. He said that his verdict concerning the manner of her death became quite another matter.

Given the accepted evidence, his options remained limited. They included taking one's own life, unlawful killing, and an open verdict.

As a matter of English law, suicide must be proved by the evidence. When a person dies an unnatural death, the signs of suicide must be there for all to see, not entertained as a mere possibility, or even on the face of it, as a likely explanation. If suicide cannot be proven beyond a reasonable doubt by the evidence, then it remains the coroner's duty to exclude it as an official finding.

He said that he was not satisfied by the evidence, and that therefore suicide was an improper verdict in Sharri's death. Mrs. Darcy looked relieved. Benjamin appeared annoyed. Chilgress and Kennington remained expressionless.

Unlawful killing covers a number of options, but for the Coroner's purposes in this case, the choice came down to murder, or manslaughter. Both amounted to the same thing except for the determination of intent.

According to English law, a murder is committed when " . . . a person of sound memory and discretion unlawfully killeth any reasonable creature in being and under the king's peace with malice aforethought either express or implied, the death occurring within one year and a day." Manslaughter amounted to the same thing without "malice aforethought."

To reach such a verdict, the coroner had to be satisfied beyond a reasonable doubt that the unlawful act of another person entered the chain of causes resulting in Sharri's death. He told the audience, citing the extensive police inquiries, that he remained unsatisfied, and therefore could not find that Sharri Tempelton Darcy had been unlawfully killed. Only one of the three verdict options remained.

An open verdict obtains when the available evidence fails to point unequivocally to the manner of death. The evidence did not point clearly to either a suicidal or a homicidal chain of events linking the last hours of her life with her death. He found no evidence of a struggle, and none of another's presence. He uncovered no unassailable evidence of suicide. With that, he declared an open verdict and adjourned the official inquest.

The unofficial inquest continued beyond the coroner's court. The debate raged among the public as well as among the police. Opinions clashed in pubs with the fanaticism of conflicts between Protestants and Catholics in Northern Ireland. Those favoring suicide battled those preferring some flavor of homicide. Other positions joined the fray holding that Sharri's death had been autoerotic, while still others added an elusive partner to the sordid mix. Almost everyone who had heard of the case had an opinion. Many proponents of these views remained unrestrained by the actual evidence.

Some felt that the police must have caused her death because obviously the experts concealed their true findings from the public. For this reason, others felt passionately that Prince Charles had to be involved. Or maybe a jealous Diana put out a contract. The politically paranoid concocted great government conspiracies, while the extraterrestrially inclined posited a sadistic visit from cruel space aliens. Such positions from the lunatic fringe become paradigms of irrationality, an aneurysm on the aorta of human intellectual evolution.

But when investigators and forensic experts disagree among themselves, expert opinion looks just as arbitrary, and appears equally as unreasonable as these bizarre accounts. When the same data support opposing explanations, the experts' credibility, honesty, and integrity come under general attack.

General attacks fail to advance the debate. Personal assaults merely degenerate the discussion into the irrational name-calling and accusatory finger-pointing characteristic of a barroom brawl. While the specific scrutiny of each expert's context of observation and alternative expectations may not resolve the disagreement, it may at least illuminate the relevant differences. This is often the best that we can get.

Peirce would say that many expert disagreements involve conflicting observations, different readings of the same sign. Holmes' enviable ability to read the signs correctly and to overpower Watson's paltry efforts depends on exhibiting Watson's inappropriate expectations as much as on applying his own superior background. No master looks good unless confronted with a bad student. Sharri Tempelton Darcy's case, like many others, had no willing Watsons among the crowd. With too many masters and no willing students available, the solution remained invisible.

According to Peirce, disagreement remains an important sign, one among the many others to be reckoned with, when struggling to solve a mystery like the death of Sharri Tempelton Darcy. That sign endured. Not a day passed for the last nine years that Kennington didn't think about the case and the disagreements it generated. He continues to reshuffle the images; the pond, the lay-by, the car, the diary, and the cables; viewing them in different lights, hoping to see something missed by everyone, still lurking among the shadows.

NOTES

1. See Jon J. Nordby, "Can We Believe What We See If We See What We Believe?—Expert Disagreement," *Journal of Forensic Sciences*, JFSCA, Vol. 37, No. 4, July 1992, pp. 1115–1124.
2. See Nordby, p. 1115–1116, and note.
3. Such inappropriate expectations are called "expectation-laden observations." See Nordby, p. 1120.
4. An investigator's appeal to experience can differ from a pure scientist's appeal: The investigator observes spontaneous facts scattered throughout a case, while the pure or theoretical scientist may observe facts created and manipulated by a particular experiment. Certainly the interests also may overlap.
5. Sir Arthur Conan Doyle, "The Disappearance of Lady Frances Carfax," in *The Complete Sherlock Holmes*, Vol. II, Doubleday & Co. Inc., Garden City, NY., N.D.

Annotated Bibliography

The following philosophical works address issues of method discussed in *Dead Reckoning*. Some are more technical than others. This short bibliography is meant to help the reader investigate puzzles in the analysis of "rational method" raised by scientists and philosophers over the last 2,000 years.

Achinstein, Peter. *The Nature of Explanation*. Oxford, 1983.
A rigorous philosophical treatment investigating explanation.

Achinstein, Peter. "Concepts of Evidence." *Mind* 87 (1978): 22–45.
Discusses potential and actual evidence; links evidence to explanation.

Achinstein, Peter. *The Concept of Evidence*. Oxford, 1983.
A collection of classic and contemporary essays by Kempel, Carnap, Salmon, and Achinstein.

Brent, Joseph. *Charles Sanders Peirce: A Life*. Indiana University Press, 1993.
A biography of Peirce focusing on his philosophical and scientific work; the author attempts to explain Peirce's theories as they developed over his lifetime.

Brody, Baruch A. "Confirmation and Explanation." *Journal of Philosophy* 65 (1968): 282–299.
Argues for a link between these two concepts.

Carnap, Rudolph. *Logical Foundations of Probability, Second ed*. Chicago, 1962.
A difficult work, but a standard in the field which inspired multiple reinvestigations of the concept of probability.

Cartwright, Nancy. *How the Laws of Physics Lie*. Oxford, 1983.
Defends inferences to causal explanations while critical of other attempts at abduction; an effective response to van Fraassen.

Cohen, L. Jonathan. *The Probable and the Provable*. Oxford, 1977.
Argues for a methodological distinction between these two notions.

Corrington, Robert S. *An introduction to C. S. Peirce: Philosopher, Semiotician, and Ecstatic Naturalist*. Rowman & Littlefield, 1993.
A brief overview of the man, his moods, and the substance of his theories.

Doppelt, Gerald. "Kuhn's Epistemological Relativism: An Interpretation and Defense." *Inquiry* Vol. 21 (1978): 33–86.
Argues that Kuhn espouses neither relativism nor the irrationality of rigorous scientific method.

Dretske, Fred. "Laws of Nature." *Philosophy of Science* 44 (1977): 248–268.
A nonempiricist analysis of laws of nature, making confirmation the converse of explanation; he says: "Statements of law, by talking about the relevant properties rather than the sets of things that have those properties, have a far wider scope than any true generalization about the actual work." He continues: "To confirm a hypothesis is to bring forward data for which the hypothesis is the best (or one of the better) competing explanations."

Earman, John, ed. "Testing Scientific Theories," *Minnesota Studies in the Philosophy of Science* Vol. X. Minnesota, 1983.
A collection of essays on Clark Glymour's views of evidence and explanation.

Eco, Umberto and Thomas A. Sebeok, eds. *Dupin, Holmes, Peirce: The Sign of Three.* Indiana University Press, Bloomington 1983.
An engaging collection of essays focusing on the logic of abduction and Peirce's philosophy of science illustrated by fictional inferences celebrated in works by Edgar Allen Poe and Sir Arthur Conan Doyle.

Glymour, Clark. *Theory and Evidence.* Princeton, 1980.
Defends a "bootstrap" account of confirmation: Hypotheses are confirmed relative to other theories.

Hacking, Ian. *The Logic of Statistical Inference.* Cambridge University Press, 1965.
An unusually clear look at the logical foundations of statistics.

Harman, Gilbert. "The Inference to the Best Explanation," *Philosophical Review.* Vol. 74, No. 1 (January 1965).
Harman's persuasive argument to prove that abduction is a necessary inference for making any induction is possible.

Harre, Rom, and Edward H. Madden. *Causal Powers: A Theory of Natural Necessity.* Rowman & Littlefield, 1975.
Defends a non-Humean account of causality in terms of specific properties rather than general laws.

Hume, David. *Treatise of Human Nature, Book I.* Oxford University Press, 1888, 1968.
Famous rejection of an entity called "cause."

Jackson, Frank. "A Causal Theory of Counterfactuals." *Australasian Journal of Philosophy* 55 (1977): 3–21.
Defines a "Hume world" and argues for an irreducible causal element in most counterfactual reasoning (i.e., "if I would have detonated the explosives, we all would be dead"). Also argues that this causal element is present in many probability judgments.

Kent, Beverley. *Charles S. Peirce: Logic and the Classification of the Sciences.* Montreal McGill-Queen's University Press. 1987.
A detailed presentation, clarification, and assessment of Peirce's logic and its foundation in his philosophy of natural science.

Kneale, William. *Probability and Induction.* Oxford, 1949.
Classic in the field; argues that numerical measures of probability are secondary to nonnumerical probability judgments involving "the desire to explain."

Kuhn, Thomas. *The Structure of Scientific Revolutions.* University of Chicago Press, 1970.
A relatively recent stimulus for contemporary discussions of science and scientific method.

Kuanvig, Jonathon L. "How to be a Reliabilist." *American Philosophical Quarterly*. Vol. 23, No. 2 (April 1986).

Distinguishes "degree of probability" judgments from reliability judgments as a measure of scientific certainty.

Kyburg, Henry E. *Epistemology and Inference*. Minnesota, 1983.

Especially Parts III and IV present valuable articles covering epistemic probability and induction.

Lacey, F. B. "Scientific Evidence." *Jurimetrics Journal*. Vol. 24, No. 3 (Spring 1984) 254–272. [NCJ-94054]

Discusses the "Frye" test for evidence applied to computer data.

Lakotaos, Imre. "Changes in the Problem of Inductive Logic." Chapter 8 of *Mathematics, Science, and Epistemology*. Cambridge, 1978.

Illuminating discussion of one of the classic puzzles in philosophy—the puzzle of how rationally to justify inductive reasoning.

Laudan, Larry. *Science and Values: The Aims of Science and Their Scientific Debate*. University of California Press, 1984.

Discusses uniquely scientific values essential for the practice of science.

Leplin, Jarrett, ed. *Scientific Realism*. California, 1984.

Offers a balanced clarification and treatment of the issues surrounding the realist vs. antirealist debate in the philosophy of science. Includes discussions and essays by McMullin, Boyd, and van Frassen.

Mackie, J. L. "The Relevance Criterion of Confirmation." *British Journal for the Philosophy of Science* 20 (1969): 27–40.

A derivation, using standard probability calculus, showing that a theory which makes data highly probable is confirmed by that data.

McMullin, Ernan. "A Case for Scientific Realism." in Jarrett Leplin, ed., *Scientific Realism*. California, 1984, 8–40.

Clear, accessible essay by one of the leading defenders of scientific realism.

McMullin, Ernan. *The Inference that Makes Science, The Aquinas Lecture, 1992*. Marquette University Press, Milwaukee 1992.

A brief history and analysis of scientific demonstration, supporting abduction as "the inference that makes science."

Mill, J. S. *A System of Logic*. London, 1843.

The classic discussion of inductive reasoning in terms of what we now call "Mill's Methods."

Mirabelli, Andre. "Belief and incremental Confirmation of One Hypothesis Relative to Another," in Peter D. Asquith and Ian Hacking, eds. *PSA Proceedings 1978: Volume One*. Philosophy of Science Association, 1978.

Discusses epistemic characteristics of hypotheses which cascade one from another.

Newton-Smith, W. H. *The Rationality of Science*. Routledge & Kegan Paul, 1981.

Defends scientific rationality, discussing Popper, Lakatos, Kuhn and Feyerabend; includes a treatment of the sociology of knowledge.

Popper, Karl R. *Realism and the Aim of Science*. Rowman & Littlefield, 1983.

Classic presentation of the case against induction and for corroboration, defending his "propensity interpretation" of probability.

Putnam, Hilary. *Mathematics, Matter and Method.* Cambridge, 1975.
Chapter 16, "The Corroboration of Theories," links confirmation and explanation while critically evaluating Popper and Kuhn; Chapter 17, "Degree of Confirmation and Inductive Logic," argues against Carnap that inductive practice cannot be represented by any measure function; presents a rational method for selecting from among competing hypotheses.

Rescher, Nicholas. *Scientific Explanation.* Free Press, 1970.
Technical discussions of probabilistic explanation and the logic of evidence; defends something similar to Bayes' Theorem, but it does not fit the standard probability calculus; includes a 45-page appendix "On the Epistemology of the Inexact Sciences" and a thorough bibliography.

Ryle, Gilbert. "Induction and Hypothesis." *Proceedings of the Aristotelian Society,* Supplementary vol. 16 (1937): 36–62.
Defends the use of inductive methods to assess competing hypotheses.

Salmon, Wesley C. *The Foundations of Scientific Inference.* Pittsburgh, 1967.
Accessible treatment of probability theory and the problem of induction; defends an abductive account of confirmation, including reference to Bayes' Theorem.

Salmon, Wesley C. *Scientific Explanation and the Causal Structure of the World.* Princeton, 1984.
Defends the reality of non-Humean causes and modifies his early account of causal explanation.

Smokler, Howard. "Conflicting Conceptions of Confirmation." *Journal of Philosophy* 65. (1968): 300–312.
Attempts to resolve paradoxes of confirmation by distinguishing between two types of confirmation—one straightforwardly inductive, the other linked to explanation.

Thagard, Paul R. "The Best Explanation: Criteria for Theory Choice." *Journal of Philosophy* 75. (1978): 76–92.
Defends and expands on Gilbert Harman's account of abductive inference.

Tursman, Richard. *Peirce's Theory of Scientific Discovery: A System of Logic Conceived as Semiotic.* Bloomington Indiana University Press. 1987.
A robust treatment of Peirce's logic as the fundamental structure of scientific method.

van Fraassen, Bas C. *The Scientific Image.* Oxford, 1980.
Attempts to refute foundations for "inference to the best explanation" by supporting a pragmatic account of explanation; a leading antirealist who shuns the tag "instrumentalist."

von Wright, G. H. *The Logical Problem of Induction.* Basil Blackwell, 1965.
Argues that the impossibility of conclusive rational justifications for induction is a pseudo problem that does not count against the reliability of inductive inferences.

Weatherford, Ray. *Philosophical Foundations of Probability Theory.* Routledge & Kegan Paul, 1982.
Advanced analysis of competing theories of probability.

Whewell, William. *The Philosophical Foundations of the Inductive Sciences Founded on Their History,* Vol. I–II, Second ed. London, 1847.
The classic text: argues against Mill and critically evaluates what we now call "Mill's Methods."

Index

A

B

C

H

I

J

K

L

M

N

O

P

Q

R

S